Contents

Crisis and Renewal in France, 1918-1962

S. Alexander

Berghahn Books
New York • Oxford

First published in 2002 by

Berghahn Books
www.berghahnbooks.com

Library of Congress Cataloging-in-Publication Data

Crisis and renewal : France, 1918-1962 / edited by Kenneth Mouré and Martin S. Alexander.
p. cm.
Includes bibliographical references.
ISBN 1-57181-146-X (alk. paper) -- ISBN 1-57181-297-0 (pbk.: alk. paper)
1. France--Politics and government--20th century. I. Mouré, Kenneth. II. Alexander, Martin S.

DC369 .C75 2001
944.08--dc21 00–050792

British Library Cataloguing in Publication Data

A catalogue record for this book is available from the British Library.

Printed in the United States on acid-free paper.

Dedicated to

John C. Cairns

Abbreviations

2e Bureau	*Deuxième bureau*
ALN	*Armée de la libération nationale*
APD	*Association de la paix par le droit*
BAV	*Brigade des agressions et violences*
BEF	British Expeditionary Force
CDETJ	*Comité de défense des enfants traduits en justice*
CDLs	*Comités départmentales de la Libération*
CFLN	*Comité français de libération nationale*
CFTC	*Confédération française des travailleurs chrétiens*
CGPF	*Confédération générale du patronat français*
CGT	*Confédération générale du travail*
CIV	*Centre d'identification de Vincennes*
CLLs	*Comités locales de la Libération*
CNR	*Conseil national de la resistance*
CNRA	*Conseil nationale de la révolution algérienne*
CRS	*Compagnies républicaines de sûreté*
CSAR	*Comité secret d'action révolutionnaire*
CVIA	*Comité de vigilance des intellectuels antifascistes*
DAPC	*Direction des affaires politiques et commercials*
DGA	*Direction générale de l'armement*
DST	*Direction de la sûreté de territoire*
ECSC	European Coal and Steel Community
EDC	European Defense Community
EEC	European Economic Community
ERP	European Recovery Program
FFI	*Forces française de l'intérieur*
FLN	*Front de la libération nationale*
FNACA	*Fédération nationale des anciens combattants d'Algérie*
FNC	*Fédération nationale des contribuables*
FPA	*Force de police auxiliaire*
FPVM	*Fédération des porteurs de valuers mobilières*

FR	*Fédération républicaine*
FRS	*Forces républicaines de sécurité*
GIMRP	*Groupe des industries métallurgiques de la région parisienne*
GPRA	Algerian Provisional Government
INED	*Institut national des études démographiques*
INSEE	*Institut national des statistiques and des études économiques*
IPES	*Institutions publique d'éducation surveillée*
ISES	*Institutions spéciales d'education surveillée*
JOC	*Jeunesse ouvrière chrétienne*
LDH	*Ligue des droits de l'homme*
LICP	*Ligue internationale des combattants de la paix*
LIFPL	*Ligue internationale des femmes pour la paix et la liberté*
MNA	*Mouvement national algérien*
MPF	*Mouvement populaire des familles*
MRAP	*Mouvement contre le racisme, l'antisémitisme et pour la paix*
MRP	*Mouvement républicain et populaire*
MSR	*Mouvement social révolutionnaire*
MTA	*Mouvement des travailleurs arabes*
NCOs	Non-commissioned officers
OAS	*Organisation de l'armée secrète*
OEEC	Office for European Economic Cooperation
OSARN, or OSAR	*Organisation secrète d'action révolutionnaire nationale*
PCF	*Parti communiste française*
PDP	*Parti démocrate populaire*
PNRS	*Parti national révolutionnaire et social*
PS	*Parti socialiste*
PSU	*Parti socialiste unifié*
RNP	*Rassemblement national populaire*
SAT	*Service d'assistance technique*
SEDCOG	*Société d'études documentaires et critiques sur les origines de la guerre*
SF	*Sans frontière*
SFIO	*Section française de l'internationale ouvrière*
SIM	*Servizio informazione militare*
SNCF	*Société nationale des chemins de fer*
STO	*Service du travail obligatoire*
TEA	*Tribunal pour enfants et adolescents*
UCAD	*Union des comités d'action défensive*
UFF	*Union des femmes françaises*
UFF	*Union française féminine*
UIA	*L'union des infants d'Auvergne*
UNEF	*Union nationale des étudiants de France*
UPA	*L'union des patriotes d'Auvergne*

Crisis and Renewal in France Since the First World War

Kenneth Mouré and *Martin S. Alexander*

The story line in Charles de Gaulle's *War Memoirs* traces a pattern recurrent in French political history. The crises of defeat and German occupation in *The Call to Honor* lead to a gathering of French resources to combat the forces of occupation in his second volume, *Unity*. The third volume, *Salvation*, brings liberation and victory, followed almost inevitably by discord, disunion, and de Gaulle's departure from politics. On his final page, writing from self-appointed political retreat in Colombey, de Gaulle evoked the fundamental lessons of nature that gained in significance as he grew older. He likened the return of spring, the ever-recurring return of light and life to a cold and darkened world, to his own life and hopes, and to France itself, "weighed down with history, prostrated by wars and revolutions, endlessly vacillating from greatness to decline, but revived, century after century, by the genius of renewal!"[1] De Gaulle returned to active politics before the volume appeared in print, and his engineering of the Fifth Republic produced a political renewal to parallel the French economic miracle that reached fruition in the 1960s.

France takes pride in a revolutionary tradition that has made of French experience an exceptional model for political modernization; exceptional in rendering French experience *exemplary*, rather than unique and separate.[2] If for more than a century after the Revolution, France experienced unusual political instability that demonstrated a "uniquely revolution-prone political culture,"[3] the political

Notes for this chapter begin on page 13.

aspirations prompting revolution were exemplary rather than unique. The crises leading to revolutions were unplanned and unexpected, often catching the revolutionaries and the forces of order unprepared. In contrast to this turbulent political record, the French path for economic and social development displayed notable stability, particularly in the gradual pace of change in its agricultural and artisanal manufacturing sectors, which slowed the twin processes of urbanization and industrialization. This gradual social and economic transformation, in conjunction with the frequency of the political crises, suggests that de Gaulle's sense of Providence having created France "either for complete successes or for exemplary misfortunes" was often true for the latter.[4]

Although renewal in twentieth-century France has achieved great success, for many years the need for renewal prompted great uncertainty. In a landmark volume of essays published in 1963, *In Search of France*, it was by no means clear that France had successfully met the challenges it had faced since the turn of the century. Economic growth surpassed pessimistic postwar expectations, but social and political modernization had not kept pace.[5] Economically the "sick man of Europe" in the late 1930s, France became one of the most spectacular cases of economic recovery and growth in the "golden age" following World War II.[6] France ranks now as the fourth-largest exporter in the world after the USA, Japan and Germany, and works in close partnership with Germany to lead integration in the European Union.

But the extent of French success remained in doubt in 1963, with the uncertain future of French politics threatening to compromise the obvious economic and social advances achieved since the war. Stanley Hoffmann ended his essay "The Paradoxes of the French Political Community" with his judgment suspended on whether the Fifth Republic would endure, fashioning a new political consensus to replace the Third Republic's "stalemate society." Six years later, following the crisis of May 1968 and de Gaulle's resignation, Raymond Aron was uncertain whether these events would mark a new departure or would return France to the stalemate politics of the Fourth Republic.[7] Michel Crozier explained May 1968 as a revolt against the "stalemate society" in which crises were the only means to effect reform, adding that reforms tended to be narrowly limited within an overly-centralized and rigid bureaucratic state; changes tended to occur within, rather than overturning, the existing system.[8]

Yet the Fifth Republic survived, stabilized, developed and prospered far beyond its critics' expectations. Twenty-five years beyond the *In Search of France* essays, French historians could write of "the end of French exceptionalism" and the "banalization" of French politics.[9] Observers in search of "the New France," if uncertain of precisely what had been gained, were clear that the "stalemate society" had been left behind, having "crumbled under the weight of economic and social change."[10] The factors that produced recurrent crises in twentieth-century France had altered, and the major problems facing France since François Mitterrand's election in 1981—prolonged unemployment, increasing income disparities, the rise of anti-immigrant political movements on the extreme right, and social exclusion—have parallels in most wealthy, industrialized nations.

The year 1940 marked a significant milestone in the process of French modernization. A decisive military defeat led to military occupation by a regime more brutally exploitative than any previously experienced, to a change in political regime and civil administration that would perturb and divide the French polity, and to a retrospective condemnation of the politics, the economic policies and the social immobility of the interwar years. "Modernisation politics," Peter Morris has noted, "had in France to grow out of the humiliation of system collapse."[11] But acute crises and system collapse do not by themselves invent and impose new policies or politics. The traumatic events of 1940 in France produced a series of crises that prompted many changes, not all leading to renewal. Apart from the military defeat, the clearest crisis was political. The Vichy regime was established as a political negation of the Third Republic, but it proved to be an interregnum, followed by an abortive renewal of Third Republic parties and practice. The Fourth Republic collapsed in turn through a combination of internal stalemate and a threat from *without*—the war in Algeria—bringing back Charles de Gaulle to create the Fifth Republic. Even then, the new system would need many years of operation to develop as political practice and to prove its stability and durability.

The changes produced in the years 1940 to 1944 had roots stretching deep into the interwar period and earlier. Economic renewal, to take one significant example, was not simply a product of "new men and new ideas" arriving with the forces of Liberation in 1944. The new men and ideas were products of French recovery from the First World War, the economic successes of the 1920s, economic decline in the 1930s, attempted renovation under Vichy, and planning for reconstruction and modernization in the Resistance and Free France. Their accomplishments after 1945 owed a great deal to particular postwar opportunities for changes in the personnel and organization of the state, the urgency of directing limited investment funds to meet critical needs, and the availability of investment funds enhanced by the European Recovery Program.[12] Defeat in 1940 had confirmed the failure of the interwar economy to provide the economic strength needed to resist the German threat, but economic renewal was not a necessary or inevitable result. It developed from discontents and the development of new ideas in the long French depression of the 1930s, the accelerated decline of the French economy exploited to serve German war needs, the advance of new ideas and organization in the Vichy period (an interregnum in which neither *l'État français* nor the French *patronat* had the power to effect major changes), and a renewed struggle to decide who would determine policy after the Liberation. Nineteen-forty was but one link in a long, complex evolution, and its determining element—the German victory—was an example of external force intervening to transform the dynamics for policy-making within the French state and society.

This volume did not set out with a template to define crises, renewal, and the linkages between the two. Nor is it structured to analyze a predetermined set of crises, defined with the wisdom of hindsight to have been *the* critical crises and turning points that sparked renewal in twentieth-century France. Nor is "renewal" linked mechanically to the problematic concept of "modernization" as a single process yielding a new and improved society, with the success of French modernization measurable against an ideal type. Rather, the case studies that follow explore the relationship between particular crises and the convoluted path to renewal from 1918 to the early years of the Fifth Republic. Major political crises have been deliberately excluded, except as they impacted the timing and nature of renewal on other levels. Political crises are without doubt the most visible and the most dramatic crises in modern French history.[13] Yet even when crises succeed in changing political regimes, as happened in 1870-71, 1940, and 1958, their direct contribution to renewal is political, with deeper changes following indirectly if at all.

This volume deals with case studies of what might be termed sub-strata of crises, assessing the process of crisis and renewal and the links between the two in areas beneath the surface upheavals of politics: areas such as women's participation in politics, economic thought and policy, strategic planning for war, military experience in terms of what soldiers fight for, the administration of juvenile justice, and the policing of dissident, oppositional and marginalized groups. The purpose is to elucidate how France responded to the challenges of twentieth-century political, social, and economic development. The results of these individual studies provide a new perspective on larger issues of French crisis and renewal. The essays suggest that similar structural determinants were at work in the reactions to various crises and in the effectiveness of efforts at renewal across the range of subjects considered. They also show that considerable care is needed to specify the nature of particular crises and the reasons for the responses they generate, if one is to understand how and to what degree those responses led to successful renewal.

I. Crisis

Contributors to this volume were asked to address the theme of "crisis and renewal" in case studies in their area of expertise, with freedom to concentrate on the aspects of crisis and/or renewal as appropriate to their material. Most give greater attention to renewal than to crisis, a fitting allocation of effort given the successes of French renewal. Even in the essays that demonstrate little or no renewal, such as those by Sally Marks, Kenneth Mouré, William Irvine, Norman Ingram and Patricia Prestwich, more attention is given to explaining the lack of renewal than to the nature of the crises invoked. One of the key issues in the collection is how one chooses to characterize what, precisely, constitutes a given crisis.

Political crises are more clearly identifiable than other types of crisis. They are recognized by the significant challenge they pose to a political regime or government, which, if the forces seeking to benefit from the crisis are successful, is thereby overthrown. Such a crisis is clearly marked in its timing and its outcome, if not in its nature. Political crises threaten the regime or government in power. Michel Winock's analysis of such crises in France since 1870 demonstrates both the variety of political crises in France and the limitations inherent in looking at crises as purely political. Winock presents a *crisométrie* measuring duration, the number of condemnations, and the number of victims (deaths),[14] but the most important measure is clearly the political outcome. And as Danielle Tartakowsky has pointed out, street demonstrations, one of the most visible manifestations of "crisis" and protest, have rarely coincided with political crises and have tended to support and renew rather than challenge republican institutions since 1870.[15] The meaning of political crises, in their impact on the lives of citizens, remains unclear until one penetrates beneath the surface events of politics to the deeper layers of policy, practice, and lived experience.

In August 1944, to take one example, de Gaulle pointedly refused invitations from Resistance leaders who had gathered at the Hôtel de Ville in Paris to proclaim a new Republic. He insisted that the existing Republic had never died. Herrick Chapman's contribution to this volume shows de Gaulle's care in reestablishing the authority of the state on his own terms. Yet, disillusioned by 1946, de Gaulle set about rethinking the concept of Republicanism. In 1958, Odile Rudelle has suggested, de Gaulle returned to power seeking to implement his new brand of Republicanism through what she terms a "national ecumenical discourse" so that the Republic could do what Adolphe Thiers had initially hoped it would do after 1870—unite rather than divide the country.[16] This was also what Raymond Poincaré had done in 1914 with the *union sacrée* and what he hoped, in vain, to preserve after the return of peace in 1918.[17]

However, the extent to which de Gaulle succeeded in transforming the meaning of Republicanism in 1958 may be questioned. Furthermore, focusing on the familiar political *moments clés,* the presumed turning points, risks paying excessive attention to the political surface events marking the passage of modern France, and too little to the unseen engines and fuel within the ship of state that moved France from the crises of the interwar decades and the Fourth Republic to the relatively placid waters of the mid-1960s. Even there, it is well to recall that de Gaulle sedulously cultivated the myth of an abrupt change, a near-instantaneous restoration of order, and clear purpose and control on his part in 1958 for his own purposes. De Gaulle's return to power "was not the beginning of the end but only the end of the beginning. The turbulence of the early years of his presidency cannot be over stressed. The serene self-confidence of his own public statements and the final outcome of Algeria make it easy to forget the multiplicity—and the danger—of the challenges he faced."[18] The events in May 1968 would follow, casting in doubt the stability achieved and leading de Gaulle to withdraw again from politics in 1969.

The crises examined in this volume are identified by a number of criteria. While these are still linked to the posing of a threat, the object threatened need no longer be a government or political regime. The sense of crisis remains connected to perceived danger. But the element at risk might be a political belief, a sense of political, social, economic or moral order, particular conditions of existence, or something as vague as a *certain idea of France.* And the crisis need not mark a turning point. Indeed, the threat of change and a potential "turning" might be the danger perceived. As the nature of the crisis varies, so too does its intensity, the fears it arouses, the degree to which it mobilizes popular forces to effect or resist change, and the duration of the period of crisis. Deciding what constitutes a crisis, its extent and timing, and ultimately its significance, involves an element of distinctly subjective judgment—for the contemporaries who experienced the crises as much as for the historians who seek to categorize and analyze them.

This subjective quality is important to understanding the linkages between crises and renewal. It has repercussions on the outcome of any given crisis and on the extent and quality of renewal the crisis sparked. The interwar *Ligue des droits de l'homme* and the post-1945 *Mouvement républicain populaire* saw no crisis in representation to suggest that they should do more to integrate women into French politics on a basis of full equality. For the LDH, Irvine shows that the integration of women was clearly a problem rather than an opportunity for renewal or, even more significantly, an important question of political equality and justice. For the postwar MRP, Prestwich explores how women's suffrage and representation were adopted as new terrain from which to attract women voters without altering conventional, male-dominated politics. Mouré shows how French economic policy makers in the interwar period refused to recognize the monetary origins of the economic crisis in France and misperceived the nature of the global economic crisis. Their conviction that the origins of the crisis lay abroad reduced their incentive to alter monetary policy in France, devoting their attention instead to maintaining belief in the gold standard and pressing successive ministers of finance to balance their budgets. The crises in these examples were neither acute enough nor perceived as significant enough to require change. To put this another way, these cases demonstrate that change could be successfully opposed, postponed, or diluted when the barriers to change had not yet been critically weakened and the arguments for the status quo rendered threadbare.

Several cases provide sharp, easily recognized crises. Sally Marks terms the Ruhr crisis of 1923 "France's first great interwar crisis." At risk, in the French view, was the enforcement of the Versailles Treaty and the receipt of German reparations on which French finance depended to cover state spending to rehabilitate the extensive war-damaged regions of northern France. Poincaré's invasion of the Ruhr attempted to meet this crisis by decisive action in order to assure the collection of reparations. Yet, as Marks shows, Poincaré's leadership was not decisive, and the result was financial loss, increased dependence on allies who were alienated by the French action (Britain in particular), and thus increased diplomatic isolation.[19]

For the Cagoule in 1937, Joel Blatt shows that their attempt to overthrow the Popular Front did not constitute a political crisis for the French state, for the Cagoule posed no significant threat. The Cagoule and its failed coup attempt demonstrated, rather, the existential crisis experienced by right-wing plotters who found themselves bereft, in 1937, of the threat from the extreme left they needed in order to attract broader support. In this sense the failure of the Popular Front to deliver the reforms it portended in the summer of 1936 was paradoxically a disappointment for extremists on the right as well as the left. For French pacifists, a less marginal group, the coming of war in 1939 and the military defeat and occupation in 1940 brought crisis in the shape of the failure of their cause.[20] Their divergent paths in coping with this, from collaboration with the Nazi victors in hopes of assuring a future European peace, to retreat and silence, and on rare occasions to joining with the Resistance to take up arms against an enemy worse than war, are explored with care and nuance by Norman Ingram.

Talbot Imlay's account of French defense policy after Munich details the shaken confidence of French military and political leaders with their hopes for a second front on Germany's eastern border crippled by the Munich agreement. The crisis for French defense policy could not have been more stark. Remarkably, after exploring the prospects for retreat from their commitments in Eastern Europe, French leaders decided to reaffirm the commitments despite the diminished prospects for a militarily effective eastern front. In doing so they led, rather than followed, the so-called *gouvernante anglaise*. The crisis brought reassessment and a recommitment to their earlier strategy, without the means to renew that strategy and make it effective. Ultimately, this strategy needed military assistance from the Soviet Union.

Looking at these crises alone, one might wonder whether the line of causation ran the other way, with failures of renewal leading to crises rather than crises to renewal, and whether the frequency of crises reflected a persistent failure of renewal—politically, economically, socially. One might also question whether a categorization of crises according to type would clarify just what, in any given case, was really in crisis. A typology of crises, employing tried, and at times trite rather than true conventional categories, might posit four broad types: political, economic, military, and diplomatic crises. Such categories necessarily overlap, to varying degrees, in any given crisis. More importantly, they leave out crises of equal importance to the perceptions of those involved: moral crises or crises of conscience is one such facet, crises of prestige or rank another, both broadly similar as crises of *identity*. Lastly, given that the concept of renewal implies an important policy aspect, one could create categories to include crises in specific policy realms, institutions and career paths (influencing decision-makers' choices).

The case studies dealt with in this volume can all be fitted in more than one of these categories. To characterize them according to one type would obscure the multi-dimensional character that heightened the sense of acute danger and that made particular situations seem to be truly circumstances of intense crisis. The Cagoulard conspiracy examined by Blatt, for example, is not explicable as simply a political crisis. There was no threat of a Communist *coup* in November 1937 when the Cagoule mobilized to seize power; the crisis lay principally in Cagoulard perceptions of their own diminishing possibilities for effective action and influence, in their own enraged, impotent sense of frustration, making the crisis for the Cagoule one chiefly of identity and purpose. In a similarly complex fashion, the massacre of Algerians in Paris in October 1961 can be seen as the conjuncture of a series of crises: within the Paris police, regarding their own security and control; within the Algerian community in seeking justice as citizens equal before the forces of order in the French state; and within the operational practice of the French state which had imported a distinctly colonial system of control to regulate the lives of Algerians within the *métropole*—what Martin Evans has referred to as France's post-1962 "colonial syndrome."[21] As the essay by Jim House and Neil MacMaster demonstrates, the sense of corporate, institutional or "group" crisis within the Paris police force in 1961 was the most important of the crises leading to the massacre of 17 October.

The French decision to push forward with economic integration and the Treaty of Rome was, in Will Hitchcock's view, less a crisis of economic management (on which policy makers were divided as to the nature of the crisis and the means of resolution) than a crisis of foreign policy, over the country's world rank and, ultimately, over elite perceptions of France's national stature and identity. In the case of reform to the juvenile judicial system, Sarah Fishman shows how reform required a succession of crises: the evolution of expert opinion on rehabilitation of delinquents, a series of scandals to attract public attention in the 1930s, stalled Popular Front reform initiatives and, finally, the fall of France leading to Vichy's emphasis on the moral regeneration of people and nation.

The impulses for change or for renewal were not felt equally by all involved, and this helps explain the unpredictability of the development of actual crises and the linkage between crisis and renewal when renewal followed. In fact, the process of renewal seems in many cases to have depended on a preceding crisis only insofar as the crisis acted as a catalyst to speed the breaking down of long-standing resistance to change, and thus to promote ideas and impulses for renovation or renewal already underway.

II. The Process of Renewal

The concept of "renewal" can be more clearly defined in the abstract and recognized in practice. In contrast to the term "modernization," with its connotations of a single process of transformation and in which different countries can be more or, more often, *less* successful in following a reproducible ideal pattern, "renewal" implies that a good deal of the past and of the particular characteristics of a state or society are carried forward and adapted to meet new needs and demands.[22] Our use of "renewal" borrows unabashedly from Stanley Hoffmann's *Decline or Renewal? France Since the 1930s*.[23] We stress renewal as a process of redevelopment, renovation, reorientation, in order to refashion France and its place in a changing world. This allows the possibility of renewal even on a conservative basis: Pétain, often portrayed as the arch-conservative seeking to recreate a romanticized, idealized France in 1940-41, preferred to label his efforts at Vichy as a "national renovation." More importantly, it allows for an essential uncertainty as to where the changes undertaken will lead. "Modernization" too easily implies that there is a specific destination intended, a station to be arrived at once and for all, rather than a continuous process of adaptation and development into a future that remains uncertain in its details and in constant movement ahead of present plans.

Two salient characteristics of the renewal process recur in these essays and merit clear statement at the outset. First, that renewal can be better understood as a cumulative process, one in which changes occur by an aggregation of impulses, pressures and ideas that converge or find their conjuncture—rather than as a sharp turn or a new departure. Secondly, that resistance to renewal had at times tremendous strength in France.

Treated as a cumulative process, there is no fixed point of departure for renewal, nor any predetermined or ideal point of destination. The schematic concepts of modernization and the models developed in the 1960s, the most common and most commonly refuted being Walt Rostow's "stages of growth" argument to explain industrialization, prove to be more misleading than helpful in understanding specific historical cases.[24] Particularly in the essays concerning questions of state policy, renewal was a distinctly evolutionary process. It required the development of new ideas for policy reform, the persuasion of key administrative and institutional constituencies, and the acceptance of these new ideas in broader interest groups, be they the public-at-large, politicians, a partisan press, or a constituent group particularly affected by the policies under consideration.

Examples from the case studies presented here demonstrate the point. Interwar monetary authorities, trapped in the gold-standard rhetoric of automatic adjustments and monetary normalcy, dismissed economists' ideas on targeting policy to achieve price stability as the misguided schemes of "currency cranks" with no experience of the real world. As Mouré shows, the success of the Poincaré stabilization delayed the rethinking of monetary management in France that gained momentum elsewhere, particularly in Britain and the United States, when currencies were forced off gold.

The shift in official policy for the treatment of juvenile offenders was also protracted. Fishman's study of the juvenile justice system demonstrates the insufficiency of a shift in expert opinion during the interwar period, despite the clear sense that France was falling behind other countries. Fishman quotes a lament by legal specialist André Perreau that it was "unfortunate that the country that gave birth to Descartes has let itself be surpassed in the application of Cartesian principles by countries like England, the United States, Belgium, Italy." The trend toward the use of diagnosis and treatment, rather than trial and punishment, prompted many reform ideas in the 1930s and early 1940s, and the Popular Front aspired to reform the standing legislation and managed to open new houses for juvenile offenders. But it was the Vichy regime's quest for moral regeneration that provided the energy needed to effect both legal and administrative reforms, aided, paradoxically, by the authoritarian nature of the regime, which obviated the need to gain support from officials and the public. Even then, a change in correctional personnel powered in part by avoidance of Vichy's compulsory labor service (STO), was needed to transform the actual administration of the system within the correctional houses, and the reforms did not obtain full legislative revision until after the Liberation, in 1945.

While Fishman presents a case for the cumulative character of renewal, Chapman's focus on the period of Liberation itself as a "moment" in state-building highlights the complexity of the factors conditioning the expectations and the opportunities for state action to foster renewal. Rather than focus on the development of a particular policy field or series of reforms, Chapman looks at the reestablishment of the legitimacy of the state, in its role not just to govern reflecting the interests of the constituencies it represents, but to lead social, economic, and cultural development in the interests of the nation as a whole. He argues that reform initiatives after the war benefited from a reconceptualization of the role of the state, treating in detail the reassertion of state authority from above with de Gaulle's return to France and the new demands made from below for greater state intervention in the public interest. His concluding remarks on the space in policy determination opened to the influence of reformers *within* the state, often new personnel brought in successively by Vichy and by de Gaulle's restoration of state authority, offer a tantalizing foretaste of his new work on the development of reform in social and economic policy after the war.

Prestwich's study of women in the MRP is particularly revealing as a case of the frustration of renewal. Women were granted the same civic rights as men by decree in April 1944, a long overdue reform to catch up with democratic representation elsewhere that did not involve any sense of crisis. Women joining the MRP and running for political office during the Fourth Republic were quickly disillusioned: the MRP and Fourth Republic politics remained under the control of male politicians seeking to maintain traditional gender roles; they encouraged women's participation in subordinate roles in order to attract new members and mobilize women voters without threatening men's positions of power in determining issues, candidacy and representation. Unable to break down male resistance to women's political participation, MRP *militantes* had to seek alternative forums for political activism.

In his contribution, Martin Alexander suggests that, even before the crisis in military discipline in 1958-61, French military officers had divided between "colonialist" and "European" outlooks. The former professed attachment to empire as the key attribute of French world stature and sought in Algeria to expunge the legacy of defeat in Indochina and the deeper, lingering trauma of defeat in 1940. The "European" officers put their faith in new technology (supersonic aircraft and nuclear weapons) and sought to recast military organization and doctrine to serve European and NATO purposes in the Cold War. The political engagement of "colonialist" officers' in 1960-61 clinched the case for a purge of the military leadership, enabling de Gaulle to promote *technocrates en képi* and remove the officers deluded by *fantasmes politiques*, and thus recast the French armed forces to serve his European designs with renewed technical capacity and prestige.

Within renewal as a cumulative process, crises need not act as catalysts for change; they could have little or no influence, or even retard renewal. Their role appears to have been more significant in relation to the second characteristic evident in these essays, the strength of resistance to renewal. In any given case, particular institutions, interest groups, individuals, constituencies, were in influential positions to stall, block or preempt renewal. Crises seem to have played their most significant role in breaking down resistance to renewal, particularly where this resistance had become institutionalized. They discredited old values or convictions by exposing their flaws, their problems, even their irrelevance; by persuading those putting up resistance that new ideas were needed and preferable to established practice; by changing personnel in positions to influence policy and practice, whether by sweeping out old personnel and bringing in new or by altering or abolishing old institutional structures; and by challenging conventional wisdom and traditional mind sets that proved unequal to the crises they confronted.

Resistance came on a variety of fronts. Traditional foreign policy views and visceral anti-Communism in the personnel of the French ministry of foreign affairs and the political leadership of all French parties in the 1920s stiffened resolve to treat the Soviet Union as a pariah state regardless of the new state's potential to provide a powerful eastern ally against the threat of German military revival. Even in the late 1930s, when French leaders accepted the need for coordinated, international resistance to German expansionism after Munich, close military alliance with the Soviet Union remained an option to be circled warily rather than tackled directly.[25] Opposition to devaluation in France was coordinated from an institutional base in the Bank of France, but thrived because fears of the incalculable results of monetary instability convinced professional economists, civil servants, businessmen and the public at large that inflation posed a much greater danger than the monetary stringency and economic contraction needed to preserve the franc. The granting of suffrage to women in France encountered open protest from many conservative political leaders in the interwar period, and more subtle resistance from its self-proclaimed supporters in the *Ligue des Droits de l'Homme*. Where crises did not break down the various forms of institutional, ideological and practical resistance, renewal could make no headway.

In understanding renewal as a cumulative process, with the most important role for crises being that of breaking down resistance to change, two factors are clearly important in the relationship between crisis and renewal. The first is ideas. Particularly where renewal is linked to changes in policy, the development of new ideas is a critical step, involving the analysis required to attain a good understanding of the problem(s) needing solution and the rethinking of policy to provide solutions. The development of new ideas to reorient policy takes time, and it is only once these ideas have developed as conceivable alternatives and started to gain influential support that a crisis can provide the opportunity to sweep resistance aside and speed adoption and implementation.

This underscores the importance of the second factor, the persons and the institutional networks that provide the support needed to effect renewal and the resistance that retards or obstructs change. The linkage between crisis and renewal, as exposed in these essays, comes chiefly through crises breaking down resistance to change, and while this can happen as an immediate product of a crisis in a given policy realm, it can result as well from crises in other realms, particularly the political, which bring changes in personnel and institutions that sweep away resistance. Renewal as a cumulative process can be seen as taking place in recurrent waves, with crises having an influence on the height and the force of the waves striking existing structures, but the success of renewal depending on the shape and strength of the structures resisting change, and on the direction of the underlying tide of renewal.

This volume is presented, with affection and as a tribute, to John Campbell Cairns, Professor Emeritus at the University of Toronto. As a friend and guide for many of the contributors to this volume, he has played an important role as a colleague, critic and mentor. His own ground-breaking reassessment of the French crisis of 1940, interpreting it as an allied political-military failure rather than a French defeat, and his dedication to archival research have influenced all of us in pursuing our own scholarly paths toward deeper understanding of crises and renewal in France since the First World War. The collection begins with a contribution by P.M.H. Bell, who provides a personal reflection and reminiscence on the impact of one early Cairns essay, "Great Britain and the Fall of France: A Study in Allied Disunity."

Notes

1. Charles de Gaulle, *The Complete War Memoirs of Charles de Gaulle 1940-1946*, vol. 3, *Salvation 1944-1946*, trans. Richard Howard (New York, 1967), 998.
2. Furet's formulation in François Furet, Jacques Julliard and Pierre Rosanvallon, *La République du centre: La fin de l'exception française* (Paris, 1988), 54.
3. Robert Gildea, *France 1814-1914* (Essex, 1996), 32.
4. De Gaulle, *Complete War Memoirs, vol. 3*, 3.
5. Stanley Hoffmann et. al., *In Search of France* (Cambridge, MA, 1963).
6. See Barry Eichengreen, ed., *Europe's Postwar Recovery* (Cambridge, 1995).
7. Raymond Aron, *The Elusive Revolution: Anatomy of a Student Revolt*, trans. Gordon Clough (New York, 1969), xix.
8. Michel Crozier, *The Stalled Society* (New York, 1973).
9. Furet et. al., *La République du centre*, particularly 11 and 51-55.
10. James F. Hollifield, "Conclusion: Still Searching for the New France," in *Searching for the New France*, James F. Hollifield and George Ross, eds. (New York and London, 1991), 275.

11. Peter Morris, "Defeat and the Modernisers: A Review Article," *Modern & Contemporary France* 41 (April 1990), 63-5.
12. See Richard F. Kuisel, *Capitalism and the State in Modern France: Renovation and Economic Management in the Twentieth Century* (Cambridge and New York, 1981); Michel Margairaz, *L'État, les finances et l'économie: Histoire d'une conversion, 1932-1952* (Paris, 1991); Philippe Mioche, *Le Plan Monnet: Genèse et élaboration 1941-1947* (Paris, 1987); and Andrew Shennan, *Rethinking France: Plans for Renewal 1940-1946* (Oxford, 1989).
13. For analysis of the major political crises since 1870, see Michel Winock, *La fièvre hexagonale: Les grandes crises politiques 1871-1968* (Paris, 1986), esp. chap. 9.
14. Winock, *La fièvre hexagonale*, 389-90.
15. Danielle Tartakowsky, *Le pouvoir est dans la rue: Crises politiques et manifestations en France* (Paris, 1998).
16. Odile Rudelle, *Mai 58, de Gaulle et la République* (Paris, 1988); Thiers had famously predicted that the Provisional Republic of 1871-75 would endure by virtue of being the regime that would divide the French the least (compared to the alternatives of another monarchist Restoration or a Bonapartist dictatorship).
17. See John F.V. Keiger, *Raymond Poincaré* (Cambridge, 1997).
18. Peter Morris, "De Gaulle and the Reality of Things: A Review Article," *Modern & Contemporary France* (1990), 50-53.
19. See also Keiger, *Raymond Poincaré.*
20. For the developing crisis of conscience versus action as it affected one influential and highly-organized group within the French electorate, the 1914-18 veterans, see Lyn Gorman, "The *Anciens Combattants* and Appeasement: From Munich to War," *War & Society* 10, no. 2 (1992), 73-89.
21. Martin Evans, "The French Empire: From Colonialism to Post-Colonialism," in *French History since Napoleon*, Martin S. Alexander, ed. (London, 1999), 412.
22. See Herrick Chapman, "Modernity and National Identity in Postwar France," *French Historical Studies* 22, no. 2 (1999), 292-314.
23. Stanley Hoffmann, *Decline or Renewal? France Since the 1930s* (New York, 1974), which Hoffmann in turn has adopted from de Gaulle's *Memoirs of Hope: Renewal and Endeavor*, trans. Terence Kilmartin (New York, 1971), of which Hoffmann notes (264-5), "All his life this disciple of Bergson scrutinized the future and worked to project France into the vanguard of modern times, to predict coming trends so as to take better advantage of them."
24. W.W. Rostow, *The Stages of Economic Growth: A Non-Communist Manifesto* (Cambridge, 1960), and idem., ed., *The Economics of Take-Off into Sustained Growth* (New York, 1963).
25. See Michael Jabara Carley, "End of the 'Low, Dishonest Decade': Failure of the Anglo-French-Soviet Alliance in 1939," *Europe-Asia Studies* 45, no. 2 (1993): 303-41; and *1939: The Alliance That Never Was and the Coming of World War II* (Chicago, 1999).

Chapter 1

John Cairns and the Historiography of Great Britain and the Fall of France

'Il n'y a que le premier pas qui coûte'

P.M.H. Bell

The story is told that when Saint Denis, the patron saint of France, was martyred by having his head cut off, he set out to walk some two leagues to the place where he wished to be buried, carrying his head in his hands. When onlookers cried out in amazement and admiration, the saint observed with becoming modesty: '*La distance n'y fait rien; il n'y a que le premier pas qui coûte.*'[1] The same is often true in the development of historical understanding. It is the first step which is difficult, and the first step which counts—to take two ways in which Saint Denis's remark may be translated. In the early 1950s, the historical questions presented by the state of Franco-British relations during the great crisis of May-June 1940, and the role played by Britain in the defeat of France, were shrouded in an apparently impenetrable obscurity. Historians grappled with sources which were at once voluminous and unenlightening. It was a struggle even to establish what had happened, never mind to understand it. There seemed to be no perspective in which to see the events of 1940, and little structure to form the basis of historical analysis.[2]

Then in December 1955 John Cairns, published in the *Journal of Modern History*, a massive article (far longer than any normal publication in a learned journal) on 'Great Britain and the Fall of France: A Study in Allied Disunity.'[3]

Notes for this chapter begin on page 26.

Suddenly the whole subject was illuminated, not only by the depth and perspicacity of the author's research, but by the clarity of his analysis and by a historical perspective which was remarkable only fifteen years after the events. It was a first step of crucial importance, and it is right in this volume that we should look back to see how difficult it was and how much it counted.

I. The State of the Evidence and Historical Discussion, c.1954-55

In 1954-55 the evidence available to historians of Britain and the fall of France was large in quantity but highly variable in quality. The government archives of both countries for 1940 were firmly closed to researchers. In Britain, the 50 Year Rule prevailed, under which papers were closed until fifty years after the year in which they were produced, so that the files for 1940 would become available in January 1990. (If maintained, this would have meant that only now, in 1999, would we be absorbing the considered results of research on the events of 1940.) In France, there was in effect no fixed rule. Many government papers, especially those of the Quai d'Orsay, had been destroyed in 1940; many had been captured by the Germans; many had been dispersed and disorganized during the confusion caused by conquest, occupation and liberation. To restore order amid this chaos was bound to take a long time. Moreover, there was a powerful if usually unspoken belief that the archives contained material which was better left in obscurity, for the sake of France as well as of individuals. Access by historians to French government archives was therefore likely to be put off to the Greek kalends. In both Britain and France, the owners of the private papers of politicians, civil servants and military men usually followed the practices of their governments.

Historians were thus forced to make do with material which was patchy in its coverage and difficult to evaluate because it had usually been produced for some strong personal or political motive. This was particularly true in France, where most of the principal participants in the events of 1940 speedily published their memoirs in order to justify their own actions, and sometimes also to provide a whole design by which events should be explained. Paul Reynaud, the French Premier during the great crisis, wrote two long, versions of his own account of events—and the title of the first, *La France a sauvé l'Europe,* was intended to shock the reader into attention by claiming for France a victory within the defeat of 1940. Reynaud's argument was that France, by absorbing the first force of the German blow in the west, had gained time which enabled the British, and behind them the Americans, to survive and ultimately gain the victory—a victory in which France could claim a share.[4] General Weygand, the French Commander-in-Chief after the departure of Gamelin, placed the battle of

France in the context of his whole career by dealing with it in only a part of a three-volume set of memoirs, of which that dealing with the events of 1940 was entitled *Rappelé au Service,* striking the note of duty done.[5] Paul Baudouin, who served under Reynaud before becoming Pétain's first Foreign Minister, published his account in the form of a diary. François Charles-Roux, who took over as Secretary-General at the Quai d'Orsay in the midst of the crisis, composed a solid volume of diplomatic memoirs, worthy of an earlier age. General de Gaulle dealt with the defeat in only the first two chapters of the first volume of his carefully sculpted *Mémoires de Guerre,* in which the fall of France was only the prologue to a longer and greater story.[6] Each had his own axe to grind, and most concealed as much as they revealed.

The events of 1940 and the subsequent German occupation of France also produced trials of those who were accused of responsibility for the defeat or for the treason involved in collaboration. The Vichy authorities staged the trial at Riom of General Gamelin, Edouard Daladier, Léon Blum and other ministers from the last years of the Third Republic, for their alleged role in bringing about the defeat of 1940.[7] After the Liberation and the victory of 1945, Marshal Pétain, Pierre Laval and lesser figures of the Vichy regime were tried on charges of collaboration and treason.[8] After the war, the newly elected National Assembly set up a *Commission d'Enquête parlementaire sur les événements survenus en France de 1933 à 1945,* made up of members of the Assembly and representatives of various Resistance groups, which eventually produced a Report (including documents) and nine volumes of testimony and cross-examination.[9] These proceedings produced a certain amount of documentation (for example, signals sent by the French Ministry of Marine at the end of June 1940); a mass of narrative and assertion, much of it hard to verify; and a multitude of accusations, protestations and evasions. The material was difficult to use, through its sheer bulk and the modes of procedure—some individuals testified in a number of trials, and then to the commission of inquiry on more than one occasion. There were a few gold nuggets for the historian to dig out, but only by means of infinite toil and careful sifting.

In November 1950 there appeared the first number of a new journal, the *Revue d'Histoire de la Deuxième Guerre Mondiale,* published by the Presses Universitaires de France, edited by Henri Michel and with the distinguished figures of Pierre Renouvin and Maurice Baumont among its editorial committee. Issue No. 1 of the *Revue* was devoted to '*Aspects de la Résistance française,*' a subject on which Henri Michel had already written a book and to which he was to remain devoted during the whole of his long editorship. There followed special numbers on Japan in the war (No.2); the armistice of June 1940 (No.3); the campaign of 1940 in France (Nos. 10-11); and the German concentration camp system (Nos. 15-16); as well as issues not devoted to a particular theme. The *Revue* thus opened discussion on widely different aspects of the war, while showing a natural concentration on the role of France, and a special care for the history of the French Resistance. Through a long and distinguished life, the *Revue d'Histoire de la Deuxième Guerre Mondiale* was to bring an increasingly rigorous scholarly appraisal to bear on its whole vast subject-matter, including the events of 1940; but by January 1955 it had published only seventeen numbers, and its work was only in its pioneering phase. A historian of Great Britain and the fall of France could find only limited guidance in its pages.

Almost the whole of this endeavor—the writing of memoirs, the holding of trials and inquiries, and even the beginnings of scholarly investigation—was directed towards the arraignment or self- justification of individuals, or towards claims as to what had gone wrong at the time of the fall of France, or towards the heroic reactions to that defeat which took shape in the Resistance. From a deeper examination of the state of France before and after the defeat, the nature of the Vichy regime, and the limits of Resistance activity, French politicians, historians and public opinion in general shrank back. In the delicate state of French politics in the post-war years, which were also the time of the onset of the Cold War and a new relationship with Germany, memories were carefully selective. Moreover, even within the limited discussion which took place, the role of Franco-British relations in the defeat of France was allotted only a limited part, sometimes amounting to little more than blaming the British for letting down, or even betraying, the French.

The position of Britain was very different. For the British, defeat in the Battle of France was almost swallowed up by later victory in the Battle of Britain. An intense pride in the country's finest hour took the place of the French sense of tragedy.[10] The British were thus saved from the worst excesses of self-justification and point-scoring which afflicted the French, and the British accounts produced much solid evidence on Britain and the fall of France, available in the reporting and immediate reflections of journalists; the memoirs of two leading participants, Winston Churchill and Sir Edward Spears; and the official history of the British part in the Battle of France. These sources provided much for historians to work on, but were still subject to grave shortcomings and problems.

The newspaper reporting of the defeat of France at the time showed a remarkable degree of sympathy for the French plight, and an acknowledgment of the paucity of the British contribution to the battle. On 3 June the *Daily Herald* declared that 'We do not forget that French armies helped to cover the retreat [to Dunkirk].' On 14 June the *Daily Mirror* said that 'The French do not need our tributes and our praise. They need aeroplanes, tanks, guns, men.' There was a strong sense that both Britain and France had made grave mistakes and failed to prepare for modem warfare, but that it was France which was paying the price.

Indeed, at the very moment of the French defeat there was a fuller acceptance of the French point of view on these matters, and a keener acknowledgment of British inadequacies, than there was to be in later times.[11] But there was also a strong sense of British superiority. In its analysis of the causes of the French defeat, the press almost unanimously condemned the French for their 'Maginot mentality' (or 'Maginot folly'); and was equally firmly convinced that France had been rotted from within before being struck from without. Disunity, treachery, and failure of leadership had all opened the way for the German victory. The French censorship of press and radio had encouraged rumor, sapped morale and prevented healthy criticism of government policy. Opinions differed as to whether such diseases of the body politic were to be found also in Britain and might produce similar results—some thought they did, and advocated a purge of appeasers and guilty men; but in general there was an optimistic conviction that 'it can't happen here.'[12]

Among the best-informed commentators of the time were Alexander Werth, a correspondent for the *Manchester Guardian* and the *New Statesman,* and the author of influential (and still valuable) books on France in the 1930s; and Denis Brogan, an academic writer who was also a popularizer in the best sense. In September 1940 Werth published *The Last Days of Paris,* printing his diary for May and June, with some later reflections.[13] Brogan published an article, '*Il y avait la France,*' and a book review which became a discussion of the fall of France.[14] Werth's book was a vivid piece of description, shot through with flashes of insight and explanation. The author had an agonized sense that France was fighting almost alone. 'God, why is there no decent-sized British Army in France?' But equally he was convinced that something was badly wrong within France itself. 'What is one St. Exupéry to a million Chautemps [Camille Chautemps, who achieved the status of the archetypal politician of the last phase of the Third Republic]? Hasn't pacifism rotted the guts of the French soul?' In his Epilogue, Werth argued that in defeat France had turned in upon itself. '*La France aux français*' had become the slogan of Pétain's government at the time when two-thirds of French territory had been placed under German occupation.[15] Brogan for his part wrote that under the cover of two great military reputations (those of Pétain and Weygand) the forces of those who had long despaired of France had decided 'to try the daring and despicable experiment of saving all but honour.' The French state had lost its authority, and opened the way to those who sympathized with foreign powers more than with their own country.[16]

There was much here for historians to seize on: France fighting virtually alone; a rot within; 'la France aux français.' But these points can now be picked out with the grace of sixty years of hindsight. A mere fourteen or fifteen years after the events there was no such clarity. Journalists (from whom no secrets were hid—or so they believed) had written a great deal, and parts of it were true—but which parts? In 1954 it was very difficult to tell.

By that date the ephemeral contributions of the press had been reinforced by two substantial books of memoirs by those who had played central roles in Franco-British relations in 1940: Churchill himself, and Sir Edward Spears, whom Churchill appointed as his personal liaison officer with Reynaud.[17] These volumes carried the authority of firsthand knowledge, buttressed by the citation of contemporary documents; and indeed they marked a great advance in historical understanding. But each had its own emphasis and message, implicit in its title: for Churchill, *Their Finest Hour;* for Spears, *Assignment to Catastrophe.*

Book One of *Their Finest Hour* is entitled 'The Fall of France,' but in fact France shared the stage with other matters. Eight chapters were devoted to French affairs, and seven to the formation of Churchill's coalition government, defense against invasion and preparations for eventual counterattack, and relations with other countries. Even within the chapters dealing with France, there was much material on the BEF and the British side of the evacuation from Dunkirk. Churchill wrote about the fall of France, but his main subject was the survival of Britain. He was prepared to admit a number of British faults and failures in the battle of France: neglecting to thrash out with the French the whole Allied plan of campaign and distribution of forces, especially the implications of the agreement to advance to the River Dyle in the event of a German attack on Belgium; and above all the tiny British contribution to the land battle—only ten divisions in May 1940. Throughout his account there ran a thread of sympathy for France and the French people in their agony. But there was also a stern indictment of French failures. One of the most enduring images conveyed by the book, etched indelibly into the historical record, was Churchill's account of his meeting with French leaders in Paris on 16 May. He recalled his question to General Gamelin: '"Where is the strategic reserve?" … "*Où est la masse de manoeuvre?*"And then the answer: 'General Gamelin turned to me and, with a shake of the head and a shrug, said: "*Aucune.*"' Churchill then drove the point home by repetition and capital letters—'NO STRATEGIC RESERVE. "*Aucune.*"'[18] It is unforgettable. There were other pictures of French failure, less vivid but still insistent—weakness in tackling the German tanks, crowds of French prisoners with scarcely an escort in sight, Weygand's delays while events and the enemy took control, a lack of will to continue the struggle outside France.

In contrast, Churchill drew a discreet veil over the agonized discussions in the War Cabinet of 26-28 May on whether to inquire after peace terms through the mediation of Mussolini, and presented solely a picture of British resolve to fight on alone. He emphasized the steadfastness of ministers, parliament and people alike, and the sound strategic judgment of the Chiefs of Staff. Equally powerful was his evocation of the evacuation from Dunkirk: 'In the midst of our defeat glory came to the Island people, united and unconquerable ... ' And when the last British troops had been taken off there came 'a sense of deliverance ... a feeling of intense relief, melting almost into triumph.'[19] As a constant theme in the background to events, Churchill referred repeatedly to his communications with President Roosevelt and the Prime Ministers of the Dominions, the English-speaking alliance which was eventually to carry the country to victory. Churchill's narrative was primarily, and with ample justification, a British story. It was striking that, before he turned to the events themselves, he opened his account with five pages on the total contribution to the war as a whole by 'the people of this small island, upon whom in the crisis of the world's history the brunt fell.'[20]

Churchill was at the center of British government during the crisis. From 25 May to 17 June, Spears was in France, responsible for liaison between the Prime Minister and Paul Reynaud, and present at all the meetings of the Supreme War Council. No one was better placed to give an account of Franco-British relations which took into account the French position, because he was in constant contact with French politicians, soldiers, officials and journalists. His experience as a liaison officer in the Great War (related in two substantial books, *Liaison 1914* and *Prelude to Victory*), together with his perfect command of the French language arising from a bilingual upbringing, and his own repeated assertions on the point, combined to give Spears an unrivaled reputation as a devoted Francophile, who had as great an affection for France as for his own country.[21] He was also a very considerable artist with words. The extraordinary vividness and pace of his narrative in *Assignment to Catastrophe,* the weight of detail and the verbatim reports of conversations, can still carry the reader along almost unresisting.

Historians were at once aware, on the book's publication in 1954, that they were in the presence of a first-class source, and Spears's reputation as a lover of France gave it a stamp of fairness and evenhandedness. It was only slowly that a different picture took shape. On careful reading, the appearance of evenhandedness dissolved. In fact, Spears directed a steady fire of barbed comments against the French. In his chapters on the phony war, before his main narrative got under way, Spears was already drawing contrasts between British unity and French discord. As soon as he plunged into the main stream of events, Spears introduced Commandant Fauvelle, an emissary from General Blanchard's headquarters in the North-East: 'I have in my time seen broken men, but never before one deliquescent, that is, in a state where he was fit only to be scraped up with a spoon, or mopped up.' The description of the deliquescent Fauvelle continued for some six pages, and resumed a little later on. But a few pages later again, the reader met Major Archdale, a British liaison officer with the French Armies: 'If I had tried to imagine something that was the exact opposite of Commandant Fauvelle, here it was. Resolution, clarity of thought, utter determination, a spirit that banished all trace of fatigue …'[22] The contrast was vividly drawn, and left a lasting impression of two individuals forming the very embodiment of opposite national responses to the military crisis. Spears emphasized his own bewilderment in the face of French collapse. 'Every other minute a voice within me asked "What has happened to France?" But no answer came. It was like questioning death.'[23] Again, the message was inescapable—as Spears stated in his title, he was on an *Assignment to Catastrophe*.

These passages were followed by many others in the same tone. Spears remarked on Admiral Abrial, said to be directing operations at Dunkirk from the protection of thirty feet of concrete—'"C'est l'Amiral Abri."'[24] He repeatedly emphasized the French (and especially Weygand's) tendency to escape from their own responsibilities by throwing the blame for French defeats onto the British. He was prepared to accept that General Vuillemin, the Commander of the French Air Force, had a fine record in the Great War, but added at once that 'the brave are not necessarily intelligent.'[25] The final scenes of French breakdown and flight were vividly and ferociously described: 'fat convoys and their sleek personnel ambulating like cows towards Bordeaux.'[26] All the time, Spears contrasted the French collapse with British resolution, and showed how Churchill's oratory (as translated by himself) could stiffen the French leaders—but only temporarily. From time to time there were warning signs of a breach between Spears and the France of his earlier affections. Describing a brief visit to London on 7 June, he observed: 'Until these last few days I had always felt almost as much at home in France as in England, but this time I had left strangers behind me and was now at home.'[27]

It is by no means the case that Spears's memoirs are rendered valueless by this *parti pris*. Indeed, even in distant retrospect, and with much archive material available, much of his account stands up very well, and the details are usually corroborated. The trouble is that the drip-feed of Spears's animosity towards France, usually administered under cover of protestations of affection, renders the source something other than it appeared at first sight. It was doubtless possible to pick up the warning signs; but how many did so on first or even second reading?

In 1954-55 the British archives were open, at any rate in large part, to the historians commissioned to write the official histories of the war. In 1953 L.F. Ellis's *The War in France and Flanders, 1939-1940* was published in the military series of these official histories. It had the virtues of careful narrative and sober reflection within its own imposed limits. When one needs a clear, brief account of the Escaut and Dyle plans formulated during autumn 1939, it may be found in Ellis. The British side of the controversial affair of the counterattack at Arras on 21-22 May was well and fairly expounded, with the telling details that the actual force involved was only two battalions of infantry and 76 tanks—not enough to make a deep or lasting impact.[28] The author even entered imaginatively into the very different meaning of the evacuation from Dunkirk for the British and French troops involved, quoting the haunting lines of Louis Aragon:

> La France sous nos pieds, comme une étoffe usée,
> C'est petit à petit à nos pas refusée.[29]

Ellis's criticisms of Gamelin and Weygand were measured and sensible, and everyone would now agree that as early as 25 May Weygand had decided that nothing could avert defeat, and all his actions were colored by that certainty. But the author let Gort down lightly, offering some mild critical comment, but concluding that 'All his major decisions were both wise and well-timed,' which was doubtless loyal on the part of the official historian, but surely open to question.[30] The whole book provided a solid basis of information on its prescribed subject: the operations of the British forces engaged in the campaign; but almost by definition it went little further than that.

All these British sources allotted much space and attention to relations between Britain and France during the crisis of 1940—more proportionately than the French material. From the two sets of sources together, historians in 1954-55 could learn much, but only in patches. It often remained hard even to ascertain the chronological order of events, that simple but vital starting-point for understanding. Perspective was lacking, and there seemed no framework for the analytical approach which is the instrument of historical explanation. The task of a researcher was akin to trying to draw a map of an unknown land from a boat, without being able to set foot on land. The coastline (the outline of the principal events) could be discerned, though not in its entirety. Sometimes a great river (corresponding to a valuable volume of memoirs) allowed a view of the hinterland, but only from a limited angle. It was very difficult to put the pieces together, and impossible to produce a map which conveyed a proper picture of the terrain as a whole.

II. John Cairns and 'le premier pas'

It was this obscure scene which John Cairns illuminated by his article on 'Great Britain and the Fall of France.' His achievement was not only to master the evidence, however difficult (for example, there were no fewer than eighteen references to *Les événements survenus en France,* that notoriously cumbrous and difficult source), but also to apply the historical methods of analysis, criticism and perspective to draw out the meaning and shape of events.

The analytical structure of the article was its most immediately striking virtue. The problems of military cooperation were reviewed in careful, almost relentless order: the crucial issue of the Dyle Plan; the vagueness in the Allied chain of command; the problem of the point at which Gort began to take an independent line; the simple inability of commanders and their staffs to *find* one another. Dunkirk was presented as 'the nadir of Anglo-French military relations' as well as, for the British, 'a gloriously successful evacuation.'[31] (Incidentally, Cairns always wrote 'Dunkerque,' not 'Dunkirk.' It is a French town, so he used the French name—a tiny but characteristic point.) The sharpness of comment was sometimes arresting.—'Gort was, so far as the situation of the northern armies was concerned, defeatist from the advent of Weygand's command at the latest.'[32] The immediate reaction of a British reader at the time was one of surprise, shading into indignation. How could Gort, with his Victoria Cross and his unshakeable courage, be called defeatist? But the force of the comment lay in the qualifying clause—'so far as the situation of the northern armies was concerned.' When Gort set out to save the BEF, which from a British point of view was a crucial decision, it meant that he had accepted the defeat of the northern armies. It was a remarkable example of evenhanded, almost clinical analysis.

Failures of communication were scrutinized in the same manner, from the absurdity of the single telephone at the Château du Muguet—'classic in its own comic and terrible way'[33] to the wider issues of the muddle over the so-called Breton Redoubt and the British failure to grasp at an early date 'the magnitude of the defeatist spirit rising in the political and military circles of France.'[34] On another issue of communication, the British telegrams of 16 June agreeing to a French approach for an armistice provided that the fleet was sent forthwith to British harbors, and the withdrawal and later fate of those messages, Cairns was the first to penetrate the multiple confusions of the evidence to point out that *it did not matter* what happened to the telegrams, because 'The French could not have dared to lose their ships to the British'.[35] Conflicts of personality were similarly passed in review. Finally and crucially, Cairns came to the analysis of the different concepts of the war held by France and Britain. The crucial point was that 'between the French and British governments there was no common conception of the war being fought.'[36] The French could see nothing beyond the immediate disaster; the British were confident in ultimate victory. In such circumstances it was almost inevitable that they should follow divergent paths, and much of the commentary concerned with distributing praise and blame was irrelevant. The point was pressed home in a remarkable passage pointing out that the armistice was 'the nationalist conclusion to France's war.'[37] Equally, and in complete contrast, resistance was the conclusion for Britain.

Much of this was not strictly speaking new. Churchill and Ellis had both drawn attention to the problems of the Dyle Plan. Alexander Werth had pointed out in September 1940 that the slogan of Pétain's government was 'La France aux français'—the nationalist conclusion. The triumph of Cairns's vision was to pick out from the mass of fact, argument and assertion which was available to all observers the key elements which permitted analysis, which in turn opened the way to understanding.

The analytical structure of the article was its most obvious feature, but its unobtrusive critical commentary on the evidence was equally significant. A crucial example was Cairns's passage on the role of Spears as liaison officer, in which he challenged for the first time Spears's reputation as a devoted friend of both France and Britain and an unfailing intermediary between them. Cairns coolly reviewed the tale of Spears's stormy confrontations with French leaders, concluding with the restrained but telling comment that 'It is possible to feel that they were far more harmful than helpful.'[38] After this review, it was not only Spears's actions but his account of events that appeared in a different light, and one of the crucial sources for the history of Franco-British relations took on a new aspect.

Alongside critical appraisal of the sources there came flashes of insight into what was left unsaid. Cairns's section on the question of whether France and Britain should make an approach to Mussolini to keep him out of the war (in simple terms to buy him off) could not get far, in view of the limits imposed by the evidence. But he pointed out that in Paris Colonel de Villelume had urged Reynaud to sound the British 'on the prospect of asking Italy to mediate in the struggle with Germany'—something which went much further than buying off the Italians, and raised the possibility of an attempt at a general peace through Mussolini's mediation. Cairns also picked up, though only speculatively, the divisions within the British War Cabinet on the issue of an approach to Italy, with Halifax in favor of the French proposing terms, Chamberlain undecided, and Churchill squarely opposed.[39] Churchill himself, in his war memoirs, was completely silent on the War Cabinet meetings on 26, 27 and 28 May 1940, when the British ministers debated the question, not only of buying Italy off, but of using Mussolini as a mediator with Hitler. It was indeed one of the most crucial moments in British history, and by extension in the history of Europe and even the world. The evidence available in 1954 and early 1955 did not reveal what had happened, but Cairns sensed that *something* had been afoot, and left hints for others to pursue.

Finally, what Cairns brought to the whole discussion was the quality of perspective, demonstrating that this could be achieved by the adoption of a sound historical standpoint rather than simply waiting for the passage of time. At the beginning of his article, Cairns deplored the unhistorical tendency 'to discuss the course of the war from the perspective of the post-war period alone.'[40] He argued that the fall of France had been unsympathetically handled in the English-speaking countries, and that it was necessary to reconsider events from the point of view of the defeated as well as that of those who had held on and secured the final victory. These themes ran through the whole article, in which the author made a remarkable and successful effort, first to see events from the perspective of their own time, and second to be evenhanded as between the British and the French. He argued powerfully that the opposed British and French views about the defeat of France could be understood only by immersing oneself in the circumstances of 1940. That in turn led to the belief that Franco-British relations in 1940 formed 'an essentially tragic situation'—a view whose truth has emerged ever more clearly with the passage of time.[41]

Cairns's article on 'Great Britain and the Fall of France' is now itself a landmark in the historiography of the subject. Some (but by no means all) of the evidence which he and others used at that time has now been superseded as the archives have been opened and historians exploit the wealth of documentation available in government and private archives in both countries. Historical research and understanding have moved on, but it is right that we should remember with respect and gratitude the historian who took the crucial first step towards understanding the nature of the problem and some of its solutions.

Notes

1. The saint's remark appears in various forms. This version is in Anthony Lejeune, ed., *The Concise Dictionary of Foreign Quotations* (London, 1998), 81.
2. This passage arises from vivid personal memory. In the early 1950s I was one of those historians trying to make sense of Franco-British relations in 1940; and my own notes, drafts and early articles bear testimony to the problems besetting research at that time.
3. John C. Cairns, 'Great Britain and the Fall of France: A Study in Allied Disunity,' *Journal* of *Modern History* xxvii, no. 4 (December 1955): 365-409. The distinction of this article was speedily recognized by the award of the Higby Prize. See *ibid.*, xxix, no. 1 (March 1957): 82.
4. Paul Reynaud, *La France a sauvé l'Europe*, 2 vols. (Paris, 1947); *Au coeur de la mêlée* (Paris, 1951).
5. Maxime Weygand, *Rappelé au service* (Paris, 1950).
6. Paul Baudouin, *Neuf mois au gouvernement, avril-décembre 1940* (Paris, 1948); François Charles-Roux, *Cinq mois tragiques aux affaires étrangères, 21 mai-1 novembre* 1940 (Paris, 1949); Charles de Gaulle, *Mémoires de guerre*, vol. 1, *L'appel, 1940-1942* (Paris, 1954).
7. *Le procès de Riom* (Paris, 1945).
8. *Le procès du Maréchal Pétain* (Paris, 1949); *Le procès Laval* (Paris, 1946); *Le procès Flandin* (Paris, 1947).
9. *Commission d'enquête parlementaire sur les événements survenus en France de 1933 à 1945* (Paris, 1951-52), *Rapport de M. Charles Serre* (2 vols.), *Témoignage* (9 vols.).

10. It was symbolic that the second volume of Churchill's war memoirs was entitled in English *Their Finest Hour,* and in its French translation *L'heure tragique.*
11. It is true that the press was partly responding to government guidance on the need to keep up French morale and maintain the solidity of the alliance; but British newspapers did not always follow the guidance of the Ministry of Information, and on this occasion their comments were virtually unanimous and transparently sincere. See the discussion in P.M.H. Bell, A *Certain Eventuality: Britain and the Fall of France* (Farnborough, 1974), 119-22.
12. See the summary, *ibid.*, 129-32.
13. Alexander Werth, *The Last Days of Paris:* A *Journalist's Diary* (London, 1940).
14. These articles are reprinted in D.W. Brogan, *French Personalities and Problems* (London, 1946): 'Il y avait la France,' 133-5; 'France, 1940,' 147-55.
15. Werth, *Last Days,* 40, 76, 267-68.
16. Brogan, *French Personalities,* 133, 154.
17. Winston S. Churchill, *The Second World War,* vol. 2, *Their Finest Hour* (London, 1949); Sir Edward Spears, *Assignment to Catastrophe,* vol.1, *Prelude to Dunkirk,* vol. 2, *The Fall of France* (London, 1954).
18. Churchill, vol. 2, 42.
19. *Ibid.*, 92, 122.
20. *Ibid.*, 4-8.
21. Sir Edward Spears, *Liaison 1914: A Narrative of the Great Retreat* (London, 1930); *Prelude to Victory* (London, 1939).
22. Spears, *Assignment,* vol. 1, 188-94, 197-98, 224.
23. *Ibid.*, 202.
24. Spears, *Assignment,* vol. 2, 6.
25. *Ibid.*, 17.
26. *Ibid.*, 237.
27. *Ibid.*, 115.
28. L. F. Ellis, *The War in France and Flanders, 1939-1940* (London, 1953), 87-89.
29. *Ibid.*, 247.
30. *Ibid.*, 323.
31. Cairns, 'Great Britain and the Fall of France' (see note 3, above), 373.
32. *Ibid.*, 377.
33. *Ibid.*, 384.
34. *Ibid.*, 387.
35. *Ibid.*, 394.
36. *Ibid.*, 402.
37. *Ibid.*, 406.
38. *Ibid.*, 399-400.
39. *Ibid.*, 382.
40. *Ibid.*, 365.
41. *Ibid.*, 409.

Chapter 2

POINCARE-LA-PEUR

France and the Ruhr Crisis of 1923

Sally Marks

On occasion, the eye of the historian has an excessively narrow focus in space and time. This has frequently been true of historians of interwar France who tend to study its external policies *in vacuo* or in relation to Germany alone.[1] Beyond geographic isolation comes chronological. All too often, the early 1920s and the late 1930s are treated as if they occurred in different, disconnected centuries, and some historians are prone to assume that the problems culminating in the Third Republic's collapse arose in 1934 or 1936.

In fact, there were numerous early signs of later weakness, many of them visible in the Ruhr venture of 1923, which was the first great crisis of interwar France and the Third Republic's last real effort to assert an independent policy against a major power.[2] As in 1936, existing treaties would be enforced by France or nobody, and the failure of 1923-1924 foreshadowed the absence of action in 1936; so also did the fact that 1923 represented the first of several military downturns as terms of service were cut and equipment aged without extensive replacement. Both eras displayed the fraying of France's twin bulwarks: the Versailles treaty and key alliances. Early and late, hesitant politicians were unwilling to run political risks, especially that of full mobilization, and cautious generals opposed acting against Germany without crushing military superiority. Governmental and economic disorganization did not change, nor did underestimation of the importance of propaganda. There was no diminution of the stubborn French belief that

Notes for this chapter begin on page 39.

whatever France needed would somehow come to be simply because France needed it, a faith which reached its ultimate disastrous absurdity in the strategy of 1940 when, as Joel Blatt has remarked, France needed "close to a 'perfect war'," with key variables falling to her favor.[3]

It is important occasionally to attempt a broader focus in space as well as time because France's greatest problem in the interwar era, in its struggle to remain the great power most assumed it to be, was its heavy dependence on other states, which generally is not an attribute of genuine great powers. Indeed, the degree of dependency, although obscured by short-term power *vacua* east of the Rhine and France's briefly dominant army, raised questions about whether France really remained a great power, even if lovers of France (including historians) were, and sometimes are, reluctant to face cruel facts. France remained dependent on Russia for cannon fodder to overcome the demographic deficit and for a second German front in the lengthy war it posited, on Germany for coking coal and markets, on the United States for money and military equipment. French military doctrine generated geographic dependence on Belgium to provide France's battlefield in the next war and to be an obedient satellite in other, often nonmilitary, respects. Dependence on Britain came in several forms: its empire and ties to the United States could be decisive in that long war; only the Royal Navy could in practice provide access to the French empire, whereas the British merchant marine was needed to carry oil from the British-dominated Middle East to France. Yet from start almost to finish, France choked on the ideological factor regarding Russia, had strained political and either unresolved or unsatisfactory economic relations with Germany, and faced Anglo-American hostility to any French action to uphold the Versailles treaty or restrain German resurgence. From 1920 on, Belgium was a reluctant, often recalcitrant ally with no enthusiasm for its allotted role. Nor had Britain any taste for its assignment as France's primary protector.

All French prime ministers of the early 1920s understood French dependency, though they reacted in diverse ways—and had more choices than their successors of the late 1930s since the threat to France's independence was less immediate. Yet all knew that allies and potential allies had a constraining effect on French policy. In the short run, Britain mattered most, for lack of any other major ally. Much has been written about how World War I haunted France and affected its interwar policies; students of French history in this era need to consider as well how the Great War affected Britain. Early and late, memories of the bloodletting and recognition of what the war had cost generated hostility to France and Belgium, who were blamed for what Britain had suffered, and appeasement of Germany to ensure that it did not suffer again. This factor, combined with British smugness, sense of superiority, and sureness that it was right, strained relations and narrowed French policy options from 1920 on.

In addition, historians need to consider their sources and seek as diverse an array as possible when dealing with an international crisis, be it that of 1923 or that of 1938. This is particularly true in the twentieth century when propaganda has played so large a role, and "truths" have emerged and established themselves on the basis of partial records which do not square with the full weight of available evidence, a situation well-illustrated by the Ruhr episode of 1923. The long-standing stereotype of Poincaré-la-guerre, France's strong man avid to enter the Ruhr and dismember Germany, still lingers on, reinforced by Poincaré's rhetoric, Anglo-German propaganda, and monographs based on British and German diplomatic reporting, not on intimate knowledge of French governing circles.[4] In fact, his policies differed little from those of his predecessors, but his pronouncements and image did, and until recently that has been determining. French and Belgian files, however, present a different picture of Poincaré the procrastinator[5] who did not wish to enter the Ruhr, especially militarily, and, once there, did not know what to do. The strong man emerges as timid, irresolute, inclined to half-measures in the early months, and indecisive. Once driven to decisions, he clung to those already made and resisted making any more. Many factors prolonged the Ruhr agony and prevented France from capitalizing on its victory, but Raymond Poincaré's fear of risks was among them.

The history of France's first great interwar crisis in 1923 has been shaped by the fact that British and German archives opened long before French ones did. Hostile reporting based on dislike of Poincaré, distrust of France, and limited knowledge has been only partially offset by a belated opening of the French files. Further, because the Ruhr crisis was essentially a Franco-German collision about the outcome of World War I, scholars have often treated it as a bilateral struggle between two powers only. In fact, Italy contributed two engineers to the Ruhr force and then played both sides, retaining German coal deliveries, trade, and capital investment. Britain's supposed neutrality favored Germany diplomatically, but in practical terms it aided France actively and by omission. Further, Belgium, the junior member of the Entente, was France's essential if reluctant ally, guaranteeing control of the Reparation and Rhineland Commissions and providing sorely needed troops and rail access as well as an international aspect to the operation. Poincaré maintained distant relations with the British and Italian ambassadors and the German chargé, but he and his top aides, Emmanuel de Peretti de la Rocca and Jacques Seydoux, could not ignore the Belgians, much as Poincaré would have preferred to do so.

Fortunately for posterity, the Belgian ambassador, Baron [Edmond] de Gaiffier d'Hestroy, was a seasoned, shrewd, and energetic observer. During the Ruhr crisis, he visited the Quai d'Orsay twice daily for chats with Peretti and Seydoux. His voluminous despatches[6] provide an essential supplement to the sparse and often cryptic French internal documents. De Gaiffier had been head of mission in Paris since 1916 whereas other key diplomats were new to their posts as the Ruhr venture began and thus were, as British ambassador Lord Crewe said of himself, "not on 'dropping in' terms with the Quai d'Orsay."[7] For this reason among others, British and Italian (as well as German) reports in 1923 lack the detail and reliability of the Belgian records.

Beyond the limitations of the sources used by historians lies another problem. The image of a vindictive and imperialistic France trying to humiliate and partition a prostrate Germany under the forceful leadership of Poincaré-la-guerre owes much to the skill of Anglo-Saxon propaganda and the lack of any concomitant French response.[8] Germany, more adept at inflicting punishment than absorbing it, portrayed itself with British aid as helpless victim under the heel of a brutal oppressor. The traditional image was not dented even by Lord Vansittart's oft-quoted remark, "We all blamed France ... for being vindictive when her real motive was funk."[9] Vansittart was essentially correct, though "funk" is a cruel term for a realistic reading of the power equation. French policy in the five years after the Armistice was based upon fear and upon realization that France was not the victor of 1918 and might well become the loser. In its last desperate effort to avoid that fate, France was led in 1923 by a very frightened man whose erratic course arose in part from awareness that his nation lacked the strength to carry out its German policy without British aid. Like other postwar French leaders, he sensed that France was no longer truly a great power and more rescued than victor in the war. Its brief artificial continental preponderance rested on a shrinking army, short-term east European power *vacua*, and temporary Versailles treaty clauses which were eroding quickly, not least those concerning reparations which were designed to redress the economic balance somewhat. The Ruhr venture presented a brief opportunity to impose treaty compliance and favorable economic terms, but instead of forcing a swift conclusion to the crisis and reaping its fruits, Poincaré froze into immobility. He and his military commander were precursors of the hesitant politicians and cautious generals of 1936-1940 and, to a surprising degree, in 1923 as in 1939-1940 the initiative was left to Germany.

A reparations crisis at the start of 1923 was visible well in advance, for the 1921 London Schedule of Payments broke down quickly. The Entente and Germany limped through 1922 on various expedients whereby Germany made small cash payments, then none. These expired on 1 January 1923 when the London Schedule would resume effect unless another solution were found. There was no agreement on anything except the impossibility of reverting to the London Schedule.[10] As the prospect of trouble ahead became clear before 1922 was half over, French war minister André Maginot prodded Poincaré to review existing French plans dating from early 1921 when a Ruhr occupation had been envisaged to force acceptance of the London Schedule.[11]

When the German government on 12 July 1922 sought a moratorium on cash payments through 1924, Poincaré ordered revision of contingency plans.[12] Three schemes emerged. He refused the most drastic, a full Ruhr occupation, as too costly in money and troops, but never chose between encirclement and seizure of Essen, using features of both plans.[13] None of the plans said how French troops would gain the Ruhr, which could be reached by rail only through the Belgian and especially British zones; allied consent to what France required was apparently assumed. Much else remained unsettled. In late November, Poincaré obtained French authorization for a Ruhr venture but had not decided to use it.[14] His refusal to grant Germany a long moratorium without productive guarantees to ensure that payments would resume was firm, but he still hoped for limited unanimous Allied economic sanctions such as seizing customs receipts and sending a few engineers to Essen to ensure essential coal deliveries.[15] But he was not wedded to Essen and would work with other economic plans, notably an Italian one, if Britain joined in.[16] After prime minister David Lloyd George's fall in October, he convinced himself that chances of British participation had increased.[17] His oratory in Paris became more noncommittal, though he took a stronger line on weekends in the provinces.[18] As late as Christmas, neither his aides nor Allied ambassadors knew his intentions, because he did not know them himself.[19]

Poincaré's goals then and thereafter were sharply limited, for his primary concern, as always, was security for France against renewed German attack. He hoped to salvage the Versailles treaty, symbol of Allied victory and France's chief bulwark, and to gain German compliance with it. He sought coking coal, which France sorely needed, and eventual monies on reparations account, though he had no illusions that the Ruhr operation itself would yield much cash. His intentions did not include hegemony, annexation, the break-up of Germany, or a military and political occupation of any size. He told aides he opposed a military operation but that a few military posts should not cost much.[20]

Since he dreaded drastic action, Poincaré persuaded himself in the teeth of the evidence that Britain would endorse both treaty enforcement and France's rejection of an unsecured moratorium implying the effective end of reparations.[21] He hoped French support of Britain at the Lausanne conference would bring British backing of France's German policy, particularly as he indicated that, failing British involvement, France must take stronger measures.[22] Poincaré knew France was war-weary and tired of reparations crises, either inconclusive or diluting Germany's treaty obligations; he equally knew France's need for cash and coal, both threatened by German and British reparations plans. He understood the larger issue was avoiding defeat in World War I, but he thought a team at Essen would cramp German industrialists enough to induce cooperation and return of their expatriated capital; that, in turn, should pressure the Berlin government into restoring its finances and currency, issuing a domestic loan, and resuming reparations payments, or at least negotiating on a French plan.[23] Fearing both action and a split with Britain, on whom France relied for security against Germany, Poincaré convinced himself that a modest Allied economic action was achievable. Failing British support, troops must protect the engineers, but despite warnings he foresaw no difficulties, citing the smooth Allied occupation of Düsseldorf in 1921[24] although success there had owed much to British participation.

Poincaré's first moment of truth came at the Paris conference which opened on 2 January 1923 and collapsed two days later. Britain brushed aside French and Italian schemes for economic sanctions and insisted on its own plan, which it published at once. Born of the Francophobia of Britain's Reparation Commission delegate, Sir John Bradbury, and the inertia and inexperience of the new prime minister, Andrew Bonar Law, its goal was Anglo-German control of reparations toward rapid reduction and cancellation. All continental Allies rejected it.[25] Trapped by his own rhetoric, Britain's policy, and intense pressure from president Alexandre Millerand and Maginot,[26] Poincaré decided late on 4 January to send engineers with protecting troops to Essen. On 5 January, orders went forth to General J-J-M Degoutte, commanding on the Rhine.[27] Only then did Poincaré seek Belgian and Italian participation,[28] even though, given Rhineland zonal boundaries and rail routes, any Ruhr operation was impossible without Belgian cooperation and extremely difficult without British consent to rail transit.[29] That was sought on 7 January and duly afforded.[30] This last, plus Bonar Law's cordial words to minimize the breach, reinforced Poincaré's unfounded hope of British participation soon.[31]

The ease of the initial operation and the first week at Essen only heightened his optimism.[32] Berlin refused to finance coal shipments on reparations account to France and Belgium, so France agreed to pay for them. Then Germany forbade shipments; France requisitioned, which led to rail strikes and spreading passive resistance, called for and financed by the German government.[33] As problems mounted and coal shipments to France and Belgium virtually ceased, Poincaré took a few steps to strengthen France's position but did nothing dramatic, hoping to restore calm and prevent more strikes. German resistance only became bolder.[34] In response, orders from Paris merely advised "to persevere and be patient."[35]

As the situation worsened, Belgium demanded to know French plans, accusing Poincaré of failing to consult and inform. It discovered there were no plans and nothing to inform. The interministerial committee met twice daily to read reports from the Ruhr. It discussed and dithered but did not decide; nor did Poincaré.[36] Having thought he could send engineers with military escort to Essen, collect the coal, and pressure the Ruhr magnates into forcing Berlin to meet France's needs, he was amazed by what had occurred and did not know what to do. Thus he did nothing. Brussels was daily assured that there was no change in French plans, despite the sharply altered circumstances.[37] In effect, the initiative lay in German hands.

A sharp disjunction between French and Belgian views emerged. Brussels wanted to end the crisis and so pressed "to proceed quickly and forcefully," but Poincaré told his agents to act "slowly and gently."[38] As the Belgian tail could not wag the French dog, he prevailed. French policy through the Ruhr crisis was dictated by lack of troops. France stripped her metropolitan army for the entry and first reinforcements; there were no more units to send.[39] The Belgian cabinet, torn by domestic crisis and facing a divided public opinion, could not recall reserves and survive;[40] Poincaré would not.[41] He was far stronger politically with opinion united, but the recall of a military class in May 1921 had been unpopular, so he would not run the political risk of mobilizing reserves.[42] Thus Belgian pleas for strong action were countered by French fear of riots or new strikes in the Ruhr, which the French army thought it could not handle without reinforcement.[43]

Those involved used military terms to describe the Ruhr episode and called it a battle.[44] As the postwar became the continuation of war by other means, the Ruhr was the last battle of World War I, albeit without bullets. Yet France's actions were curiously halfhearted, despite much propaganda to the contrary, which Poincaré failed to counter. In theory, France could have ended the resistance by cutting off food and cash shipments from unoccupied Germany and starving the Ruhr into submission. In practice, France never contemplated forcing surrender by starvation; on the contrary, it feared that Berlin would end the food and money shipments. From the outset, Degoutte's forces, with Poincaré's approval, created soup kitchens for the very poor and made plans to feed the entire Ruhr population if need be. In addition, officials in Paris fretted endlessly about whether to create a sound currency for the Ruhr and Rhineland, a question fraught with political as well as financial and economic implications, without bringing Poincaré to any decision.[45] His procrastination and hope that problems would evaporate was reinforced by fear of further breach with Britain and lack of troops, which in his eyes dictated a conciliatory policy in the Ruhr. Equally loath to face problems at home, he never imposed a unified command on France's chaotic Ruhr operations, which remained plagued by division of authority and competition among agents of various ministries.[46] Some firm action against Germany was taken at Belgian insistence. For example, Belgian exasperation forced a decision to cut off coal shipments to unoccupied Germany on 1 February;[47] this led to all-out passive resistance, licensing of Ruhr exports, the Franco-Belgian rail Régie, and more crisis. Brussels proposed fining obstructive Ruhr industrialists, protested trips by German cabinet ministers to Essen to preach resistance, to which France did not object, and wished to expel the German representative at the Rhineland High Commission who was a focal point for resistance. Poincaré consulted the British, who demurred but said they would abstain in the Commission, as they always did on measures affecting the Ruhr. Thereupon, France delayed for months before acting, lest London take offense.[48]

Even crisis in the French and Belgian iron and steel industries did not spur France to action. Since no problems had been anticipated, French industrialists had not stockpiled coal and coke. As France entered Essen, they were alerted to prepare for a flood of coal, but the German ban on shipments, plus mine and rail strikes when France requisitioned, meant only a dismal trickle. French and Belgian blast furnaces were soon dimmed, then extinguished from lack of supplies.[49] At the end of February, Brussels learned that one or two million metric tons of coal were above ground in Ruhr coalyards. It insisted this be loaded and shipped on the Régie to provide temporary relief. Both Paris and General Degoutte, commanding in the Ruhr, feared riots and more strikes, but Belgian pressure gradually produced action, first in their zone, then in thinly populated Ruhr districts.[50] By mid-April, some French blast furnaces were relit after a two month shutdown.[51] But France, unlike Belgium, refused to counter German sabotage in the coal yards, citing the danger of more sabotage and the lack of troops to patrol all yards.[52]

Clearly, the Ruhr occupation, or rather encirclement, Poincaré got was not what he had intended. Faced with an unforeseen situation, he did as little as possible, reluctant to act without overwhelming force which he could not obtain without political risk. Belgian leaders were equally unhappy. Until late April, they begged for firmer action, but became restive as the impasse continued. At a Franco-Belgian session in February about how to obtain coal, in which Poincaré's conciliatory policy prevailed, he asked what should be done if Germany yielded.[53] Belgian efforts turned toward forcing Poincaré to face that question.

Despite his caution, Poincaré was clear about certain key points. He knew France had played her last trump in entering the Ruhr and must win on this card or go down to permanent defeat by a more populous, potentially stronger foe. Though averse to drastic action, he hung grimly on, and in time events forced his hand. Continuing coal shortages and German resistance dictated supervision of Ruhr mines and cokeries in mid-April and direct exploitation of a few.[54] Throughout, he declined to treat with unofficial emissaries who could be disavowed by Berlin, and insisted on governmental communications.[55] Though still optimistic about British participation, he refused Entente conferences as a snare and resisted London's efforts to mediate; he suspected these were aimed at restoring Britain to its historic position at the fulcrum of the continental power balance and equally designed to give Germany equality with France.[56] Inadequate German proposals were swiftly rejected since hesitation, gentle words, or efforts to meet British wishes would encourage German resistance.[57] In diplomatic exchanges, Poincaré was adamant, clinging to prior positions; in the Ruhr itself, he was indecisive in the first months. But he came to accept that France was in a fight to the finish, that it must break the resistance or be defeated, and that Weimar must be brought to heel.[58]

However, he was slow to answer his own question about what to do when that day arrived. In part, he was exhausted and consumed by the daily decisions; in part, he procrastinated. In early March, Belgian pressure produced a joint declaration, after Poincaré seized upon the German formula of 1871, that the Ruhr would be evacuated "gradually as Germany executes its reparations obligations."[59] Poincaré clung to this ambiguous statement for months. In time, his closest aides became frustrated by the inaction. Seydoux told de Gaiffier, "If you are asked about the French plan, you can reply: Article 1. There is no French plan. Article 2. Nobody is charged with executing the present decree."[60] In June, he finally produced a set of terms, amounting to full German submission, acceptance of treaty obligations, a complete end to passive resistance, and resumption of payments. After all that, unspecified alleviations in the regime would occur and evacuation would proceed according to the existing formula, which could mean anything.[61]

After a summer of squabbles with Britain over how to resolve the impasse,[62] and the distraction of the Corfu crisis wherein French policy was dictated by the need to keep Italy in tow as the Ruhr battle reached its climax,[63] on 4 September the new German government under Gustav Stresemann signalled a desire to dicker.[64] Brushing aside Belgian efforts to ease Stresemann's task,[65] Poincaré awaited surrender which came, or appeared to come, on 26 September with word that the resistance ordinances were being repealed.[66] Poincaré had at last won a bigger battle than he had expected, but within months he lost the war, because once again he had no plans and did not know what to do, so he did nothing. Partly he was distracted by the Corfu crisis, the return of the crown prince to Germany, the separatist fiasco, efforts by German industrialists to regain a ten hour day while blaming France, a series of German efforts toward unofficial negotiations, and other episodes of an eventful autumn, and partly he was exhausted. But primarily he lacked any flexibility or capacity for swift, decisive moves. His inaction soon gave Germany chances to escape the consequences of defeat.

Rigid and legalistic to the core, he first insisted on a complete end to passive resistance. This meant repeal of all resistance ordinances, acceptance of all Allied ordinances, a full return to work in the Ruhr, and regular coal shipments.[67]

Because Berlin dragged its feet and refused to finance coal deliveries, meeting Poincaré's requirements consumed two and a half critical months of Germany's brief prostration when France could have exploited its victory, had Poincaré not been fearful of decision.[68] Crucially, he did not draw up a new reparations plan. He would negotiate only in the slow-moving allied Reparation Commission, the authorized entity under the Versailles treaty, where France held a commanding position, but not until resistance was completely ended,[69] by which time France's moment had passed. Until reparations were settled, he would not address other economic matters. Thus even in November as the Reich seemed to approach disintegration, he refused to try to impose a favorable Franco-German trade treaty while he had the opportunity. Faced by conflicting demands from the Comité des Forges, the Comité des Houillères, and the Lorraine mine owners, he let slip a brief chance to gain substantial shares in Ruhr and Rhineland heavy industry, which in December sought infusions of French capital.[70] The situation required a bold leader to act rapidly and take risks, not Poincaré-la-peur, who dared neither to offend Britain nor to make decisions. Similarly, he hesitated about introducing a Rhenish currency, even when separatism brought new implications.[71] In time, the Rentenmark took hold in Germany and the franc fell, destroying its appeal to the Rhinelanders who had long preferred it to worthless inflation marks.[72]

Support for Rhenish separatism, a departure from previous policy, also weakened France's position. Poincaré did not hope for an independent Rhineland, for he understood British hostility and separatist incompetence.[73] Aware that the Ruhr occupation could not last indefinitely after passive resistance ceased, he had long since decided the permanent gain, aside from resumed reparations, should be continuation of the Ruhr-Rhine rail Régie as an international, French-dominated company, affording much profit and especially security against German attack, always his paramount concern.[74] But, surprised by a separatist outbreak not under French control in the Belgian Rhineland zone, the one prospect he had never considered, he panicked and plunged into support of a Rhenish republic at Coblenz, whose short, squabbly life impressed nobody. Having made a decision, he stuck to it, announcing French neutrality and lack of involvement, but as evidence to the contrary mounted, he lost credibility.[75]

Most decisive in France's defeat, aside from Poincaré's costly hesitations early and late in the year, was the fact that the Allies turned against it in the autumn. Britain had long been haunted by inflated ideas of French predominance and was now horrified by German prostration. Forgetting that both were temporary conditions, it rushed at German request to tilt the power balance and approached the United States about a new reparations inquiry with American involvement; this was granted on an unofficial basis, adding American financial power to British views.[76] Italy, ever fainthearted about the Ruhr occupation, and Belgium, which had lost heart halfway through,[77] endorsed the investigation.[78] Bereft of allies and facing a united front, Poincaré himself proposed the inquiry to the Reparation Commission in hopes of restricting its scope on 11 November,[79] five years to the day after the triumphant Armistice.

As 1924 began, the Dawes committee set to work and the French franc collapsed, leaving French policy at Anglo-American mercy. Diplomatic isolation, national weariness, and above all financial crisis drove Poincaré from office in June. Others presided over France's defeat at the London conference of 1924,[80] where the Versailles treaty was revised to German benefit at the insistence of American bankers and British leaders, and led France to Locarno in 1925. There Britain succeeded in restoring Germany to equality and itself to the center of the power equation. When the Locarno treaties were signed on 1 December 1925, the Ruhr occupation had ended in all respects. The Régie was gone, along with France's preponderant position in the Reparation Commission, and any prospect of action against future German default. In addition, reparations payments had been sharply reduced, with more reductions to come. Germany now held the upper hand in economic negotiations vital to the health of the French iron and steel industry, and the Allies were evacuating the first Rhineland zone despite German disarmament defaults.[81] Once more, Germans had suffered but, again, emerged with no lasting sense of defeat, only a sense of grievance, blaming France, as did western opinion.

The last battle of the continuation of war by other means was over, but France had not won it. This crisis had brought neither renewal nor resolution of France's diplomatic, military, economic, or organizational problems, which remained to impede decisive action another day. Despite the fainthearted diffidence with which Poincaré conducted the Ruhr venture, he had brought Germany to heel and to near collapse; that afforded a rare chance perhaps for internal French economic reorganization, certainly for a vastly improved external economic relationship with France's most dangerous rival, but this unique opportunity was squandered in inactivity. Domestic disorganization and factors beyond France's control played a role, as did Poincaré's legalism, disregard of propaganda, and dependence on Britain, inasmuch as France lacked the strength for solo conduct of its foreign policy. But above all, Raymond Poincaré's rigidity, indecision, lack of daring or any real brutality, and especially his timidity and procrastination, meant that a venture designed in part to teach Germany who won the Great War failed in the end to uphold the military verdict of 1918. At the same time, it failed to maintain the Versailles treaty, frayed the crucial British and Belgian alliances, left unaddressed basic deficiencies narrowing France's already limited power, and greatly increased dependence on and deference to Britain. Thus in some respects the events of 1923-1925, more by inaction than action, set France on the path toward 1940.

Notes

1. For example, Robert J. Young, *France and the Origins of the Second World War* (New York, 1996).
2. The tenor of this paragraph and some of its particulars owe much to Prof. Martin S. Alexander's comment at a panel on "Crisis and Response in Interwar France" at the meeting of the Society for French Historical Studies, Ottawa, 28 March 1998.
3. Joel Blatt, "Introduction," in Joel Blatt, ed., *The French Defeat of 1940: Reassessments* (Providence, RI, 1998).
4. Weimar Republic, Akten der Reichskanzlei, *Die Kabinette Wirth I und II*, 2 vols. (Boppard am Rhein, 1973), 2: 739-40, 776n., 804, 858, 974-9, 988, 1044, 1149-50; *Das Kabinett Cuno* (Boppard am Rhein, 1968), 9, 12, 17, 21, 60, 63, 92, 136-8. For a recent study based on British archives which assumes them to be infallible as to fact and interpretation, see G. H. Bennett, *British Foreign Policy during the Curzon Period, 1919-24* (London, 1995). British reporting improved when Lord Crewe was absent and Sir Eric Phipps was in charge. The German ambassador departed in response to French entry into the Ruhr, leaving Leopold von Hoesch as chargé. Though respected by the French, he lacked access at this time. Stanislas Jeannesson, *Poincaré, la France et la Ruhr (1922-1924: Histoire d'un occupation* (Strasbourg, 1998) unfortunately was not available in time for consultation.
5. Curiously, one German observer saw this as well. Carl Bergmann, *Der Weg der Reparation* (Frankfurt, 1926), 218-19. For more recent interpretations, see Marc Trachtenberg, *Reparation in World Politics* (New York, 1980), 291, which stresses prudence and moderation, and J. F. V. Keiger's excellent *Raymond Poincaré* (Cambridge, 1997), 290-9, which agrees about the timidity and lack of plan.
6. Brussels, archive, Belgian Ministry of Foreign Affairs [hereafter BMAE], Correspondance politique, France, 1923 [hereafter France/1923] and série B, file 10.071 [hereafter B-10.071].
7. Cambridge, Cambridge University Library [hereafter CUL], Crewe to Phipps, 18 June 1923, Crewe Papers/C41.
8. The role of Anglo-German propaganda and the lack of French counter-thrust need study. On the weakness of French propaganda under Jean Giraudoux, who ran the Quai d'Orsay's cultural diplomacy 1922-24, see Anthony Adamthwaite, *Grandeur and Misery* (London, 1995), 86.
9. Alan Sharp, "Lord Curzon and British Policy Towards the Franco-Belgian Occupation of the Ruhr in 1923," *Diplomacy and Statecraft* 8, no. 2 (1997), 85.
10. For details, see Sally Marks, "Reparation in 1922," in Carole Fink, Axel Frohn, and Jurgen Heideking, eds., *Genoa, Rapallo, and European Reconstruction in 1922* (Cambridge, 1991), 65-76. Germany had paid little cash, mostly borrowed. Britain was preoccupied by the Greco-Turkish crisis and Lloyd George's fall; it gave little attention to the looming reparations crisis.
11. Paris, archive, Ministry of Foreign Affairs [hereafter FMAE], Maginot to Poincaré, 17 June 1922, #665-5/II, sous-série B, vol. 69 [hereafter B/69].
12. Poincaré to Foch, 12 July 1922, FMAE, B/69; London, Public Record Office [hereafter PRO], Foreign Office memo, 15 July 1922, FO 371/7680.
13. French-Belgian meetings, 23 Nov., 23 Dec. 1922, Vignon note, 24 Dec. 1922, FMAE, Papiers d'agents, Millerand Papers, vol. 24 [hereafter Millerand/24]; FMAE meeting, 22 Dec. 1922, FMAE B/141; de Gaiffier to Jaspar, 24 Nov. 1922, #15089/7018, BMAE France/1922; Poincaré to Herbette, 9 Jan. 1923, tel. 35, FMAE Série Z, Allemagne, vol. 237 [hereafter Z/Alle/237].
14. Notes of the 27 November 1922 meeting are in Millerand/43, closed to most searchers. Prof. Stephen Schuker, who had access, says only an authorization was at issue and that translations in Ludwig Zimmermann, *Frankreichs Ruhrpolitik* (Göttingen, 1971), made during World War

II when Germany had the French files, are distorted; hence, this source is not used. When Poincaré took his decision is disputed. Denise Artaud, citing a Poincaré speech, says early June ["A propos de l'occupation de la Ruhr," *Revue d'histoire moderne et contemporaine* 17 (1970): 2-21]. Jacques Bariéty, *Les relations franco-allemands après la première guerre mondiale* (Paris, 1977), 107-8, and Charles S. Maier, *Recasting Bourgeois Europe* (Princeton, 1975), 291, favor November. Walter A. McDougall, *France's Rhineland Diplomacy, 1914-1924* (Princeton, 1978) votes for both 27 November and 3 January. Marc Trachtenberg, "Poincaré eut-il en 1923 une politique rhénane?" *Revue d'histoire diplomatique* nos. 2-4 (1981): 225, and Keiger, *Poincaré*, 292-7, opt for late November with further hesitations, which the evidence confirms. See fn. 13, 16, 26, 27, 29.

15. De Gaiffier to Jaspar, Nov.-Dec. 1922, *passim*, BMAE France/1922; Poincaré to Saint- Aulaire, 26 Dec. 1922, tel. 2681, FMAE B/140; Curzon to Phipps, 27 Dec. 1922, House of Lords Record Office, Bonar Law Papers 111/12/51; Rolin-Jaequemyns to Jaspar, 29 Dec. 1922, BMAE B-10.071. Return of the Lorraine iron fields to France created dependence on Ruhr coal, especially as all Saar mines save one were anthracite, not bituminous coking coal, and French mines were not yet restored.
16. De Gaiffier to Jaspar, 16 Dec. 1922, #16254/7524, BMAE France/1922; Italy, Ministero degli affari esteri, *I documenti diplomatici italiani*, settima serie [hereafter DDI], 1: nos. 245, 256, 271, 296, 298, 302.
17. De Gaiffier to Jaspar, 31 Oct., 24 Nov., 1 Dec. 1922, #14030/6524, 5089/7018, 15459/7178 BMAE France/1922.
18. De Gaiffier to Jaspar, Nov.-Dec. 1922, *passim*, BMAE France/1922.
19. Ibid.; Vignon notes, 3, 4, 7, 23, 25 Dec. 1922, Millerand/24.
20. Vignon note, 24 Dec. 1922, Franco-Belgian meetings, 23 Nov., 23 Dec. 1922 Millerand/24; de Gaiffier to Jaspar, 15 Dec. 1922, tel. 2020, 5 Jan. 1923, no. 207/97, BMAE France/1922, 1923.
21. Saint-Aulaire to Poincaré, 24 Dec. 1922, tel. 1171-7, FMAE B-140, Curzon to Phipps, 27 Dec., 1922, Bonar Law 111/12/51; de Gaiffier to Jaspar, 23 Dec. 1922, #16670/7709, BMAE France/1922, 6 Jan. 1923, #209/98, BMAE France/1923.
22. Vicomte de Saint-Aulaire, *Confession d'un vieux diplomate* (Paris, 1953), 645-9; Poincaré to Saint-Aulaire, 26 Dec. 1922, tel. 2681, FMAE B/140; de Gaiffier to Jaspar, 6 Jan. 1923, #209/98, BMAE B-366/IX.
23. Vignon note, 24 Dec. 1922, Millerand/24; de Gaiffier to Jaspar, Nov. 1922-Jan. 1923 *passim*, BMAE France/1922, 1923.
24. Minutes, Franco-Belgian meetings, 23 Nov., 23 Dec. 1922, Vignon note, 24 Dec. 1922, Millerand/24; de Gaiffier to Jaspar, Dec. 1922 passim, BMAE France/1922.
25. See fn. 23. Texts of Entente plans and minutes in Great Britain, Parliament, Cmd. 1812, *Inter-Allied Conferences of Reparations and Inter-Allied Debts, Held in London and Paris, December 1922 and January 1923* (London, 1923) and France, Ministère des Affaires Etrangères, *Documents diplomatiques. Demande de moratorium du gouvernement allemande à la Commission des Réparations, 14 novembre 1922. Conférence de Londres, 9-11 décembre 1922. Conférence de Paris, 2-4 janvier 1923* Paris, 1924). Summaries of all plans, including the German one never submitted, in Bergmann, *Der Weg.* The British plan, revising one already rejected by France and Belgium, was shown in advance to Germany (*Das Kabinett Cuno*, 61) but not to the Entente. France did not seek it, but Belgium and Italy did. LeTellier to Jaspar, 23 Dec. 1922, #4597/1917, de Gaiffier to Jaspar, 6 Jan. 1923, #209/98, BMAE B-10.071; G. Grahame to Curzon, 7 Jan. 1923, tel. 6, PRO, FO 371/8626; DDI, 1, no. 261.
26. De Gaiffier to Jaspar, Dec. 1922-Jan. 1923, *passim*, BMAE France/1922, 1923; DDI, I, no. 245; Millerand to Poincaré, 11 Dec. 1922, tel. 2601-1, FMAE B/139; Vignon note, 24 Dec. 1922,

Millerand/24; Phipps to Tyrrell, 8 Sept. 1923, Phipps to Crowe, 6 Nov. 1923, Phipps Papers, Churchill College, Cambridge; G. Grahame to Curzon, 1 Mar. 1923, tel. 39, F.O. 371/8718. See also Michael J. Carley, "The Shoe on the other foot: a letter from Raymond Poincaré to Alexandre Millerand, December 1922," *Canadian Journal of History*, 206:3 (1991), 581-7.

27. Château de Vincennes, Service Historique de l'Armée [hereafter SHA], Etat-Majeur memo, 4 Jan. 1923, #1412/3, Poincaré to Degoutte, 5 Jan. 1923, #2.263, Degoutte Papers, 7N3489.
28. Gen. J. Degoutte, *L'occupation de la Ruhr* (Düsseldorf, 1924), 56 (SHA, Degoutte/40072); de Gaiffier to Jaspar, 5 Jan 1923, #207/97, BMAE France/1923; 2 meetings, 5 Jan. 1923, FMAE B/141; Poincaré to Coste, 8 Jan. 1923, FMAE B/197.
29. Seydoux note, 29 Dec. 1922, Millerand/52; Rhineland rail map, 1922, F.O. 371/8711. Save for a line through the Belgian zone, partly single track, railways to the Ruhr crossed the British zone, mostly through Cologne.
30. The French request to use British-controlled railways was made to British military authorities in the Rhineland and approved by the pro-French War Office without referral to the Cabinet or request for Foreign Office views. Godley to W.O., 7 Jan. 1923, c.o. 37/7/1, F.O. 371/8703; Kilmarnock to Lampson, 8 Jan. 1923, F.O. 371/8702. In February as French traffic mounted, Britain ceded a corner of its zone to the French for the duration so a line from the Ruhr would not cross British-controlled territory en route from the Belgian to the French zone and, after negotiations in London, allowed substantial use of lines administered from Cologne for transit of troops, supplies, technicians, and coal. See FMAE: Z/Ruhr/9-12, 15, B/145-6, 197-8, Z/Grande-Bretagne/51 [hereafter Z/GB/51]; Archives Nationales [hereafter AN], Haute Commission interalliée des Territoires Rhénans, Haut Commissariat français dans les provinces du Rhin, sous-série AJ^9, file 3224 [hereafter AJ^9/3224]; PRO: F.O. 37l/8711-13; BMAE: B-10.071. Britain permitted collection of customs receipts in its zone. Saint-Aulaire to Poincaré, 17 Jan. 1923, tel. 50-53, FMAE Z/Alle/237. Also, as the Ruhr entry occurred one day after the third anniversary of the entry into force of the Versailles treaty, Britain could now demand repayment of the French war debt—but chose not to. CUL, Crowe note, 31 May 1923, Baldwin Papers/F3/125; Mouy note, 5 July 1924, French Ministry of Finance B33041.
31. De Gaiffier to Jaspar, 5, 6 Jan. 1923, #207/97, 210/99, BMAE France/1923. On 19 February, Poincaré told a Chamber committee that British engineers would join those in the Ruhr. Hoover Institution [hereafter HI], Logan to Strong, 23 Feb. 1923, Logan Papers 2/287.
32. Tirard to Poincaré, 12, 13, 14, Jan. 1923, tels. 10, 11, 13, 14, FMAE B/141; Nollet to Poincaré 13, 17, 18 Jan, 1923, #2283, 2485, 2489, FMAE B/185; de Gaiffier to Jaspar, 17, 20 Jan. 1923, #854/418, 20 Jan. 1923, #1035/527, BMAE France/1923.
33. Poincaré to Herbette, 15 Jan. 1923, tels. 50, 52, Poincaré to Tirard, 31 Jan. 1923, tel. 115-18, FMAE Z/Alle/237; RC annex 1735b, 15 Jan. 1923, AN Délégation française à la Commission des Réparations, sous-série AJ^5, file 414 [hereafter AJ^5/414]; Tirard to Poincaré, 12 July 1923, #2160, AJ^5/315; Genoyer (Düsseldorf) to Poincaré, 22 Jan. 1923, tel. 3, FMAE B/143; Nollet to Poincaré, 17 Jan. 1923, #2485, FMAE B/185; de Gaiffier to Jaspar, 15 Jan. 1923, tel. 19, BMAE B-10.071. See also *Das Kabinett Cuno*, 129, 174-7, 202-3, 210-12, 236-7.
34. F.O. Summary, 25 Jan. 1923, F.O. 371/8707; de Gaiffier to Jaspar, 17 Jan. 1923, tel. 24, Hannecart note, n.d. (18-21 Feb. 1923), BMAE B-10.071.
35. De Gaiffier to Jaspar, 26 Jan. 1923, tel. 41, BMAE B-10.097.
36. Belgian demands for information from 12 January to early March in BMAE B-10.071, France/1923, FMAE Z/Belgique/59 [hereafter Z/Belg/59], Z/Ruhr/7, B/142-3. Procès-verbaux of the Interministerial Committee on the Ruhr in FMAE B/141-3 and Millerand/25 confirm de Gaiffier's reports. He concluded (27 Jan. 1923, #1382/708): "These idle talks are useless."
37. Instances too numerous to list contained in files cited in fn. 26.

38. Belgian policy: Rolin-Jaequemyns to Jaspar, 2 Mar. 1923, BMAE B-10.071, quoting Jaspar. French policy: de Gaiffier to Jaspar, 24 Jan. 1923, #1195/611, BMAE France/1923, citing Peretti.
39. Poincaré to Jusserand, 14 Jan. 1923, tel. 36, FMAE Z/Alle/237; de Gaiffier to Jaspar, 17 Jan. 1923, #854/418, BMAE B-10.071; de Gaiffier to Jaspar, 15 Jan. 1923, #715/336, BMAE France/1923. Initial French contingents in the Ruhr amounted to 20,885 troops, which soon rose to about 45,000, plus about 5,000 Belgians. Peak figures were 57,815 French and 7,063 Belgians. The Ruhr, which lacked exact boundaries, consisted of about 2,500 km^2 or 138 square miles, and had a population of 4 or 5 million. SHA, Degoutte to Maginot, n.d. [29 or 30 May 1923], #323, 7N3489, Note on Troops, 1 Apr. 1923, 4N94; Forthomme to Hymans, 7 July 1924, Brussels, Archives Générales du Royaume [hereafter AGR], Hymans Papers/157; Germany, Auswärtiges Amt, Selected Foreign Ministry Records, T-120 [hereafter T-120], Reich Statistical Office Fact Sheet, 13 Jan. 1923, W.127, Reel 1524/Serial 3116H/D635910-12. France patrolled the lion's share of the Rhineland and on 24 January 1923 took over the US zone.
40. *Passim*: FMAE: Z/Ruhr/3-7, 10, 12, 26, B/142, 146, Millerand/28-29; AN: AJ^5/342, 386; PRO: FO 371/8627, 8643, 8657, 8703-5, 8709, 8711, 9382; BMAE: France/1923, B-10.071.
41. De Gaiffier to Jaspar, 22 Jan. 1923, #1065/541, 1 Mar. 1923, #2960/1430, BMAE France/1923; de Gaiffier to Jaspar, 27 Jan. 1923, #2852/1381, BMAE B-10.071.
42. FMAE note, 8 Jan. 1923, FMAE B/141; Loucheur to Poincaré, 10 Apr. 1923, HI, Loucheur Papers 7/197; Saint-Aulaire, *Confession*, 650; de Gaiffier to Jaspar, Jan-Feb. 1923 *passim*, BMAE B-10.071. On the worsening shortage of troops, see procès-verbal, Franco-Belgian meeting, 19 Apr. 1923, FMAE B/148.
43. De Gaiffier to Jaspar, Jan.-Feb. 1923 *passim*, Jaspar note, 28 Feb. 1923, procès-verbal, Franco-Belgian meeting, 30 Jan. 1923, BMAE B-10.071; Poincaré to Herbette, 26 Jan. 1923, tel. 169-70, FMAE Z/Ruhr/7.
44. For example, de Gaiffier to Jaspar (citing Poincaré), 25 Jan. 1923, #1201/618, BMAE B-10.071; de Gaiffier to Jaspar, 22 Jan., 9 Oct. 1923, #1065/541, 13208/6054, BMAE France/1923; Degoutte to Maginot, 19 Jan. 1923, #8.587/D, FMAE B/142; Bergmann, *Der Weg*, 225-6.
45. On the food: SHA Degoutte to Maginot, 7 Jan. 1923, #99 3/4, Maginot to Degoutte, 17, 24 Jan. 1923, E7642, 182 PC/4, Degoutte/7N3489; Payot instruction, 8 Jan. 1923, #8727/CRW, FMAE B/141, 151, 157, *passim*. On the money: Dec. 1922 meeting, FMAE B/141; Tirard to Poincaré, 30 Jan. 1923, tel. 58, FMAE B/197; de Gaiffier to Jaspar, 7 Feb. 1923, #1877/970, BMAE France/1923; Delacroix to Theunis, 6 Feb. 1923, #60105, BMAE B-10.071.
46. Crewe to Curzon, 8 Mar. 1923, tel. 270, FO 371/8720; Rolin-Jaequemyns to Jaspar, 2 Mar. 1923, 8 Mar. 1923, #215, Jaspar to de Gaiffier, 3 Mar. 1923, BMAE B-10.071.
47. Franco-Belgian meeting, 30 Jan. 1923, BMAE B-10.071; de Gaiffier to Jaspar, 31 Jan. 1923, #1556/813, BMAE France/1923.
48. On fining industrialists: Jaspar to de Gaiffier, 20, 21 Jan. 1923, tels. 18, 29, BMAE B-10.0071. On licenses: Poincaré to Herbette, 4 Feb. 1923, tel. 244, FMAE Z/Ruhr/19; Poincaré to Tirard, 11 Feb. 1923, tel. 161-3, FMAE Z/Alle/238. On the Régie: Poincaré to Degoutte, 22 Feb. 1923, tel. 99-100, FMAE B/197, Kilmarnock to Curzon, 1 Mar. 1923, FO 371/8718. On trips by German cabinet members, which were eventually banned but not stopped: Peretti note, 7 Feb. 1923, Herbette to Poincaré, 6 Feb. 1923, tel. 99-101, FMAE B-145; Peretti note, 19 Feb. 1923, FMAE B/146; Seydoux to Poincaré, 28 Feb. 1923, FMAE B/147; Jaspar to de Gaiffier, 19 Feb. 1923, tel. 61, BMAE B-10.071. On the German commissioner, removed in mid-April, Jaspar to de Gaiffier, 22 Jan. 1923, tel. 20, Jaspar to Rolin-Jaequemyns, 27 Jan. 1923, tel. 34, BMAE B-10.071; Montille to Poincaré, 14 Feb 1923, tel. 270, Poincaré to

Saint-Aulaire, 14 Feb. 1923, tel. 546, FMAE B/146; Franco-Belgian meeting, 14 Apr. 1923, FMAE B/148.

49. Logan to Strong, 23 Feb., 9 Mar. 1923, HI Logan Papers 2/287, 328; Nollet to Poincaré, Jan.-Mar. 1923 *passim*, FMAE B/185-6; de Gaiffier to Jaspar, Jan.-Feb. 1923 passim, BMAE France/1923; London, India Office Library, Crewe to Curzon, 29 June 1923, Curzon Papers F112/210a. France and Belgium were buying costly British coal, but that did not suffice.
50. Mar. 1923 *passim*, BMAE B-10.071; Peretti note, 2 Mar. 1923, FMAE B/147; Nollet to Poincaré, Mar. 1923 *passim*, FMAE B/186.
51. De Gaiffier to Jaspar, 16 Apr. 1923, #50067/2342, BMAE France/1923.
52. De Gaiffier to Jaspar, 27 Apr. 1923, #5611/2592, BMAE France/1923.
53. Theunis-Poincaré meeting, 21 Feb. 1923, BMAE B-10.090. On the growing split, Bradbury to Baldwin, 25 May 1923, CUL Baldwin Papers, file F3/125.
54. FO Summary, 9 Jan. 1924, FO 371/9713; Nollet to Poincaré, 27 Mar. 1923, #2618, FMAE B/186; Seydoux to Poincaré, 6 Aug. 1923, FMAE B/150; meeting, 25 July 1923, Degoutte to Poincaré, 3 Aug. 1923, #5509, Peretti to Poincaré, 14 Sept. 1923, FMAE B/209.
55. Poincaré to Margerie, 27 Feb. 1923, tel. 340-1, FMAE Z/Ruhr/13; Poincaré to Saint-Aulaire, 18 Mar. 1923, tel. 843, FMAE Z/Ruhr/16; de Gaiffier to Jaspar, 24 Mar. 1923, #4110/1945, BMAE France/1923; Degoutte to Poincaré, 28 Aug. 1923, tel. 391, FMAE Millerand/30.
56. Logan to Strong, 23 Feb. 1923, HI Logan Papers 2/287; de Gaiffier to Jaspar, 7 Apr., 15 June 1923, #4716/2194, 7903/3625, BMAE France/1923; Phipps to Curzon, 19 Aug. 1923, Phipps Papers; G. Grahame to Curzon, 5 May 1923, tel. 99, FO 371/8634; Crewe to Curzon, 10 May 1923, tel. 484, FO 371/8635; Poincaré to Saint-Aulaire, 15 Feb. 1923, tel. 566-7, FMAE Z/Ruhr/11; Poincaré to Saint-Aulaire, 14 Apr. 1923, tel. 935-40, FMAE Z/Ruhr/17.
57. Poincaré to Hoesch, 6 May 1923, FMAE B/337. Poincaré promptly rejected Berlin's 7 June 1923 note, partially drafted by John Maynard Keynes (T-120, 1526/3116H/D637557, D638687, D638697), but Allied dissension over a response consumed the summer.
58. Poincaré to Saint-Aulaire, 14 Apr. 1923, tel. 935-40, FMAE Z/GB/51; Poincaré to Saint-Aulaire, 5 May 1923, tel. 1006, Millerand/26; de Gaiffier to Jaspar, 14 Feb., 9 June 1923, #2164/1093, 7648/3508, BMAE France/1923; Poincaré to Herbette, 29 June 1923, Millerand/17.
59. Poincaré to Margerie, 27 Feb. 1923, tel. 340-41, FMAE Ruhr/13; quotation from minutes of Franco-Belgian meeting, 12 Mar. 1923, and communiqué, FMAE B/152.
60. Plans were drawn up but not approved by Poincaré. De Gaiffier to Jaspar, Mar.-May 1923 *passim*, BMAE France/1923; French plan, 24 Apr. 1923, AJ5/342; Vignon note, 1 May 1923, Poincaré to Saint-Aulaire, 1 May 1923, tel. 971-3, Millerand/26. Quotation from de Gaiffier to Jaspar, 30 Apr. 1923, #5695/2622, BMAE France/1923.
61. Poincaré to Saint-Aulaire, 10 June 1923, tel. 1215-21, FMAE Millerand/26. The British fired back a detailed questionnaire demanding precisions. Curzon to Saint-Aulaire, 13 June 1923, FO371/8636. Thereafter, Poincaré stalled, dragging out the talks until after passive resistance ended, adamantly clinging to prior positions. By June, the stereotypical image of Poincaré had taken on partial but frozen reality. Vignon notes, 15, 25 June 1923, Peretti note, 28 June 1923, Poincaré to Herbette, 29 June, 1923, FMAE Millerand/27.
62. The interminable exchange of ever lengthier diplomatic notes is ably summarized in Etienne Weill-Raynall, *Les réparations allemandes et la France*, 3 vols. (Paris, 1947), 2: 415-57.
63. On the relationship between Corfu and the Ruhr, see Joel Blatt, "France and the Corfu-Fiume Crisis of 1923," *The Historian*, 50, no. 2 (1988) and Sally Marks, "Quasi niente per quasi niente: Mussolini and the Ruhr Crisis," *The International History Review* 8, no.1 (1986).
64. Stresemann to della Faille, 4 Sep. 1923, AGR, Jaspar Papers, file 229A; Margerie to Poincaré, 4 Sep. 1923, tel. 1143-53, 1154, FMAE, Papiers d'agents, Margerie/II.

65. Sep. 1923 *passim,* FMAE Z/Ruhr/28-9; Margerie to Poincaré, 12 Sep. 1923, tel. 1177-9, FMAE Papiers d'agents, Margerie Papers, file II; Poincaré to Margerie, 14 Sep. 1923, tel. 728-9, FMAE Millerand/30; de Gaiffier to Jaspar, 26. Sep. 1923, #12645/5796, Jaspar/229A.
66. Della Faille to Jaspar, 27 Sep. 1923, tel. 130, Jaspar/229B. Though Berlin said all resistance ordinances were being abrogated, its decrees seemed incomplete. Also, much resistance had been organized by secret circulars. Seydoux to Poincaré, 28 Sep. 1923, Margerie to Poincaré, 29 Sep. 1923, tel. 1274-5, FMAE B/347. The 19 September Poincaré-Baldwin meeting, never mentioned in German debates on ending resistance, played little or no role in the German decision. *Die Kabinette Stresemann I und II,* 2 vols. (Boppard am Rhein, 1978), 1: 312-77.
67. Poincaré to Margerie, 28 Sep. 1923, tels. 752-3, 755-6, FMAE B/347; Seydoux note, 23 Oct. 1923, FMAE B/348.
68. The last so-called MICUM agreements with German industrialists were signed on 23 November 1923. On 1 December full agreement was reached about the Régie. On 5 December, Poincaré conceded that passive resistance had ended and ordered alleviations in the regime, agreeing finally on 15 December to receive German proposals about reparations. FO memo, 9 Jan. 1924, FO 371/9813; FO memo, 13 June 1924, FO 371/9766; Poincaré to Degoutte, 6 Dec. 1923, tel. 649, FMAE Millerand/33; Poincaré to Hoesch, 15 Dec. 1923, FMAE B/348.
69. Poincaré to Barthou, 5 Oct. 1923, Vignon note, 8 Oct. 1923, Millerand/31; Poincaré to Herbette, 17 Oct. 1923, tel. 1545-6, FMAE Z/Ruhr/31; Poincaré to Margerie, 13 Dec. 1923, tel. 945-7, FMAE Z/Ruhr/33. The technical work for a new reparations plan existed in the Etudes belges, prepared during the spring. Poincaré was wedded to 26 milliard gold marks for France if it was relieved of its war debts. Beyond that his economic thinking did not go.
70. See FMAE files B/157, 220-21, Millerand/33, Z/Ruhr/35, *passim.*
71. The currency question had been studied for a year without addressing *how* to introduce a new currency—mainly because Poincaré did not make decisions. Besides, he knew little about money. For the long debates, see PRO FO 371/8685-90; FMAE B/157, 268 (especially), Z/Ruhr/30-31, Millerand/27-33; AN AJ^5/315, 330, 389, AJ^9/3231, 3236, 6383; BMAE B-10.090.
72. Interministerial committee, 10 Nov. 1923, 12, 23 Jan. 1924, FMAE B/157-8; Margerie to Poincaré, 12 Dec. 1923, tel. 1571, FMAE Z/Ruhr/33. The Rentenmark was not circulated in the occupied territories at first. French and Belgian francs were popular in the Rhineland even before the Ruhr occupation. *Das Kabinett Cuno,* 23-4. The German hyperinflation predated the Ruhr venture but was greatly aggravated by Berlin's policy in response to it.
73. There is disagreement about Poincaré's views on separatism, some arguing that because he backed it in late October, he must have favored it all along. McDougall, *Rhineland Diplomacy,* 280-6, 300-4, which is inaccurate. Trachtenberg, *Reparation,* 324-5, deems French policy confused but seems to think Poincaré sought a Rhenish buffer state. Maier, *Recasting,* 392-5, hedges but sees a more forceful and consistent policy than seems likely. Bariéty, *Les relations franco-allemandes,* 250-55, who alone considers the events at Aachen, stresses that France did not start the separatist train moving but jumped aboard as it accelerated, and then improvised and temporized. The scattered evidence (especially FMAE Z/Rive gauche du Rhin) indicates that Poincaré opposed French annexation, favored Rhenish autonomy within the Reich (as did the Rhinelanders), would not object to spontaneous establishment of an independent Rhineland but considered that unlikely and probably not viable. During the summer, he had not encouraged separatist efforts; his contempt for Dorten, Mathes, et al. was blistering and often expressed. Degoutte agreed. Degoutte note, 20 Nov. 1923, #6, SHA Degoutte/7N3489.
74. The theme of the permanent Régie (15-30 years), whose creation Belgium opposed, appears from March 1923 on. Examples: Franco-Belgian meetings, 13 Apr, 6 June. 1923, FMAE B/152, 149; Seydoux note, 21 Jan. 1924, #24/17, AN AJ^5/389, Degoutte to Poincaré, 4 Mar.

1924, #3.938, AJ[9]/3224; de Gaiffier to Jaspar, Mar.-June 1923 *passim*, BMAE France/1923; Logan to Strong, 23 Feb. 1923, Logan 2/287. Régie lines normally were much the most profitable in the German system. Georgi memo, 6 May 1924, FO 371/9827.

75. Pieces of the separatist puzzle in: PRO FO 371/8681-8; FMAE Z/Rive gauche du Rhin/32-7, Z/Belg./59, B/352-3, Millerand/31-2; AN AJ[9]/3776-81, 3790, 3795, 3804-5, 4331, 5268; BMAE France/1923, B-10.440-44; AGR Jaspar/235, 240, 240B. Poincaré was surprised and displeased by General de Metz's independent plunge into separatism in the Palatinate.
76. See FO summary, 9 Jan. 1924, FO 371/9738. Among the main files: PRO FO 379/8659-61; FMAE B/348, Millerand/32, Z/Alle/482; AN AJ[5]/362; BMAE France/1923, B-10.074; AGR Jaspar/124B; Library of Congress, C. E. Hughes Papers, Boxes 174-5. Among many evidences of British fear of France: DDI, 3, no. 477; PRO CAB 21/260-1, *passim*, CAB 24/160.
77. De Gaiffier to Jaspar, 13, 17 Jan. 1923, #650/313, 8554/418, BMAE B-10.071; procès-verbal, Franco-Belgian meeting, 6 June 1923, Millerand/52; Herbette to Poincaré, 3 Aug. 1923, tel. 451-5, FMAE B/342; Herbette to Poincaré, 3 Aug. 1923, tel. 455, FMAE Millerand/29. On Italian nervousness, see also Marks, "Quasi niente."
78. *Die Kabinette Stresemann* 2: 674, 894-9; Moncheur to Jaspar, 25 Oct. 1923, tel. 110, Jaspar/214B; R. Graham to Curzon, 10 Nov. 1923, tel. 277, FO 371/8661; FO Summary, 9 Jan. 1924, FO 371/9738; Peter Krüger. *Die Aussenpolitik der Republik von Weimar* (Darmstadt, 1985), 225-7.
79. Poincaré to Barthou, 11 Nov. 1923, #1337, AN AJ[5]/362.
80. On the events of 1924, see Stephen A. Schuker, *The End of French Predominance* (Chapel Hill, NC, 1976).
81. The Ruhr occupation ended in August 1925. At the London conference, July-August 1924, Edouard Herriot failed to salvage the Régie or gain a German trade treaty before Versailles treaty economic clauses expired on 10 January 1925, leaving Weimar free to dictate terms for access of Lorraine ore and semi-finished iron to German markets. The August 1924 agreements destroyed the Reparation Commission's power by creating a new structure to bypass it. Another casualty was Poincaré's argument that the 5-10-15 year terms for the Rhineland occupation would not begin to run until Germany complied with the Versailles treaty. Herriot gained an IMCC investigation of German disarmament, but Stresemann's offer of a Rhineland pact early in 1925 diverted the Entente from defaults it uncovered. Evacuation of the first Rhineland zone began on 1 December 1925 as the Locarno treaties were signed and ended on 31 January 1926.

Chapter 3

WOMEN'S RIGHT AND THE 'RIGHTS OF MAN'

William D. Irvine

One of the most important ways in which Third Republic France did *not* modernize was with respect to the political rights of women. Prior to 1914 France was, by any standards, one of the most advanced political democracies in the world, far more democratic that her major European neighbors: Germany, Italy, Russia or even Great Britain. After 1918 all of that changed. Almost everywhere women were granted the same voting rights as men: Germany, Great Britain, the United States, the Soviet Union but also in such unlikely places as the Irish Republic, Palestine and six provinces of Republican China. Even her Latin neighbors, Italy and Republican Spain, accorded women the vote at the local level. France was virtually alone in denying political rights to half of its adult population.[1]

Why was the cause of women's suffrage so unsuccessful in France? Vocal advocates were not lacking. Although the suffragette movement in France was arguably weaker than in Britain and the United States, there were, from the late nineteenth century onwards, a number of women's groups which, with various degrees of intensity, advocated the vote for women. By some calculations, no fewer than 350,000 women were enrolled in feminist organizations between the two wars.[2] Nor did the cause lack influential supporters among mainstream politicians. The leaders of the two major conservative parties, Louis Marin and

Notes for this chapter begin on page 62.

Pierre-Etienne Flandin, were principled proponents of women's suffrage, as was Léon Blum, leader of the Socialists. So too was Raymond Poincaré, president during World War I and frequently premier during the 1920's. Indeed, the roster of prominent politicians who supported political equality for women was rather more impressive than the handful who formally opposed it. Women's suffrage was rarely on the center stage of interwar French politics, but proposals for enfranchising women were almost always pending. The Chamber of Deputies or the Senate would debate several score bills calling for at least some degree of women's political participation and as the most recent historian of the subject, Paul Smith, has remarked, "votes for women was seldom off the political agenda between the two world wars, forming part of an open and sometimes vicious debate over the gender of citizenship."[3]

A standard explanation of the failure of women to get the vote in France has stressed the anticlericalism of the French left, primarily, although not exclusively, the Radical party. Radicals feared that a female electorate would be more susceptible to clerical influence than its male counterpart, and therefore likely to vote for parties of the right. By way of proof they cited the general enthusiasm for women's suffrage on the part of conservative politicians as well as selected electoral statistics from Weimar Germany purporting to demonstrate a feminine propensity to vote for right-wing parties.[4] Radicals were well positioned to block suffrage reform because, even after their representation in the Chamber of Deputies began to wane, they maintained an effective stranglehold on the Senate. As a consequence, Radical deputies could vote for women's suffrage in the Chamber, confident that their electorally more secure colleague in the Senate would defeat, or more likely, bury the bills emanating from the lower house.[5] An alternate explanation suggests that the failure of women's suffrage lies with the inherent weakness of the various feminist organizations. Predominantly middle class and urban, the various suffragist groups were strongest in the urban regions and lacked a solid implantation in rural France, most notably the regions south of the Loire which were most hostile to suffrage reform. The failure to achieve women's suffrage, on this reading, owed less to the perfidious nature of the Radicals and more to the inability of French feminists to put effective pressure on local politicians.[6] Either way, it would appear that what the cause of French women's suffrage really needed was a powerful auxiliary: a large, politically influential organization, solidly implanted in the provinces which was at the same time prepared to put principle ahead of partisan political concerns. But in fact, such an organization did exist. It was called the League of the Rights of Man.

The League of the Rights of Man (*Ligue des droits de l'homme*) was founded in June 1898 to defend the unfairly convicted Jewish army officer, Captain Alfred Dreyfus.[7] It soon blossomed into a full-fledged civil liberties organization.

Within a decade of its founding the League had 80,000 members. At its peak in the mid 1930's it had 180,000 members, a total which exceeded the membership of either the Radicals or the Socialists. Nor were these members concentrated exclusively in Paris and the large cities. By 1910 there were some 800 sections; by 1935, 2,500. Rare was the small town or even the modest village that did not have a section of the League. League sections were especially evident in the south where feminist organizations were notably scarce.[8] Some sections were dormant but anyone reading the provincial press and the local bulletins of the League cannot help but be impressed by the energy displayed at the local level—regular meetings, an annual congress and a steady stream of resolutions directed towards the League's governing body, the Central Committee. Moreover, the League was singularly well-positioned to be politically influential. A large number of deputies and senators belonged to the League. By 1933 the League's *groupe parlementaire* had 173 deputies and 24 senators; the actual number of League members in the two chambers was probably higher. The League also was well-represented among the premiers and cabinet ministers. About half the interwar governments of France, for example, were led by members or former members of the League. Some of these had only weak or distant connections to the League[9] but others like Paul Painlevé, Edouard Herriot, and Léon Blum were long standing members of the League and had sat on its Central Committee. Similarly, the League was well-represented among the cabinet ministers in many interwar governments, especially left-center ones. Two thirds of the cabinet in Daladier's 1933 government belonged to the League; only a handful of Léon Blum's 1936 Popular Front cabinet were not members of the League. Again, some of these cabinet ministers had rather tepid associations with the League and were provincial politicians for whom a membership card in the League was primarily a useful electoral accoutrement. Rather more, however, were high profile members of the League. Significantly, no fewer than five of Blum's ministers were sitting on the Central Committee at the time of their appointment. The League was therefore extremely well-connected politically and blessed with ready access to ministerial antechambers.[10]

The League could not, of course, claim to be representative of the entire French political spectrum. It was, in principle, open to all provided always that they accepted the democratic republic. In its early years it represented more or less faithfully the "Dreyfusard coalition" ranging from the center-right (known quixotically in contemporary parlance as the "*centre-gauche*"), through to some but not all of the Socialists. After 1905, as thorny issues of church and state and labor relations displaced the initial concerns of the Dreyfusards, most of the more conservative elements distanced themselves from the League. By 1911 the great majority of League members were Radicals or Socialists, with the organization's political center of gravity almost exactly situated in the assorted splinter formations that existed between the two major parties of the left.[11]

In spite of, and perhaps because of, the distinctly left-wing orientation of the League, the organization at all times stressed that it was manifestly not a political formation. *Ici on ne fait pas de la politique* was easily the most widely echoed phrase at virtually every meeting of the League. The League, its leaders reminded everyone at every opportunity, was not on the left nor was it on the right. It was on the ceiling. It stood above and entirely outside of politics. If most members of the League happened to be on the left, League spokesmen insisted, this merely reflected the fact that the left-wing parties were more consistent champions of the rights of man than were their conservative counterparts. But the League's mission was not to pursue left-wing causes or right-wing ones. It was to pursue justice and the League's role was to serve as the conscience of democracy. Partisan politics and partisan political advantage had no place in such a cause.

Indeed, representatives of the League were always insistent on the fact that the League would champion any cause, regardless of the political consequences and would do so even when the beneficiaries were on the extreme right. In 1909 the Minister of War, General Picquart, a former Dreyfusard, sanctioned a group of army officers in Laôn for attending mass (in civilian dress) and for later participating in a private meeting of the very conservative and clerical *Jeunesses Catholiques*. The current President of the League, Francis de Pressensé publicly upbraided then premier Georges Clemenceau in the Chamber of Deputies. The League carried no candle either for army officers or for highly politicized Catholic organizations. But, Pressensé would insist, Picquart's actions represented a clear violation of the elementary principles of the right to association which applied to all citizens, even Catholic army officers.[12] Pressensé's defense of the officers of Laôn became an oft-told story in subsequent years, an integral part of League lore.[13] Victor Basch, League President after 1925, was fond of reminding everyone that issues of public and political morality were at the heart of the League's mandate and ought not to be sacrificed to partisan political considerations. In 1929 he demanded that the Central Committee pronounce on the impending debate on the ratification of the inter-allied wartime debts. Repayment to the United States of loans contracted during the First World War was a widely unpopular cause within France and was opposed by his own party, the Socialists, the more so because it was the project of Raymond Poincaré's conservative coalition government. But Basch would insist that fidelity to freely consented contracts was a critical moral principle and one the League must address.[14] This kind of dedication to principle, notoriously absent from political formations like the Radicals, made the League an obvious potential ally of advocates of women's suffrage.

To be sure, the League was predominantly a male organization. Women belonged to it from its inception although it took a quarter century for the League to amend its statutes to indicate that the League was an association of men and women as opposed to one that women were permitted to join.[15] Three women sat on the League's first Central Committee although one was the wife of the treasurer and the other two, school teachers, soon ceased to attend meetings.[16] The League did not again reach this level of female representation on the Central Committee until 1935 when three of the fifty-eight members were women. Of the 110 members who sat on the Central Committee in the 1920's, only two were women. Nor were women more prominent in the local sections. In 1923 of 995 known presidents of sections, five were women; in 1929 the figures were nine of 1,871, in both cases about half of one percent. Women were always present at the League's annual congresses although only in the mid-1930's did their numbers exceed 10% of the delegates. Many appear to have been present in their capacity as wives of male delegates.[17] Of the 60 or 70 delegates who took the floor at an average congress, rarely were there more than four or five women and never did they speak at the same length as did male colleagues. Still, the League was hardly unique in underrepresenting women, nor did this prevent it from championing the cause of women's suffrage.

Indeed, women's suffrage was, for a number of reasons, an obvious cause for the League to embrace. In the first place, the League had always recognized that the "homme" in "droits de l'homme" referred to members of the human race and not to the male species. In 1924 Victor Basch, soon to become the president of the League said: "If our League is called the League of the Rights of *Man,* it is solely because there is no word in the French language that corresponds to the Latin *homo* or the German *Mensch.*"[18] Secondly, members of the League, while usually highly critical of the operation of French democracy were nonetheless also proud, and justifiably so, of France's status as one of the leading democracies in the world. It was therefore a source of considerable chagrin when, in the years immediately following the First World War, it became obvious that on the question of women's political rights, France lagged behind all but a handful of the nations in the world. Thirdly, the arguments advanced against women's suffrage were transparently specious. Women, it was traditionally alleged, neither desired the vote nor were prepared for it. In so far as any of this was true at all, members of the League could not help but reply, it had been even more true of men before 1848. One could hardly, on these grounds, oppose extending the franchise to women without simultaneously admitting that one's republican ancestors had made a serious error in 1848.

Finally, of course, there was the whole question of the forces that stood in the way of women's suffrage. The obstruction of women's suffrage bills by the Senate outraged the League on two counts. The Senate was an undemocratic body, elected by a highly restricted suffrage, and a holdover from the days of the reluctant republicans who had founded the regime. Its democratization—or better yet its elimination—had been a traditional League demand. Moreover, the fact that so many of the deputies who so readily voted women's suffrage in the Chamber did so only because they were confident that their political counterparts in the Senate would reject the measure was precisely the kind of political hypocrisy and opportunism that the League specialized in denouncing.

It is not therefore surprising that early on the League, or at least a number of it prominent leaders, embraced the cause of women's suffrage. Ferdinand Buisson, one the League's founders and its president from 1911 until his death in 1926 quite literally wrote the "book" on the subject, the 1909 report of the parliamentary commission on universal suffrage.[19] In 1909 the League designated the distinguished French feminist, Marie Vérone, as *rapporteur* for its commission on women's rights for that year's annual congress. On her initiative the League accepted the principle of women's suffrage and recommended immediate implementation of it for all three levels of local government.[20] It reiterated its demand at its 1914 congress.[21]

At the 1924 congress of the League in Marseille and in the wake of the Senate's effective obstruction of the suffrage bill, Victor Basch gave a classically passionate speech on the suffrage issue. Denying women the vote, he insisted, had always been a grave flaw in French democracy. Women were in all respects the equal of men and were therefore entitled to equal political rights. The stock argument against women's suffrage, he noted, was the clerical issue. But, even were it true that women were excessively under the influence of the clergy, whose fault was that if not that of men who refused to treat them as political equals? Making no allowances for the fact that he was in the south, traditionally refractory to women's suffrage, Basch was particularly harsh on the men of the Midi whose "ancestral, Arab … and, Roman" traditions led them to treat women like virtual servants, unworthy of eating at the same table as men. Moreover, even granting clerical influence, in the League, Basch intoned, "we do not have the right to bend our principles in the face of facts." "For us principles are eternal and we do not permit them to be affected by the opportunity of the moment. Otherwise there would be no point in having a League of the Rights of Man … If we become opportunistic, we might as well close the doors of the League and dissolve it."[22] All of this was classic League rhetoric, repeated endlessly at every congress and, one suspects, calculated to put the better part of the audience to sleep.

Actually, Basch seems to have hoped so since shortly thereafter he found himself saying that while the League was, of course, above politics, its individual members belonged to political parties (by which he meant the Radicals and the

Socialists) and had therefore "the duty to consider the destiny of their party." "I confess," he added, "that to give women all electoral votes right away, without any transition, without steps and without stages constitutes a serious risk." Consequently, although the League remained as committed as ever to the principle of women's suffrage, he thought it appropriate to limit women's voting for the moment to municipal elections. The aging historian, Alphonse Aulard, if for no better reason than to prove he at least had stayed awake, could not resist wondering just what Basch might have proposed had he in fact fallen into the trap of opportunism. Nonetheless the congress voted overwhelmingly both for the broader principle of women's suffrage and its very gradual implementation. A halfhearted attempt to get the congress to commit itself to demanding women's suffrage for the *next* municipal consultation (i.e. 1925) failed to find enough support. Neither Basch nor anyone else seemed to notice that this resolution, municipal voting only, represented a significant retreat from the 1909 and 1914 positions which had envisaged voting at all levels of local government.[23]

Some indication of the impact of even so moderate a resolution can be seen in a talk on feminism given by *citoyen* Jean Zay, later to become minister of national education in Léon Blum's government, before his fellow leaguers in the section of Orléans. Feminism had made gigantic strides in recent years and, insofar as feminism sought to ensure women's equality with men within society, he thought this to be truly admirable. Unfortunately, he noted, the feminist movement had in recent years concentrated excessively on the conquest of political rights. This bothered him. Women, he insisted, were not inferior to men—in some respects they were superior. But, alas, the one area in which they were deficient was the ability to reason, and reasoning, he opined, was critical for political decision-making. Moreover, women had no interest whatsoever in social questions. They did not want the vote and would not exercise it if they received it. Giving them the vote, at any level, was a "leap in the dark" and very dangerous. The vice president of the section, *citoyenne* Cormier, promptly rebutted his arguments as did several of her male colleagues, without however convincing Zay.[24]

As the Zay incident shows, Basch's position on the suffrage issue, however conditional it may have been, was a good deal in advance of that of most of his fellow leaguers. This was clearly illustrated in 1929 at a meeting of Marie Vérone's *Ligue française pour les droits des femmes.* Basch's support for suffrage reform, cautious when speaking to the League, could be effusive before a feminist audience. Here Basch noted that some republicans feared that in a Latin and Catholic country like France giving women the vote might imperil the democratic regime. But he was having none of that and openly questioned the republican commitment of anyone who challenge the democratic necessity of equal political rights for women. "Better the republic should perish," he ended by saying, "rather than have her principles perish because without those principles there can be no republic." It was, of course, just as well he said this since the next speaker up was the cranky old right-wing—but equally suffragist—deputy, Louis Marin, armed, as he always was, with a long list of Roman Catholic countries whose internal politics had not been significantly altered by their adoption of women's suffrage. All in all, though, it was a good night for Basch until near the end of the meeting when a letter was read from one of those who had been invited to speak but had been unable to attend. The letter was from Maurice Viollette, former governor of Algeria, currently deputy from Eure-et-Loire, and also a member of the Central Committee of the League. Viollette allowed as how he was of course in favor of the principle of women's suffrage but also a believer in "prudence." It was his impression that most women were indifferent to the vote and, were they given it, between 70% and 80% would not exercise the right. Even the municipal vote was fraught with peril because municipal councilors elected senators and "to give women the right to determine the political orientation of the country and even of its constitution is, at this time, a very dangerous thing to do, the more so because I think that the only women who will participate in elections are from among the extremist elements." By unhappy accident, he ended his letter with the words: "I am not one of those who says: Better the colonies should perish than their principles."[25]

It is entirely possible that Viollette's concern about the sanctity of the Senate was related to the fact that shortly thereafter he became a member of that august body. In his capacity as senator, Viollette drafted a bill permitting women to vote in municipal elections. The bill provided for a separate college of women electors and candidates. Women would be entitled to one quarter of the positions on the municipal council, on the condition that they would not have a say in choosing the mayor and would not vote in senatorial elections. No less authoritative a figure than Henri Guernut, secretary general of the League, drew the Viollette proposal to the attention of all Leaguers, noting in passing that some would find it inadequate, including, presumably, those members of the League who could remember the resolutions so solemnly passed eight years before, to say nothing of those passed eighteen and twenty-three years previously. Still, Guernut gamely insisted, the Viollette bill would be a useful trial run which, if it did not work out (and he thought it would), could cause no real harm, would certainly give women a chance to acquire their "political education" and would ensure that France would no longer be in last place among nations when it came to women's suffrage.[26]

Zay, Viollette, and Guernut were not, the 1924 resolutions notwithstanding, all that far out of line with the thinking of many members of the League. The League's *Cahiers* certainly opened its columns to proponents of women's suffrage but they were also open, although not perhaps in equal measure, to opponents like Pierre Flottes who belligerently met the aforementioned precedent of 1848 by wondering if anyone remembered Louis Napoleon.[27] To judge from a reading of thousands of *compte rendu* of local sections, women's suffrage was not a favorite topic and when it was discussed, more often than not the emphasis was on the inherent dangers. The director of a local women's teaching college in the Charente-Maritime and vice-president of the League's section in La Rochelle, recalled bitterly how the mere news that a local suffragist group was holding classes on civic education for women prompted members of her section into wholesale denunciations of women's suffrage.[28] One of her colleagues recalled being told by a fellow leaguer that even municipal suffrage for women was out of the question because "in our villages it would mean the end of republican municipalities and waiting for parliament itself to become anti-republican."[29] The president of the League's federation of the Creuse found himself in hot water because he had the temerity to *read* out loud the League's official position on suffrage reform at a local meeting. His colleagues somehow felt that this was an oblique and disloyal attack on Alfred Grand, senator from the department and also a leaguer who had consistently voted against women's suffrage. It was nothing of the kind, the flustered president protested. Surely everyone realized that League principles were one thing and that the timing and modalities of their application were something else again. All he had really wanted to say, he pleaded, was that women's suffrage was going to come sooner or later and that the League should prepare for it.[30] In this respect he was like many, if not most, of that minority in the League who spoke in favor of women's suffrage. Rather than present suffrage reform as a good idea in its own right, they typically chose to treat it as something which, whether the League liked it or not, was inevitable. That being the case, they suggested, the League should stop opposing the measure because as one speaker in Chartres observed, "when the day comes that they get [suffrage reform] in spite of you" women might be lost to the republican cause.[31]

For every trenchant argument in favor of women's suffrage[32] there was at least another insisting that it would be "dangerous to grant all women the right to vote even in municipal elections" or reminding everyone "that history reminds us of the too-numerous and disastrous examples of the vote prematurely granted."[33] But such articles, pro or con, were the exception. Women's suffrage never generated the passion within the League that other issues: pacifism, clericalism, or labor union rights did. Women were underrepresented in the columns of the League's press but they were not absent. Yet they were more likely to write about peace or the struggle against fascism than about the vote; calls for suffrage reform were whispered, reflecting either lack of interest or, more likely, a recognition that this was a controversial topic. What pressure there was to do something about women's political rights tended to come from the top, rather than the grass roots.

By 1935 it was therefore apparent that women's suffrage was at best the lowest possible priority within the League and, at worst, a reform that Leaguers were fighting all the way. In April of that year the two (out of fifty-eight!) women on the League's Central Committee finally raised the question of suffrage reform. What, Odette René-Bloch and Suzanne Collette wanted to know, was the Central Committee's position on suffrage reform, what had been done about it since 1924 and how was it that so many of the League's deputies and senators somehow managed to continue to vote against suffrage reform? For their pains, they were treated to a series of tortuous disquisitions on the problems of suffrage reform. Emile Guerry for example readily admitted that denying women the vote had been a "monstrosity" but at the same time he was under "the impression that most women did not want the vote." Of course he acknowledged that the same could have been said of men in 1848 but he also insisted that the vote for women now "risked bringing about the same political regression in France that has happened elsewhere." Alfred Bayet, a left-wing Radical, pointed out to the two women that the very fact that the Central Committee was discussing the issue (for the first time in eleven years) was solid proof that the League believed in "the principle of the equality of men and women." But the League believed in other things too, such as freedom of conscience. "Now," he insisted, "we are more or less certain of losing that freedom of conscience in France if the right to vote is granted to women." He had nothing against feminism but was tired of the extremists; what he wanted was the "true and good feminism", the "feminism without danger." Jacques Hadamard, of the Collège de France, pointedly reminded both women that voting was not just a right but also a duty and what, he wanted to know, had his female colleagues been doing about the "political education" of the fairer sex? Emile Kahn, the secretary general of the League reminded the two women—one of whom he would soon marry—that the League had other things on its mind besides suffrage reform and was frustrated by the fact that any proposal short of full and complete equality was greeted by French feminists with hostility and suspicion.

The debate was taken in hand by ex-secretary, Henri Guernut, now a Radical deputy and soon to be minister of national education. As a deputy he had consistently voted for suffrage reform which, he felt, gave him a certain moral authority in these matters. He first chastised the two women for being so tactless as to bring up the voting records of League deputies. This was a sensitive issue. The two chambers of parliament were full of members of the League and it was a matter of some notoriety that many of them felt under no obligation whatsoever to ensure that their voting patterns conformed to League principles. Calling League deputies to account for their votes was not, he bluntly declared, League policy—unlike women's suffrage which apparently was.[34] He did concede that something had to be done about the suffrage issue and that one had to start somewhere. He proposed what amounted to a modified version of the Viollette bill, expanding women's representation to one third of the municipal councilors, dropping the prohibition on women voting for the mayor, but continuing to exclude then from senatorial elections.

In short, and with a straight face, Guernut was putting forth a proposal that represented a dramatic regression from even the very limited reforms recommended in the previous decade. It nonetheless received the support of everyone present with the entirely understandable exception of René-Bloch and Collette, who discreetly abstained. Now, unanimous votes were, to say the very least, not the norm in the Central Committee which was legendary for its disputatious sessions. But, that on this issue, the two women could go so far as to *abstain* was more than Emile Kahn would bear. "All of the work of the Committee," he declared, "risks being destroyed by the abstention of our two female colleagues." In the end, Bloch and Collette were persuaded—not to say bullied—into accepting a compromise formulation.[35] As for the work of the committee, apparently so dear to Kahn, this was the very last time it ever mentioned the suffrage issue. Worse, Suzanne Collette, having endured the pious lectures of males in the Central Committee, was subjected to roughly the same kinds of arguments a few days later from a female delegate at the League's annual congress at Hyères. Collette was visibly displeased when Jeanne Deghilage, a retired school teacher from the Nord, and recently elected to the Central Committee, trotted out the traditional prudential arguments against full women's suffrage, but there was no denying that her anti-clerical fulminations struck a resonant chord with most of the other delegates.[36]

The clerical peril, evoked explicitly or implicitly, by most of those who opposed extending the franchise to women, was clearly central to the debate and an important part of League orthodoxy. Even in the last years of the republic, members of the League, notably those in the north and west, insisted on the undiminished threat from the church and bristled at the suggestion that nineteenth-century anti-clericalism might be outmoded. The fact that the parties of the extreme right, Louis Marin's *Fédération Républicaine* in particular, supported women's suffrage only seemed to prove the point. Did members of the League actually believe any of this? The possibility cannot be discounted, however hard French feminists worked to demonstrate the frailty of that assumption. Even Suzanne Collette, whose *bona fides* are not in doubt, could write, as late as 1944, on the eve of the first electoral consultation involving women, that "if by chance the first result of women's suffrage should be the compromising of the republican regime" women around the world would never forgive their French sisters.[37] This article was leapt upon eagerly by male leaguers for whom it legitimized their prewar reservations about the wisdom of women's suffrage.[38] But spokesmen for the League were never entirely clear about this. In 1928 Henri Guernut, while attempting to sell a local section of the League on the municipal franchise for women, noted that the chief difficulty with women voters was they were likely to go "to the two extremes, that is to say to the Communists and the nationalists."[39] Guernut never quite got around to explaining how a feminine electorate, apparently under the yoke of a priestly caste, would be inclined to vote Communist.

The pleas by French feminists—and a handful of leaguers—that French women were, on the evidence, unlikely to vote much differently than did men, usually went unheard. Even when heard, the message could have unpredictable results. Fernand Corcos, another member of the Central Committee, certainly believed that women were unlikely to vote very differently than men but for him this was a terrible reason for giving women the vote. Corcos, of course, was a principled pacifist, given to writing books documenting in excruciating detail the degree to which French women had been at least as ardent in the support of the World War I as had been men—if not more so. That French women had attempted to parlay their contributions to the war effort into postwar political rights struck him as being frankly "criminal."[40] He saw little evidence that women were any more pacifist than men and unless, and until, French feminists gave evidence of being true pacifists—by which he meant subscribing to his own brand of pacifism—he really could not see the point of giving women the vote.

There were, of course, elements in the League who did not quite grasp Corcos's message and took his plea that women ought to be pacifists to mean that they in fact were. One section in the Charente-Maritime, apparently inspired by a misreading of Corcos, voted overwhelmingly in favor of women's suffrage in 1937 on the grounds that it was the best way to salvage the peace. But a neighboring section, apparently less partial to pacifism, replied with a resolution which read, in part: "Considering that the political and civic education of women is in general far too incomplete and the acquisition by women of political rights would put the republican regime in danger, [the section] concludes that in the current state of things, it is simply impossible to grant women civil and political rights even though they may be the apostles of peace." Yet a third section, evidently by way of compromise, suggested that women should be granted the municipal vote but only on the understanding that women municipal politicians should have but a "consultative" say and there only on matters involving women and children.[41]

What is so striking about the League's position on women's suffrage is that the entire debate was conditional upon the presumed voting patterns of women. Women's participation in the electoral process was a good thing only if they did not vote for conservatives, if they did not vote for Communists, and if they did vote for pacifists. But not otherwise. That women had the right to vote, and to vote for whomever they chose, seems to have been a proposition alien to virtually all members of the League. In their great majority, leaguers believed that having proclaimed, in the abstract, women's political rights, they had done their duty and could comfortably await the moment when such rights would be to their political advantage, before making much effort to insist that they be applied. Overlooked was the fact that this kind of political calculation was in flagrant contradiction to the oft-proclaimed League policy that it was above politics, interested only in justice and prepared, should the two conflict, to sacrifice politics to justice.

The League would play no role in the decision of the Provisional Government to enfranchise women on 21 April 1944. In fact, the decree occasioned remarkably little debate.[42] But even had the issue been more contentious, the League was by 1944 neither materially nor morally in a position to play the prominent public role that had characterized its first forty years. The organization had been dissolved by the Occupation authorities, its archives seized and its leader, Basch, brutally murdered in January 1944. Individual members had played an important role in the Resistance, but a number of equally high-profile former members of the League, motivated by pacifism and a disillusionment with the democratic regime, had actively supported the Vichy regime and collaborated with the Germans.

Still, the question remains: had the League, in the years before 1940, been more consistent and more principled, had it given more than lip service to the cause, had it championed women's rights with the same energy it displayed for male victims of injustice or for the cause of peace or disarmament, how much difference would it have made? Almost certainly it would have made some difference. It might have helped move the issue off the political back burner on which it perpetually sat and it might have exposed more clearly the glaring hypocrisy of so many politicians. But it is far from certain that the end result would have been much different. The League's access to the corridors of power looked more impressive than it was in reality. League politicians were fond of saying that if they were responsible *politically* before their constituents and, in the case of ministers, before the Chamber, they were responsible *morally* before the League. This was a seductive formula but it could not mask the fact that, for most of them, political considerations came first and would, should they clash with abstractions of morality, usually prevail. The more ardent *militants* within the League were perennially frustrated by the glaring gaps between the principles enunciated at League congresses and the votes and actions of their numbers in parliament. The League had been outraged by the fall of the center-left coalition occasioned by the riots of 6 February 1934. It was even more hostile to the conservative governments that followed. At best they owed their legitimacy to counterrevolutionary violence in the streets; at worst they were paving the way for the triumph of fascism. What could not be overlooked, however, was the fact that sitting in all of those governments were members, sometimes prominent ones, of the League.[43] Nor could the League do very much about it. Controlling the actions of deputies and ministers was very difficult for almost all French political parties; it was next to impossible for a nominally nonpartisan organization like the League. There were of course repeated efforts from the mid 1920's on to sanction deputies and ministers whose votes and actions were, or appeared to be, inconsistent with, if not in flagrant violation of, League principles. But such attempts achieved little more than to increase the political divisions within the League and to reduce much of its activity to internecine feuding. In principle having a parliamentary group representing the League was an effective way to enhance its influence. In practice, it provided a convenient target for some League *militants*, the practical consequence of which was to permit partisan quarrels to spill over into the life of the association. The decision to dissolve the parliamentary group in 1935 was precipitated by the impertinent questions of the female members of the Central Committee but was greeted with some relief by those who hoped, more or less in vain, to restore some critical detachment to the League.

So the cause of women's suffrage might have failed even *with* the active support of the League. But the critical point is that it failed *without* that support. Why did the League prove itself to be so flabby on this issue? A simple answer would be that its claim to being above partisan politics was simply fraudulent and that the League was from very nearly the beginning deeply immersed in the partisan political culture of the nation. Certainly it would be hard to deny that on the suffrage issue many in the League unselfconsciously parroted the traditional mantra of the Radicals. Nor was it the case that the League's calculated opportunism on this issue represented a unique blind spot. It was, in fact, part of a much larger pattern. Its rhetoric notwithstanding, the League routinely sacrificed principles to politics. One example among many—and one not unrelated to the suffrage question—would be the League's position on the Senate. This highly, and deliberately, undemocratic institution, was the source of innumerable platonic resolutions calling for its democratization or abolition. Yet it is worth listening to George Gombault, the militant socialist journalist on the Central Committee on this subject—significantly within the context of a debate on women's suffrage. The Senate, he insisted, might be socially conservative but in matters political it had always been republican. What did "republican" mean in this context? That it was full of Radicals? That it consistently rejected women's suffrage? Victor Basch himself, speaking of the Senate some months after it had overturned the government of Léon Blum, would insist that the Senate, for all its flaws, was "an instrument for moderation and reflection" and "a guarantee against rash actions." It cannot have escaped him that this had been precisely the argument made by the illiberal right in the formative years of the Republic. In the same debate, Fernand Corcos insisted that "the most attentive observers of the universal crisis of democracy have doubts about the clairvoyance of the masses."[44] One could multiply the examples endlessly. Nearly four decades of defending the political freedom of civil servants did not prevent League sections from demanding massive *épurations* once the Popular Front was in power.[45] In short, narrow concerns for short-term political advantage help account for the League's failure on this issue as on many others.

It might also follow from the above that the League, its public pronouncements notwithstanding, actually exemplified the essentially bankrupt and hypocritical political culture of the late Third Republic. There is some truth to this kind of argument but it is uncommonly difficult to prove that France was unique in this respect. The Radicals' penchant for campaigning on the left but governing on the right, for example, was and is shared by political parties around the world. It is not obvious that the stance of much of the French left on women's suffrage, hypocritical though it incontestably was, was more odious than the contemporary position of the American Democrats on civil rights in the South. And the League was hardly the only civil liberties organization to have problems distinguishing politics from principle.[46]

Perhaps the issue should be put differently. The real problem of the League was that its political vision, far from being too narrow, was too broad. From the beginning the League had declared that its mandate went well beyond dealing with individual cases of injustice, of which the Dreyfus Affair was a classic example. The League always defined the Rights of Man very broadly and insisted that a host of stances on international affairs, the modern economy, and church and state, were consistent with, when not the very embodiment of, the 1789 Declaration of the Rights of Man. [47] Local sections, with a less exalted vision, were forever invoking the rights of man in support of resolutions on spelling reform, postal rates and heavy truck traffic. In time it became nearly impossible for the League to define an issue that was not within its remit. At one level this was a positive development, not least because it made women's suffrage a legitimate cause for the League. But one consequence of this vast array of principled positions was that many a statement of principle, ardently advocated by but a few, received the platonic support of the many who believed, more often than not correctly, that little of significance would come of these positions. It takes nothing away from the sincerity of the delegates at the League's 1928 congress who called passionately for the "abolition of the wage system" to suggest that few of them thought this measure likely to be implemented very soon. Something similar could probably be said of the delegates who voted for limited women's suffrage in 1924.

Moreover, drafting lofty declarations of principle was one thing; translating them into effective action was another. Prior to 1914 it was effortless for the League to denounce war and to call for international arbitration to end all conflicts. But in 1916 did this mean calling for international arbitration *now* or did it mean awaiting a victorious, albeit Wilsonian, peace before exploring the merits of arbitration? There were no easy answers to this as the wartime rift in the League would show. Opposition to war and fascism was an effortless principle to evoke but after 1933 which came first? Peace at any price or collective security? Both could be reconciled with League principles although the point was lost on many in the League whose growing belief in one of the two aforementioned strategies would lead their respective advocates into either an incongruous indulgence towards Nazi Germany or an only slightly less incongruous indulgence towards Stalin's Russia.[48] Among other things, this was not a climate in which the suffrage issue or the League's apparent inconsistencies thereon would seem worthy of much concern.

For many in the League the choice was always between conflicting principles. Women's suffrage was certainly one, but so too was the defense of the very much beleaguered Republic. Which came first? In retrospect this appears as a false dichotomy. There is little evidence that female voting would have threatened the regime and certainly postwar women's voting patterns provide little support for the contention. It cannot be excluded that members of the League wrapped themselves in the republican flag in order to mask their fundamental misogyny. Still, it is just as possible that those who argued, in effect, for women's suffrage eventually, but not when the regime was threatened, were no less honest than those, the great majority, who in 1916 called for international arbitration eventually but not when the Germans are occupying much of northern France. Those who had, often enough in the past, denounced Soviet justice simply did not think that 1936, with France desperately in need of an ally and a fragile Popular Front in power, was quite the appropriate moment to annoy the Soviet Union and the French Communist party by posing awkward questions about the Moscow show trials. Those who in 1938 began to discover some hitherto undetected progressive aspects to Hitler's Germany had not, or had not yet and not for the most part, scrapped their League principles. They simply believed that one of those principles, peace, was by the late 1930's primordial. With the threat of what promised to be an utterly destructive war looming, it did not seem like the ideal time to cultivate a war psychosis by encouraging a major hate campaign against France's eastern neighbor.

Public policy is all about choices and while some of these choices are more odious than others, they are easy enough to understand. But they are harder to justify if only because the League, by its own definition, was not supposed to be making choices of public policy but defending transcendent principles of justice. After all, reopening the Dreyfus case and perhaps exposing the army's scandalous misconduct was not without potentially disruptive consequence for French political life, for the nation's security and, it is to the point, for the political future of the then ruling conservative republicans. These consequences go some ways to explain what now seems like the obdurate "choice" of those late-nineteenth-century governments. The Dreyfusards and the League, to their everlasting credit, were having nothing to do with such choices. It was not that the French right in general did not have a great deal to lose from a reconsideration of Dreyfus's guilt; the political developments of the next five years would show how much: arguably a good deal more than women's suffrage would, in the worst case scenario, have cost the interwar left. But it was the League's position that political advantage must never trump issues of justice. This was a noble position but one easier to embrace when out of power than when, if not exactly in power,[49] at least a good deal closer to it than the League had been in 1898. All too often, on critical issues, the League appears to have lost sight of its founding principle. The cause of women's suffrage was a victim. So too was the League itself.

Notes

1. The best sources for the women's suffrage movement in France are Steven C. Hause with Anne R. Kenney, *Women's Suffrage and Social Politics in the French Third Republic* (Princeton, 1984) and Paul Smith, *Feminism and the Third Republic: Women's Political and Civil Rights in France, 1918-1945* (Oxford, 1996). A spirited recent synthesis of the subject is Albert et Nicole du Roy, *Citoyennes. Il y a 50 ans, le vote des femmes* (Paris, 1994). See also C. Sowerine, *Sisters or Citizens? Women and Socialism in France since 1876* (Cambridge, 1982); J. F. Macmillan, *Housewife or Harlot, the Place of Women in French Society, 1870-1940,* (Brighton, 1981); Siân Reynolds, "Marianne's Citizens? Women, the Republic and universal suffrage in France" in S. Reynolds, ed., *Women, State and Revolution: Essays in Gender and Power in Europe since 1789* (Brighton, 1986); S. Reynolds, "Women and the Popular Front in France: The Case of Three Women Ministers," *French History* 8, no. 2 (1994): 196-224; Paul Smith, "Political Parties, Parliament and Women's Suffrage in France, 1919-1939," *French History* 11, no. 3 (1997): 338-58.
2. Smith, *Feminism,* 253.
3. Smith, *Feminism,* 10.
4. Radical suspicion of women's suffrage was not allayed by the fact that, especially between 1928 and 1932, proposals for votes for women were linked to elimination of the second ballot, a measure transparently designed to weaken Radical parliamentary representation. For an excellent discussion, see Smith, *Feminism,* 132 ff.
5. In May 1919, the Chamber voted 329 to 95 in favor of women's suffrage. Nearly 60% of the Radicals who voted supported the bill. Three years later, the Senate voted 156 to 134 against even debating that bill. Nearly 70% of the Radicals who voted opposed considering the bill, including a number who had voted for it when, three years earlier, they had been members of the Chamber. See Hause, *Women's Suffrage,* 212-47.

6. This is the burden of Hause's argument, *Women's Suffrage*, 269-77. Cf. Smith, *Feminism*, 150-162 where he argues that Hause's argument, while perhaps valid for the early 1920's, does not hold up for later efforts to gain the suffrage for women. The Radicals and their ingrained anti-clericalism, he insists, were at the heart of the suffrage problem.
7. The *Ligue des droits de l'homme* has yet to find its historian. In 1927 Henri Sée provided a well-informed, if decidedly "in house" summary of the League's first quarter century, *Histoire de la Ligue des droits de l'homme* (Paris, 1927). Françoise Basch has recently produced a scholarly biography of her grandfather, Victor Basch, president of the League from 1925 until his death in 1944, *Victor Basch: De l'affaire Dreyfus au crime de la Milice.* (Paris, 1994). The most recent literature on the League can be found in a special issue of *Le Mouvement social* no. 183 ("Les droits de l'homme en politique," April-June, 1998.) It is worth noting that virtually all the literature on the League takes its self identification as "the conscience of democracy" to be inherently unproblematic.
8. By way of example, the Charente-Maritime where feminist activity was relatively weak, was the home of the largest and most active departmental federation of the League.
9. By the time they attained the premiership, neither Pierre Laval nor ex-President of the Republic, Gaston Doumergue, now both very conservative, were viewed very warmly within the League. But Doumergue had been, although no one chose to recall it at the time, a member of the League's Central Committee before 1914; the League's central bulletin chose to congratulate the then still leaguer, Laval, when he first became a minister in 1925. See the League's bulletin, *Cahiers des droits de l'homme*, 1925, 231.
10. This kind of access to ministerial antechambers was widely remarked upon in the League, not all of whose members regarded it as an unalloyed asset. A minority frequently complained that the effective lines of influence ran in the wrong direction and deprived the League of the appropriate degree of militancy.
11. After 1920 some members of the League chose to join the fledgling Communist party, but in 1922 the party declared that membership was incompatible with belonging either to the League or the Freemasons.
12. *Bulletin officiel de la Ligue des droits de l'homme*, 1909, 214.
13. What did quickly get lost in the retelling was the fact that Pressensé's actions outraged a large number of the League's sections who did not share his indulgence towards Catholic army officers and who also believed, not altogether improbably, that Pressensé's apparently principled stance owed not a little to the fact that he, as socialist deputy from the Rhône, was a bitter ideological enemy of Clemenceau, "the strike breaker."
14. *Cahiers*, 1929, 470 ff. In spite of Basch's claims to hold the moral high ground, his actual arguments before the Central Committee differed little from the pragmatic arguments put forth by Poincaré, although Basch chose not to acknowledge this fact. Nor would Basch demonstrate an abiding concern for the "sacred" quality of the debt since two years later he would insist that talk about "the respect for contracts" was little more than "vain and demagogic phraseology." *Cahiers*, 1932, 461, 675.
15. The point did escape some local sections who, as late as the 1920's, were still informing their members that at their monthly meetings "les dames sont admises." *Bulletin mensuel de la section de Boulogne-sur-Mer*, March 1922. Ironically, the same issue contained a careful discussion of the fact that "homme" in the League's title really meant "le genre humain." As late as 1932 Mme. B. Lop, one of the three women on the 22 person central committee of the League's very large section in Marseille, complained that most women were still misled by the association's name and did not realize that the League was open to them. *Le Ligueur* (Marseilles), November-December 1932.

16. On the origins of the League, see Henri Sée, *Histoire de la Ligue des droits de l'homme*, but also and especially the account of Emile Kahn, then secretary general, in Georges Boris' left-wing weekly, *La Lumière*, 10, 17, 24 June, 1 July 1938.
17. At most congresses between a half and a third of the women present (63% in 1932; 44% in 1933) had the same last name as a male delegate. To be sure, this does not prove that they were not delegates in their own name or that it was not the men who were present in a spousal capacity. Certainly the hosts of these congresses were careful to organize various diversions for wives on the explicitly stated grounds that they were unlikely to share their husbands' enthusiasm for sessions of the congress. See, for example, the welcoming address at the 1930 congress of Biarritz, *Ligue des droits de l'homme. Congrès national, 1930* (Paris, 1930), 9; or the prospectus for the 1933 departmental congress in the Gironde, *Ligue des droits de l'homme* (Gironde), February 1933.
18. *Ligue des droits de l'homme. Congrès national, 1924,* 206.
19. The best recent assessment of Buisson can be found in Judith F. Stone, *Sons of the Revolution: Radical Democrats in France, 1862-1914* (Baton Rouge, 1996), 176 ff.
20. *Bulletin officiel de la Ligue des droits de l'homme,* 15 August 1909, 991-5. Women could therefore vote at the municipal, arrondissement and departmental level. To the surprise of Vérone, a male delegate added an amendment calling for women's *eligibility* for the Chamber and the Senate. It passed despite the insistence of then President, Francis de Pressensé, that if one were going to call for eligibility in national elections then one might as well, as he personally preferred, grant them the right to vote at that level as well.
21. The issue of eligibility at the national level was discreetly dropped in 1914.
22. *Ligue des droits de l'homme. Congrès national, 1924,* (Paris, 1924): 208-9.
23. The point did not escape Marie Vérone, who noted a few years later that the whole idea of vote by stages, an acceptable expedient in 1909, was now hopelessly out of date. *Le droit des femmes,* March 1929.
24. *La Ligue d'Orléans,* November 1926.
25. *Le droit des femmes,* June 1936.
26. *La Ligue des droits de l'homme* (Drôme), July 1932. Of course, by 1932, granting of limited municipal voting rights to women would still leave France tied for last place with fascist Italy!
27. *Cahiers,* 1924, 473.
28. *Les droits de l'homme* (Charente-Maritime*)* December 1927.
29. *Ibid,* November 1932.
30. *La Ligue française des droits de l'homme* (Gueret), May 1929.
31. Cited in *Le droit des femmes,* July-August 1934.
32. Elie Réynier, pugnacious pacifist and hard-nosed boss of the Federation of the Ardèche once, but only once, made a withering assault on the opponents of women's suffrage within the League. *Ligue des droits de l'homme* (Drôme), April 1925 (The Federation of the Ardèche shared editorial space with the bulletin of the neighboring department.)
33. *Les droits de l'homme* (Morbihan), 1927 (reporting on the decisions made at the departmental congress of 22 May 1927); *Les droits de l'homme* (Meurthe-et-Moselle), February, 1933.
34. It is probably not accidental that within two months of this debate the League opted to dissolve its parliamentary group. *Cahiers,* 30 August 1935, 594.
35. *Cahiers,* 20 May 1935, 348-52.
36. *Ligue des droits de l'homme, Congrès national, 1935* (Paris, 1935): 89.
37. *Espoir,* July 1944.
38. *Le ligueur artésien* (Pas de Calais), January-February 1945.
39. *Les droits de l'homme* (Charente-Maritime), July 1928.

40. Fernando Corcos, *La paix? Oui, si les femmes voulaient* (Paris, 1929). In the same vein see also his *Les femmes en guerre* (Paris, 1927) and *La paix ordonnée par les mères* (Paris, 1934).
41. *Les droits de l'homme* (Charente-Maritime), May 1937. The resolutions are those respectively of the sections of Jonzac, St. Fort-sur-St. Dizant, and Néré.
42. Given the pressing issues faced by the Provisional Government in the spring of 1944, the question of women's suffrage was of secondary importance. Ironically the question seems to have become one that divided the French least. Félix Gouin's 1943 constitutional drafts, prepared for the Free French, called for women's suffrage but so too did the stillborn constitutional proposals prepared by Vichy in January of 1944. A number of prominent prewar members of the League, notably André Philip, Pierre Cot, and Jules Moch, were active in the constitutional committee of the *Comité Français de Libération Nationale* but they directed their energies to the more pressing issues of the role of a President, the question of a second chamber, proportional representation and strengthening of party discipline. For a thorough discussion see Andrew Shennan, *Rethinking France: Plans for Renewal 1940-1946* (Oxford, 1989), chap. 5.
43. Edouard Herriot, for example, was sitting as Minister of State in the government of "national salvation" headed by Gaston Doumerge (and ex-member of the League) which was formed in the wake of the 6 February riots. His presence there (and he was hardly the only leaguer) was one—but only one—reason for a major internal which ravaged the League for the next three years.
44. *Cahiers*, 1-15 July 1938, 446.
45. To cite but one example, the Federation of the Alpes-Maritimes began by May 1936 to demand "regional tribunals of Public Safety to seek out, judge and punish" right-wing civil servants. Its Nice branch felt that the Federation should work with the new government to "ensure, as soon as possible the dismissal, relocation or punishment where necessary of the civil servants of the Alpes -Maritimes." *Le Ligueur*, May, July 1936. Calls for "épuration" were widespread in the League's local sections. See for example, *Bulletin trimestriel de la Fédération de la Seine-et-Marne*, 2nd trimester, 1937; *Les droits de l'homme* (Charente-Maritime), May 1937; *Ligue des droits de l'homme* (Gironde), May, November 1937; *Les droits de l'homme*, (Meurthe-et-Moselle), June, November 1936.
46. Aryeh Neier, *Defending My Enemy* (New York, 1979), 69-104, has some pertinent observations about the inability of members of the American Civil Liberties Union to grasp that freedom of assembly actually extended to members of the American Nazi Party.
47. Given that the 1789 declaration was actually silent on these issues, as it was on women's suffrage, it required some dialectical sophistication, present in abundance in the League, to make this argument.
48. From 1934 until 1937 the League was very nearly torn apart by political feuds. The departure of some of the most prominent dissidents at the end of 1937 reduced, but did not end, the tensions within the League. Some indication of the nature and the intensity of the internal struggles in the last years of the republic is the fact that after 1940 some prominent members of the prewar League chose to support the Vichy regime and became active within the "collaborationist left." On the origins of these feuds see Emmanuel Naquet, "Entre justice et patrie: La Ligue des droits de l'homme et la Grande Guerre," *Le Mouvement social*, no. 183 (April-June, 1998): 93-109, and in the same issue, Roland Faivre, "Le pacifisme et la Ligue des droits de l'homme en Charente-Inférieure pendant les années 1920," 135-8. For a summary of the crisis faced by the League in the 1930's, see Madeleine Rébérioux, "Victor Basch et les droits de l'homme" in Michel Denis, Michel Lagrée and Jean-Yves Veillard, eds., *L'Affaire Dreyfus et l'opinion publique en France et à l'étranger* (Rennes, 1996), 99-112 and William D. Irvine, "Politics of Human Rights: A Dilemma for the Ligue des droits de l'homme," *Historical Reflections / Réflexions historiques* 20, no. 1 (Winter 1994): 5-28.
49. Although having a majority of ministers in a cabinet constitutes, by some definitions, "being in power."

Chapter 4

The Gold Standard Illusion

France and the Gold Standard in an Era of Currency Instability, 1914-1939[1]

Kenneth Mouré

In *The Gravediggers of France*, his wartime indictment of France's "guilty men," the journalist André Geraud (Pertinax) criticized a French "financial oligarchy," which included regents of the Bank of France, private bankers, and officials at the Treasury for having clung obstinately to "the ancient teachings of liberal economics, to the classic doctrine of the gold standard" as if the world had not changed since the nineteenth century.[2] As other countries abandoned the gold standard in the early 1930s, France steadfastly maintained the gold parity of the Poincaré franc, conceiving defense of the franc as a new battle of the Marne and insisting that the link to gold would prevent monetary chaos. The battle for the franc cost France dearly. The high interest rates it required particularly hurt investment; the depression persisted in France longer than elsewhere, lasting through the 1930s and weakening French financial and industrial power in the years leading back to war.[3]

French fidelity to the gold standard offers a revealing case study of French response to crises in the interwar period. The gold standard itself was in crisis. Restored in the 1920s as a bulwark against inflation and monetary instability, it was believed to prevent the monetary laxity that had produced postwar inflation and currency depreciation. In John Maynard Keynes's phrase, gold standard advocates

Notes for this chapter begin on page 82.

saw it as "the sole prophylactic against the plague of fiat moneys."[4] Abandoned in the 1930s when the defense of gold parities required severe economic contraction, the gold standard fell out of favor. Monetary authorities developed active monetary management practices, including exchange-rate adjustment, in order to maintain domestic prices and give priority to domestic stability and employment rather than sacrificing these to exchange-rate stability. Leaving gold was a critical step in the development of fiscal and monetary management to promote economic growth and greater stability of economic activity and employment.

Faith in the gold standard as an automatic adjustment mechanism slowed the development of modern central banking and monetary management in France. The suspension of convertibility in August 1914 was seen as a temporary measure entailing prompt restoration after the war. Inflation, reconstruction, and the political difficulties in obtaining parliamentary support for increased taxation delayed the return to gold until June 1928. Legal stabilization at one fifth the franc's prewar parity was understood as a national impoverishment, an amputation of four fifths of the nation's wealth. In fact, depreciation eased the burden of public debt by allowing repayment in depreciated francs, taxing holders of state debt for their faith in the government, and increasing French exports and employment. In the 1920s the growth of French gross domestic product and industrial output outstripped that of its economic rivals.[5] But the inflation, budget deficits and currency instability that followed the war left as their legacy a firm resolve to preserve the gold value of the restabilized franc. The gold standard represented an absolute value for the franc and an essential mechanism to adjust prices in order to maintain the balance of payments and the budget in equilibrium. French monetary policy concentrated on defense of the franc, which was threatened above all by inflation. The 1928 currency reform undervalued the franc, inducing a strong inflow of gold as the French repatriated capital sent abroad and investors sent short-term capital seeking speculative gain. Gratifying as this gold inflow may have seemed in France as a sign of sound monetary management, it increased the contractionary squeeze exerted by the gold standard system on money and prices abroad.[6] As countries suffering depression and reserve losses were forced off gold, France embraced deflation, seeking to match falling world prices and currency depreciation by lowering prices in France. This policy deepened and prolonged the slump, weakening France in its ability to prepare for the growing threat of war with Nazi Germany.[7]

France maintained its gold standard belief more doggedly and more durably than any other country in the interwar years. It also did more to disrupt the functioning of the international gold standard. French gold acquisition in the late 1920s played a major role in the international monetary contraction that produced the Great Depression in 1929 and the breakdown of the gold standard in 1931. This seeming paradox is explained by the particular character of gold standard belief in France and its influence on French policy. This essay traces the French commitment to gold and belief in the gold standard through the fourteen years of the *cours forcé*, from 1914 to 1928, in its first section. The second section examines French gold policy during the eight years of the Poincaré franc, arguing that French faith depended on assumptions that can be aptly characterized as "illusions," as they fitted poorly with actual experience and were maintained *as illusions* even when their substance had all but vanished. The final section reviews the decline of faith in the gold standard after 1936 and the importance of the *gold standard illusion* in delaying French progress toward modern monetary management.

I. The Commitment to Return to Gold, 1914-1928

France suspended convertibility of the franc in August 1914 as one of a series of measures to finance mobilization, convinced that the franc would return to gold at its prewar parity at the end of hostilities. In the course of the war, official gold reserves increased: the Bank of France gathered 2,400 million francs in gold from the public, roughly one-half the estimated private holdings of gold in 1914, in a carefully-orchestrated campaign to "harvest gold." When initial enthusiasm to exchange gold coin for paper francs subsided, the Bank of France helped organize local committees to distribute propaganda urging citizens to give their gold and subscribe to Bons de la Défense Nationale. "Verser de l'or, c'est gagner sans rien perdre," claimed one slogan of the national committee coordinating for these efforts.[8] Even the Catholic clergy was mobilized to encourage the surrender of hoarded gold: sermons, pamphlets, and articles in local editions of the weekly *La Semaine religieuse* advised good Catholics to make themselves "apostles of gold payments for the country."[9] These campaigns, sponsored indirectly by the Bank, demonstrated an unqualified commitment to restore the franc to its prewar parity. French citizens were promised that exchanging gold for bank notes at the Bank of France was a patriotic act, accomplished "without losing even the smallest part of their savings, without running any risk, without having to pay more dearly for what they wish to buy."[10] Although postwar financial policy would render the return to prewar parity impossible, the wartime commitment to do so had been made in good faith and would not be easily abandoned.

Postwar faith in the gold standard was nearly universal. In Britain, the Cunliffe Committee [on Currency and Foreign Exchanges after the War] recommended restoration of the gold standard as "the machinery which long experience has shown to be the only effective remedy for an adverse balance of trade and an undue growth of credit."[11] Accounts of how the prewar system had worked tended to be superficial, based on wishful thinking and nostalgia for prewar security rather than sound analysis. Most of the world went back to gold in the 1920s based on an illusion: restoring gold convertibility would correct all that had gone wrong in the monetary world since August 1914.

For the Bank of France, the path for postwar policy was clear. Wartime advances to the state had inflated currency and prices. The restoration of the gold standard offered two clear advantages: it would return monetary authority to the Bank, retrieving it from government where it was subject to political demands and inflationary mismanagement, and it would provide an automatic and effective system to regulate prices and correct any balance of payments disequilibrium. As Jules Décamps explained, under the gold standard, "Monetary policy is reduced ... to surveying and maintaining the sound functioning of the gold standard; in this way, one guarantees a relative stability of prices and of the exchange rate."[12] To restore the gold parity of the franc after wartime inflation, one simply reversed the process by which the inflation had taken place: repay Bank advances to the state and retire the franc notes from circulation. Governor Pallain announced in the Bank's annual report at the end of the war that "Reimbursement of the state debt to the Bank is the necessary condition ... *and the unique means* to reestablish a normal monetary regime."[13] But the inflationary process did not work smoothly in reverse, although this was more easily recognized by economists than policy-makers.[14] In France, political demands for reconstruction expenditure proved irresistible, and the Treasury met state financial needs by a combination of short-term public borrowing and new advances from the Bank. The German default on reparations merely aggravated the problem. Eventually, poor financial management, driven home by crises that expanded to become simultaneously financial, political and monetary, would destroy the illusion that deflation could restore the franc to its prewar parity.

The terms "deflation" and "inflation" were attached specifically to the supply of notes in circulation, rather than to prices; thus the Bank of France's insistence on repayment of its advances to the state.[15] The greatest part of the franc's depreciation took place in 1919-20 [see Figure 1], and the increase in note circulation roughly equaled the Bank's advances to the state, making it seem that the process of inflation need simply be reversed.[16] At the Genoa Conference in April 1922, French delegates insisted the franc would be returned to par, although this would require a 60% reduction in French prices, and they repudiated suggestions that devaluation was a more realistic policy. At a semi-official conference to discuss French policy in June 1922, support for deflation was nearly unanimous: the choice between deflation and devaluation was posed as a choice between a return to sound money or currency inflation leading ineluctably to the destruction of the franc. To question the wisdom of deflation was "a crime against the credit of France."[17]

Figure 1 Gold value of franc, 1914-1940 (annual averages, 1914 = 100)

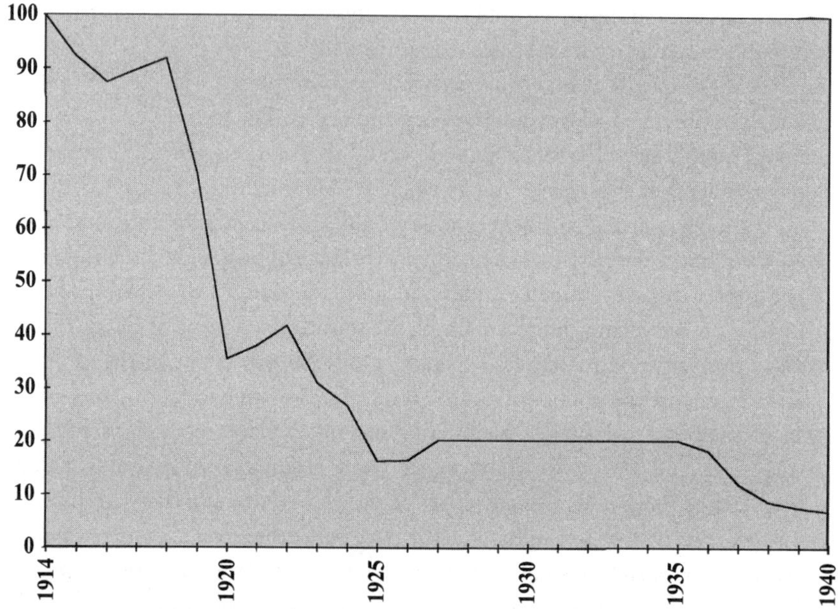

Fear of inflation and fidelity to gold were nowhere more clearly displayed than in the first Cartel des Gauches government after their election victory of 11 May 1924. Radical party leader Edouard Herriot and his minister of finance, Etienne Clémentel, rejected sound financial advice from their director of the Treasury, relying instead on that of the governor of the Bank of France, Georges Robineau. They tried to maintain "confidence" rather than attack the key Treasury problem of the floating debt, which required the renewal of 55 to 60 billion francs in short-term government paper each year providing a monthly plebiscite on state financial management. Fixation on the number of Bank notes in circulation, which crept ever-closer to the legal maximum of 41 billion francs, distracted attention from the serious problem of how to manage the constant maturities of the floating debt. When it came to light that the Bank had falsified its weekly balances and exceeded the ceiling on the note issue, Herriot and Clémentel tried in vain to push this number back below its ceiling. In December 1924 Herriot, Clémentel, and Robineau declared dramatically that they would resign rather than engage in inflation. But the increase in note circulation they forswore had already taken place, and the key questions at issue were management of the floating debt and finding the courage needed to take political responsibility for raising the legal note ceiling.[18]

Blame for the *faux bilans*, a measure initiated by the Bank before the Cartel took power, was unwittingly assumed by Herriot and Clémentel in choosing to continue the deception. When forced, finally, to raise the ceiling on the note issue in April 1925, Herriot's government fell. Confidence in Cartel management, never strong, began a rapid descent given graphic representation in the fall of the franc.[19] The Bank, dedicated to restoring the prewar franc, gave less and less help to successive Cartel governments, arguing that "confidence" could be restored only by sound government policy, believing that sound policy required a government situated further to the right. By May 1926, as the final crisis began to break, the extent to which prices would have to fall to restore prewar parity was in the order of 85%. François de Wendel, a regent of the Bank representing industrial interests, still argued for "a clearly deflationary policy," conceding that this would mean "short-term" difficulties, including reduced domestic consumption, the loss of foreign markets, a crisis of production, and increased unemployment. But inflation was "a danger infinitely more serious that we must avert at all costs."[20]

The Bank's commitment to deflation was broken by changing its governor. The appointment of Emile Moreau to replace Robineau, with the economist Charles Rist as his deputy governor, reoriented Bank leadership in favor of stabilization.[21] Both had served on the Sergent Committee, appointed in May 1926 to chart a program for financial and monetary stabilization, and they sought to implement its recommendations. Raymond Poincaré, returning as premier and minister of finance to "save the franc" in July 1926, adopted most of the Sergent Committee's report, except with regard to monetary stabilization. Poincaré wished to restore the franc to the fullest extent practicable. In contrast, Moreau and his advisors sought rapid stabilization to facilitate the adaptation of French industry and commerce to conditions of stability.[22] For Moreau, Rist, and Pierre Quesnay (appointed director of economic studies), the gold standard would prevent government interference in central bank direction of monetary policy, and the Bank's primary role would be defense of the gold parity of the franc. Government and Bank thus temporarily opposed each other directly regarding monetary policy, with the government holding decisive authority on the issue. But Poincaré was an astute politician, seeking optimal economic conditions as a way to avoid political crises. *De facto* stabilization, begun in response to a sharp crisis in December 1926, proved politically advantageous: it offered *stabilisateurs* temporary stability and *revalorisateurs* the promise of future improvement in the franc's exchange rate.[23]

Maintained for eighteen months, *de facto* stability was purgatory between the hell of inflation and the heaven of gold convertibility.[24] The Bank used the period to absolve itself of past sins and establish the conditions for entering the state of heavenly grace. Its actions are revealing of its gold standard views. The recovery of the franc in 1926 and its undervaluation in December encouraged the return of French flight capital and speculative demand for francs. The Bank accumulated foreign exchange, chiefly sterling. In preparation for the restoration of convertibility, Moreau increased his gold reserves and limited the increase in the volume of notes in circulation. Gold deposited in England as security against wartime loans was redeemed in 1927, and gold and silver were purchased from the French public at market rates. In May 1927, when high-level hints that the franc would be allowed to rise prompted a surge in demand for francs that threatened *de facto* stability, the Bank tried to raise interest rates in London by converting £20 million in sterling reserves to gold at the Bank of England. Moreau and his advisors saw this as the "gold standard solution" to their problem: withdrawing French funds in gold would tighten credit in London and thus, in turn, in Continental markets, to curb the speculation. Moreau attributed the demand for francs to the high interest rate in Paris and the prospect of revalorization, but sought to raise interest rates abroad rather than lower them in Paris.[25] As a "gold standard solution" the strategy illuminates the Bank's views: movements of capital and gold were not signals to prompt a policy change intended to maintain the international system in balance. If so, the Bank of France would have lowered its discount rate to conform with rates elsewhere. Rather, the system contained a strong element of hierarchical power. Countries drawing gold or capital were playing the game successfully, and were thus entitled to have their way; countries losing gold had to adjust policy to retain gold.[26] Countries gaining gold acquired the right to impose adjustments elsewhere; by converting sterling, Moreau sought to force the Bank of England to act on Continental markets, Berlin in particular. Governor Montagu Norman of the Bank of England refused.

Although the conflict was part of a campaign by the Bank of France to gain status and influence equal to that of the Bank of England, a cooperative solution prevailed. Norman raised the market rate of discount in London, while Moreau cooperated with the Federal Reserve Bank of New York to concentrate French gold purchases in New York.[27] The lesson drawn by Moreau did not emphasize cooperation. Rather, it stressed that the gold exchange standard worked to the advantage of the gold centers, which benefited from increased deposits without being required to redeem the claims of foreign central banks in gold. Central banks holding foreign exchange as reserves drew the secondary benefit of earning interest, but clearly stood in the second rank in terms of prestige and power. The Bank of England had traditionally relied on slender gold reserves to back its currency, able to draw capital from abroad by changes in its discount rate. But since Britain's return to gold in 1925 this mechanism had not operated; Governor Norman had been reluctant to incur political criticism for rate increases. There was no guarantee that sterling balances held by foreign central banks were really convertible into gold. Central banks holding sterling as reserves seemed to Moreau not to be on the gold standard at all.[28] The experience convinced the Bank of France that the gold exchange standard was suitable only for second-rank nations seeking to shelter in the orbit of a stronger currency.

The Bank of France categorically rejected the gold exchange standard, informing Poincaré: "There can be no question of adopting a monetary system condemned by the experience of the last few years, the policy of *de facto* stabilization by the Bank of France having been the integral application of the gold exchange standard."[29] The monetary reform of 25 June 1928 restored convertibility, defining the franc in terms of gold. The reform undervalued the franc: further appreciation would have rewarded speculators and increased export difficulties, while the slight devaluation proposed by the Bank might have lost Poincaré political support.[30]

Understanding the French stabilization leads, according to William Adams Brown Jr., "straight to the heart of the postwar gold standard labyrinth;" Gustav Cassel believed the French undervaluation resulted in the breakdown of the gold standard system.[31] But the measure was not intended to gain competitive advantage, nor was world deflation "an understood consequence of adoption of the French Monetary Law."[32] The monetary reform sought to restore gold convertibility as an essential restraint on state fiscal policy, and to reintegrate France in the gold standard world. French prices were recognized to be lower than those abroad, but the Bank argued that this was normal, and that they could be kept below world prices indefinitely.[33] This understanding of the gold standard not only held that adjustment was the responsibility of countries losing gold, but implied that the gold standard did not work automatically to balance prices and payments internationally. The gold standard's key benefit was the prevention of inflation. France was most concerned not with a potential decline of world prices, which key French economists believed natural and inevitable, but with the dangers of inflation.

II. The Poincaré Franc and the Gold Standard Illusion

Once back on gold, French monetary authorities intended to stay there. Since 1914, experience had demonstrated the inflationary hazards of discretionary monetary policy. The return to gold and subsequent experience would show French faith in the gold standard to depend on assumptions that can be aptly characterized as "illusions." First, their assumptions did not accord with actual experience: even in 1928, there was a clear gap between proponents' claims as to how the system should work and actual practice. This was true not only in observing gold standard policies abroad, which conflicted with French standards for how the system should work, but even within France in the distance between Bank claims for the gold standard and Bank policy. Second, the maintenance of the gold standard in France after its abandonment elsewhere showed that the appearance of a smoothly-functioning, efficient system needed to be fabricated when it was not evident of its own accord. This was particularly true in France not just because the gold standard was maintained when experience abroad suggested the benefits of going off gold exceeded the costs, but because psychological factors were recognized to play a more important role in public confidence in France than elsewhere. The assumptions on which French policy operated can be separated into three specific problems.

The first assumption was that the gold standard worked as a single, smoothly-functioning system. The essential minimum for the existence of an international gold standard is to have currencies freely convertible into gold at fixed rates; this then establishes relatively fixed rates of exchange between gold currencies. Gold losses impose an external constraint, requiring a policy response in order to maintain the legally-required level of gold reserves in relation to currency in circulation. But there were no binding, or even commonly-agreed upon "rules of the game" specifying when and how a central bank should tighten monetary or credit policy in response to gold losses. The restoration of the gold standard was accomplished in the 1920s with conflicting views on how it should work. The Genoa resolutions to economize gold were never put into effect consistently, and by 1928 the Bank of France, the Reichsbank, and the Federal Reserve Bank of New York had all turned against the gold exchange standard.[34] This did not mean a return to pre-1914 central bank practice. Rather, policy-makers were increasingly concerned with domestic problems, particularly levels of economic activity and unemployment, which influenced their discount rate policy.

The second illusion, closely related, was that the gold standard was automatic, rather than a "managed" system. That this was an illusion should have been apparent by 1928. The gold exchange standard was believed in France to promote credit inflation in countries holding foreign exchange reserves without imposing a reciprocal contraction in the gold centers where those reserves were convertible.[35] This perception increased reluctance to use domestic measures to discourage the gold flow to France: if the problem causing the gold inflow lay in flawed policy abroad, then nothing should be done in France, as gold losses would eventually require correction of the misconceived policies. The Bank thus responded passively to the large gold inflows of 1929 and 1930, doing nothing to counter the deflationary effect of gold losses abroad. As the world crisis deepened, deliberate policy increased the flow of gold to France, particularly when the Bank decided to reduce its foreign exchange holdings to an absolute minimum after sterling had gone off gold in September 1931.[36] French gold policy undoubtedly contributed to the severity of the depression, but policy-makers were unconcerned by the impact of their policies abroad. Keynes predicted that only the "grinding pressure of events," i.e. the impossibility of sustaining a prolonged deflation, would force a change in French views: "They think that if everyone had behaved as they have, everyone would have as much gold as they have. Their own accumulations are the reward of virtue, and the losses which the rest of us have suffered are the penalty of imprudence."[37]

Governor Benjamin Strong of the Federal Reserve Bank of New York had long recognized the need for a "managed" gold standard; Montagu Norman was less frank about the degree of management in which he engaged, but he clearly sought alternative policies in order to avoid discount rate changes in England, and British policy concentrated on cheap money and exchange-rate management to promote domestic recovery after their departure from gold.[38] The Bank of France, too, exercised discretionary management within the constraints of its gold standard belief. Although it sought changes in discount rates abroad in order to improve the working of the gold standard, it tried to maintain a stable discount rate at home until change became absolutely necessary. The Bank had been created to provide stable conditions of credit; during the short "classical era" of the gold standard, 1880-1914, its discount rate was changed thirty-two times (to 31 July 1914); the Bank of England's discount rate changed 199 times in the same period.[39] This tradition of rate stability was continued in the interwar period, and the infrequency of changes remained a source of considerable pride. The inflow of gold in 1929-31 was deemed a result of low discount rates elsewhere, particularly in London; the efflux of French gold beginning in 1933 was accepted as the delayed reversal of the inflow, and the discount rate was raised only in periods of acute crisis to defend gold reserves, *not* as a measure for domestic adjustment.[40] Faith in the gold standard and concern to limit the domestic impact of rate changes forestalled the very actions that the gold standard was supposed to effect "automatically."

The illusion that the system was self-regulating rendered cooperation between central banks suspect. Cooperation had been sporadic and self-interested before the war; it was on the initiative of Benjamin Strong that continuous contacts between central banks were established beginning in 1916.[41] The Genoa resolutions called for closer central bank cooperation, but the resolutions were never put into full effect, lacking a consensus on appropriate policy and the benefits of cooperation among the leading central banks. Currency stabilizations in the 1920s were accomplished on a cooperative basis with the provision of central bank credits, with the franc one significant exception to the pattern. Strong and Norman refused assistance when Raoul Péret appealed to them in the chaotic conditions of May 1926 for assistance in defending the beleaguered franc; Moreau believed central bank credits essential to stabilization, but revised his view when the Bank rapidly accumulated foreign exchange in 1927. French experience seemed to prove that tough domestic measures were the necessary and sufficient solution to monetary difficulties; cooperation would delay adoption of the measures needed.[42]

The Bank of France did cooperate in efforts to contain the financial crisis that swept from Austria to Germany and then Britain in 1931. Its cooperation to assist Germany was half-hearted, seeking political concessions. But its cooperation to defend sterling was willing and sincere, despite the perception that Britain had brought the crisis upon itself by failing to restrict credit sufficiently to lower British prices and limit foreign lending. Jacques Rueff, serving as *attaché financier* to the French embassy in London and an ardent advocate of the gold standard, argued that Britain had maintained a low discount rate and used open market purchases deliberately to prevent the monetary contraction required by the gold standard: "Under the name of a managed currency, they no longer submit to the facts." [43] Observers at the Bank of France agreed that the Bank of England had persistently obstructed the natural correction process of the gold standard by open market purchases, and concluded that, "In not taking the measures necessary to defend the pound sterling, in brutally suspending the gold standard and thus plunging many countries into monetary disorder, the Bank of England has failed in its task."[44] International financial cooperation, Rueff declared, was a term devoid of sense. International solidarity was invoked "always when one wishes to profit from the prosperity of neighboring states, but never when one can come to their assistance."[45] Even when the tables were turned two years later and France sought greater cooperation within the gold bloc, her cooperative efforts were perfunctory, seeking to maintain an illusion of productive effort and group solidarity in order to hide inaction.

The third illusion was consciously manufactured propaganda, conceived as "education" rather than illusion. This met the need to persuade political and public opinion that the gold standard remained necessary, that departure from it would produce a monetary cataclysm, and that even as it disintegrated in the 1930s, the gold standard merited preservation. In the 1920s, the Bank had developed contacts with the press in order to educate opinion regarding the need to repay Bank advances to the state and return of the franc to prewar parity. During the *de facto* stabilization, Moreau made systematic use of the press to argue his case for stabilization against the wishes of Poincaré, several regents, and significant political figures of the center and right who supported revalorization.[46] With the franc back on gold, propaganda activity declined. The Bank's annual reports made customary claims regarding the necessity of the gold standard: "We remain more than ever convinced," Governor Clément Moret stated in January 1934, "that convertibility of the currency into gold is an indispensable condition for sound economic and social discipline ... It alone, it seems to us, can with continuity promote the just and orderly development of human society." Moret flatly rejected "the artificial expedients which history shows that nations have always been inclined to adopt in period of crisis."[47] Leaving gold was the easy way out, a lamentable backsliding that would return the world to the unstable currencies and inflation of the postwar years. The global crisis was a product of the "abuse of credit" under the gold exchange standard, and attempts by monetary authorities abroad to improve on the operation of the gold standard by discretionary management. France would preserve the gold standard as the anchor for the international monetary system, to which errant currencies would one day gratefully return.

Unfortunately, the gold standard itself was a major part of the problem. Its asymmetrical operation, forcing contraction on countries losing gold without inducing reciprocal credit expansion in creditor countries, now bears much of the blame for the downward spiral of prices, economic activity and employment in the Great Depression.[48] France, too, would succumb to the difficulty of meeting gold standard demands for domestic contraction, aggravated by the depreciation of currencies abroad, and finally negotiate a devaluation of the franc in the guise of an international stabilization in September 1936. Before giving in, the Bank expended great effort to sustain public belief in the gold standard and to persuade skeptics that the system worked. From May 1933, when devaluation was first proposed in the Chamber of Deputies, to May 1936, the Bank assiduously opposed devaluation, but the economic costs of defending the franc proved unsustainable, and the practical measures for doing so proved politically unsustainable.

The gold bloc, established under French leadership when the World Economic Conference in 1933 disintegrated over the issue of temporary exchange-rate stabilization, exemplifies the impulse to pretend that effective measures were being taken. It consisted of six countries—France, Belgium, Holland, Switzerland, Poland and Italy—dedicated to preserving their gold parities and the remnants of the international gold standard system. As Belgian Minister of Finance Camille Gutt commented, "The gold bloc was anything but a bloc," its members united only by their continued link to gold.[49] Central bank measures to calm speculation, particularly against the Dutch florin, were the product of an agreement between the Bank of France and the Nederlandsche Bank. A meeting of gold bloc central bankers on 8 July 1933 in Paris merely consolidated agreement to provide mutual support of each other's currencies and encouraged better communications between central banks. Governor Moret, as host, insisted that their meeting in and of itself would have a favorable psychological effect, and that their press declaration should give no details as to the nature of their agreement: "Speculation, thanks to the secrecy we will observe, will suppose that effective technical measures have been taken. The efficacy of central bank action will be that much greater if it remains shrouded in mystery." Charles Farnier agreed that secrecy was indispensable, "in order that the meeting produce its full effect on public opinion."[50] In 1934, the gold bloc attempted to increase trade within the bloc without success, and France could offer no significant assistance to Belgium to prevent their devaluation in March 1935. The gold bloc was never more than a hollow shell.[51]

The Bank of France attributed the Belgian defection to a national campaign in Belgium for devaluation, and resolved to combat the widening devaluation debate at home. In France, the case being made for devaluation had gained a powerful new advocate in the summer of 1934 when Paul Reynaud, former minister of finance and defender of French gold policy, began to advocate devaluation.[52] The Bank's response was to print, promote and distribute 75,000 copies of regent René Duchemin's anti-devaluationist tract, *Y aurait-il intérêt à dévaluer le franc?*[53] Governor Tannery, appointed in January 1935, mobilized Bank resources for a concerted effort to battle growing public interest in devaluation.[54] The Bank revived contacts with the French press in order to place articles written in the Bank's economic studies section, and sought to block the publication of unfavorable material; Bank spending on propaganda from its *Fonds S* (for secret) increased dramatically.[55] Chambers of commerce and agriculture were encouraged to send resolutions against devaluation to the minister of finance.

The most significant Bank initiative, a campaign of public lectures, was launched in 1935 to serve a dual purpose: to counter the spread of devaluationist views among the population at large and to persuade politicians as national elections approached in 1936 that there was massive public opposition to devaluation. The economic studies section asked branch directors to identify local notables who could speak in defense of the franc. Although the initial campaign was organized and underwritten by the Bank, the Bank stressed that its part should remain unseen. Directors were encouraged to work through local organizations, chambers of commerce in particular, to rent facilities, advertise for the lectures and introduce the speakers. It was soon apparent that there was little local talent suited to the task, particularly in regions where tourism and exports had been badly hurt by the overvaluation of the franc. Speakers were sent from Paris, and in 1936 the *Fédération des porteurs de valeurs mobilières* [FPVM] took over the campaign, coordinating a series of ninety-six lectures reinforced by an extensive publicity barrage. The lectures were strictly organized to maximize their propaganda impact; ninety of the assemblies voted prepared resolutions condemning devaluation unanimously. The FPVM noted with pride that "All the political parties—and we limit ourselves to recalling how much they hesitated to do so in the past—have put defense of the franc in their program."[56] The lectures tended to preach to the converted and were avoided by advocates of devaluation. The reports from local branch directors to Paris suggest that the campaign did little to alter public views. But the propaganda effort paid off: widespread attention to devaluation seemed to indicate strong public opposition. The Popular Front government elected in May 1936 took office convinced that devaluation, even if economically essential, was "politically impossible."[57]

III. France Off Gold

The Popular Front reoriented French monetary policy, hoping to promote recovery with cheap money and increased purchasing power. With wage increases, rising government expenditure (particularly for rearmament) and an overvalued franc, the Popular Front pledge of "*Ni déflation, ni dévaluation*" was economically impossible. The franc was devalued on 1 October 1936, allowed to float (i.e. depreciate) on 30 June 1937, and deliberately undervalued in a new stabilization attempt on 4 May 1938. In October 1936 a *fonds de stabilisations des changes* had been established to support the franc and obscure the gold movements for and against the franc. State reliance on borrowing, particularly to pay the costs of rearmament, and a lack of confidence in Popular Front financial management continued to push depreciation of the franc. Confidence was not restored until Paul Reynaud became minister of finance in November 1938. The Bank's most formidable adversary in the debate over devaluation took charge to direct a dramatic recovery of confidence, production, currency stability and gold reserves.[58]

French belief in the gold standard suffered. However much true believers might lament the disintegration of the gold standard, the trend abroad was a distinct move toward active monetary management to stabilize domestic prices, promote economic activity, and effect adjustments with the international economy via the exchange rate. The last prewar congress of French economists concluded unanimously that the gold standard had ceased to exist.[59] Bertrand Nogaro, an economist and Radical deputy, analyzed the relationships between gold, currency units, and prices and discovered that managed currencies in the 1930s showed greater stability of purchasing power than those tied to gold. He asked whether the gold standard, as traditionally understood in France, had ever existed at all.[60]

The gold standard had been restored in the 1920s with widespread belief that it would provide the stability essential for the recovery of world trade and prevent monetary inflation and currency instability. The discipline of the gold standard would guarantee stability, preventing the discretionary use of monetary policy that produced inflation and currency depreciation after World War I. The "gold standard vision"[61] that inspired policy-makers in the 1920s was an illusion, particularly deceiving in the simplicity with which it promised to solve complex problems. The discretionary power that produced inflation during and after World War I turned out to be needed after 1929 in order to combat a systemic deflationary compulsion that would otherwise squeeze not only prices, but trade, production and employment. Economists promoting "managed currency" ideas in preference to restoration of the gold standard were easily dismissed by central bankers as "currency cranks" in the 1920s. In the 1930s, as monetary authorities took stock of the economic costs of prolonged deflation, and as gold losses forced them to tighten credit to defend their currencies, although this would mean a sharper domestic contraction, the gold standard exacted too high a price for the benefits it conferred. Trade links encouraged some countries to follow their chief trading partners off gold and join managed currency blocs in order to obtain exchange-rate stability to facilitate trade. Countries leaving gold learned that monetary management could provide relative price stability and easier credit conditions, and could thus promote investment, employment and recovery.[62] The logic of the gold standard required that policy-makers give priority to exchange-rate stability. The Depression promoted a change in priorities from the external balance to the stability of domestic prices, activity and employment.[63]

Commitment to, and faith in, the gold standard, and success with a gold policy that accumulated huge reserves from 1928 to 1932, made France slower to learn this lesson. Large gold reserves rendered the Bank of France less sensitive and less vulnerable to the contractionary policies demanded by the external constraint of gold losses, and the Bank showed no sympathy for countries suffering such losses. Financial authorities abroad, in turn, demonstrated little sympathy for the French problems resulting from the overvalued franc, particularly authorities in Britain. On the vital issue of the price level, Governor Moret explicitly rejected price stability as an objective for central bank policy, claiming it was "hardly desirable, and impossible to achieve."[64] The gold standard became, for true believers, an ideal system able to solve all monetary problems, if left free to do its work. But as critics pointed out at the time, and as economic historians have generally agreed, the gold standard was not the solution, but the problem.

The restored gold standard distracted attention from urgent problems that could not be resolved within the constraints it imposed. Trade deficits, falling prices, high interest rates, and rising unemployment all became secondary effects of the working of the gold standard mechanism, to be resolved in the longer-term if only the gold standard were permitted to work, unfettered by state interference abroad. French belief in the efficacy and the necessity of the gold standard prolonged the Depression in France because it prevented policies to promote recovery through deficit spending and cheap money, and thus reduced France's financial and industrial capacity to rearm for war.

Experience had taught French monetary authorities that human failings were responsible for inflation and currency depreciation during and after the war; the gold standard seemed to provide an automatic disciplinary system to prevent such failings. The continued defense of the franc Poincaré and the gold standard in the mid-1930s was not only illusory in seeking benefits the gold standard could not provide, but in seeking to foster belief that all was well and that circumstances particular to France made devaluation there unworkable. The crisis in gold standard belief abroad was interpreted as a failure of will. Jules Décamps had noted in 1921 of those who claimed there had been a failure of the principles of economic science, "It is obviously easier to deny the determining force of these principles than to bend oneself to the discipline of labor and economy which they require."[65] A similar view prevailed through the early years of the depression, when French economists insisted that the economic crisis and departures from gold elsewhere demonstrated a failure to follow correct policy. The economic crisis and the breakdown of the gold standard abroad confirmed French policy on a course that would take France deeper into depression.

This course, set by gold standard orthodoxy, finally altered in response to a combination of growing dissent within France (Reynaud's devaluation advocacy being the most obvious challenge), the examples of successful monetary management abroad which could not be dismissed as irrelevant to French experience indefinitely, and the force of financial pressures. Departure from gold in 1936 and the decline of the franc that followed weakened faith in the gold standard and its virtues; defeat in 1940 prompted a fundamental rethinking of France's place in the international monetary system and French needs for the postwar world.[66] In the postwar world, France would resort more readily to inflation, with periodic devaluation to restore its external balance when rising domestic costs hurt international competitiveness, sacrificing both price stability and the external value of the franc to domestic growth.

Notes

1. The author would like to thank the German Marshall Fund of the United States for their support; this essay was written while a German Marshall Fund Research Fellow in 1998-99.
2. Pertinax, *The Gravediggers of France: Gamelin, Daladier, Reynaud, Pétain and Laval* (New York, 1942 [reissued 1968]), 364.
3. See Pierre Villa, *Une analyse macroéconomique de la France au XXe siècle* (Paris, 1993), particularly 91-103, 189-95. Villa stresses the importance of the decline in exports and investment, both results of the overvaluation of the franc in the 1930s.
4. John Maynard Keynes, *A Treatise on Money* (New York, 1930) vol. 2, 290-1.
5. Barry Eichengreen and Charles Wyplosz, "The Economic Consequences of the Franc Poincaré," in Barry Eichengreen, *Elusive Stability: Essays in the History of International Finance, 1919-1939* (Cambridge, 1990), 154. The strong French growth rates reflected recovery from the war.
6. Criticism of French gold policy came mainly from Britain, see for example the works of Paul Einzig, including *Behind the Scenes of International Finance* (London, 1932), v, xi-xii; *The Fight for Financial Supremacy* (London, 1931), ch. 10; also the Committee on Finance and Industry, *Report* (London, 1931), 70-79, Sir Henry Strakosch, "The Economic Consequences of Changes in the Value of Gold," in League of Nations, *Selected Documents Submitted to the Gold Delegation of the Financial Committee* (Geneva, 1930), 20-36; and idem., "Gold and the Price Level," supplement to the *Economist*, 5 July 1930. From recent literature, H. Clark Johnson, *Gold, France, and the Great Depression, 1919-1932* (New Haven, 1997) provides an extreme case against France for having caused the world depression.
7. Eichengreen and Wyplosz; "Economic Consequences," 154; French industrial production increased at an annual rate of 1.2% from 1931 to 1938, compared with 6.6% in Britain, 7.7% in the U.S., and 14.9% in Germany.
8. "To give gold is to gain without losing a thing." Archives de la Banque de France [BdF], 1060193601/11.
9. Copy of lecture by Canon Gaudeau, undated; details of the mobilization of the clergy can be found in BdF, 1060193601/5.
10. Notice of the Comité national de l'or to French mayors in 1916, encouraging them in their *duty* to promote the exchange of gold for currency notes, and the purchase of Bons de la Défense Nationale; BdF, 1060193601/11.
11. Committee on Currency and Foreign Exchanges after the War, *First Interim Report* (London, 1918), 5.
12. Jules Décamps, director of the Bank's *service des études économiques*, in a lecture to the Société des économistes in December 1921; *Journal des économistes* (Dec. 1921), 460-61.
13. Banque de France, *Compte rendu des opérations de la Banque de France pendant l'année 1918* (Paris, 1919), 9; my emphasis.
14. For economists' warnings, see Gustav Cassel, *The World's Monetary Problems: Two Memoranda* (New York, 1921), 63-69 and 112-20; John Maynard Keynes, *A Tract on Monetary Reform* (London, 1923) and Charles Rist, *La déflation en pratique*, 2nd ed. (Paris, 1927 [1923]).
15. See Rist, *Déflation en pratique*, 1-7; Cassel, *The World's Monetary Problems*, 33-35.
16. At the end of 1920, the note circulation of the Bank was nearly 38 billion francs, and Bank advances to the state were close to 27 billion francs. The advances were very close to the difference between the note circulation and its prewar level of notes plus gold and silver coin in circulation (roughly 12 billion francs).
17. Semaine de la Monnaie, *La politique financière et monétaire de la France* (Paris, 1922), 143, 550.

18. See Jean-Noël Jeanneney, *François de Wendel en République: L'argent et le pouvoir, 1914-1940* (Paris, 1976), 200-36; further detail on how the *faux bilans* were manipulated is provided in Bertrand Blancheton, "Les mécanismes des faux bilans de la Banque de France entre le 13 mars 1924 et le 2 avril 1925," *Etudes et Documents IX* (1997), 455-70.
19. Herriot and Clémentel did not learn that falsification of the balances had started before they took power until the summer of 1925. Poincaré and his ministers of finance in March 1924 were not told of the deception, which was the brainchild of the Bank's secretary-general, Albert Aupetit. See Etienne Clémentel, "Note pour mon dossier relative à l'inflation," 2 July 1925; Archives Départementales de Puys de Dôme, 5 J 52, and François de Wendel, "Conclusions à tirer de ma visite du 22 Mars 1932 à M. James Leclerc, Gouverneur du Crédit Foncier, 19, rue des Capucines, à Paris, sur l'affaire des situations inexactes de la Banque de France," 26 March 1932. Archives Nationales [AN] 190 AQ 20.
20. BdF, Délibérations du Conseil Général [DCG], annex to 20 May 1926.
21. Robineau was retired; first deputy governor Ernest Picard was appointed to Moreau's former position as governor of the Banque de l'Algérie; the second deputy governor, James Leclerc, who was instrumental in exposing the *faux bilans*, took Picard's position.
22. See Kenneth Mouré, *La politique du franc Poincaré (1926-1936)* (Paris, 1998), ch. 1; Jeanneney, *François de Wendel*, 296-354; and Emile Moreau, *Souvenirs d'un gouverneur de la Banque de France: Histoire de la stabilisation du franc (1926-1928)* (Paris, 1954).
23. Mouré, *La politique du franc Poincaré*, 70-80.
24. Columbus wrote long before that gold provided he who possessed it with all he needed in this world, including "the means of rescuing souls from Purgatory and restoring them to the enjoyment of Paradise." Cited in R.H. Tawney, *Religion and the Rise of Capitalism: A Historical Study* (London, 1933), 89.
25. See Moreau, *Souvenirs*, 324-26 and 332, and Banque de France, *Compte rendu des opérations de la Banque de France pendant l'année 1928* (Paris, 1929), 5.
26. Part of the problem, Moreau admitted, was that the franc was not on gold and that the demand for francs could force a revalorization, which he opposed. But the logic as to *who* should act would remain the same with the franc on gold.
27. The clash of views can be followed in the notes and correspondence in Archives of the Bank of England [BoE], G1/34 and in the Quesnay papers, AN 374 AP 6.
28. Quesnay's conclusions after an extended discussion of the gold exchange standard with H.A. Siepmann of the Bank of England. Their correspondence on this can be found in BoE, OV48/1 and AN 374 AP 6 and 9. See particularly Quesnay's margin comments on Siepmann's summary, "Monsieur Quesnay on the Gold Exchange Standard," 22 Sept. 1927, in AN 374 AP 9.
29. "Méthodes propres à assurer le maintien de la stabilité du franc," June 1928; AN 374 AP 8.
30. Undervaluation meant that the exchange rate was fixed at a level that gave France a competitive advantage in international trade.
31. William Adams Brown Jr., *The International Gold Standard Reinterpreted 1914-1934* (New York, 1940), vol. 1, 433; Gustav Cassel, *The Downfall of the Gold Standard* (New York, 1936 [1966 reprint]), 47.
32. As argued in Johnson, *France, Gold*, 139.
33. "Répercussions possibles de la réforme monétaire sur les prix, les salaires et les mouvements de capitaux," June 1928; AN 374 AP 8 and BdF, 1397199404/76.
34. See Harold James, *The Reichsbank and Public Finance in Germany 1924-1933: A Study of the Politics of Economics during the Great Depression* (Frankfurt am Main, 1985), 27-28, and Stephen V.O. Clarke, *Central Bank Cooperation 1924-31* (New York, 1967), 38-39.

35. Jacques Rueff, "Défense et illustration de l'étalon or," and Edmond Lebée, "Le gold exchange standard," in *Les Doctrines monétaires à l'épreuve des faits* (Paris, 1932). Rueff remained opposed to the gold exchange standard, claiming in 1965 that "the gold-exchange standard attains to such a degree of absurdity that no human brain having the power to reason can defend it." Jacques Rueff and Fred Hirsch, "The Role and the Rule of Gold: An Argument," *Essays in International Finance* no. 47 (Princeton, June 1965), 2-3.
36. Kenneth Mouré, *Managing the Franc Poincaré: Economic Understanding and Political Constraint in French Monetary Policy, 1928-1936* (Cambridge, 1991), 70-77.
37. J. Maynard Keynes, lecture in *The World Economic Crisis and the Way of Escape* (London, 1932), 87.
38. See Strong to Carl Snyder, 4 Feb. 1924; Central Records Office of the Federal Reserve Bank of New York [FRBNY], Strong papers, 320.45.4, and Strong to Shepard Morgan, 16 Feb. 1924; FRBNY, Strong Papers, 320.24.1. On Bank of England policy 1925-31, see Susan Howson, *Monetary Management in Britain 1919-38* (Cambridge, 1975), chs. 3 and 4; D.E. Moggridge, *British Monetary Policy 1924-1931: The Norman Conquest of $4.86* (Cambridge, 1972), and Theo Balderston, "German and British Monetary Policy, 1919-1932," in Charles H. Feinstein, ed., *Banking, Currency and Finance in Europe Between the Wars* (Oxford, 1995), 151-86.
39. R.S. Sayers, *The Bank of England, 1891-1944* (Cambridge, 1976), vol. 3, 345-47, and "Variations des taux d'avances et d'escompte de la Banque de France," BdF, 1069198803/14.
40. Mouré, *Managing the Franc Poincaré*, 47-65, 120-55.
41. See Kenneth Mouré, "The Limits to Central Bank Co-operation, 1916-1936," *Contemporary European History* I, no. 3 (Nov. 1992), 259-79; and on prewar experience, Marc Flandreau, "Central Bank Cooperation in Historical Perspective: A Sceptical View," *Economic History Review* L, no. 4 (1997): 735-63.
42. Mouré, *La politique du franc Poincaré*, 74.
43. Rueff, "Sur les causes et les enseignements de la crise financière anglaise," 1 October 1931, reprinted in Rueff, *De l'aube au crépuscule: Autobiographie* (Paris, 1977), 299-320.
44. Georges Lacout, "La Banque d'Angleterre et la défense de la livre sterling," 30 September 1931; BdF, 1397199403/163.
45. Rueff, "Sur les causes," 319.
46. The key regents were Baron Édouard de Rothschild and François de Wendel; on Moreau's campaign, see his *Souvenirs*, and Jeanneney's *François de Wendel*. For its importance in the victory over revalorisateur interests, see Kenneth Mouré, "*Le chef d'orchestre invisible et le son de la cloche officiel*: The Bank of France and the Campaign Against Devaluation, 1935-1936," *French History* 9, no. 3 (1995), 345-46, and Siepmann, "Conversation with Monsieur Quesnay," 20 June 1928; BoE, OV45/2.
47. Banque de France, *Compte rendu des opérations de la Banque de France pendant l'année 1933* (Paris, 1934), 22.
48. The essential synthesis for this interpretation is Barry Eichengreen, *Golden Fetters: The Gold Standard and the Great Depression, 1919-1939* (Oxford, 1992). See also Barry Eichengreen, "The Origins and the Nature of the Great Slump Revisited," *Economic History Review* XLV, no. 2 (1992): 213-39; Peter Temin, *Lessons from the Great Depression* (Cambridge, MA, 1989), Peter Temin, "Transmission of the Great Depression," *Journal of Economic Perspectives* 7, no. 2 (1993): 87-102; James D. Hamilton, "Role of the International Gold Standard in Propagating the Great Depression," *Contemporary Policy Issues* 6 (April 1988), 67-89; and Ben Bernanke and Harold James, "The Gold Standard, Deflation, and Financial Crises in the Great Depression," in *Financial Markets and Financial Crises*, ed. R. Glenn Hubbard (Chicago, 1991), 17-56.
49. Camille Gutt, *Pourquoi le franc belge est tombée* (Brussels, 1935), 81.

50. "Compte-rendu de la réunion des gouverneurs des banques d'émission des pays à l'étalon-or, tenue, à la Banque de France, le 8 Juilliet 1933," and Charles Farnier, "Suggestions en vue de la réunion des Banques Centrales," 6 July 1933; BdF, 1397199403/10.
51. See Mouré, *Managing the Franc Poincaré*, 109-17.
52. On the development of Reynaud's views and their influence see Mouré, *Managing the Franc Poincaré*, 196ff, and Julian Jackson, *The Politics of Depression in France, 1932-1936* (Cambridge, 1985), 180-88.
53. "Tirage et répartition de la brochure de M. Duchemin," 23 October 1934, and "Tirage et répartition de la brochure de M. Duchemin," 13 December 1934; BdF, 1069198810/no carton number. Of the 75,000 copies, more than 10,000 were distributed through Bank of France branches, but most were sent to the Ministry of Finance, which took charge of sending more than 50,000 copies out to senators, deputies, journalists, mayors and chambers of commerce.
54. Robert Lacour-Gayet, "D'une guerre à l'autre: Souvenirs d'un jeune inspecteur des finances," *Études et Documents III* (1991), 455-56. Lacour-Gayet was director of economic studies in the Bank, 1930-36.
55. See Mouré, "*Le chef d'orchestre*," 349-51. Spending from the *Fonds S* was 1,595,000 in 1934; 5,475,000 in 1935, and nearly 5 million francs in the first four months of 1936.
56. FPVM, *Correspondance no. 69* (May 1936); see Mouré, "*Le chef d'orchestre*," 351-57.
57. See Mouré, "*Le chef d'orchestre*," 358-59.
58. The government reviewed its record after Reynaud had been minister for five months in *Le bilan économique et financier des cinq premiers mois du plan de trois ans* (Paris, 1939), copy in Service des Archives économiques et financières [SAEF], B 21848.
59. M. Ansiaux, "Comment se pose actuellement la question des étalons de valeur?" *Revue d'économie politique* LII (1938), 1523-34.
60. B. Nogaro, "L'étalon d'or a-t-il existé? Étude sur la signification théorique du régime dit de l'étalon d'or," *Revue d'économie politique* LIV (1940), 161-84.
61. The phrase is Stephen Clarke's from his *Central Bank Cooperation*, 27.
62. See Howson, *Domestic Monetary Management*, 79-119, for British experience, and Eichengreen, *Golden Fetters*, 21-26, 285-93, 302-10, and Barry Eichengreen and Jeffrey Sachs, "Exchange Rates and Economic Recovery in the 1930s," *Journal of Economic History* 45 (1985), 925-46, for more general application.
63. This shift, begun in the 1930s and completed after the Second World War, changed the main priority for macroeconomic policy (monetary and fiscal) from fighting inflation to maintaining full employment; see Douglas J. Forsyth and Ton Notermans, "Introduction" and "Macroeconomic Policy Regimes and Financial Regulation in Europe, 1931-1994," in *Regime Changes: Macroeconomic Policy and Financial Regulation in Europe from the 1930s to the 1990s*, ed. Douglas J. Forsyth and Ton Notermans (Providence, R.I, 1997), 1-68.
64. Clément Moret to Georges Bonnet, 8 April 1933, cited in Mouré, *Managing the Franc Poincaré*, 90. Rueff argued the same point still more vehemently in 1932; see ibid., 33-34. Most central bankers had shared this view in the 1920s.
65. Jules Décamps, *Les changes étrangers*, 2nd ed. (Paris, 1922), 271.
66. For the shift in French monetary planning, see Robert Frank, "Contraintes monétaires, désirs de croissance et rêves européens (1931-1949), in *Le capitalisme français, 19e-20e siècle: Blocages et dynamismes d'une croissance*, ed. Patrick Fridenson and André Straus (Paris, 1987), 287-306; Chiarella Esposito, "French International Monetary Policies in the 1940s," *French Historical Studies* 17, no. 1 (1991), 117-40; and Michel Margairaz, *L'état, les finances et l'économie: Histoire d'une conversion, 1932-1952* (Paris, 1991), 747-55.

Chapter 5

THE CAGOULE PLOT, 1936-1937[1]

Joel Blatt

In January or February 1937, a woman arrived at the residence of General Benoit de la Laurencie, commander of the First Cavalry Division stationed in Paris, claiming to be soliciting contributions to fight tuberculosis. She spoke openly for Eugène Deloncle, principal leader of the "Cagoule," warning the general that he and three other generals were targets for Communist assassination. At a subsequent rendezvous, Deloncle bluntly asked, "In the case of an anti-Communist movement, can we count on you?" "Can we count on you if there was a furious storm (*coup de chien*) against the government?" The general replied, "The Army … is essentially loyal towards the institutions of our country … We are not an Army of Pronunciamento."[2]

The encounter encapsulates the Cagoule conspiracy: a quest for the violent overthrow of the Republic, provocation, anticommunism, and ultimate failure. The Cagoule plot of 1936-1937 was the most serious attempt by an element of the French extreme Right to seize power through a coup d'état during the 1930s. One of the least known, significant affairs in modern French history, the episode illuminates the intense crisis from 1934-1937, and provides a window into the weaknesses and strengths of "Marianne" during her last years. This essay turns now to tracing the Cagoule's roots, its leadership and organization, the main strands of the plot, and its denouement.

The *Organisation Secrète d'Action Révolutionnaire Nationale* (OSARN shortened to OSAR), sometimes called the *Comité Secret d'Action Révolutionnaire*

Notes for this chapter begin on page 99.

(CSAR) and nicknamed "the Cagoule,"[3] formed in 1936. Dissidents from Charles Maurras' Action Française, which the *cagoulards* called *maison mère* (mother house),[4] the OSARN emerged from the 17th Equipe of the Camelots du Roi (the Action Française's strong arm force) in Paris' 16th Arrondissement led by Jean Filiol. During the mammoth riot in Paris on 6 February 1934, Filiol hurled his troops against police barricades on the Concorde bridge. Over the next twenty months, the 17th Equipe's allegations of passivity and "immobilism" against the Action Française provoked an "expulsion-resignation."[5]

A bitter turf war ensued. On 13 February 1936, during the funeral for Jacques Bainville, the prominent royalist historian and journalist, the *cagoulards* claim to have attempted the premeditated assassination of Léon Blum, motivated by desires to provoke a government crackdown against the Action Française and to kill the Socialist Party leader hated so profligately by the Right for his beliefs and Jewish origins.[6]

The Action Française found lasting revenge. Charles Maurras warned his faithful against a new "masonry."[7] Maurice Pujo, Editor-in-Chief of *L'Action Française*, coined the term *cagoule* (hooded ones), ridiculing the new organization whose Nice affiliate donned Ku Klux Klan-like garb during rituals (the members of the OSAR's disciplinary council also wore hoods).[8]

The Cagoule plot from April/May 1936 through November 1937 paralleled the rise and fall of the Popular Front in France and took shape amidst European political polarization. The OSARN crystallized as the Popular Front coalition of Socialists, Communists, and Radicals won elections on 26 April and 3 May 1936, and outlawed right-wing leagues on 18 June 1936. On 18 May Deloncle and company established the *Parti National révolutionnaire et social* (P.N.R.S.), and soon thereafter the clandestine OSARN.[9]

Educated by Maurras,[10] the Cagoule was monarchist, authoritarian—even totalitarian, nationalist, anticommunist, antisocialist, antidemocratic, anti-liberal, anti-Semitic, and anti-Masonic. Nonetheless, action beckoned far more than theory.

Eugène Deloncle shaped the OSARN. Born in 1890, he lost his Navy father in a shipwreck in 1898. He graduated from the École Polytechnique, was wounded and won citations during World War I. Afterwards, he pursued highly successful naval engineering and business careers, occupying prominent positions on Boards of Directors.[11]

It is difficult to cross the chasm separating thought from action, bemoaned Deloncle in a psychologically redolent address of 1941. Perhaps he even remembered the period before World War I when, according to "Agathon," a generation of elite youth chose action, faith, and nation over "pessimism," skepticism, and intellectual paralysis.[12] Deloncle ascribed his "taste for action" to the times.[13]

Calling himself "one of the awakened of 1934,"[14] he asserted, "Revolution or war, war or revolution, perhaps the two" had faced France and galvanized his cohort. He lamented the loss of Fascist Italy to Germany. Moreover, in March 1936, France should either have contested Hitler's remilitarization of the Rhineland or sought "a true peace with Germany." The arrival of "Blum and his clique" had deepened the gulf "between the two nations." He claimed to have led "a plot for the security of the nation" even though arrested for "a plot against the security of the nation." He cherished the memory of:

> 1936-1937! Remember the stormy atmosphere of our political and social battles. France was then a boiling cauldron, neighbor to a partially exploded cauldron that spewed out jets of burning steam, Spain.[15]

Ominously, Deloncle ruminated on the "taste for betrayal." "The patron" cultivated a phantasmagoria of enemies filtered through his extreme rightist lens and an extraordinary taste for Byzantine plotting.[16]

Deloncle's close associates in the Action Française, and others, played prominent roles in the OSAR. Foremost, Jean Filiol, formerly a paper salesman, pressed him to seize power. Filiol shared the fascist mentality of the most aggressive Italian squadristi and Nazi stormtroopers, which made the Cagoule essentially fascist.[17] Deloncle and his wife, Mercedes, invited a young furniture salesman into their home, and Jacques Corrèze served as a key troubleshooter.[18] Henri Martin, rightist archconspirator, co-headed the Cagoule's intelligence bureau, with Aristide Corre (pseudonym Dagore).[19] Henri Deloncle, Eugène's brother, and Gabriel Jeantet, formerly an Action Française student leader, carried out important tasks.[20] François Méténier conducted foreign policy.

The OSARN followed five paths towards a coup d'état. They constructed an organization, smuggled weapons, courted foreign backing, approached the army, and developed strategy and tactics. Influenced by Curzio Malaparte's *Technique du Coup d'État,* which analyzed the Bolshevik Revolution, the Cagoule thought effective organization, strategy, and tactics, plus devoted militants, could seize power.[21]

First, the OSAR fashioned a state outside the state. A First Bureau recruited members from recently dissolved right-wing leagues.[22] The OSAR administered an oath of "loyalty, obedience, and discretion" in the presence of a tricolor flag, and threatened death in case of transgression. The Second Bureau, intelligence, gathered information and carried out surveillance. The Third Bureau planned an "insurrection" and trained recruits. The Fourth Bureau transported weapons and planned movement during the coup d'état. A special section carried out assassinations. A council of discipline "judged" errant *cagoulards.* A medical service treated the wounded. A profile of this military-style general staff includes distinguished participation in World War I, retired military officers, continued military service as officers in the reserves, and prominent business careers.[23]

The Cagoule plot required substantial money, although amounts and names remain in doubt. Jacques Corrèze mentioned an armaments bill of ten million francs in August 1937. Deloncle cited 40 million francs, while another source estimated possibly 80 millions in contributions. Police informers implicated major industrialists. Authorities suspected Pierre Michelin, and investigated the books of the Michelin and Citroën companies. Individuals at Renault came under suspicion. Jacques Lemaigre-Dubreuil, head of the *Fédération Nationale des Contribuables* (a taxpayers group) and of Huiles Lesieur (Lesieur Oil), donated and solicited money. Marshal Louis Franchet d'Esperey gave 1,500,000 francs to Major Georges Loustaunau-Lacau, who had established an anti-Communist group in the Army. Did the Marshal, or his financial sources, also back the OSAR? From the defeat of 1940 until 1942, Eugène Schueller, the founder of "L'Oréal," provided substantial financial support for the *Mouvement Social Révolutionnaire* (MSR), the OSAR's successor. It is unclear whether Schueller similarly bankrolled the Cagoule.[24]

The OSAR also coordinated like-minded groups, forming one conspiracy. The most important was the *Union des Comités d'Action Défensive* (UCAD), whose President, the much-decorated World War I veteran, retired air force general Edouard Duseigneur, provided respectability.[25] Madame Mercedes Deloncle called the OSARN and the UCAD "twin sisters," portraying her husband and Duseigneur as virtually interchangeable parts.[26] Exaggeration, but Duseigneur contributed to the seriousness of the Cagoule plot. The general legally registered the UCAD in December 1936; however, it served as a front for the OSARN. It could enroll a range of rightist dissidents, many of whom thought they were joining a self-defense organization against Communism. The UCAD did attract more than twice as many members as the 1260 names (a list of the OSAR) found at the residence of Aristide Corre.[27]

Another significant affiliate was the *Chevaliers du Glaive* (Knights of the Sword) of Nice. Its members wore hoods, and swore oaths before a sword laid out on a black sheet.[28] Several, particularly Dr. Jean Faraut, established contacts with the Nazis. The Cagoule's first two major arms merchants, Léon Jean-Baptiste and Adolphe Juif, had ties to Nice. Joseph Darnand, future head of the Milice under Vichy, was the group's preponderant figure. His trucking company smuggled weapons into France, and Darnand served as an intermediary with Italian Fascist Intelligence.[29]

A third affiliate, *L'Union des Enfants d' Auvergne* or *L'Union des Patriotes d'Auvergne* of Clermont-Ferrand, contributed François Méténier to the OSARN. In

September 1937, Méténier summoned Réné Locuty, an engineer at Michelin, who constructed bombs exploded near the Etoile. Sources indicated the Clermont-Ferrand-Lyons region as a major financial resource for the OSAR.[30]

Jean Filiol cultivated *L'Algérie Française*, an organization apparently originated to fight for the rights of native Algerians as French citizens. Attempting to mobilize native Algerians for the Cagoule's putsch, Filiol and Fernand Jakubiez, a prominent *cagoulard*, placed Mohamed El Maadi at the group's helm. Using threats and subsidies, Filiol wanted "350 décidés" ("350 decided men").[31]

A French "deep throat" might have whispered, "Follow the weapons."[32] The OSARN scoured Europe for firearms, grenades, and munitions. In August 1936, Léon Gabriel Jean-Baptiste, the OSARN's principal arms merchant, and Adolphe Juif (pseudonym "Israel"!), his primary aide, bought weapons in Belgium, mainly of German origin. The two arms merchants also attended the Nazi Nuremberg rally. Then, during September and October, they contacted the Beretta Company in Italy and divided their time between Fascist Italy and Belgium.

Jean-Baptist's world, however, was crumbling. On 21 September 1936, Belgian authorities blocked transfer of 300 Schmeisser *mitraillettes. Cagoulard* leaders discovered that their arms merchants had over-billed the organization. Moreover, in Italy Jean-Baptiste had become infatuated with the mistress of an Austrian baron, who threatened to intervene with Fascist leaders. Deloncle and Duseigneur, in Rome seeking an audience with Mussolini, suddenly returned home. A telegram, signed "Marie," one of Deloncle's pseudonyms, recalled Jean-Baptiste from Brussels. In Paris, on the evening of 26 October 1936, after dining with Corrèze and leaving with him for a meeting with Deloncle, Jean-Baptiste disappeared, almost certainly "tried" by the OSAR's council of discipline and executed.[33] Juif relocated to San Remo in northern Italy, but disappeared on 14 December 1936, his bullet marked body discovered in a ditch on 8 February 1937. French authorities ascribed Juif's demise to his colleagues in the *Chevaliers du Glaive*, working with the Cagoule.[34]

These murders had unintended consequences. In October 1936, two trunks, addressed to Jean-Baptiste and mailed from Italy before his disappearance, arrived at the Lille railroad station unclaimed. When opened three months later, beneath fancy clothes, French customs inspectors found weapons receipts, the address of a major Belgian arms dealer, and the names of French rightists.[35] Jean-Baptiste achieved revenge from his unmarked grave. Soon thereafter, the Sûreté Nationale also unraveled the threads of Juif's death. By May 1937, French investigators linked Jean-Baptiste and Juif to Deloncle and company.[36]

Gabriel Jeantet and others continued purchasing weapons and the complex task of smuggling them into France, concentrating on Belgium, Switzerland, Fascist Italy, and Nationalist Spain.[37]

The OSAR sought foreign backing and Fascist Italy and Nationalist Spain (more than Nazi Germany) became the foci. Deloncle and Duseigneur visited Nationalist Spain in January 1937. Spanish Nationalists provided weapons, perhaps financial support, and eventually exile. Arms, often made in Germany, crossed the porous Spanish frontier into southwestern France. In return, the OSAR aided French volunteers for Franco's side, and joined Italian and Spanish Nationalist agents in destroying material destined for the Loyalists. In September 1937, the Cagoule supported Spanish Nationalists in an unsuccessful attempt to hijack a Loyalist Government submarine in the French port of Brest.[38]

Italian Fascists and the Cagoule found each other early in 1937 as Mussolini and Foreign Minister Count Galeazzo Ciano bogged down in Spain. The Third Section (Counterintelligence) of the *Servizio Informazione Militare* (SIM), Italian Army Intelligence, headed by Santo Emanuele and seconded by Roberto Navale, developed a sabotage plan, targeting Carlo Rosselli for assassination.[39] Italian Fascism may have feared him more than any other Italian anti-Fascist. From exile in France, the indefatigable Rosselli, charismatic, action-oriented, maverick liberal socialist, led a movement, *Giustizia e Libertà*, which organized propaganda ventures in Italy and, from deeper clandestinity, plotted the Duce's assassination.[40] Rosselli volunteered immediately for the Spanish Civil War, and helped link Italian anti-Fascists and the Loyalist government. Nello Rosselli, a pathbreaking historian, resolutely supported his brother Carlo, but was less militant and lived in Italy. In June 1937, he visited his brother, who was undertaking a cure in Bagnoles de l'Orne to relieve blood clots from a wound in Spain.

Deloncle and company regarded Fascist Italy as a fount of weapons and an ideological ally in an international as well as national civil war. During the first months of 1937, Filippo Anfuso, Ciano's chief aide, met with Méténier and Darnand. The OSAR informed Anfuso of its intention to overthrow the Third Republic, establish a regime similar to Italian Fascism's, and asked for Italian aid. The idea of "an Italo-French bloc" linked to "Belgium with Degrelle, Holland with Mussert, Spain with Franco," plus "the 'fascisant' activity of ... Mosley in England" and "in alliance" with Hitler's Germany attracted Anfuso, who described Mussolini as intrigued by such a "Franco-Italian alliance."[41] On 22 March 1937, after Italian Antifascists had embarrassed Italian Fascists at the Battle of Guadalajara, the OSAR, probably Méténier, "solemnly engaged" to assassinate Rosselli in return for "100 semiautomatic Beretta rifles."[42] Mussolini almost certainly ordered the assassination in conjunction with Ciano.[43] For the OSAR, 100 weapons, significant in themselves, also represented a down payment, while SIM paid as little as possible.[44]

Sabotage explosions soon rippled across southern France to the Spanish frontier.[45] These bombings climaxed ten years of episodic Italian Fascist bombings in

France.[46] The Rosselli assassinations, though, represented the primary outcome of the Blackshirt/Cagoule connection.

On 9 June, an assassination team, led by Jean Filiol, composed of Filiol, Jakubiez, François Baillet, Robert Puireux, Jacques Fauran, Renée Alice Lamy, and Jean Bouvyer, ambushed and slaughtered the Rosselli brothers on a desolate country road in Normandy. Filiol shot and stabbed Carlo Rosselli, and shot and (together with Jakubiez) stabbed Nello. The OSAR, possibly not the Blackshirts, may have chosen to kill both brothers, instead of Carlo alone. The Cagoule immediately sent evidence of its authorship to Ciano and Mussolini.[47]

Two months later, the OSAR assured SIM of their admiration for the Duce as "our master" and "Fascism" as "a norm not only of Italian, but of European political life," which should be "copied and applied in France." Santo Emanuele reported, "After the conquest of power, the movement wants to combat in France communism, freemasonry, Judaism, parliamentarism, the '*politicaillerie*' of the professionals." Thus, the OSAR assassinated the Rossellis as part of its "preparation" for a putsch, and to secure a future alliance with Fascist Italy.[48]

Similarly at home, the Cagoule chased an alliance with the French Army. This essay began with Deloncle's blunt courtship of General de la Laurencie. General Gaston Prételat, Vice-Military Commander of Paris, maintained that in June 1937 he rejected a similar proposal. In September, three sticks of dynamite were found outside Prételat's residence.[49]

Deloncle had better luck with Marshal Louis Franchet d'Esperey, a World War I hero and a member of the advisory Conseil Supérieur de la Guerre, who sent Colonel Georges Groussard to assess the Cagoule. After fifteen meetings between May and November 1936, hardly a casual look-see, Groussard claimed he advised against a relationship.[50]

Nonetheless, in March 1937, according to Commandant (Major) Georges Loustaunau-Lacau, a member of Marshal Philippe Pétain's staff who had organized the Corvignolles ostensibly to root communists out of the Army, Franchet d'Esperey pressed him and Deloncle to collaborate "for France." The OSAR's head spoke openly about overthrowing the state. A civil war would profit Germany, Loustaunau-Lacau claimed he responded, while Deloncle argued that French survival required "renewal" of the state.[51]

In June 1937, Deloncle and Loustaunau-Lacau reached a significant agreement. According to the Major, the OSAR freed its members on active military service from their loyalty oaths. In return, Loustaunau-Lacau opened a conduit into the Deuxième Bureau (Intelligence) of the Army General Staff of Paris. Thus, weekly, the Cagoule fed information about alleged communist activity into the military intelligence hopper.[52]

How much headway did the OSAR make with the French military? Weeding out OSAR hyperbole is not always easy. Loustaunau-Lacau emphatically denied membership, I think accurately, but the extent of his collaboration with the OSAR remains moot.[53] Deloncle and Duseigneur contacted higher ranking officers rather than the rank and file. A handful probably joined the OSAR, while others intimated cooperation if faced by a Communist coup d'état. As an example, General Henri Giraud, Military Governor of Metz, appears to have given the OSAR a hearing without uttering a categorical rejection.[54] Still others watched the Popular Front unfold with anxiety.[55] Some knew about the OSAR's preparations without apparently informing France's civilian leaders. For example, in January 1937, Pétain sent Loustaunau-Lacau on a fact finding mission to General Duseigneur who frankly avowed that the OSAR was gathering weapons. Informed, Pétain quipped, "That's too bad because when one has weapons one tends to use them." [56] The OSAR very likely avoided contacting Lieutenant-Colonel Charles De Gaulle.[57]

General Maurice Gamelin, head of the French Army General Staff, provides a clue to the mentality of the officer corps as he (and Pétain) unsuccessfully urged Edouard Daladier, Minister of National Defense and War in 1938, to transfer the politicized Loustaunau-Lacau to a provincial command rather than remove him from active duty. On Loustaunau-Lacau's behalf, Gamelin claimed that there had been a moment of communist effervescence in the Army in 1936.[58] If the Popular Front had been stronger or more radical, France's military commanders might have been more receptive to the OSAR's siren song.

Throughout 1937, the OSAR rushed ahead on its conspiracy, attempting to create an atmosphere of instability that would be blamed on Communists. On 25 January 1937, the Cagoule murdered Dimitry Navachine, a Russian émigré economist with Soviet and Popular Front contacts.[59] On 16 March 1937, the OSAR may have helped provoke the clash at Clichy between police and leftist demonstrators resulting in dead and wounded.[60] On 17 May 1937, the OSAR slashed the throat of Laetitia Toureaux in the Paris metro, perhaps apprehensive about what she might know and wishing to stoke public malaise.[61] Continuing to collaborate with SIM, after the 9 June Rosselli assassinations, on 29 August 1937, at the French airfield of Toussus le Noble, the OSAR, led by Filiol, sabotaged two airplanes destined for Loyalist Spain.[62] On 11 September 1937, the Cagoule exploded bombs near the Etoile at the headquarters of two major business organizations, the Confédération Générale du Patronat Français and the Groupe des Industries Métallurgiques de la Région Parisienne, with the unintended deaths of two policemen. From his naval background, Deloncle called it a *coup de semonce* ("a warning shot across the bow"), sowing disorder and threatening the *patronat*.[63]

Preparatory to their putsch, the OSAR gathered information on ministers, ministries, the electricity, telephone, metro, and sewer systems of Paris, on the approaches to the Palais Bourbon (Parliament), the Matignon Hotel (the Premier's offices), and the Elysée Palace (home of the President). They constructed a command post, weapons depots, and a medical service. They also built a prison, telling workers that it would hold "communists" and "certain political personalities." Filiol indicated that after the seizure of power, leaders of the Left and Jews would be "suppressed" (*supprimés*).[64] They trained their cadres to use weapons and explosives, and considered resort to biological toxins.[65]

Why did the Cagoule choose 15-16 November 1937 as "J" day? Prior to their abortive coup d'état, the OSAR wallowed in an environment increasingly inhospitable to their conspiracy. The Popular Front waned; Léon Blum's government fell in June 1937. Quiet reigned on the communist front in France; the Ministries of the Interior and National Defense saw no signs of a Communist putsch.[66] The acute fears of the OSAR's backers subsided.[67] Inside their cabal, *cagoulards* discussed hustling history; in the absence of a Communist rising, the OSAR would manufacture a Communist threat.[68] The Etoile bombings capped this tactic. Further, the OSAR considered assassinating leaders of the Action Française and blowing up the Matignon Hotel, exploits to be imputed to Communists.[69] Even in their foreign policy, the Cagoule's courtship of Italian Fascism conflicted with its approaches to the French Army, which was becoming increasingly wary of Fascist Italy.[70] In September 1937, French authorities began arresting and questioning *cagoulards* (including Deloncle), and seized a list of OSAR members. Moreover, Henry Charbonneau, a *cagoulard*, portrayed Henri Martin, head of the Cagoule's "intelligence" section in November 1937, as "an incorrigible mythomane," and Deloncle as a devotee of "intelligence."[71] Perhaps information from Martin forecasting a Communist coup influenced Deloncle at a moment when time worked against their cause.

The Cagoule based its strategy of 1936-1937 on an audacious but flimsy plan of agent provocateurism. Fomenting violent disorder as a means to call for order, the OSAR trumpeted a Communist peril, in which they at least partially believed, and sought a pretext to launch a coup d' état. The Cagoule flooded military and police intelligence channels with vivid information about a scheduled Communist takeover on 15-16 November 1937, a mirror image of their own plans. Deloncle and Duseigneur disseminated "intelligence" material widely, including top generals.[72] The OSAR probably achieved some limited success in offering the organization as an auxiliary force to military commanders in the Paris region in the event of a Communist putsch.[73] The *cagoulards* hoped army barracks and armories would be opened to them. Either the Army would believe outright in a Communist plot, or escalating civil conflict would elicit a Communist response, thereby encouraging the military to collaborate with the OSAR.[74] In the ensuing commotion, the Cagoule would break through to power.

During the evening of 15-16 November 1937, the OSAR mobilized its forces. Prior Cagoule planning entailed forced entry into ministries and firing on gardes mobiles if necessary,[75] but during the long overnight *cagoulards* waited at their posts. Deloncle failed to convince the Army and other authorities that France faced a Communist insurrection and no Communist assault materialized. Nevertheless, he came under intense pressure from Filiol. "You will always be the same," Filiol argued. "You will wait until they come to slit your throat in your own home. We must act and act rapidly. The people who have sworn their oaths should descend into the street when we will give the order, whatever the reason, offensive or defensive." Deloncle replied, "If we descend first into the street, no one will follow us; whereas if it is to defend ourselves, everyone will march." Towards 5 A. M., 16 November, apparently realizing that the Cagoule lacked sufficient weight and military support, Deloncle demobilized his troops.[76]

From at least as early as January 1937 when French customs officials uncovered the contents of Jean-Baptiste's luggage, French authorities investigated the OSAR plot with intensity as a threat to the Third Republic and to the Popular Front. Léon Blum recalled receiving reports nightly from Marx Dormoy, the Minister of the Interior.[77] By late 1937, effective police work broke the conspiracy, leading to the arrests of Deloncle, Duseigneur, and others, while prominent *cagoulards*, including Filiol, fled to Fascist Italy and Nationalist Spain.[78] An additional tragedy struck on 27 January 1938 when explosives and thousands of grenades, previously uncovered in the OSAR's arms caches, exploded in Villejuif killing fourteen.[79]

Faced with political divisions at home and war abroad, French governments failed to try the *cagoulards* before World War II. Authorities released General Duseigneur from prison in 1938 and Deloncle and others after war began. Only in 1948 did surviving *cagoulards* stand trial. This is not the place to explore the aftermaths of the Cagoule plot during the subsequent sixty years.

In conclusion, with regard to "crisis and renewal in France since the First World War," one may ask of the Cagoule conspiracy: which crisis? how much renewal? The Cagoule plot marked a climax of acute political and social ruptures from distant and recent sources and may be placed within historical units extending back to the Revolution of 1789. It represented one of the last battles of the French Revolution.[80] It also harkened back to the Far Right around 1900 with the OSAR resembling the early Action Française.[81]

The Cagoule fits best into steep divisions in France from 1934-1938, particularly during the year following the Popular Front victory. The Third French Republic began in total military defeat and civil war, significant residues of which remained sixty-five years later. French politics polarized in three intensifying, related waves: before World War I, during the 1920s, and during the 1930s.[82] The French crisis of the 1930s had domestic and foreign roots. What Stanley Hoffmann calls the "Republican synthesis," "a stalemate society," "plenty of brakes and not much of a motor," responded with difficulty to the Great Depression.[83] Contemporaneously, fifteen years after the pyrrhic victory of 1918, a huge hurricane blew up from Germany while the preponderance of French leaders, because of the Communist Revolution, would not countenance a military alliance with the Soviet Union. But Russia remained the necessary continental counterweight to Hitler's Germany.

The Cagoule responded to the crisis of the 1930s by plotting to overthrow the Republic and establish a nationalist dictatorship. The OSAR represented social defense and a consuming hatred of communism, socialism, and liberal democracy so strong as to bend the *cagoulards'* image of reality. Historians disagree on whether the Cagoule was fascist.[84] Contacts with Italian Fascism indicate "like minds" with non-identical interests; however, the *cagoulards*, Blackshirts, and the Nazis resembled each other more than they differed. All three advocated national revivals, entailing increased national power, excluding groups from the national community, and intense dictatorships. The OSAR's monarchism and elitism, between traditional and mass politics, are less significant differences than similar mentalities. "Mussolini's regime" appealed to Henry Charbonneau as "a muscular monarchy."[85] The OSAR, Italian Fascism and Nazism shared proclivities for violence and extreme solutions. They wished to be brutal, a prominent characteristic of European Fascism. Deloncle threatened, "Nous sommes méchants" ("We are wicked").[86] Filiol led French fascist squads during his expeditions. Considering methods and goals, the OSAR was "ultra right" and essentially fascist.

Deloncle, similar to Mussolini and Hitler, manipulated the calculus of anti-communism, anti-socialism, and anti-liberal democracy to reach power. An engineer, Deloncle had absorbed the lessons of Mussolini's and Hitler's rise to power. Portray a widespread communist menace. Generate substantial disorder as a means to de-legitimize a vulnerable liberal regime while calling for order. Approach conservative custodians of power.

The Cagoule plot has been underestimated. Certainly, the organization was small. In June 1937, Corre lamented fewer than 2000 "shock troops,"[87] and perhaps many fewer mobilized on 15-16 November. Moreover, proselytizing failed to convert most military officers. Still, the conspiracy attracted devoted militants, found sympathy from a small number of superior officers, and, in Paris alone, gathered explosives, many hundreds of weapons, thousands of grenades, and hundreds of thousands of cartridges.[88] The conspiracy attempted to overthrow the state, cooperated with foreign governments, and committed substantial crimes. Why did the Cagoule plot fail?

First: one of the least significant explanations is the OSAR's resemblance at times to "the gang that could not shoot straight." Jean-Baptiste swindled the Cagoule and fell inappropriately in love in Rome. Corre kept a diary, and police eventually seized a list of members at his home. Jakubiez dribbled cartridges through a hole in the false bottom of an auto from Switzerland into France.[89] The youngest of the Rosselli assassins, Bouvyer, boasted about his role in the crime. Still, the OSAR should be regarded as a lethal and serious conspiracy.

Second: Deloncle battled over turf with the Action Française and with the largest rightist movement of the 1930s, Colonel de la Rocque's Croix de Feu/Parti Social Français, and weakened the OSAR.[90] Evidence supports historians who have emphasized divisions on the French Far Right. In seeking "space" for itself, the OSAR struck extreme rightist obstacles.

Third: respectable conservatives held the keys to fascists seizing power. The Cagoule plot provides an excellent historical laboratory for assessing why French fascists or "ultra-rightists" failed to reach power prior to defeat and Vichy. Postwar Italian and German governments allowed the emergence of paramilitary forces outside the state; furthermore, conservatives, King Victor Emmanuel III and President Paul von Hindenburg, literally gave Mussolini and Hitler power. For French extreme Rightists to break through, they needed an effective coalition of conservatives, reactionaries, and the Far Right. Robert Paxton suggests that the "rooting" and "acquisition of power" by fascist movements in France were blocked by conservatives already occupying the "space," and by governments (including the Popular Front) and the state actively protecting order.[91] At the beginning of the Third Republic, Adolphe Thiers asserted, "The Third Republic would be conservative or it would not be."[92] During the 1930s, the Republic contained enough ballast to restrain conservatives from shaking the Cagoule's aggressively proffered hand.

Fourth: the military represents the OSAR's failure to achieve sufficient conservative backing. Historians disagree about the Army's responses to the crisis of the 1930s. For Paul-Marie de la Gorce, the Cagoule affair marked "the moral rupture between an important segment of the army and the republican state."[93] In contrast, Martin Alexander portrays General Maurice Gamelin as working within the Republic, while Minister of National Defense Daladier, and Blum's support for rearmament, soothed the Army Chief of Staff's relations with the Popular Front Government.[94] Philip Bankwitz elaborates General Maxime Weygand's many discontents with "Marianne," and from 6 February 1934 the conscious and unconscious erosion of restraint by the military towards the Republic's civilian leadership. Bankwitz concludes, "… Definite antiregime plans did not exist in the command," but "clear signs of the approaching confrontation of the civil and military powers" emerged.[95] Alexander, citing Jean Lacouture, notes the need to know more about "the Army's state of mind," but both historians indicate rightist sympathies within the military.[96] D. L. L. Parry finds "loyalty increasingly conditional."[97] Additional factors should be considered. Antoine Prost reminds us that many French veterans were antimilitarists, not rightist leaguers.[98] Unlike Germany, and nationalist resentments in postwar Italy despite victory, France won World War I and the French military helped formulate foreign policy during the 1930s. France significantly rearmed from 1936-1940. And the omnipresent German enemy at the gates diminished the military's taste for domestic adventures.[99]

Fifth: Timing! During the first seven months of the Popular Front Government, June-December 1936, the military and conservatives hesitated. The Right reacted viscerally to the huge surge of popular enthusiasm, the raised fists, the singing of the "International," the red flags, the sit-down strikes of May-June, the Matignon accords and subsequent social legislation.[100] Martin Alexander suggested that the Cagoule might have missed its moment, the autumn of 1936 when episodic strikes continued and industrialists counterattacked.[101] Did the Cagoule miss a window of opportunity during the gathering conservative backlash? The climate proved propitious for fundraising and organization, but autumn 1936 caught the *cagoulards* unprepared to reach for power. In addition, the *patronat*'s "counterattack" showed once again the capacity of conservatives for self-preservation without resort to a Cagoule coup.[102] By 1937, clearheaded conservatives and generals could foresee fissures sundering the Popular Front coalition and power ricocheting back towards a Radical-moderate conservative coalition. They also could perceive real Communist activity falling far short of the imagined Communist putsch.

Sixth: the Third Republic retained enough vitality to withstand the OSAR's assault. The police and the judiciary effectively investigated the OSAR, and most of the Army remained at least circumspectly loyal. Moreover, enough people continued to believe in the Republic as an ideal or acquiesce in it. Even during her last years, the reputation of the much maligned "Marianne" deserves a certain refurbishing, but only so far.

The Daladier-Reynaud Cabinet following the Popular Front's collapse partially resolved the crisis of the mid-1930s. It rallied the wagon trains around a center and center-right axis including national defense, hostility to the Left, and Paul Reynaud's liberal economic policy.[103] Still, France paid a price for the Cagoule conspiracy.

French governments took sharp political divisions into account. For example, during the Cagoule trial of 1948, Blum ascribed his reticence during the Spanish Civil War to worry about civil war at home.[104] Significantly, from 1935-1938,

French governments assiduously avoided pursuit of a military alliance with the Soviet Union.[105] Stalin led one of the most brutal regimes in history, but France had only barely survived in 1914 with both Great Britain and Russia as allies. One cannot blame France's unsuccessful foreign policy solely on the OSAR. Nevertheless, the Cagoule conspiracy symbolizes the extent to which political polarization in France during the mid-1930s sapped the Third Republic's resiliency, depriving France of necessary vigor and additional allies.

The Cagoule plot bore harbingers of the defeat of 1940 and of Vichy. Although *cagoulards* fought hard during the Battle of France, "towards October 1939 Deloncle had confided":

> ... It was impossible to foresee an effective resistance against the German armies before 1941 and therefore, without prohibiting the members of the organization from doing their duty, it was necessary to be thrifty with their lives because, after the war that could only end with a German victory, it would be necessary to appeal to all the energies in order to save France.[106]

From Vichy on 10 July 1940, Deloncle wrote a letter to his wife:

> full of joy in the sadness. The Republic is no more. Today I saw these puppets (*pantins*) commit suicide. I was present at their death throes ... My dream is half realized ... I cannot tell you my role in the affair ... It was not negligible ... The future will tell if I was right."[107]

Notes

1. Brigitte Lainé, an archivist at the Archives de Paris whose knowledge has guided numerous researchers, aided me substantially. I would also like to thank another archivist, Philippe Grand, and successive Directors and staffs at the Archives de Paris and at the repository of Villemoisson.
2. Déposition, Benoit de la Laurencie to Judge Robert Lévy, 18 June 1946, Archives de Paris (henceforth AP), 212/79/3, carton 49.
3. There is uncertainty about the association's accurate name. Deloncle claimed OSARN, shortened in July 1937 to OSAR. The band was also called the CSAR. It is possible that the group first called itself the CSAR and OSARN and later the OSAR, reflecting a desire to broaden image. The OSARN, OSAR, and CSAR are synonyms for the same organization. See Christian Bernadac, "Avant-Propos," Dagore (Aristide Corre), *Les carnets secrets de la cagoule* (Paris, 1977), 15-16; Philippe Bourdrel, *La Cagoule* (Paris, 1992, 1970), 58; Frédéric Monier, *Le complot dans la République: Stratégies du secret de Boulanger à la Cagoule* (Paris, 1998), 285; Réquisitoire définitif, L' Affaire de l' OSARN, 1 July 1939, 62-63, AP, 212/79/3, carton 46; also see

Franco Bandini, *Il cono d' ombra: Chi armò la mano degli assassini dei fratelli Rosselli* (Milan, 1990), 444, note 2 (but Bandini's interpretations must be considered with utmost caution).

4. For the Cagoule, see Bourdrel, ibid.; Monier, ibid., 267-9 and chaps. 13 and 14; D.L.L. Parry, "Counter Revolution By Conspiracy, 1935-37," in *The Right in France 1789-1997*, ed. Nicholas Atkin and Frank Tallett (London-New York, 1998), 161-81; Frédérick Freigneaux, "La Cagoule: Enquête sur une conspiration d'extrême droite," *L' Histoire*, 159, October 1992, 6-17; J.R. Tournoux, *L' histoire secrète* (Paris, 1962); Robert Soucy, *French Fascism:The Second Wave, 1933-1939* (New Haven-London, 1995), 46-53. For "maison mère," see Dagore, ibid., 38.
5. The phrase "expulsion-resignation" is Dagore's (Corre's), *Les carnets secrets,* 38. Also see Bernadac, 19-21; Bourdrel (1992), chap. 2; Eugen Weber, *Action Française: Royalism and Reaction in Twentieth Century France* (Stanford, 1962), 368.
6. Bernadac, 22; Weber, 363-4; Bourdrel (1992), 34-8.
7. Charles Maurras, *L'Action Française,* 28 July 1936, 1.
8. Maurice Pujo, *L'Action Française,* 20 November 1936, 1; 18 November 1937, 1; Bernadac, 15; Weber, 398; Bourdrel (1992), 58.
9. Philippe Bourdrel describes clearly the historical context in which the OSARN emerged (chap. 1 of each edition of *La Cagoule*); also see Barnadac, 22-3.
10. Bourdrel (1970), 29.
11. Réquisitoire définitif, 1939, 619-47; Bourdrel (1970), 66-9, and (1992), 60-3; Bernadac, 17.
12. When I asked Jan Goldstein about Deloncle's psychology, she pointed to *Les jeunes gens d' aujourd'hui* of 1912-1913. Under the pseudonym of Agathon, Henri Massis and Alfred de Tarde interviewed students from elite Parisian schools and concluded that their generation surmounted "the supposed antinomy of thought and action" by renewing faiths in nation, Catholicism, "heroism," and even war. See Massis and de Tarde, "The Young People of Today," in *Twentieth Century Europe,* volume 9, *The University of Chicago Readings in Western Civilization,* ed. John W. Boyer and Jan Goldstein (Chicago,1987), 16-35, and Robert Wohl, *The Generation of 1914* (Cambridge, Massachusetts, 1979), chap. 1, particularly 5-18.
13. Eugène Deloncle, "Les Idées et l' action" (Paris, 1941), 7.
14. Ramon Fernandez, *La Gerbe,* 25 September 1941, and cited in Bourdrel (1970), 70.
15. Deloncle, "Les idées et l' action," 9.
16. Deloncle, ibid., and Bourdrel (1970), 66-74, (1992), 62-4.
17. For Filiol, see Réquisitoire définitif, 1939, 731-41; Report 15478, Borel, 13 April 1938, AP, 212/79/3, carton 44; Bourdrel (1992), 59-60.
18. Extrait des Minutes du Greffé, Cour d'Appel de Paris, 28 July 1939, AP, 212/79/3, carton 52; Bourdrel (1992), 64-5.
19. Pierre Péan, *Le mystérieux Docteur Martin 1895-1969* (Paris, 1993); Bernadac, "Avant Propos," and Dagore, 37; Bourdrel (1992), 65-7.
20. Extrait des Minutes du Greffé, La Cour d' Appel de Paris, 28 July 1939, AP, 212/79/3, carton 52; Bourdrel (1992), 66, 74-5.
21. Monier, 302-6; Tournoux, 84; Weber, 275; Bourdrel (1992), 68-71.
22. Réquisitoire définitif, 1939, 67.
23. Réquisitoire définitif, 1939; Reports, René le Poittevin, 31 May 1946 and 6 March 1947, AP, 212/79/3, carton 49.
24. See AP, 212/79/3, carton 24, and Réquisitoire définitif, 1939, 275-83; Parry, 172-3; Monier, 178-9; Pierre Milza, "L' ultra-droite des années trente," in *Histoire de l' extrême droite en France,* ed. Michel Winock (Paris, 1993), 178; Bourdrel (1992), 106-8; Péan, *Docteur Martin,* 107-8; Soucy, *The Second Wave,* 51. Also see, Georges Loustaunau-Lacau, *Mémoires d' un français rebelle 1914-1918* (Geneva,1972, 1948), 98. For Schueller and the MSR, see Bertram M. Gor-

don, *Collaboration in France during the Second World War* (Ithaca, 1980), 36, 71-2, 108, 206-7; Joel Blatt, "Mouvement Social Révolutionnaire," in *Historical Dictionary of World War II France*, ed. Bertram M. Gordon(Greenwich, 1998), 253; Michael Bar-Zohar, *Bitter Scent: The Case of L' Oréal, Nazis, and the Arab Boycott* (New York et al., 1996), 46-8; "Schueller, Eugène," in *Dictionnaire de la Politique Française*, ed. Henry Coston (Paris, 1967), 966-7.

25. For Duseigneur and his Vice-President, Duke Joseph Pozzo di Borgo, see Bourdrel, (1992), 57-8.
26. Réquisitoire définitif, 1939, 245, and Letter, probably Madame Deloncle to Jacques Corrèze, 26 September 1938, AP. 212/79/3, carton 14.
27. Réquisitoire définitif, 1939, 232-45; Report, Le Procureur de la République to the Procureur Général, 31 January 1938, 36-41, AP, 1320W, carton 119. For the numbers of *cagoulards*, see Parry, 162-4; Monier, 288-92.
28. Réquisitoire définitif, 1939, 132-3.
29. Ibid., 129-56, 335-49, 610-18; AP, 212/79/3, carton 29; Bourdrel (1992), 94-5, 128-31, and Bourdrel (1970), 115-16.
30. Réquisitoire définitif, 1939, 245-8; Bourdrel (1992), 91-2.
31. Réquisitoire définitif, 1939, 250-3, and AP, 212/79/3, carton 44. For the affiliates of the OSAR, also see Parry, 164, and Monier, 275 and 278-82.
32. "Deep throat," the nickname of a Watergate Affair source, advised the journalists Woodward and Bernstein to "follow the money."
33. The OSAR claimed Jean-Baptiste had died in Spain.
34. For Jean-Baptiste and Juif, see AP, 212/79/3, carton 11; Réquisitoire définitif, 1939, 103-24, 129-34, and 319-50, and for the OSAR's pursuit of weapons and munitions, 103-86; Henry Charbonneau, *Les mémoires de Porthos*, volume 1 (Paris, 1967), 200.
35. Report 803, Procureur Général, La Cour d' Appel of Douai, to Minister of Justice, 5 March 1937, Archives Nationales (henceforth AN), BB18 3061, carton 2.
36. Report 1623, Procureur Général, La Cour d' Appel of Douai, to Minister of Justice, 12 May 1937, AN, BB18 3061, carton 2.
37. Réquisitoire définitif, 1939, 103-86.
38. Ibid., 156-65; Report, Valentin, 6 July 1937, Fonds Panthéon, MI 25393, Archives at the Ministry of the Interior (Paris), Dossier—Troncoso 1 (I believe that the Fonds Panthéon are now kept at Fontainebleu and are accessible through the Archives Nationales); also see the second Troncoso dossier in MI 25394; Dagore (Corre), 303; Bourdrel, (1992), 173-9, 227.
39. Reports, 29 January and 3 February 1937, Counterintelligence, SIM, AP, 212/79/3, carton 50. Tournoux, *L' histoire secrète* and Clara Conti, *Servizio segreto* (Rome, 1946) published some relevant documents.
40. For content and literature on Carlo Rosselli, see Joel Blatt, "The Battle of Turin, 1933-1936: Carlo Rosselli, Giustizia e Libertà, OVRA and the Origins of Mussolini's Anti-Semitic Campaign," *Journal of Modern Italian Studies*, 1 (1) 1995: 22-57; Joel Blatt, "Carlo Rosselli's Socialism," in *Italian Socialism: Between Politics and History*, ed. Spencer Di Scala (Amherst, 1996), 80-99.
41. Procès-verbal, Filippo Anfuso before Robert Lévy, 9 November 1945, and Procès-verbal, Anfuso before Léon Dauzas, 19 October 1945, AP, 212/79/3, carton 49.
42. Tournoux, 357.
43. I am writing a book, "The Assassination of Carlo and Nello Rosselli."
44. Tournoux, 357.
45. Report, "Activité terroriste dans le midi de la France," Valentin, 6 July 1937, Fonds Panthéon, MI 25393, and the second Troncoso dossier in MI 25394; Dagore (Corre), 303; Bourdrel (1992), 173-9, 227.

46. Italian Fascist bombings in France began in 1927, inciting French authorities to expel Italian Antifascists. A larger study would be necessary to present the evidence for ascribing these bombings to Italian Fascism.
47. Dagore (Corre), 83-6.
48. Reports, Santo Emanuele and his office, 12 August 1937, AP, 212/79/3, carton 50; Tournoux, 335.
49. Extrait des minutes du Greffé, La Cour d' Appel de Paris, 28 July 1939, 53-4, AP, 212/79/3, carton 52; Parry, 168.
50. Déposition, Colonel Georges Groussard to Robert Lévy, 11 February 1945, AP, 212/79/3, carton 49.
51. Loustaunau-Lacau, *Mémoires*, 97, and 85-108 for the Corvignolles; Déposition, Georges Loustaunau-Lacau, 4 February 1946, AP, 212/79/3, carton 49.
52. Réquisitoire définitif, Le Procureur de la République, 7 March 1948, AP, 212/79/3, carton 49; Déposition, Loustaunau-Lacau, 30 July 1945, Trial of Marshal Pétain, AP, 212/79/3, carton 47.
53. Loustaunau-Lacau, *Mémoires*, 95-8, 107; Déposition, Loustaunau-Lacau, Pétain trial, ibid. Bourdrel (1992), 189-205, places Loustaunau-Lacau prominently in what he calls "la cagoule militaire," but the Corvignolles and OSAR were different organizations.
54. Déposition, Henri Giraud, 20 June 1946, and Note, 8 March 1945, AP, 212/79/3, carton 49; Charbonneau, 192; Pierre Ordioni, *Le pouvoir militaire en France de Charles VII à Charles de Gaulle*, volume 2, *De la Commune de Paris à la Liberation* (Paris, 1981), 388-9.
55. See Philip Bankwitz's portrait of the retired Army Chief of Staff, General Maxime Weygand's response to the Popular Front in *Maxime Weygand and Civil-Military Relations in Modern France* (Cambridge, Massachusetts, 1967), 224, 244-7, and chaps. 5-7.
56. Aide Mémoire, Loustaunau-Lacau, May 1945, and Réquisitoire définitif, Le Procureur de la République, 7 March 1948, both in AP, 212/79/3, carton 49; Loustaunau-Lacau, *Mémoires*, 95; Déposition, Loustaunau-Lacau, Pétain trial, ibid.
57. Jean Lacouture, *De Gaulle: The Rebel 1890-1944*, translated by Patrick O'Brian (New York, 1990), 127-8.
58. Procès-verbal 122, Georges Depre, 15 June 1946, AP, 212/79/3, carton 49; Martin S. Alexander, *The Republic in Danger: General Maurice Gamelin and the Politics of French Defence, 1933-1940* (Cambridge, 1992), 101-2; Elisabeth du Réau, *Edouard Daladier 1884-1970* (Paris, 1993), 326-8.
59. The French police investigation concluded that Filiol shot and stabbed Navachine in the Bois de Boulogne with a group of *cagoulards* nearby. See Report 1291, Louis Simon, 13 January 1939, and Report, Bascou, 3 March 1939, both in AP, 212/79/3, carton 43; also see Tournoux, 313. Articles in *Candide* after the crime demonized Navachine from a Rightist perspective: Soviet and British agent, freemason, intermediary for Soviet support of the Spanish Loyalists. The portrait's accuracy is moot (Alain Selby, *Candide*, 25 February, 1937, 1,8; 4 March, 1,12; 11 March, 13; 25 March 1937, 8). John Braun discussed Navachine in a paper, "French Leftist Economists and the Breakdown of the International Monetary System, 1931-1933," American Historical Association, Chicago, 29 December 1991. Also see Monier, 298-9; Dagore (Corre), 38-9; Péan, *Docteur Martin*, 117-26.
60. Bourdrel (1992), 112-17; Monier, 299-300.
61. AN, F7 14816, Dossier, Meurtres attribués au CSAR, Navachine, Laetitia Toureaux, 1937-1939; Bourdrel (1992), 137-9.
62. Réquisitoire définitif, 1939, 418-29.
63. Ibid., 318 and 369-417. Falling debris killed the two policeman. The bombings provoked huge responses by the press, government and police. D.L.L. Parry (173) and the Réquisitoire définitif, 1939 (417) suggest that the OSAR chose their targets in part with declining financial contributions in mind.

64. Réquisitoire définitif, 1939, 285-6, 309.
65. Ibid., 283-308.
66. Réquisitoire définitif, 1939, 304-5.
67. Henry Charbonneau, *Les mémoires de Porthos*, 199-200.
68. Réquisitoire définitif, 1939, 292-4, 317-18.
69. Ibid., 292-4, 317-18, 738.
70. In comments at the Society for French Historical Studies in Ottawa, March 1998, Martin Alexander emphasized the contradiction between the OSAR's approaches to both Italian Fascism and the French Army at a moment when the latter was abandoning the close Franco-Italian cooperation of 1935.
71. Charbonneau, 194-5; Péan, 110-15; Parry, 176.
72. No. D/F13475, Minister of the Interior to Minister of Justice, 7 April 1938, sending Renseignements (Intelligence) dated 11 and 12 November 1937; Letter, Beteille to Procureur de la République, 4 June 1938, all in AN, BB18 3061, Carton 2. Also see Parry, 166-7; Du Réau, *Edouard Daladier*, 328; Bourdrel (1992), 210-13; Freigneaux, "La Cagoule," 12; Monier, 316-17; Péan, 160-4.
73. Report, René Le Poittevin, 6 March 1947, AP, 212/79/3, carton 49.
74. Bourdrel (1992), 225; Parry, 175-6.
75. Réquisitoire définitif, 1939, 302-3, 307.
76. Ibid., 273; also see Parry, 166-7, 170; Bourdrel (1992), 222-3; Monier, 316-17; Péan, 159-66; Tournoux, 92-100; Charbonneau, 203-4. The sources are unclear whether all these words were spoken during the overnight of 15-16 November, or some of them on other occasions.
77. Draft speech or article, Papiers Léon Blum, consulted at the Fondation National des Sciences Politiques, now held at the Archives Nationales, 4BL7, Dossier 1, sous-dossier D.
78. Corre (Dagore) provides extensive information about the *cagoulards* in exile.
79. Bourdrel (1992), 256-7.
80. Stanley Hoffmann, "Paradoxes of the French Political Community," *In Search of France* (New York, 1963) suggests that the French Revolution only ended after World War II; also see François Furet, *Interpreting the French Revolution*, trans. Elborg Forster (Cambridge et al., 1981), 4-5.
81. For the early Action Française, see Eugen Weber, *Action Française*; Joel Blatt, "Relatives and Rivals: The Responses of the Action Française to Italian Fascism, 1919-1926," *European Studies Review* 11, no. 3 (July 1981), 265-7; Robert Soucy, *French Fascism: The First Wave, 1924-1933* (New Haven and London, 1986), chap. 1.
82. Hoffmann, 25; Soucy, ibid.
83. Hoffmann, 17.
84. Pierre Milza portrays the OSAR as "more fascist" in "methods" than in its "very bourgeois clientele," "counterrevolutionary ideology," and "political project" ("L'ultra droite des années trente," 178). D.L.L. Parry places the Cagoule "well inside the right wing" except for its "extreme" "methods"(174). Robert Soucy situates the Cagoule as a "minor" fascist movement (*French Fascism: The Second Wave, 1933-1939*, 46-53).
85. Charbonneau, 158.
86. Bourdrel (1992), 61.
87. Dagore (Corre), 97; Parry, 164.
88. Réquisitoire définitif, 221 and 103-232; Monier, 290.
89. Bourdrel (1992), 219-20.
90. For the Cagoule's conflict with the Action Française, see notes 4 through 8 above, and with the Croix de Feu/PSF, Réquisitoire définitif, 1939, 68-70. For the Croix de Feu, see Robert Soucy, "French Fascism and the Croix de Feu: A Dissenting Interpretation," *Journal of Contemporary*

History, 26 (1991): 159-188; William Irvine, "Fascism in France and the Strange Case of the Croix de Feu," *Journal of Modern History*, 63, no. 2 (June 1991): 271-295; Kevin Passmore, *From Liberalism to Fascism: The Right in a French Province, 1928-1939* (Cambridge, 1997), chaps. 8, 9.

91. Robert Paxton, "The Five Stages of Fascism," *Journal of Modern History*, 70, no. 1 (March 1998), particularly 13-17. Also see William Irvine, *French Conservatism in Crisis* (Baton Rouge, 1979), and Roger Austin, "The Conservative Right and the Far Right in France: the Search for Power, 1934-44," in *Fascists and Conservatives: The Radical Right and the Establishment in Twentieth-Century Europe*, ed. Martin Blinkhorn (London, 1990), 176-99.
92. Gordon Wright, *France in Modern Times*, 5th. ed. (New York and London, 1995), 206.
93. Paul-Marie de la Gorce, *The French Army. A Military-Political History* (New York and London, 1963), 250-2; Parry, 169-70; Martin Alexander, "Duty, Discipline and Authority: French Officer Elites between Professionalism and Politics, 1900-1962," in *The Right in France 1789-1997*, ed. Atkin and Tallett, 129.
94. Alexander, *The Republic in Danger*, chap. 4; Martin Alexander, "Soldiers and Socialists: The French Officer Corps and Leftist Government, 1935-37," in *The French and Spanish Popular Fronts: Comparative Perspectives*, ed. Martin Alexander and Helen Graham (Cambridge, 1989), 62-78; also see Henry Dutailly, *Les problèmes de l'Armée de Terre française (1935-1939)* (Paris, 1980), 275-9.
95. Bankwitz, *Maxime Weygand*, 276, 277, chaps. 5-7; Alexander, "Soldiers and Socialists," 74.
96. Alexander, "Soldiers and Socialists," 72-3; Jean Lacouture, *Léon Blum*, trans.George Holoch (New York and London, 1982), 320-1.
97. Parry, 170.
98. Antoine Prost, *In the Wake of War: 'Les Anciens Combattants' and French Society, 1914-1939*, trans. Helen McPhail (Providence and Oxford, 1992), 137, and Prost, *Les anciens combattants et la société française 1914-1939*, 3 vols. (Paris, 1977).
99. Alexander, "Soldiers and Socialists," 75.
100. See Georges Lefranc, *Histoire du Front populaire (1934-1938)* (Paris, 1965), part 2, chaps. I, II, III; Joel Colton, *Léon Blum: Humanist in Politics* (Durham, 1987), chaps. IV-VI; Lacouture, *Blum*, 195-399; Charbonneau, 183-6.
101. Commenting at the Society for French Historical Studies' meeting in Ottawa, March 1998, Alexander quipped, "Not only was the Cagoule 'the gang that could not shoot straight,' but they also missed the bus." He emphasized ongoing strikes during the Fall 1936 outside the control of the unions and the Left political parties, and the hardening conservative response; for example, the conservative takeover of the renamed *Confédération Générale du Patronat Français.*
102. For conservative responses to the Popular Front, see Richard Vinen, *The Politics of French Business 1936-1945* (Cambridge, 1991), chap. 4; Jacques Delperrie de Bayac, *Histoire du Front populaire* (Paris, 1972), chap. 13; Guy Bourdé, *La défaite du Front populaire* (Paris, 1977), 26-31.
103. William Irvine argues the provocative, revisionist case that France entered World War II relatively united. See Irvine, "Domestic Politics and the Fall of France in 1940," in *The French Defeat of 1940: Reassessments*, ed. Joel Blatt (Providence and Oxford, 1998), 85-99.
104. Bourdrel (1970), 365-7.
105. See Michael Carley, "Prelude to Defeat: Franco-Soviet Relations, 1919-1939," in *The French Defeat of 1940: Reassessments*, 171-203; also see my "Introduction" to the same volume, 9-10.
106. The source was Michel Harispe, a prominent *cagoulard.* See Letter, 2 November 1945 (attached to another Letter of 1 December 1945 from the Director of the Judicial Police to Robert Lévy), Roger Wybot, AP, 212/79/3, carton 47.
107. Procureur Général at the Cour d' Appel of Paris, 26 April 1948, AP, 212/79/3, carton 51.

Chapter 6

RETREAT OR RESISTANCE

Strategic Re-Appraisal and the Crisis of French Power in Eastern Europe, September 1938 to August 1939

Talbot Imlay

Thousands gathered at Le Bourget airport, just outside of Paris, on the morning of 30 September 1938, to greet Edouard Daladier on his return from the Munich Conference. It is said that the French Premier, catching sight of the massive crowd from the window of his approaching plane, expected to be lynched. When the crowd fêted him instead, a surly Daladier muttered "fools."[1] His reaction stands in stark contrast to that of Neville Chamberlain, the British Prime Minister. Before leaving Germany Chamberlain had told a confidant that the Munich Accords meant peace for ten years, a prediction he rashly and famously extended to "peace for our time" once back in England.[2] Temperament partly explains their different reactions: Daladier tended to brood skeptically on events whereas Chamberlain attacked them with cocksure optimism. Yet the reactions of the two men also reflected different official assessments of the Munich settlement in Paris and London. The public in both cities might equally rejoice that a European war had been averted, but what British leaders viewed as a success, their French counterparts saw as a disaster.

This essay examines French foreign and defense policies during 1938 and 1939. Its starting point is the perception of Munich as a disaster. For strategic reasons, the French during the Czech crisis had sought to maintain Czechoslovakia as a viable military power in Eastern Europe as a counterweight to Germany.

Notes for this chapter begin on page 125.

Czechoslovakia's evisceration at Munich prompted French leaders to question France's ability to resist Germany's bid for hegemony in Europe. For many, the wiser course appeared to be an accommodation with Hitler based on a free hand to Germany to expand in Eastern Europe. Yet despite considerable support for this course in military and political circles, the French in the end reaffirmed the traditional policy of resisting German expansion which, in turn, produced a recommitment to constructing a second front in Eastern Europe whose cornerstone would be the Soviet Union. That this strategy was based on questionable assumptions, as the pursuit of a Soviet alliance in the summer of 1939 would reveal, is perhaps less important than the decision to oppose Germany, for this commitment was a key factor in the origins of World War II. Much of the existing work on the prewar period focuses on Britain (and Germany) with the result that the French often receive little if any attention.[3] Although more specialist studies on France are an obvious exception, the anglo-centric bias remains strong, particularly in more general works.[4] Part and parcel to this neglect of France is the assumption that the French merely followed the British.[5] Yet the French decision to resist German expansion—a decision which set France and Germany on a collision course for war—was largely taken independently of the British. In other words, the answer to the question of how war came in September 1939 is to be found as much in Paris as in London—and perhaps more.

I

What were France's aims during the Czech crisis? Various scholars have portrayed the French as ardent appeasers, ready to betray the Czechs on the altar of Franco-German *rapprochement*, as astute strategists seeking to trade the Czech alliance for a more valuable one with Britain, or as realpolitikers persuaded by Germany's present military advantage to postpone a confrontation.[6] These three strands were certainly evident in French policy. Yet in stressing the willingness, if not eagerness, of France to abandon Czechoslovakia, they each downplay just how unwilling French leaders were to see the Czechs militarily reduced. To be sure, Foreign Minister Bonnet's ill-disguised aim was to prevent war at any price, especially if the Czechs could be made to bear the costs. But Bonnet was only one of several French leaders and by no means the most influential. If his goal of avoiding war was widely shared, it is also true that the preservation of Czechoslovakia as an independent and viable military power remained a basic aim of French policy throughout the crisis. Speaking in veiled but comprehensible tones to a parliamentary commission in late August 1938, Daladier insisted that France could not permit the "destruction of a friendly state in the middle of Europe ..."[7] Within the general staff, the 2e Bureau (intelligence) repeatedly cautioned against any solution to the crisis that resulted in Czechoslovakia's "neutralization." The same month that Daladier spoke, the 2e Bureau's chief, Colonel Gauché, remarked that a German occupation of Czechoslovakia "means the end of all things and a European war ..."[8] Echoing this assessment, a staff paper in early September, signed by General Gamelin, the Chief of the General Staff, concluded that "*[t]he essential thing is that Czechoslovakia not be neutralized as a state.*"[9]

The interest in Czechoslovakia's military viability stemmed from two sources. The first, and most basic, was the widespread belief in "*l'Allemagne éternelle*"—that Germany was and always would be an expansionist and aggressive power bent on European domination. During the twenties French officials assumed that the Germans would again seek to overturn the status quo by force once they felt powerful enough to do so. In this schema, Hitler and Nazism were not unique phenomena, but particularly violent manifestations of a perennial problem.[10] Accordingly, for much of French official opinion, the question during the thirties was how best to contain Germany's hegemonic aims and, in particular, whether to resist them by force and, if so, when and under what conditions. Directly related to the assumption of an expansionist Germany was the second source of French interest in Czechoslovakia—the need for a second front in Eastern Europe in a war against Germany. Ever since Germany's mounting demographic and industrial superiority had become evident, an eastern front had been a tenet of French strategy. Before 1914 the French had looked to Russia to provide an eastern counterweight, hence the alliance between Republican France and Tsarist Russia forged in the 1890s. After World War I, with Bolshevik Russia no longer available as an alliance partner, the French sought a replacement by signing a series of military and political agreements with the smaller states of Eastern Europe—Poland, Romania, Yugoslavia and Czechoslovakia. Later, in 1935, the growing threat of Nazi Germany led the French and Soviets to put aside their ideological divisions and sign an alliance.[11]

To be sure, scholars have identified a fair amount of ambivalence in French policies toward Eastern Europe between the wars. Torn between their need for a second front and the fear of being dragged into an unnecessary war, the French allowed relations with the smaller Eastern European states to languish for much of the interwar period. In particular, successive governments seemed unable and unwilling to pursue the diplomatic, military, commercial and economic policies needed to build a powerful and reliable alliance bloc.[12] As for relations with Moscow, after 1935 ideological hostility to bolshevism remained strong enough to prevent the conclusion of an accompanying military agreement. Notwithstanding this ambivalence, an eastern front against Germany remained central to French strategy during the thirties, even if perhaps more in theory than practice.

Hence, for example, the efforts of Blum's Popular Front government to strengthen ties with the region, including the extension of a large loan to Poland and staff talks with the Soviets. It has been argued that these and other initiatives betrayed the French General Staff's selfish plan to divert a future European war towards Eastern Europe, thereby ensuring that France's smaller allies rather than France itself would bear the brunt of suffering and destruction.[13] There is no doubt that the French sought allies to share the burden of another war or that they hoped to avoid France once again becoming a battlefield. But this does not mean that French planners believed that a European war could be limited to Eastern Europe. One purpose of an eastern front was to force Germany to disperse its military forces, thereby relieving pressure in the West where, it was expected, the great encounter battles would be waged. For the French, an eastern front was always a second front.

During 1938, mounting international tensions only reinforced the value of a second front in Eastern Europe. A Staff paper in April, for example, spoke of the need to "establish as soon as possible" a "common front from the *Baltic to the Adriatic*."[14] The cornerstone of this front would be Czechoslovakia. Of all France's friends and allies in the region Czechoslovakia was the one judged to be the surest and, aside from the Soviets, the strongest. Since 1924, the two countries had been allies; the Czechs had consistently supported French policy at Geneva and elsewhere. Once mobilized, the Czech Army in 1938 would number 38 infantry and 4 mobile divisions, over one third the French total. Not only were Czech troops extremely well-trained, they were also some of the best equipped in Europe thanks to the country's modern arms industry. French intelligence estimates of the number of divisions the Germans would need to defeat the Czech ranged from 25 to 30 to as many as 60, a significant drain in both cases.[15] French planners certainly did not ignore Czechoslovakia's military and geographic difficulties, especially after Germany's *Anschlu$* with Austria effectively outflanked Czech fortifications, but this detracted little from their overall assessment of the country's value. "[T]he Czech Army," concluded one report in September 1938, "was strong enough to draw a significant part of the German Army to Central Europe, thereby weakening the latter in other theaters of operations."[16] Admittedly, there were problems with this reasoning. In the event of a German attack on Czechoslovakia, the Czechs could only fulfill their assigned role of relieving German pressure on the West if they received outside support. A French offensive in the West was one obvious possibility, except that French planners, thinking in terms of a long war, had ruled out any early offensive action.[17] This left other states in the region as a possible source of support, notably Poland and the Soviet Union, yet little had been done in advance to ensure help from these quarters. In the end, French planners could only hope that military mobilization would force the Germans to divert forces to the West, thereby providing some relief to the Czechs. While perhaps something less than heroic, this hope does underscore the mutual dependence, in French military eyes, of a western and eastern front.

French interest in an eastern front, however, was rooted in more than immediate military considerations. The abandonment of Czechoslovakia, as René Massigli, the political director of the Foreign Ministry (Quai), argued in September, would open the door to Germany's political and economic domination of Central and Eastern Europe.[18] For several years the French had been tracking Germany's expanding political and economic influence in the region. Germany's commercial offensive, a Quai paper reported in early 1938, has been conducted with "rare audacity" and "great skill."[19] By 1938 diplomats and attachés on the spot, frustrated by the repeated failure of officials in Paris to respond to their warnings, were forwarding pessimistic assessments of the prospects of halting Germany's advance. If those in Paris (aside from Massigli) tended to be more optimistic, calculating on a combination of German economic weakness, the traditional fund of goodwill towards France in the region, and the fear aroused by Germany's aggressive ambitions, these were wasting assets. To allow Germany to reduce Czechoslovakia, Massigli argued, would irreparably damage France's prestige and rob countries like Romania and Yugoslavia of the will and means to resist further German expansion. With the obstacles removed to its complete control of Central and Eastern Europe, Germany would gain access to many of the strategic raw materials (oil, tungsten, chrome) needed to wage and win a modern industrial war. Germany's road to continental domination, in short, ran through Central and Eastern Europe. It was with these military and economic considerations no doubt in mind that Daladier warned British ministers in September that, once firmly in control of the region, Germany "would turn against France and Britain who would then have to defend themselves in conditions singularly more difficult."[20]

Thus, by dealing a powerful blow to an eastern front, Czechoslovakia's reduction would result in a significant shift in the economic and military balance of power in Germany's favor. Given the stakes, it is not surprising that the French labored to convince the British to support the Czechs. Chamberlain himself dispelled any idea that this effort at persuasion was *pro forma*. "Fortunately the Papers have had no hint of how near we came to a break over Czechoslovakia," he wrote after meeting with French ministers in late April.[21] Although the French failed to convince the British to adopt a common "policy of firmness," they clung to the goal of preserving Czechoslovakia as an independent military power. Thus while Daladier agreed with Chamberlain that a compromise solution had to be found, most likely involving the cession of Sudeten territory, it would have to be one with which Germany, the Sudeten Germans, and the Czechs all could—quite literally—live. "It is a question," the Premier insisted at a subsequent meeting in September, "of knowing what to do both to avoid war and preserve the Czech State."[22] This explains the staunch French refusal to agree to plebiscites in the disputed regions, for these left open the question of how much territory to cede. Some part of Bonnet's devious diplomacy can also be understood in this light. If this "arch-appeaser" bullied Prague to make concessions to the Sudeten Germans, he also tried to moderate Germany's ambitions by cultivating a calculated uncertainty about France's ultimate intentions—hence his (and Daladier's) repeated and public affirmations of France's loyalty to the Franco-Czech alliance. Unsure about French intentions, policy-makers in Berlin (and Prague) might be more inclined to compromise.

The sharp distinction that Daladier and Gamelin drew between the Berchtesgaden and Godesburg terms, the two successive agreements that Chamberlain brought back with him from his meetings with Hitler, suggests that they believed an acceptable compromise to be possible. Although Gamelin in general shied away from offering the government unambiguous advice, he did insist on the importance of maintaining Czechoslovakia's strategic viability. "[E]ven if it [Czechoslovakia] must abandon the Sudetenland," he told Daladier in September, "it could still survive and serve a useful military role."[23] While the Berchtesgaden terms apparently met this criterion, the Godesburg terms clearly did not. Exceptionally discarding his political reserve, Gamelin asked General Weygand, former Chief of the Army General Staff, to intervene with his "friends on the Right" in parliament to urge them to reject Germany's new demands. Weygand was told that the latter spelt Czechoslovakia's death, clearly in a way which their predecessors did not.[24] Military intelligence appears to have been instrumental in Gamelin's assessment. Consistent with its views on the strategic importance of Czechoslovakia, the 2e Bureau warned that, unlike the Berchtesgaden agreement, Hitler's new terms meant the "quasi total abandonment" of Czech fortifications, thereby jeopardizing the Czech army's ability to inflict "a very bloody encounter" on an invading German army. Another note spoke more bluntly of the "total destruction of Czech military power," and insisted that the new borders would mean Czechoslovakia's "economic asphyxiation" and its "military domination" by Germany.[25]

Daladier needed little convincing from Gamelin. At a Council of Ministers meeting on 25 September, the Premier criticized the Godesburg terms for allowing Germany to incorporate most of the Czech defenses.[26] Later, in London, he categorically rejected Hitler's new demands, pointing out that they involved the transfer of more Czech territory than had previously been agreed. His refusal to budge even under aggressive cross-examination from British Ministers removed any possibility that the Czechs would be pressed to accept Hitler's demands.[27]

Daladier, it appears, sought to stiffen British resolve in the hope that a firm Anglo-French front would compel Hitler to return to the Berchtesgaden terms. In an undelivered speech written during the night of 27-28 September, the Premier stated that peace lay in the rejection of the Godesburg terms that entailed the loss of Czechoslovakia's "defensive organization" and therefore the country's "destruction." Long after the crisis, he would maintain that he left for Munich convinced that a compromise was still possible that would not unduly weaken France's ally.[28] Significantly, he left behind Bonnet who, as everyone knew, would always choose peace at any price. For Daladier and Gamelin, territorial concessions on Prague's part might have been inevitable but Czechoslovakia's elimination from the European strategic balance was not.[29]

In Munich, however, the Premier was confronted with a *Diktat* and not a negotiation. The reasons why he nevertheless agreed to accept German demands and abandon the Czechs are well-known: French military weakness, especially in the air; the inability to offer any immediate military help to the Czechs; the British reluctance to support France; the uncertain position of the Soviet Union, Poland, Hungary and Romania; and the strength of anti-war sentiment in French official and public opinion. The French, in short, were materially and psychologically unprepared for war in September 1938.[30] Indeed, Daladier and Gamelin based their firm policy on deterrence: on the belief that German demands could be contained and Czechoslovakia's strategic viability thereby assured if the French and British presented a united front to Hitler.[31] But if the French shrank from the prospect of a European war in September 1938, the fact remains that they agonized over whether to support the Czechs. Throughout the crisis strategic considerations weighed heavily on the minds of French leaders (Bonnet excepted)—hence the distinction made between the Berchtesgaden and Godesburg terms. If, in the end, the French chose to abandon the Czechs rather than accept a European war, they did so reluctantly and in full awareness of the strategic cost. "Germany," wrote one military observer, "[has] achieved hegemony over all Central Europe" and could "now look forward to war on a single front on which it can deploy an overwhelming superiority." More ominously, another officer, Charles de Gaulle, commented that "France had ceased to be a great power."[32]

II

Well might Daladier brood on his return from Munich. The agreement had solved nothing—the "German problem" remained. Worse still, by reducing Czechoslovakia and crippling an eastern front, Germany's relative strategic position had greatly improved. Given the magnitude of the disaster, it is not surprising that afterwards many influential people, both inside and outside government circles, called for a general stock-taking by the French. At one level, this call dovetailed with the widespread desire for a national *redressement.* As Pierre Bernus, the editor of the conservative *Journal des Débats,* declared:

> There is a State to re-do, a diplomacy to re-do, finances to re-do. It is not next month but tomorrow that our country must put itself to this task so that it can be worthy of its past and ensure its future.[33]

At times the desire for a redressement expressed itself in vague and mystical terms of regeneration and awakening. Often, however, those who spoke of stocktaking had something more precise in mind as was the case with the Senate foreign affairs commission when it declared that French foreign policy "should be re-examined in light of the Munich Accords."[34] In particular, there was the question of what to do about France's remaining alliances in Eastern Europe. Recent events, explained an editorial in *Le Temps,* an influential daily reputed to be close to the Quai, "demands the revision of a number of doctrines ...and removes much of the practical value of the Franco-Polish alliance and the Franco-Russian mutual assistance pact."[35] Munich, in fact, placed the question of France's remaining eastern alliances at the forefront of public and official debate, for it was widely assumed that Germany's next challenge to the status quo would come in Eastern Europe. Rather than face another Czech crisis, it seemed wiser to decide France's position in advance.

The future of France's eastern alliances, however, involved far more than France's immediate policy. Implicated in the fate of these alliances were two related questions: whether to resist German expansion, if necessary by war, and what should be France's position in Europe. The links between these questions are evident in the case of Bonnet. For the Foreign Minister, the Czech crisis only reinforced a pacifism whose roots lay in a sincere horror of war and a profound conviction of France's internal and external weakness. As he had earlier intimated to a journalist:

> Let's not have any more heroics. We are not capable of them ... It is all very well to proclaim yourself the policeman of Europe but for this you need more than cap guns [*pistolets à amorces*], straw handcuffs and paper prisons ... France can no longer permit itself a blood bath such as that of 1914. Our demographic strength declines each year. Finally, the Popular Front placed the country in such a state that it would be wise to allow itself a period of convalescence. Any imprudence could be fatal.[36]

Accordingly, Bonnet believed that the French had to abandon their great power pretensions and accommodate themselves to a German-dominated Europe—a version of Vichy foreign policy *avant la lettre*. In practice this accommodation meant a Franco-German (and perhaps British) arrangement based on a "free hand" for Germany in Eastern Europe. Put simply, peace in the West would be purchased by a French withdrawal from its eastern commitments, allowing Germany to direct its expansionist drive eastwards.

No doubt aware that some people would find the cynicism of the proposed deal unpalatable, Bonnet proceeded cautiously after Munich. The first step in detaching the French from Eastern Europe was to reduce their liabilities in the region, a goal Bonnet pursued by urging a revision of France's eastern alliances. Characteristically, he told the Chamber's Foreign Affairs Commission in October 1938 that alliances with Warsaw and Moscow had been concluded at a time when France was much stronger, a clear hint that changes were needed.[37] In this effort, moreover, Bonnet could count on the strong support of Quai officials. Despite the postwar claims of several diplomats, after Munich few of them disagreed with the principle of Bonnet's policy, even if they grumbled about his secretive methods. Viewing themselves as "realists," Quai officials found it difficult to resist the argument that Munich had fundamentally changed things. Thus Charles Rochat, the deputy director of the powerful DAPC (*Direction des affaires politiques et commerciales*), while recognizing that an eastern front constituted a traditional pillar of French policy, nevertheless recommended the "adaptation" of France's eastern allies which, he admitted, would in practice limit French obligations. Even Massigli, before exiling himself to Ankara, informed staff officers that Munich would usher in a "period of withdrawal [*receuillement*]" for France.[38] To be sure, the "adaptation" or "revision" of France's alliances did not necessarily entail a complete French retreat from Eastern Europe: the Quai, for instance, sought to maintain something of France's economic interests in the Balkans, and in November a French economic mission was sent to Bulgaria, Romania and Yugoslavia to investigate commercial possibilities. However, in no way can this limited economic initiative be seen as part of a wider effort to counter the expansion of German interests in Eastern Europe.[39] For Bonnet and his officials the overriding goal was to reduce France's commitments in the region, thereby avoiding a repetition of the Czech crisis when the French had to choose between a possible European war and abandoning an ally.

Bonnet and Quai officials, then, worked together to "revise" France's eastern alliances. While diplomats in Paris busied themselves preparing memoranda which stressed the difficulties and disadvantages of these commitments, Bonnet ensured that despatches in a similar vein, from Warsaw and Moscow, were circulated widely inside and outside the Quai.[40] At the same time, Bonnet sought to improve relations with Germany, scoring a success in December 1938 with the signing, in Paris, of the Franco-German Declaration. The Declaration, while innocuous in wording, stirred a flurry of rumors over whether the Germans privately had been promised a "free hand" in Eastern Europe. Bonnet strenuously denied having done so, although it is interesting that Ribbentrop, the German Foreign Minister, insisted that a promise had been given. The truth is impossible to know for certain, and the word of both men is suspect. "What a Ribbentrop is said by a Bonnet to have said does not amount to much," one British official unkindly remarked.[41] Yet who said what to whom matters little, for Bonnet viewed the Declaration more as a beginning than an end—as one step in a larger process of negotiating France's role in a post-Munich Europe. In addition to sounding German intentions, its purpose was to accustom French official and public opinion to the idea of a Franco-German accommodation. An editorial in *Le Temps* referred to both purposes in commenting that the Declaration opened "the possibility of future negotiations in a spirit markedly different from the one that has prevailed until now."[42]

Determined and subtle though he was, Bonnet alone could not dictate French policy after Munich. Given the strategic issues involved, a policy of withdrawal would at least need the support of France's military leaders. Interestingly, Gamelin initially appeared to endorse Bonnet's policy. Less than two weeks after Munich, the Chief of the General Staff for National Defense drew up a "Note on the present situation" that he sent to Daladier, drawing attention to the "urgent nature of the questions with which it deals." Although cautious and somewhat elusive, Gamelin's "Note" suggested nothing less than a fundamental recasting of French strategy.[43] Munich, he opined, had resulted in a reversal of the strategic situation in Central (and Eastern) Europe. Believing a renewal of Germany's *Drang nach Osten* to be likely, Gamelin wondered whether anything could be done to resist this advance. Neither Poland nor the Soviet Union could be relied upon while Germany's increasing relative strength, which allowed it to wage war on several fronts simultaneously, prevented the French from mounting an effective response. The prospects for an eastern front, in short, appeared grim. With this bleak assessment of Germany's intentions and capabilities as a preface, Gamelin turned to his main proposal: that France "concentrate" on the Mediterranean. Faced with an expansionist Germany, the French should cut their ties to Eastern Europe and focus instead on defending themselves and their Mediterranean Empire. "[I]t is through the cohesion of its empire," he wrote, "that she [France] will remain a great power." This great power talk should not obscure the radical nature of Gamelin's proposal: in withdrawing from Eastern Europe, France would in effect trade its traditional role as a European power for the smaller—and safer—one of a Mediterranean power.

One might question this conclusion. Gamelin, for instance, did refer to the possibility of maintaining French "ties" to Eastern Europe through the Mediterranean. Yet it is clear from the "Note" and from other evidence that he contemplated abandoning any idea of constructing an eastern front. In addition to his manifest distrust of Moscow, Gamelin earlier in the month had discussed with Léon Noel, the French ambassador in Warsaw, the revision of France's "automatic obligations" to Poland. Later, in a paper to Daladier, Gamelin maintained that Polish policy was resolutely anti-French and that Warsaw's "good offices" should no longer be sought nor French military supplies be sent to Poland.[44] For Gamelin, a second front against Germany in Eastern Europe no longer seemed worth pursuing. When the critical role assigned to such a front in French strategy is recalled, a role Gamelin had worked to safeguard in September 1938, the proposal to "concentrate" on the Mediterranean implied the acceptance of a German-dominated Europe. Once Germany had gained control of Eastern Europe, it would dwarf France and any allies it might have. Gamelin himself admitted that even without control of this region, Germany's strength was "without rival." At best the French, together with the British, might construct a western bloc capable of deterring a German attack in Western Europe. But it is hard to see how France alone or in alliance could ever match Germany, let alone defeat it. Gamelin's proposal, in other words, would result in a significant shift in the European balance of power in Germany's favor. This shift, in turn, would impose a recasting of French strategy along Bonnet's lines. No longer able to pursue their traditional policy of resisting German expansion, the French would have to accommodate themselves to German hegemony.

The reception of Gamelin's "Note" offers further evidence of its significance. Recognizing its serious implications, Daladier's military cabinet recommended a meeting of France's highest political and military leaders to discuss the "Note."[45] In the meantime the views of the individual service chiefs were sought. The navy responded first. Given the *Marine's* traditional focus on Italy and the Mediterranean, naval planners could be expected to welcome a reorientation of French strategy in that direction. Some, indeed, wished to go further. Thus in January 1939 the naval staff's *section d'études* would propose that France "leave Germany free in the East" on condition that the latter not support Italy. For twenty years, its author remarked, French policy had been "ideological, terrestrial and exclusively European" when it should have been "realistic, naval and global."[46] Although Admiral Darlan, the naval chief, was a proponent of resistance to Germany, he did approve of Gamelin's "Note." Deeply frustrated by what he viewed as the French people's refusal to conceive of France as a maritime nation, Darlan simply could not reject a strategy that promised the navy a starring role.[47] For similar reasons no doubt, General Buhrer, the chief of staff of France's long-neglected colonial army, also gave his approval. Seeking to strengthen Gamelin's resolve to reorientate French strategy, Buhrer wrote that France could remain a "very great power" but only if it "takes advantage of all the resources that its immense empire provides."[48] General Vuillemin, chief of the air staff, responded next. His unfailing pessimism during the Czech crisis is well-known as is his influence on Daladier. But if the balance of air power appeared bleak during September, intelligence reports after Munich made it appear bleaker still. In this atmosphere of weakness and fear, Vuillemin doubted that, even with British support, France could ever match German (and Italian) air strength. He accordingly embraced Gamelin's "Note," maintaining that the overriding goal of French policy should be to avoid war with Germany, whatever the cost. In words that Bonnet might just as well have chosen, Vuillemin wrote that France "must have the policy that the absolute and relative state of our military forces" imposes, which, in practice, meant abandoning its eastern alliances and wooing Italy.[49]

The only dissenting voice was that of General Colson, the chief of the army staff. France, he argued in a response which fully confirms the nature of Gamelin's proposals, had two choices: to pursue its traditional policy of a second front in Eastern Europe or to retreat behinds its borders and empire. In rejecting the latter, Colson, echoing 2e Bureau arguments during the Czech crisis, warned that a French withdrawal from Eastern Europe would allow Germany to gain the resources it needed to wage a long war. In addition, France would lose the support of valuable military forces, particularly Poland's fifty divisions. Rather than withdrawal, Colson urged a diplomatic, economic and military effort to build an "eastern bloc" from the Baltic to the Balkans capable of "barring the path to the Drang nach Osten." Gamelin, in forwarding these responses to Daladier's cabinet, accurately noted that the navy, colonial and air force chiefs approved his proposed reorientation of French strategy. Yet, significantly, Gamelin chose to single out and endorse Colson's response—that France "cannot be content to retreat into itself and its empire, but must seek to reconstitute in Eastern Europe forces to resist Germanism [sic]."[50] Persuaded by Colson, it appears, Gamelin repudiated his earlier "Note" and instead recommitted himself to an eastern front and, by extension, to resisting German expansion. No longer would he speak of refocusing French strategy or of withdrawing from Eastern Europe.

Gamelin's rapid volte-face suggests that his "Note" represented more of an "essai" than a statement of fixed views. Certainly, a reorientation of strategy along the lines proposed clashed with his (and others') understanding of France's role and duty as a great power. As Gamelin explained to Daladier in December 1938:

> From the standpoint of France's overall policy … the central question is whether France wants to renounce its position as a European great power and abandon to Germany hegemony over not only Central Europe but all of Europe as well … Along with France it is human civilization as well as all the democratic states which are at risk.[51]

More practically, there was no guarantee that Germany would leave France alone once it had mastered Eastern Europe. Indeed, given the notion of "*l'Allemagne éternelle*" which reigned in staff circles, there was every reason to believe in the impossibility of any long-term accommodation with Germany. But whatever the reasons behind Gamelin's re-commitment to an eastern front, he would need the government's support to impose his strategy on Bonnet and the other service chiefs. He would, in short, need Daladier's help.

III

What would Daladier do? Gamelin might confidently have expected to receive the premier's support. After all, during the Czech crisis Daladier had repeatedly shown that he understood the strategic value of an eastern front. Despite his discouragement on his return from Munich, moreover, Daladier was determined to strengthen France militarily—hence his efforts to purchase American airplanes and to provide a fillip to French war production. But these initiatives provided no answer to the question of what France should do when, as expected, Germany next challenged the status quo. And although Daladier's instincts were almost certainly for resistance, domestic political factors made him hesitate. In addition to its strategic consequences, the Czech crisis also influenced the political balance within France. The brush with war, by fueling pacifist tendencies among the noncommunist Left, and Socialists in particular, exacerbated the growing schism within the SFIO (*Section Française de l'Internationale Ouvrière*) over the proper direction of French foreign policy.[52] With the Socialists deeply divided and the Communists depicted as warmongers for their outspoken advocacy of supporting the Czechs, the field was left to the Center-Right and Right. Although far from united on all issues, many on the Center-Right and Right could agree that France was too weak internally and externally to risk another European war for some time, if ever. Developments within Daladier's own Radical Party, the linchpin of any governing coalition, mirrored the shifting political balance. Following the electoral victory in 1936 of the Popular Front (a coalition of Socialists, Radicals and Communists), a disgruntled group of Radicals, led by Georges Bonnet and Emile Roche among others, worked to shift the Party's locus rightwards. Their growing influence within the Party meant that by the summer of 1938 they stood poised to mount a take-over. The Czech crisis provided them with the opportunity: exploiting Communist denunciations of Munich, these Radicals gathered sufficient support to break publicly with the PCF (*Parti Communiste Français*) and, by extension, with the Popular Front coalition.[53]

To remain in power Daladier had no choice but to take the Radicals into a Center-Right and Right alliance. As a result, he was politically dependent on an alliance whose members were increasingly attracted to a policy of withdrawal from Eastern Europe. That this was so is evident from the Radical Party's annual congress at the end of October 1938. Presenting the report on foreign policy, Aimé Berthod, a senator and ally of Bonnet, explained that Munich had seriously undermined the value of France's eastern alliance which, as a consequence, should be revised. At the same time, the French should seek an entente with Germany and, equally important, direct their energies towards the empire:

> Will we be accused of being little Frenchmen and being resigned to the "abdication of France" if we recognize that, as a western, maritime, African and colonial nation, the exploitation of our magnificent empire adds far more to our destiny that does the ungrateful role of policemen of Europe or even of banker which, in the intoxication of victory, we believed ourselves called upon to play everywhere where the prestige of our armies carried us.[54]

Berthod, in short, was offering the empire as a substitute for France's traditional great power role in Europe. Not by accident, moreover, did Berthod's idea of an "imperial retreat" [*repli impérial*] coincide with what historians have identified as an upsurge of public interest in France's empire in the late thirties.[55] For many, and not simply those on the Center-Right and Right, a French withdrawal from Eastern Europe after Munich and an "imperial retreat" were two sides of the same coin. Once again *Le Temps* is instructive: "It is because of the overthrow of the European order, which was established by the treaties of 1919 …," an editorial remarked in December 1938, "that imperial policy … has become one of the principal preoccupations of our people."[56]

It thus appeared unlikely that Daladier would be able to take the Radicals into a Center-Right political alliance without adopting its foreign policy. Yet just when the premier's hands seemed tied, the Italians offered him an escape. Underpinning an "imperial retreat" was the assumption that France would be left to pursue its imperial destiny in peace. Yet Fascist Italy's abusive campaign for colonial concessions from the French in late 1938, a campaign that the French believed had Germany's support, undermined this basic assumption. Germany, it appeared, could not be trusted to abide by any agreement to leave France alone. As Berthod himself would later admit:

> It is already a great deal, it is too much, that in turning to the West, as we are invited to do, we are confronted by Count Ciano's [Italy's Foreign Minister] overweening pretensions and we are told that, because of the Axis, these pretensions will not go without support. And, moreover, if we read what Germans are writing … —that an increase in Germany's power in Europe will only grant it new rights to make vast

> territorial demands outside Europe as well—we must ask ourselves what is the benefit of this so-called agreement which diverts our attention toward our empire only to ... place it in even greater danger.[57]

If, as Berthod now feared, Germany sought a "free hand" in Eastern Europe in order to be in a stronger position later to crush France, German expansion would have to be resisted. With the support of those like Berthod, Daladier was able to rally the Center-Right and Right behind a "firm policy" [*une politique de fermeté*], an important component of which was a commitment to France's eastern alliances. Referring to the latter, he told the Chamber in January 1939 that a policy of "retreat" or "renunciation" would be "disastrous for France's security." "I will not accept anything," he continued, "which might hamper our ties with other countries or anything which runs the risk of weakening our mutual engagements [*solidarités*]. The value of these grows as the hour of danger approaches."[58]

Led by Daladier and with Gamelin's support, the French by early 1939 had rejected a policy of withdrawal. The significance of this decision is worth stressing. French policy from Munich to Prague has been described as "attentiste", as marked by inertia.[59] Yet the French did in fact take a critical decision during this period—if only a negative one. By refusing to retreat within France and its Empire, by refusing to "revise" their eastern alliances, the French opted to resist German expansion. To be sure, they did not necessarily believe war to be inevitable. The possibility of deterrence remained—and Daladier certainly sold a "policy of firmness" to the Center-Right and Right on these terms.[60] Nonetheless, the rejection of Bonnet's policy certainly implied the acceptance of a possible, if not inevitable, European war—indeed, a policy of retreat drew a good deal of its "*raison d'être*" from the fear that the sole alternative was a Franco-German war. No one believed that Germany would be satisfied with the status quo for very long. Hitler, Gamelin reported to Daladier in December 1938, "is determined to pursue the execution of his hegemonic program."[61] Equally to the point, the French assumed that Germany's immediate ambitions lay eastwards, towards Poland and Romania. "Expansion eastwards and security in the West," was how General Didelet, the military attaché in Berlin, summarized reigning views of German intentions during this period.[62]

IV

By early 1939 the French had chosen to resist future German expansion with the risks of war that this entailed. Munich, moreover, was the catalyst in this decision. The strategic disaster represented by Czechoslovakia's reduction triggered a reassessment of French policy that, in turn, resulted in a recommitment to France's traditional policy of an eastern counterweight to Germany. This process raises an interesting point: the decision to resist Germany was not based on a more favorable evaluation of the present and future balance of power. Confidence was not a marked feature of French deliberations during this period—as Gamelin's October 12 "Note" indicates. If the immediate balance of European power looked grim after Munich, the future appeared even worse. Mention has already been made of the air staff's deep pessimism; in early 1938, French air intelligence estimated German aircraft production at 600/month, perhaps ten times the French figure. The military picture was hardly better. Germany's effort to expand rearmament, the 2e Bureau reported in November, represented the "greatest push we have recorded since the beginning of German rearmament." That this effort was "*clearly offensive*" followed from its focus on armored, mechanized and motorized forces.[63] Nor was there much expectation that economic, political or other factors would hamper German military preparations. If anything, the pace of the latter mesmerized the French. As the military attaché in Berlin wrote:

> Too often we imagine it [German society] as a variant of human society. It would be more accurate to compare it to a society of insects, ants or termites for example, in which every individual works without stop for the collectivity ... and whose organization permits the instantaneous passage from a state of peace to a state of war. Whereas military and mobilization measures wear down most peoples, they have no effect on Germany since the German no longer has the means to think and is, as I have said, permanently mobilized.[64]

In short, for the French, the balance of power would continue to shift in Germany's favor.

The French, of course, were not alone. They expected to have allies, most notably the British. As is well-known, French planners viewed Britain's potential contribution in a war as invaluable. Indeed, the driving purpose of French policy in the thirties has been explained in terms of the search for a solid British commitment. During the Czech crisis the French sought to extract a joint Anglo-French guarantee of Czechoslovakia from the British; afterwards Bonnet vigorously applied himself to the task of improving Anglo-French relations while Gamelin and Darlan spoke of the need for a "*close accord*."[65] This being so, Britain's newfound interest in the Entente in late 1938 and early 1939 no doubt contributed to French resolve to resist Germany. Yet the British factor can easily be exaggerated. At the time, Britain's embrace of a "continental commitment" appeared less certain than it did in retrospect. Reports from London in late 1938, for example, indicated that the British were becoming more isolationist.[66] This means that those like Gamelin made decisions about whether to resist German expansion without—in fact, despite—any guarantee of British support. While the French arguably assumed that, in the event of war, Britain would be on France's side, this raises another point: the very real limits of Britain's potential contribution to a common effort. In November a widely-circulated report from General Lelong, the military attaché in London, explained that Britain was in no state to intervene militarily on the continent nor would it be for a long time. Worse still, Lelong warned against any excessive reliance on the British in the future. For political and economic reasons, he insisted, Britain's overall contribution would be "greatly reduced" in comparison to 1914-18. "[I]t is upon us which will rest the largest part of the effort of resistance"—a conclusion general staff appreciations had been coming to for years.[67]

The point here is not that British support was unimportant but that it did not provide a satisfactory solution to the problems facing French planners. Whatever Britain's contribution—present and projected—the imbalance of forces against Germany would remain. Hence the terrible dilemma facing French planners: Germany's present military strength ruled out any quick victory, as it would have a preemptive war if anyone had proposed one, yet its mounting absolute and relative strength also made a French (and British) victory in a long war doubtful. The immediate result was to confirm and enhance the value of an eastern front. France (and Britain), Gamelin wrote to Daladier in January 1939, could "envisage with sang-froid" the possibility of a European war but only "on condition of help from Eastern Europe."[68] Several months later a staff paper presented to the British expanded on this point:

> The construction of an extended eastern front would force Germany to keep large forces in the East and would likely lead it to carry its initial effort in this direction in order to ensure for itself the economic resources indispensable to the pursuit of a war which can only be a *long war*.

Gamelin was even more explicit in July. "[W]e have every interest in seeing the conflict begin in the East and only becoming a general one little by little. As a result we will be given the time needed to mobilize all Anglo-French forces."[69]

Inevitably, the question of the role of the Soviet Union arose. It has been argued that throughout 1939 the General Staff viewed Poland as the backbone of an eastern front. But if French planners judged Polish participation to be essential, they never believed that Poland alone could constitute a militarily viable eastern front. No one, for instance, believed that the Poles could resist an attack for very long without considerable outside help. As a 2e Bureau report observed in January 1939:

> In case of an allied or enemy Poland we have every reason to believe that the Polish armed forces will constitute a *powerful support* for a coalition but one that will dimin-

> ish unless it receives industrial and materiel supplies and support from a powerful neighbor (Germany, U.S.S.R.)[70]

The basic problem was that the smaller states of Eastern Europe were too weak. Referring to the value of a possible coalition of Poland, Romania, Yugoslavia and Hungary, Gamelin in March 1939 commented that "[w]ar today demands such industrial power and such financial resources that the small peoples can only play a secondary role." "From the military point of view," he added, "they are non-factors."[71]

Since neither the French nor the British could lend Poland any direct help, this left the Soviet Union. Before Munich the General Staff had been reluctant to cooperate with the Soviets, owing to a combination of anti-communism and doubts about Soviet military power; afterwards, however, the Soviets quickly emerged in French thinking as the critical component of an eastern front. Once again, the 2e Bureau took the lead. "In the face of German military pressure," a paper by Gauché argued in December 1938, "using voluntarily or by force the territory of Czechoslovakia and Hungary, Poland and Romania will only be able to resist if *they are willing to accept and are assured of the only effective and immediate help available*: Soviet help—even if it is limited to air and materiel support."[72] Similarly, the Air Staff began to reverse its views on the potential contribution of the Soviet Air Force. Whereas the tendency before had been to downplay this factor, by early 1939 planners were favorably considering the possibility of Soviet bombers operating from Polish airfields. "The help which the Soviet Union could offer in the event of a war by aiding Poland against Germany …" read one report, "will be very *marked*. In effect, it allows *all of German territory* to be reached." Significantly, the problem of Soviet-Polish cooperation, which before had always been stressed, was not soft-pedaled.[73] After Prague Gamelin repeatedly echoed conclusions about the indispensability of Soviet participation in an eastern front. Writing to Daladier in April 1939, he emphasized the importance of doing "[e]verything that our diplomacy can do to convince the U.S.S.R. to collaborate with Poland by sending raw materials, foodstuffs, munitions …" Three months later, meeting with British staff officers, Gamelin underlined the "importance of the Russian factor."[74]

During 1939, then, French planners were coming to view the Soviet Union as the military backbone of an eastern front. Moscow's assigned role was not simply to supply materiel and other resources to the smaller states of Eastern Europe, but also, by intervening directly with land and air forces, to prevent the rapid conquest of Poland (or Romania) and therefore ensure the continued existence of an eastern front. As General Billotte, vice-chief of staff and member of the Superior War Council, wrote in a report for Gamelin on his return from a mission to Romania:

> Soviet military intervention … would appear to provide the Polish army with the possibility of undertaking a delaying action and to re-establish a front covering its capital and its war industries zone until its thirty-two reserve divisions are ready.[75]

French planners, in fact, came to see the Soviet Union as the solution to the general strategic problem caused by Germany's superior strength. In so casting the Soviets, the French ignored the very real obstacles—geographic, military, political—to Soviet cooperation. Few, if any, seem to have been interested in whether Moscow would or could play its assigned strategic role; no one looked closely into how the Soviets would intervene—directly or indirectly—in a war in Eastern Europe. But this reflects not so much neglect as it does a growing desperation. Faced with the mounting probability of a European war in 1939, French staff officers looked to the Soviet Union to provide the basis of a viable eastern front—a traditional component of French strategy in a war against Germany.

Here can be found the strategic underpinnings of France's search for an alliance with Moscow after Prague. Some scholars continue to question the sincerity of French (and British) efforts in this regard, most often citing the visceral anti-communism of political and military leaders.[76] Yet this thesis ignores the fact that the French at least sought an alliance with mounting desperation—as their repeated concessions to Moscow indicate. In July 1939 Daladier informed General Doumenc, head of the French delegation, that the upcoming military negotiations in Moscow were "perhaps decisive" since it was absolutely vital to confront Hitler with a "two front war." Every effort, he continued, must be made to reach an agreement.[77] During the earlier diplomatic talks, the French had repeatedly pressed the British to quicken the pace. Interestingly, Bonnet took the lead. Having failed to impose a policy of withdrawal, he fell back on a Soviet alliance as the only hope of deterring Germany and avoiding the war he so feared. As early as May he indicated that he was prepared to give the Soviets the old Curzon line; in June he told the British ambassador that the Baltic States should not become an obstacle to an agreement; in July he was ready to accept the Soviet definition of indirect aggression.[78] That Daladier shared Bonnet's desperation, if not his hope in deterrence, is evident from his despondent reaction to the news of the Nazi-Soviet Pact of August 1939. The pact, he explained to the American ambassador, "placed France in a most tragic and terrible situation."[79]

Daladier's reaction raises a final point. While the quest for an alliance with Moscow might have been sensible, given France's relative weakness, it did however mean that French strategy for war (or preventing war) was partly founded on a dubious proposition—that the Soviets could be persuaded to shoulder the burden of an eastern front. Should Moscow decide otherwise, the French would be left to face a war with Germany in extremely unfavorable circumstances. Thus on the same day Germany attacked Poland, the head of the 2e Bureau could comment to General Colson that "[n]ever in any period of its history has France entered a war in which the initial conditions were so unfavorable."[80]

V

Although a close examination of British policy during this period is beyond the scope of this chapter, a few comments on the subject are necessary to understand the significance of developments in France. As Chamberlain's obvious satisfaction suggests, British leaders viewed Munich not as a defeat but as a victory. The initial result of Munich was to reinforce isolationist trends in Britain. The bases of defense policy, collectively known as "limited liability," had been spelled out the year before in the famous Inskip Report that assigned the lowest priority in rearmament to the maintenance of a field force capable of serving on the Continent.[81] While foreign policy initially lacked the clear direction given to defense policy, following Munich the Foreign Office undertook a major policy assessment aimed at reducing Britain's European commitments. "We simply cannot protect our own interests all over the world," wrote one high-ranking official, "and at the same time claim a preponderant voice in the ordering of affairs in continental Europe."[82] The result of the exercise was the articulation of what another official termed a "Defense of the West" policy based on the tacit division of Europe into blocs. In effect, the British would help build a barrier to German expansion in Western Europe and the Mediterranean, leaving Germany free to expand its political and economic influence in Central and Eastern Europe.[83] With the British focusing on their own defense, the major responsibility for defending Western Europe would fall to the French by default.

To be sure, British policy underwent significant changes in early 1939. A war scare prompted in part by false information regarding an imminent German attack in Western Europe, possibly against Britain itself, when combined with mounting fears about French resolve, forced the British to commit themselves more fully to the defense of Western Europe.[84] In February the Cabinet agreed to staff talks with the French and to expand the BEF (British Expeditionary Force) from its current four divisions (two Regular and two Territorial) to nineteen divisions (six Regular and thirteen Territorial). Once committed to Western Europe, moreover, the British found it increasingly difficult to deny the strategic value of Eastern and Soviet participation in an eastern front. In May, just two months after the Prague Coup, the Cabinet would decide to offer an alliance to Moscow. Thus it was in early 1939 that British and French policies began to converge on a shared determination to resist future German aggression.

If decisions in Whitehall were clearly important, it must be stressed that they followed those of the French. Throughout the Czech crisis, French leaders sought to reconcile their hope of avoiding war with their desire to maintain Czechoslovakia's military viability. The reluctant decision taken at Munich to abandon the Czechs represented a grave strategic blow and led to a reassessment of France's response to future German expansion in Europe. Despite important support within political and military circles for a policy of withdrawal whose first step involved renouncing France's Eastern European commitments, the French, led by Gamelin, rededicated themselves to an eastern front and, by implication, to a policy of resistance against Germany. If the French had instead chosen to withdraw, it is hard to imagine how the British could not have followed suit. The immediate road to war, in other words, ran through Paris as much as it did through London (or Berlin). Czechoslovakia's reduction, however, forced the French to make the Soviet Union the cornerstone of an eastern front, with the result that French strategy for a war against Germany came to depend on Moscow's willingness to play its assigned role. In sum, by eliminating a strong and certain French ally in Eastern Europe, Munich gravely weakened France and, in so doing, increased the value of an eastern front in French eyes at the same time that it undermined the prospects of constructing one.

Thus it was the French and not the British who first decided that Germany had to be stopped, if necessary by war. And it was the French who first realized that effective resistance to German expansion required an eastern front centered on the Soviet Union. Contrary to many accounts, which maintain that London pointed the way for Paris in 1939, the reverse is more true. The British followed where the French led. Without the decisions taken in Paris in late 1938 and early 1939, events in Europe might very well have taken a different turn regardless of what happened in London.

Notes

1. Jean-Paul Sartre, *Les chemins de la liberté*, tome II, *Le sursis* (Paris, 1945), 362-3. Also see Etienne de Crouy-Chanel, *Alexis Leger: l'autre visage de Saint-John Perse* (Paris, 1989), 234-6.
2. Chamberlain's confidant was the British military attaché in Berlin. See Imperial War Museum, London, PP/MCR/C5, reel 2, Mason-Macfarlane's unpublished draft memoirs, 26.
3. Two examples are Williamson Murray, *The Change in the European Balance of Power, 1938-1939: The Path to Ruin* (Princeton, NJ, 1984) who throughout conflates British and French policy; and D.C. Watt, *How War Came: The Immediate Origins of the Second World War, 1938-*

1939 (London, 1989), who writes on p. 385 that "[t]he war which was to break Europe into two … was in the beginning fundamentally a war between the British and German people."

4. Specialist studies include Robert J. Young, *In Command of France: French Foreign and Defence Policy, 1933-1940* (Cambridge, MA, 1978); Jean-Baptitse Duroselle, *La décadence 1932-1939* (Paris, 1979); Martin S. Alexander, *The Republic in Danger: General Maurice Gamelin and the Politics of French Defence, 1933-1940* (Cambridge, 1992); and Elisabeth du Réau, *Édouard Daladier 1884-1970* (Paris, 1993).
5. A classic statement of this view is François Bédarida, "La 'gouvernante anglaise'" in René Rémond and Janine Bourdin, eds., *Edouard Daladier, chef du gouvernement, avril 1938-septembre 1939* (Paris, 1977), 228-40.
6. See respectively, Anthony Adamthwaite, *France and the Coming of the Second World War* (London, 1977), 175-225; Young, *In Command of France*, 192-220; du Réau, *Édouard Daladier*, 273-87.
7. France, Archives de l'Assemblée Nationale [hereafter AAN], Commission de l'armée. 16e législature, carton 16, Daladier audition, 31 August 1938.
8. Gauché is in Great Britain, Public Records Office, Kew Gardens [hereafter PRO] WO 106/5413, Fraser to Van Custem (WO), 31 August 1938; also see France, Service historique de l'armée de terre, Vincennes [hereafter SHAT] séries 7N, carton 2522, dossier 2, "Note sur le problème tchécoslovaque," EMA/2, 21 September 1938.
9. See France, Archives Nationales [hereafter AN], Papiers Daladier, 496/AP/35 4DA8 Dr5 sdra, "Note sur la réorganisation éventuelle de la Tchéco-slovaquie," 8 September 1938, EMA/2. Emphasis in original.
10. For French views of Germany, see Arnold Wolfers, *Britain and France Between the Wars* (New Haven, CT, 1940), passim; Ralph Schor, *L'opinion français et les étrangers, 1919-1939* (Paris, 1985); Peter Jackson, "French Military Intelligence and Nazi Germany, 1933-1939" (Ph.D. Cambridge University, 1995). Literary sources offer one interesting window into general attitudes and stereotypes. See George Pistorius, *L'image de l'Allemagne dans le roman français entre les deux guerres (1918-1939)* (Paris, 1964); and Jörg von Uthmann, *Le diable est-il allemand?* (Paris, 1984).
11. Piotr Wandycz, *France and her Eastern Allies, 1919-1925* (Minneapolis, MN, 1962); and *The Twilight of French Eastern Alliances, 1926-1939: French-Czechoslovak-Polish Relations from Locarno to the Remilitarization of the Rhineland* (Princeton, NJ, 1988); and William E. Scott, *Alliance against Hitler: The Origins of the Franco-Soviet Pact* (Durham, NC, 1962).
12. On this subject, see Wandycz, *The Twilight of French Eastern Alliances, 1926-1939*; Philippe Marguerat, *Banque et investissement industriel. Paribas, le pétrole roumain et la politique française, 1919-1939* (Geneva, 1987); Paul Harold Segal, "The French State and French Private Investment in Czechoslovakia, 1918-1938: a study of economic diplomacy," (Ph.D. Columbia University, 1983); David E. Kaiser, *Economic Diplomacy and the Origins of the Second World War: Germany, Britain, France, and Eastern Europe, 1930-1939* (Princeton, NJ, 1980); Georges-Henri Soutou, "L'impérialisme du pauvre: la politique économique du gouvernement français en Europe centrale et orientale de 1918 à 1929: essai d'interpétation," in *Relations internationales*, no. 7 (1976): 219-39.
13. Nicole Jordan, *The Popular Front and Central Europe: The Dilemmas of French Impotence, 1918-1940* (Cambridge, 1992), passim.
14. SHAT 2N 224/1, "Note sure les Accords d'Etat Major dont la conclusion serait à rechercher par la France," CSDN 237/DN.3, 4 April 1938.
15. For assessments, see SHAT 7N 3434/3, "Note sur une action offensive pour soutenir la Tchéco-slovaquuie", CSG, undated but in 1938; 1N 90-3, "Note succincte sur l'armée tchécoslovaque," undated but 1938. Czech military strengths and weaknesses are discussed in

Milan Hauner, "La Tchécoslovaquie en tant que facteur militaire," *Revue des études slaves,* 52 (1979): 178-92; and Katriel Ben-Arie, "Czechoslovakia at the Time of 'Munich': the military situation," *Journal of Contemporary History,* 25 (1990): 431-46.

16. SHAT 2N 235-1, "Note sur l'intérêt qui presente pour la France, du point de vue militaire, le maintien de la Tchécoslovaquie," EMA/2, 9 September 1938. But see Peter Jackson, "French Military Intelligence and Czechoslovakia, 1938," *Diplomacy and Statecraft,* 5, no. 1 (1994): 81-106.
17. On the ruling out of offensive action, see SHAT 5N 579, ""Note sur l'action possible de la France en faveur de la Tchécoslovaquie," signed Gamelin, 27 April 1938.
18. France. Ministère des affaires étrangères, [hereafter MAE] Papier d'Agents – Archives Personnelles [hereafter PA-AP], Papiers Massigli, carton 19, "Note. Conséquences pour la France de l'affaiblissement de la Tchécoslovaquie," 19 September 1938.
19. MAE, Papiers 1940, Cabinet Bonnet, "Les méthodes employées par l'Allemagne pour équilibrer sa balance commericiale – Les résultats obtenus et les conséquences qui decoulent de cette politique," 25 February 1938.
20. France, *Documents diplomatiques français, 1932-1939* (Paris) [hereafter DDF], 2e série, tome XI, no. 212, "Compte-rendu des conversations franco-britanniques du 18 septembre 1938," undated.
21. University of Birmingham Library, NC 18/1/1047, Neville to Ida Chamberlain, 16 April 1939.
22. DDF, 2e série, tome XI, no. 212.
23. AN, Daladier Papers, 496/AP/28 4DA1 Dr5 sdrb, Daladier's manuscript notes, 14 September 1938. Robert Young argues that Gamelin's priority during the Crisis was to prevent any responsibility for abandoning the Czechs from falling on the General Staff. See his "Le Haut Commandement français au moment de Munich," *Revue d'histoire moderne et contemporaine,* XXIV (1977), 127-9. The best study of Gamelin is Alexander, *The Republic in Danger.*
24. SHAT, Dépot Weygand, 1K 130, carton 15, dossier 14, Weygand carnets, 28 September 1938.
25. AN, Daladier Papers, 496/AP/10 2DA3 Dr2 sdra, "Note au sujet du mémorandum allemand présenté à M. Chamberlain le 23 septembre 1938," EMA/2, 25 September 1938; SHAT 7N 2522-2, "Situation stratégique de la Tchécoslovaquie dans l'hypothèse de l'acceptation du memorandum allemand," undated but late September 1938.
26. Jean Zay, *Carnets secrets de Jean Zay* (Paris, 1942), 113-17.
27. For minutes of the Anglo-French meeting on 25 September, see DDF, 2e série, tome XI, no. 356.
28. The text of Daladier's speech is in Colonel Pierre Le Goyet, *Munich, 'un traquenard'?* (Paris, 1988), 366-71. For Daladier's expectations, see AN, Papiers Daladier, 496/AP/8 2DA1 Dr3, "Munich."
29. Benes, the Czech President, might have encouraged the French to believe that territorial cession could be reconciled with the maintenance of Czechoslovakia's strategic viability. Through an intermediary he proposed a limited cession of territory. See A.M., "Dossier Necas," *Revue des études slaves,* 52 (1979): 135-47; and Igor Lukes, *Czechoslovakia between Stalin and Hitler: The Diplomacy of Edvard Benes* (Oxford, 1996), 221-2.
30. The best studies of the French and the Czech crisis are Yvon Lacaze, *L'opinion publique française et la crise de Munich* (Berne, 1991); idem., *La France et Munich: Etude d'un processus décisionnel en matière de relations internationales* (Berne, 1992); and du Réau, *Édouard Daladier,* 234-87.
31. Even "durs" like Paul Reynaud were convinced that Germany would be deterred. Reynaud thus wrote to a British official in August that the Germans will back down if the French and British remained firm because "they know that an open German-Czech war will soon grow into a European war." See AN, Papiers Reynaud, 74/AP/16, Reynaud to Vansittart, August 14, 1938.

32. Général de Cugnac, "Le Traité de Munich. Ses conséquences militaires" and "Le Traité de Munich. Ses conséquences politiques" in *France militaire,* October 13 and October 26, 1938; Charles de Gaulle, *Lettres, notes et carnets. 1919-Juin 1940* (Paris 1980), 477, de Gaulle to his wife, October 6, 1938.
33. Bernus, "Devant le Parlement," 4 October 1938, 1.
34. Archives du Sénat, Commission des affaires étrangères, Communique, 4 October 1938.
35. "Bulletin du jour," 2 October 1938, 1.
36. Bonnet is cited in Pierre Lazareff, *De Munich à Vichy* (New York, 1944), 32-3. For Bonnet in general, see Adamthwaite, *France and the Coming of the Second World War,* 264-79; Jean-Baptiste Duroselle, *La décadence,* 381-8; and Colette Barbier, "Das französische Außenministerium und die diplomatische Aktivität vom Münchener Abkommen bis zur Kriegserklärung," in Klaus Hildebrand et al., *1939 An der Schwelle zum Weltkrieg* (Berlin, 1990), 43-54.
37. AAN, Commission des affaires étrangères, 16eme, carton 7, Bonnet appearance, 6 October 1938.
38. For Rochat, see MAE, PA-40, Hoppenot, vol. 5, "Note," by Rochat, 30 December 1938; for Massigli, see SHAT 7N 2525, réunion hebdomadaire, 5 October 1938. For "realism" among Quai officials, see the comments in Jean Chauvel, *Commentaire,* I, *De Vienne à Alger (1938-1944)* (Paris, 1971), 57-8.
39. Duroselle, *La décadence,* 272-81, overstates the importance of this economic mission.
40. For memoranda from Quai officials, see MAE, P-40, Cabinet Bonnet, vol. 16, "Le Pacte franco-soviétique," January 1939; ibid., vol. 10, "Note sur les accords franco-polonais," 28 December 1938. For circulated despatches, see MAE, P-40, Cabinet Bonnet, vol. 10, "Note. Rapport franco-polonais," 19 November 1938, a copy of which is in AN, Papiers Daladier, 496/AP/11 2DA4 Dr3 sdra.
41. PRO FO 371/21675 C15102/42/18, Cadogan minute, 9 December 1938.
42. "Bulletin du jour," 7 December 1938. For a recent history of the Declaration, see Hans F. Bellstadt, *Apaisement oder Krieg: Frankreichs Außenminister Georges Bonnet und die deutsch-französische Erklärung vom 6. Dezember 1938* (Bonn, 1993). Also see Duroselle, *La décadence,* 381-9; Adamthwaite, *France and the Coming of the Second World War,* 264-79.
43. SHAT 5N 579/1, "Note sur la situation actuelle," no. 583/DN3, 12 October 1938. Reproduced in DDF, 2, XII, no. 86. Also see Jordan, *The Popular Front and Central Europe,* 289.
44. For Gamelin and Noel's talk, see SHAT 7N 3006, ms note dated 8 November 1938. For Gamelin on Poland, see SHAT 5N 579/7-3, Gamelin to Daladier, no. 4631/s, 12 October 1938; also see Gamelin's marginalia on Rydz-Smigly's letter to him, 3 October 1938 in 5N 579/7-2.
45. SHAT 5N 579/1, "Analyse" by Daladier's military cabinet as Minister of War and National Defense, which accompanies the copy of Gamelin's note.
46. France, Service historique de la Marine, Vincennes [hereafter SHM] 1BB2208/14-25, "L'Angleterre et la France peuvent-elles soutenir un conflit contre l'Allemagne et l'Italie," 24 January 1939.
47. SHM 1BB2171, "La Situation actuelle de la politique militaire de la France," no. 146 EMG/SE, 17 October 1938. For the navy during this period, see Claude Huan and Hervé Coutau-Bérgarie, *Darlan* (Paris, 1989), 121-54; Philippe Masson, "La Marine française et la stratégie alliée (1938-1939)" in Klaus Hildebrand and Karl Ferdinand Werner, eds., *Deutschland und Frankreich* (Munich, 1981), 153-66.
48. SHAT 2N 224/1, Buhrer to Gamelin, no. 74/s, 19 October 1938.
49. Vuillemin's response is in SHAT 5N 579/1 and 17, Vuillemin to Gamelin, no. 141 EMGAA/S, 25 October 1938. For intelligence reports, see, for example, 7N 2602/1, Greffier to Air Min.,

9 November 1938 which estimates German aircraft production at 600/month, perhaps ten times that of France.

50. SHAT 5N 579/1, "Note sur la situation actuelle," 26 October 1938, signed by Colson and enclosed in a note from Gamelin to Daladier, no. 936/DN3, same date. Nicole Jordan, in citing the 12 October 1938 paper in isolation, mistakenly argues that Gamelin remained committed to a withdrawal from Eastern Europe in 1938-39.
51. SHAT 2N 224/1, Gamelin to Daladier, no. 5705/S, 19 December 1938. Earlier, in a speech in March 1938, Gamelin had declared that France "has never ceased and will never cease to be ... an essential element in the world balance, materially as well as morally." See SHAT, Fonds Gamelin, 1K 227/7, speech entitled "L'Edelweiss," 19 March 1938.
52. For the SFIO during the period, see Nathaniel Greene, *Crisis and Decline: The French Socialist Party in the Popular Front Era* (Ithaca, NY, 1969); Richard Gombin, *Les socialistes et la guerre* (Paris, 1968); B.D. Graham, *Choice and Democratic Order: The French Socialist Party, 1937-1950* (Cambridge, 1994), 224-423.
53. On the Radicals, see Serge Berstein, *Histoire du Parti radical*, 2 volumes, II (Paris, 1982), 546-79; Peter J. Larmour, *The French Radical Party in the 1930s* (Stanford, CA, 1964), 230-48; Robert Michael, *The Radicals and Nazi Germany: The Revolution in French Attitudes Toward Foreign Policy, 1933-1939* (Washington, D.C., 1982), passim. Indispensable for French politics during this period is Charles A. Micaud, *The French Right and Nazi Germany, 1933-1939: A Study of Public Opinion* (New York, 1964 edn.), passim.
54. Parti républicain radical et radical socialiste, *35e Congrès du parti républicain radical et radical socialiste tenu à Marseilles* (Paris, 1938), 518-39.
55. On public interest in the Empire, see Charles-Robert Ageron, "La perception de la puissance française en 1938-1939. Le Mythe Impérial" in Robert Frank and René Girault, eds., *La puissance en Europe: 1938-1940* (Paris: Sorbonne, 1984); idem., *France coloniale ou parti colonial?* (Paris, 1978). For evidence that this interest did not extend to military planners, see Martin Thomas, "At the Heart of Things? French Imperial Defense Planning in the Late 1930s," *French Historical Studies*, 21, no. 2 (1998), 325-61. The huge gap between political interest in the Empire and measures of economic development are explored more generally in Jacques Marseille, *Empire colonial et capitalisme français: histoire d'un divorce* (Paris, 1984).
56. "La France et l'Allemagne," 6 December 1938, 1.
57. Berthod, "L'Est européen" in *Dépêche du Toulouse*, 25 February 1939.
58. *Journal officiel*, Chambre des Députés, 1939, 248.
59. For the *attentisme* of French policy, see Robert J Young, "The Aftermath of Munich: The Course of French Diplomacy, October 1938 to March 1939," *French Historical Studies* 8, no. 2 (1973), 305-22. Peter Jackson makes a similar argument in his "Intelligence and the End of Appeasement" in Robert Boyce, ed., *French Foreign and Defence Policy, 1918-1940: the Decline and Fall of a Great Power* (London, 1998), 247.
60. See, for instance, Daladier's speech to the Radical Party's Executive Committee on 15 January 1939 in "Le comité éxécutif radical-socialiste réuni hier ..." in *L'Ere nouvelle*, 16 January 1939, 1-2.
61. SHAT 1N 43/3-6, Gamelin to Daladier, 27 December 1938.
62. SHAT 7N 2602/2, Didelet to Guerre, 10 January 1939.
63. SHAT 7N 2676, "Note sur le développement des forces terrestres allemandes," EMA/2 SAE, no. 252, 30 November 1938; ibid., "Au 1er janvier 1939," undated.
64. SHAT 7N 2602/2, Didelet to Min. de la Guerre, no. 364, 11 April 1939.
65. See Gamelin's October 12th "Note" and Darlan's response. Also see SHAT 2N 227/3, "Note sur la collaboration militaire franco-britannique," CSDN, no. 1054/DN.3, 23 November 1938.

66. See, for intance, Corbin's report in MAE, EU 30-40, Grande Bretagne, vol. 266, Corbin to MAE, 21 December 1938; and that of the naval attaché in SHM 1BB7 42, "Compte-rendu de renseignement," 3 November 1938. In Paris, meanwhile, the air staff noted apprehensively the exclusive focus of British air rearmament on the defense of Britain. See SHAA 2B 82, "Forces aériennes britanniques," 1 January 1939.
67. For Lelong, see SHAT 7N 2815, "Etude sur la participation de l'Angleterre dans l'éventualité d'une action commune franco-britannique en cas de guerre," no. 167/s, 9 November 1938, a copy of which can be found in Daladier's papers among other places. For an example of general staff appreciations, see 7N 3438/1, "Note sur l'appui éventuel de la Grande-Bretagne," EMA, 9 January 1935.
68. SHAT 2N 224/1, Gamelin to Daladier, no. 24/DN.3, 7 January 1939.
69. For the staff paper, see SHAT 2N 228/2 and 3bis, "Etude des conditions découlant d'une alliance entre la Pologne, la Grande-Bretagne et la France," D.F.15, undated; for Gamelin see 7N 3439/3, "Conversations militaires franco-britanniques. Resumé des conversations du 13 juillet 1939," undated.
70. For the report on Poland, see SHAT "Pologne," EMA/2 SAE, 30 January 1939. Also see 7N 3002, Musse to Guerre, no. 73/s, 11 May 1939; 7N 3186/1, "Situation matérielle de l'Armée polonaise," ms note, EMA/2, undated but sometime in the summer of 1939; 7N 3033 for "Rapport du Capitaine Malaguti ...," 26 August 1938; and ibid. for the report of Cpt. de Winter on his "stage" at the Polish Ecole de Guerre, 27 April 1939. The Air Force came to similar conclusions. See SHAA 2B 97, "Note sur l'aéronautique militaire polonaise," 11 July 1939.
71. SHAT 1N 38/3, minutes of CSG mtg., 13 March 1939.
72. SHAT 7N 2522/3, "Considérations sur la constitution d'un bloc oriental," EMA/2 signed by Gauché. Emphasis in original, 28 December 1938. But see Maurice Vaïsse, "La perception de la puissance soviétique par les militaires français en 1938" in *Revue historique des armées*, no. 23 (1983).
73. For pre-Munich reports, see SHAT 7N 2522/2, "Note sur le concours militaire que la France peut attendre de l'U.R.S.S. dans le domaine aérien," 10 March 1938. For post-Munich, see SHAA Z 12941, Papiers Guy LaChambre, "Étude sur l'aide que pourrait apporter l'U.R.S.S. en cas de conflit européen," undated but probably January 1939, emphasis in original; ibid. "Conférence sur l'U.R.S.S. et les puissances secondaires de l'Europe Centrale," EMAA/2, February 1939.
74. SHAT 2N 236/2, Gamelin to Daladier, no. 719/DN.3, 15 April 1939; 7N 3439/3, "Conversations militaires franco-britanniques. Résumé des conversations du 3 juillet 1939," undated.
75. SHAT 1N 43/4-7, Billotte to Gamelin, 3 June 1939 with enclosure.
76. A recent statement of this thesis is Michael Jabara Carley, *1939: The Alliance That Never Was and the Coming of World War II* (Chicago, 1999).
77. AN, Daladier Papers, 496/AP/11 2DA4 dr6 sdrc, manuscript note, "Pour l'entretien avec Doumenc," 29 July 1939.
78. For the Curzon line, see AN, 496/AP/13 2DA6 Dr3, "Extrait des notes personnelles du Ministre des Affaires Etrangères," 26 May 1939; for the Baltic States, see Centre d'archives diplomatiques de Nantes, Londres, vol. 132, Bonnet to Corbin, no. 1091-96, 7 June 1939; and ibid., vol. 134, Bonnet to Corbin, no. 1517, 19 July 1939, for indirect aggression.
79. Franklin D. Roosevelt Library, Hyde Park, NY, PSF, Box 19, Dispatches: France, Bullitt to Sec of State, no. 1543, 22 August 1939.
80. Général Maurice Gauché, *Le Deuxième Bureau au travail 1935-1940* (Paris, 1954), 103-04.
81. British defense policy is well-covered in Michael Howard, *The Continental Commitment* (London, 1972), 113-17; Peter Dennis, *Decision by Default: Conscription and British Defence, 1919-1939* (London, 1972), 109-225; N.H. Gibbs, *Grand Strategy, I, Rearmament Policy*, (London,

1976), 491-528; and Brian Bond, *British Military Policy between the Two World Wars* (Oxford, 1980), 253-70.

82. PRO FO 371/21659 C14471/42/18, Cadogan to Halifax, 15 October 1938, cover letter for paper dated 14 October. Also see Donald Lammers, "From Whitehall after Munich: The Foreign Office and the Future Course of British Policy" in *Historical Journal*, XVI, no 4 (1973), 831-56; and Zara Steiner, "Evaluation des rapports de force en Europe occidentale en 1938: le point de vue du Foreign Office" in Frank and Girault, eds., *La puissance en Europe 1938-1940*, 55-71.
83. Gladwyn Jebb coined the phrase "Defense of the West". PRO FO 371/21659 C14471/42/18, "Preliminary Outline of Suggested Paper on Policy," by Jebb, undated but late October 1938. Other FO memoranda are in this file.
84. The literature on the war scare is extensive. See Watt, *How War Came*, 99-107; Wesley K. Wark, *The Ultimate Enemy: British Intelligence and Nazi Germany, 1933-1939* (Ithaca, NY, 1985), 211-24; Sidney Aster, *1939: The Making of the Second World War* (London, 1977), 38-60; M.S. Alexander, "Les réactions à la menace stratégique allemande en Europe occidentale: la Grande Bretagne, la Belgique et le 'cas Hollande', décembre 1938-février 1939," *Cahiers d'histoire de la Seconde Guerre Mondiale*, no. 7 (1982), 5-38; Christopher Andrew, *Secret Service: The Making of the British Intelligence Community* (London, 1985), 412-17.

Chapter 7

"NOUS ALLONS VERS LES MONASTÈRES"

French Pacifism and the Crisis of the Second World War

Norman Ingram

There is nothing quite like a war to render the pacifist cause suspect and dangerous in the eyes of public opinion. In the case of France this has been complicated by the spectacle of the War-which-was-Lost-and-then-Won, the temptations represented by the moral and political quandaries posed by Vichy, and the subsequent Gaullist absolution. Compounding these historical dilemmas is a posterity which has arguably been unable to exorcise the ghost of Vichy and a postwar peace movement which has been hijacked—at least in the public mind—by the French communist party.[1] All of this has contributed to a collective amnesia about the pacifist past in France from the slumbers of which the French historical profession and political society are only now beginning to waken.

This is in stark contrast to the experiences of France's two most important neighbors, Britain and Germany. Weimar German pacifism shared many features in common with the peace movement in interwar France.[2] In post-Second World War Germany, pacifism has flourished largely *because* it was decapitated by Hitler soon after the seizure of power in 1933; its liberal and left-wing credentials have thus been enhanced immeasurably because of its time on the cross, to say nothing of in the camps. Postwar Britain presents a different picture yet again.[3] The United Kingdom has long had a dissenting religious tradition which has informed and shaped the twentieth-century peace movement. The fact that Britain was never invaded or occupied during the Second World War, and moreover emerged

Notes for this chapter begin on page 148.

victorious from the conflict, has meant that postwar British pacifism has never had to deal with the blight of a Vichy legacy. The paradox of it all is that nineteenth-century French pacifism was second only to the British variety in its importance in Europe; the French were highly visible and important players in the international peace movement from 1889 to 1914, and it was a Frenchman, Emile Arnaud, who coined the term "pacifisme" in 1901.[4] During the interwar period French pacifism was numerically significant, although perhaps typically thoroughly balkanized, and French pacifists were important voices in the councils of the international peace movement. In fact, it is no exaggeration to say that the most well-known and influential pacifist of his generation was a Frenchman, Romain Rolland, who won the Nobel Prize in Literature in 1915.[5] In a country which had borne the brunt of the Great War public opinion and politicians alike took seriously the pacifist cry *"plus jamais ça!"*

The interwar French peace movement can be divided up into three main streams. The first is what I have called *pacifisme ancien style.* It had a juridical, liberal, and internationalist epicenter, and espoused a positive pacifism which sought, by means of the slow elaboration of international law, to erect a dike against the chaos of anarchic international politics. This *Ur-pazifismus* was represented above all by the *Association de la paix par le droit* (APD), founded in 1887 in Nîmes. Emerging at least partially from this strand, by the late 1920s, was a new type of French peace activism which I have called *pacifisme nouveau style.* This latter variety posited a radical, absolute or integral rejection of any international war whatever the pretext. It is best represented in interwar France by the *Ligue internationale des combattants de la paix* (LICP) which appeared on the political landscape in late 1930. The development from old-style to new-style pacifism marks the fundamental dichotomy and development in my study of the interwar French peace movement.

There was also, however, a very important "theme and variation" on the above development. Feminist pacifism was an influential element in the interwar French peace movement, but it evolved in a direction opposite to that elaborated above. In the 1920s the women of the most important and genuinely feminist pacifist group,[6] the *Ligue internationale des femmes pour la paix et la liberté* (LIFPL), were integral pacifists before the term came into broad use. In the 1930s, however, the women of the LIFPL evolved away from the courageous integral pacifism of the first decade toward increasingly unconditional support of the Soviet Union and a Moscow-inspired view of peace and pacifism. During the Second World War, feminist pacifism, like pacifism generally, went into an eclipse. Some feminist pacifists of note, such as Andrée Jouve, struggled in occupied Paris simply to survive.[7] Others, such as the writer and journalist Henriette Sauret, lost husbands to Nazi brutality.[8] Still others, such as Marcelle Capy, had been primarily active in new-style pacifist circles before the war and continued this engagement under Vichy.[9]

This essay will not deal in a systematic way with the fate of feminist pacifism, but rather with the moral and political dilemmas faced by the representatives of both old-style and new-style pacifism. What happened to these men and women of principled pacifism from 1939 to 1945? How did their pacifist vision of France and its place in international affairs evolve in the very changed circumstances of defeat and Vichy? Is there a simple equation between pacifism and collaborationism? And if so, how does one explain this political sea change, this reading from left to right?

The answers to these questions are complex and vary almost on an individual basis. Perhaps the first point to be made is that pacifist archives for the Vichy period are very difficult to come by. Rare indeed is the pacifist who has left a full record of his wartime activity for the perusal of the curious historian. That said, it is possible to piece together a tentative picture of the 1940 to 1944 period from which at least two patterns of pacifist response to the Second World War can be discerned, responses which, either explicitly or implicitly, contain prescriptions for the renewal of France. The first of these can be entitled "Old Hopes for a New Future in Pacifisme ancien style" and the second "Pacifisme nouveau style and the New (Nazi) Europe."

Old Hopes for a New Future in Pacifisme Ancien Style

It is difficult to determine with any degree of certainty what course the representatives of old-style pacifism took during the Second World War. The *Association de la paix par le droit* (APD) published its journal only until May 1940. There then ensued a five-year period of almost total silence. The correspondence of Jules Prudhommeaux, the secretary-general of the Association, together with the archives of the APD in Nîmes, are also silent on the war years, and only begin again in 1945. Nevertheless, from the fragmentary evidence that remains, it is possible to reconstruct, in its barest outlines, the activity of France's oldest pacifist group.

The APD responded to the outbreak of the Second World War as it had to the outbreak of the first: with firm support for the French position. This is perhaps not surprising given that the members of the APD constituted part of the French republican political and social elite. War had been imposed on Poland and its French and British allies; in the face of what Théodore Ruyssen, the Association's long-standing president, called "the incommensurable disaster into which civilization risks plunging," the first duty of the noncombatant was sober speech.

That said, "the war of 1939, no more than that of 1914-1918, was neither an unforeseen accident, nor on the contrary a reason for doubting the unchanging doctrine" of the Association.[10] The APD had always preached a "positive" pacifism, one that went far beyond the "individual repugnance of the conscientious objector," or the nonviolent resignation of the Tolstoyan, to the creation of a genuine international order equipped with the means to enforce respect for international law and conventions. Why had this nascent order, incarnated in the League of Nations, failed? Since 1932 defeat had followed defeat for the League, to the point where Czechoslovakia and Poland had not even bothered to seek League intervention. The League's failures were the Association's failures, according to Ruyssen. The APD's voice had been "lost in a desert of carelessness and skepticism."[11] The failure of Geneva was ultimately that of the democracies, however; at critical junctures in the 1930s, clear-sightedness and political will had been lacking. But the time was not for recriminations, and in a letter to Edouard Daladier, Ruyssen pledged that the Association would do nothing to weaken the French war effort.[12]

The Phoney War provided the opportunity for an examination of the reasons for the advent of war in September 1939, together with the development of a sort of *Leitmotiv* regarding the kind of peace which would result from it. It never seems to have occurred to the APD's leadership that France might first have to pass through the crucible of defeat and occupation. Ruyssen, writing in January 1940, defined the peace which would follow the war—being fought moreover to "maintain the highest human values"—in the following terms:

> Now peace—we mean by that the best peace, solid and durable, to which we all aspire—will not automatically appear at the end of the war: after the armistice, which will be limited to stating the obvious capitulation of the defeated, it will remain to establish a new regime of law which will allow both parties to live henceforth side by side in a final spirit of non-aggression, of mutual respect, and, if possible, of collaboration.[13]

Far from being a complete failure, the League of Nations (LoN) had been let down by its member states, particularly the great powers. But Georges Scelle, Professor of Law at the University of Paris, argued that something *like* the LoN would have to replace it. The disintegration of the LoN was in large part the product of a misconception founded on the idea of the sovereign character of the nation-state. According to Scelle,

> We must call things by their real name. If we persist in the postwar period in viewing International Society from the angle of a juxtaposition of sovereign States, it is possible that for several years we will enjoy an uncertain pacification, thanks to the

> victory of governments of honest men, but it will certainly not last long, and the era of gangsters will return in no time.[14]

Underlining the distance which separated the old-style from the new-style pacifism, Scelle wrote that "we must hope this time that the lesson will be sufficient and that we will have learned that it is not in the utopian vision of a renovation in the human species that the remedy will be found for the cyclical crises of our frenetic humanity."[15] The answer lay in a renewed commitment to some form of federalism, a prefiguring if not of the United Nations, at least of the European Community. Betraying the essentially positivist bent of many members of the Association, Scelle wrote that no federal system would tolerate the existence within itself of such regressive, inhuman, and *antiscientific* [emphasis added] regimes as Nazism or Bolshevism. As he saw it, the future lay in a choice between federalism and endemic warfare; there was no middle ground.[16]

At the end of January 1940, the Association's one and only wartime general assembly debated the question of the future peace. Once again there seemed little awareness of the impending catastrophe. Ruyssen began the discussion of what a future peace would look like by reviewing the reasons for the failure of the "universalistic" dream incarnated by the League of Nations. Geneva had failed because of the inability of governments to transcend their own selfish interests and rivalries. The first precondition for the future peace, therefore, was that it must be realistic. In place of the universalism of the League idea, Ruyssen proposed a European federation which would be formed under the aegis of the Franco-British alliance. Four essential conditions would regulate this new enterprise: a progressive restriction on the sovereignty of national governments; verifiable disarmament of the participating states; an international force at the disposal solely of the federal power; and a "daring rationalization" of economic relations.[17]

On the eve of the invasion of France the *Association de la paix par le droit* seemed unable to conceive of the impending French defeat, while at the same time giving voice to a critique of the Third Republic's political leadership and elaborating the beginnings of a new, less universalistic, vision of international affairs based on a Eurocentric federalism. The defeat of France and the four years of the Vichy regime intervened. During this time the APD disappeared completely from the French political landscape. Ruyssen, however, did not. He does not appear to have been active politically, but he left a few traces which call into question his postwar affirmations of political purity.

For reasons which are difficult to fathom, in the autumn of 1940 Ruyssen published two articles in *L'Effort*, the collaborationist newspaper produced first in Clermont-Ferrand and later in Lyons by Charles Spinasse and Paul Rives.[18] Certainly the men and women behind *L'Effort* were not of the same political family as Ruyssen; why did he get involved with the paper? Perhaps he felt the need to air his views somewhere, *anywhere*. What is clear is that in 1940 he gave support, albeit fairly attenuated, to the National Revolution.

Ruyssen's first article of early September 1940 dealt with the establishment of the Riom court. In it he warned the "impatient," the "nervous fraction of public opinion astonished not to see the «*première charette*»" heading off for the guillotine on the Place de la Révolution, to wait quietly for the Riom verdicts. He described the new *Cour suprême de justice* set up by Vichy as "justice on the march." Among the multiple tasks facing the new government, "one of the most essential," he wrote, was "the search for, the pursuit and punishment of, the primary responsibilities which are at the root of the catastrophe from which our country will long remain afflicted."[19] His voice joined the chorus of denunciations raining down on the defunct Third Republic. He condemned the usual varieties of treason, but there were also subtle responsibilities more difficult to discern. In a disturbing conclusion for someone normally so democratic, Ruyssen leveled his severest criticism at universal suffrage, the "inveterate and profound cause of our oscillations, our abandonment, and finally of our impotence."[20] The Riom court was "highly qualified" to deal with these cases, however, because it was "in no sense a jurisdiction of circumstances"; it was not "a tribunal established to judge crimes after the fact" or a "political tribunal." On the contrary it would be more impartial than the High Court established under the 1875 Constitution because it would be immune to the pressures of political parties. Ruyssen saw great reason for confidence because the new court represented a more classic separation of the three branches of government than had obtained under the Third Republic. Riom was thus a "great experiment" whose "serenity" must not be disturbed.[21]

Just over a month later Ruyssen published a second article in *L'Effort* which dealt with the question of the nature of the "National Revolution." His thesis that France could not turn its back on the revolutionary tradition of 1789 represented a serious misunderstanding of the goals of the architects of Vichy France. That said, he again had very negative things to say about French democracy. He wrote of the "legitimate reaction" of those who saw in the Third Republic a "caricature of democracy which has dishonored the last twenty years of our history," while at the same time warning against throwing overboard three centuries of political and philosophical development and "blaming even the idea of democracy as the unique cause of our troubles."[22] Citing the American Declaration of Rights of 1774, he argued that the people "must have a say in their law-making." From this basic principle, however, Ruyssen drew corporatist conclusions which seem very much in line with the thinking at Vichy and in Mussolini's Italy: "There is no doubt much to be expected from electoral rules which will give due respect to the influence of the family, professional corporation, and to the constituent organizations of national life."[23] Somewhat equivocally, he ended the article by asserting that "it is one of our most solid traditions that any lasting government must be founded on the consent of the governed."[24] It is difficult to believe that a man imbued with the democratic tradition of Théodore Ruyssen, to say nothing of his formidable intellectual capacity, could have argued the nonconformist case for corporatism, much less in a collaborationist newspaper such as *L'Effort* in which his articles appeared side by side with those of Marcel Déat, René Château, and Victor Margueritte.[25] But such was the case.

In the immediate postwar period, therefore, Ruyssen engaged in some damage control. It was obviously important for the leadership of the APD to portray itself as having been on the side of the Resistance. Ruyssen advised Prudhommeaux in June 1946, for example, that as far as the Resistance was concerned "you can say, in effect, that I replaced [Jacques] Chevalier [Minister of Education at Vichy and hence a politically 'undesirable' professor at the University of Grenoble] and add that I gave money to the Resistance, and moreover that during the entire German occupation I hid under my own roof, and not without risks, about a dozen unfortunates being hunted by the Milice or the Gestapo, most of them Jews, Poles, Romanians, Hungarians, Germans, etc."[26] As for the political activity of the APD, Ruyssen counseled taking the high road: "say that our Association and its leadership have always held to a position above party politics," and for good measure that the review, *La Paix par le droit*, had ceased publication in June 1940 and remained "voluntarily" out of circulation until the Liberation.[27]

There was thus an ambivalence at the heart of the *Association de la paix par le droit* which Ruyssen clearly felt it necessary to address in the immediate postwar period. This explains the insistence on the "resistance credentials" of both himself and the APD. Such a position was certainly necessary in 1945 and 1946 when the APD had to justify the purity of its position during the war in order to obtain the permission of the Ministry of Information to publish its review. Prudhommeaux seemed to have no difficulty in this regard, but as he pointed out in a letter to Auguste Laune, the Association's treasurer, in June 1946, Ruyssen was the object of "vile" attacks by the leaders of the *Ligue des droits de l'homme*, notably Emile Kahn, Gombault, and Dr. Sicard de Plauzoles, who were "rabid" partisans of the Epuration.[28]

Pacifisme Nouveau Style and the New (Nazi) Europe

If the key figures of old-style pacifism left relatively little in the way of records of their wartime activity, the same cannot be said of some of the leaders of new-style pacifism. Little remains in terms of correspondence, but many of them were active in the collaborationist press, as a result of which they were tried by the courts of the Liberation. This is certainly not to say that *all* new-style pacifists were guilty of collaboration with the Germans; even among those accused of "un-French" activities after the war, most could not be convicted of active collaboration with the Nazis. Indeed, there are notable examples of new-style pacifists who were active in Resistance activities of one form or another, even if they seem to be in the minority.[29] This latter point is open to debate. Nicolas Offenstadt has shown that the leaders of the LICP by and large became collaborators to one degree or another. Yet, according to Sylvain Broussaudier, a *normalien, agrégé des lettres* and an important member of the *comité directeur* of the LICP during the 1930s, "many former pacifists entered the Resistance."[30] It would also seem to be the case that those pacifists who were most likely to resist tended to be of the Christian variety.[31] More research is clearly needed before any definitive conclusions can be reached about the activities of rank-and-file pacifists. One is left then with the leadership of the LICP and other highly visible integral pacifists, and one must ask what led the formerly democratic, leftist men and women of interwar new-style pacifism apparently to abandon their ideals and support the Vichy regime?

Four reasons suggest themselves. First, for some pacifists the Second World War was the inevitable conclusion to a process begun in 1914, one in which French (and British) policies were to blame for both wars. This position of historical dissent had colored new-style pacifism in the 1930s; under Vichy it infused the response of many pacifists to the crisis posed by the defeat and the dilemma of collaboration. Secondly, some pacifists genuinely believed that Europe would be Nazi-dominated for years to come, and that some sort of *modus vivendi* with the Germans was therefore necessary. Thirdly, there is little doubt that many collaborationist pacifists were motivated by a visceral anticommunism, despite their own original left-wing principles. And finally, some pacifists seem to have been pulled into the collaborationist press because of ties of friendship; indeed, in the case of Michel Alexandre, a French Jew who spent much of the war hiding from both the French police and the Gestapo, these same bonds came to the rescue of friends being tried before the courts of the Epuration.

To deal first with the question of historical dissent, many pacifist intellectuals and militants drew inspiration for their political positions from a dissenting reading of France's role in the origins of the Great War. Indeed, one cannot understand the political positions taken during the late 1930s and under Vichy without an appreciation of this historical dimension. The roots of historical dissent were long; indeed, they reach back as far as a dissenting reading of the meaning of the French Revolution.

This dissenting tradition began during the Great War itself under the aegis of the *Société d'études documentaires et critiques sur les origines de la guerre* (SEDCOG)[32], which was a sort of French equivalent to the British Union for Democratic Control. Under the leadership of people like Georges Demartial, Mathias Morhardt, and Michel Alexandre, the SEDCOG provided the intellectual arguments for what became new-style pacifism in the late 1920s. The essential thesis of the SEDCOG was that far from being a case of unilateral German war guilt—the basis for Article 231 of the Versailles Peace Treaty—the Great War was actually the result of a convergence of political mistakes and France and Russia bore the primary responsibility for its outbreak. Through the 1920s Demartial, Morhardt, and others published a steady stream of attacks on the notion of German war-guilt and of the "official" Pierre Renouvin interpretation of the war's origins. Most of these critiques were ignored. Demartial, however, was expelled from the *Légion d'Honneur* in 1928 ostensibly for having brought the French nation into disrepute by disputing the Poincaré version of the origins of the Great War in an article published in an American journal.[33] At this point, René Gerin, a *normalien, agrégé des lettres*, an officer wounded in action during the Great War, and a Chevalier of the *Légion d'Honneur* himself, got involved. He engaged Raymond Poincaré in a public debate on war origins which was published in 1930.[34] For his pains he, too, was eventually thrown out of the *Légion d'Honneur*.[35]

By 1930 at least three complementary lines of historical dissent began to converge, contributing to the creation of pacifisme nouveau style. First, there was the wave of dissenting historical studies coming out of the circle of intellectuals initially involved in the SEDCOG. This was augmented in the late 1920s by a new cohort of intellectuals such as René Gerin. Most of these dissenting intellectuals were active in the *Ligue internationale des combattants de la paix* which was formed at the end of 1930 and became the most important pacifist group of any sort in interwar France. Secondly, a group of intellectuals and militants, some of whom had been members of the SEDCOG during the Great War, began to achieve some success in arguing the pacifist, dissenting, nonconformist case within the extremely influential *Ligue des droits de l'homme* (LDH). The politics of pacifist dissent are thus to be found at the very heart of Republican France. The debate on peace, pacifism, and the meaning of Versailles came to a messy head—although by this point the high water mark for pacifism within French society had long since passed—at the LDH's 1937 congress in Tours in the wake of which seven influential pacifist members of the Ligue's "minority" resigned from the central committee.[36] What is interesting for our purposes is that of these seven "*minoritaires*," at least four (Georges Pioch, Léon Emery, Félicien Challaye, Gaston Bergery) went on to publish in the collaborationist press under Vichy. Finally, there is the creation of a pacifist dissenting historical esthetic which took form largely under the pen of the Revolutionary historian Georges Michon (a student of Albert Mathiez and another of the "*minoritaires*" to resign from the LDH central committee in 1937) whose work on Robespierre and the origins of the French Revolutionary wars can be, and indeed was, interpreted metaphorically to condemn France's position on Germany during the 1930s and under Vichy.

A fine line separated historical invective from political polemic by the end of the 1930s. In a book published just before the outbreak of war in 1939,[37] Demartial's despair verged on cynicism; it extended now even to the level of the common man, who until then had been the pacifist (and revolutionary) subject and agent in whom high hopes had been vested. While he had earlier taken for granted the idea that given the choice no one would vote for war, in 1939 Demartial began by suggesting that even in a democracy the people are manipulated by the press and the government.[38] He called Edouard Herriot a charlatan (among many others in the democracies) for his panegyrics in honor of "the silent virtues of our race" in September 1938, juxtaposing this with Herriot's equally vapid condemnations of the Germans as a race, "whose least fault is to indulge in vile deeds, who are thieves by vocation, unspeakably foul liars, etc."[39] The cancer at the heart of Europe continued to be the question posed by Article 231. He believed that the Germans had accepted the need to pay war reparations as losers, but not as criminals.

On the eve of another war, Demartial undertook the prosecution of an entire French historical tradition, the French militarist tradition, the politics of being the strongest, no matter what. It was a tradition which went back to Richelieu, to Louis XIV, passed through both Napoléons, and continued on to Poincaré. He cited de Tocqueville who in *L'Ancien Régime et la révolution* traced the qualities and the faults of the French people, judging them: "Good at everything, but excelling only in war." Demartial commented dryly, "That is something."[40] But the French should not claim, he said, as Briand did at the 1921 Washington Disarmament Conference that "in the course of its history the French people has never been militarist or imperialist," or that, as *Le Temps* put it, France had been "pacific from the very beginning."[41] Because the facts were otherwise; as a nonfascist Italian historian had written: "France is the country of Europe which has fought the most wars, big or small, continental or colonial, in the last three centuries."[42]

This led Demartial to conclude, in a way not a little reminiscent of the schisms affecting pacifisme nouveau style and feminist pacifism in 1938 on the question of a disengagement of pacifism from antifascism, that "democracy is one thing, and pacifism is another." This was a political conclusion which informed much of the thinking of integral pacifists under Vichy. The democratic regime by itself was no guarantor of peace. "In the Middle Ages there was Christianity and the Infidels. Today there is Democracy and Fascism." And the Soviet dictatorship ostentatiously aligned itself with the democracies.[43] He even went so far as to accept implicitly the Lebensraum argument of the Nazis, writing that the "pacifism" of the two western democracies "comes from the fact that they are satiated, and do not want their digestion disturbed."[44] Everywhere Demartial saw double-thinking and double standards being applied. Whether it be on the Anschluss, German rearmament, Munich, Prague, the colonial question, or antifascism, he saw one set of rules applied to Germany and another set applied to the democracies. Citing Michel Alexandre, Demartial concluded that "Hitler is the natural son of Poincaré."[45]

Looking back after the defeat of France, Demartial could not see the European situation differently. The creation of Czechoslovakia in 1919 had been an attempt by the victorious Allies to create an ersatz replacement for Russia after the disaster (for the West) of the Russian Revolution. Czechoslovakia armed itself therefore to the teeth and became the cornerstone of France's eastern alliance system, all designed to ring Germany in with a buffer of strong states.[46] The Munich accord of 1938 did little to bring harmony to the Czechoslovak Republic. Hungary and Poland demanded and received the return of minorities to them from the Czechs, and the whole affair ended in disaster in March 1939 with open and violent conflict between Slovaks and Czechs. Demartial asked, "The disintegration of Czechoslovakia having given Hitler the opportunity of removing, without war, the threat posed to the German border of a Czechoslovakia under the orders of his adversaries, why would he not have taken it?"[47]

If Munich, and then Prague, were perceived as major setbacks for the western democracies, the Allies made certain that a line was drawn in the sand for Danzig. But did the line make any sense? For Demartial, much as in 1914, at least half of the blame for the outbreak of war in 1939 fell on Allied shoulders. Germany took calculated risks which might lead to war; Britain and France responded. As he put it:

> Hitler had given himself the mission of liberating his country from certain clauses of an unjust treaty. He almost succeeded without war; the only thing that remained was to recover Danzig. He thought that under the conditions offered to Poland, the arrangement would take care of itself. And yet, like twenty-five years ago in the case of Serbia, here were France and England meddling again! It was not enough for them to be gorged with land and riches, to dominate the earth, to be mistresses of the seas. They came, under the mask of pacifism, to impose their law on this Central Europe where they had no business. Hitler took up the challenge. Can one really say that he bears the sole responsibility, or even the principal responsibility for the war?[48]

And, if Polish independence were really the issue, why had the western allies not at the same time declared war on the Soviet Union for its role in carving up Poland?[49]

All of this could be written off, perhaps, as misguided attempts by monomaniacs to deny the truth about the origins of both world wars, were it not for the fact that there was also an attempt to redefine French political culture in its entirety by opening up the question of the meaning of the French Revolutionary wars. The origins of this debate lie with Albert Mathiez, an early member of the LICP's *comité directeur*, who left the organization after a trip to Germany in 1931 convinced him that the Germans were still dangerously nationalistic.[50] The torch was taken up however by his student Georges Michon. As early as 1920 Michon had published an article in the *Annales révolutionnaires* which contained many of the themes which he would elaborate in the late 1930s and under Vichy.[51] Michon developed these themes further in two books published just before and during the Second World War,[52] both of which argued that the French Revolutionary wars had been launched by an unholy alliance of the left, conservatives, and the *émigrés*. Georges Albertini, reviewing Michon's 1941 book, understood very clearly the contemporary implications. It made gripping reading

> for French people who want not only to know about the origins of the revolutionary war of 1792, but also to understand those of the war of 1939 ... One understands thereby how public opinion was intoxicated little by little by the press, to the point where it believed that the kings of Europe wanted to make war on France, which was not at all the case. And the press firebrands did not fail to insist both on the desire for aggression and the weakness of the aggressor. The reader of 1941 cannot help but think of the years 1935-1939, of MM de Kérillis and Péri, of the policy of firmness, and of other strategic anticipations.[53]

By the advent of Vichy a dissenting historical tradition had thus become a cornerstone of the pacifist world view which helps to explain the sectarian condemnations of French foreign policy which had brought the nation to such a pass. Given the crushing defeat of 1940, however, there was also a strong current within pacifist opinion which argued for the acceptance of Vichy and of France's role in the new Nazi-dominated Europe. The *politique du fait accompli* explains much of what was written by such important pacifists as Léon Emery and Félicien Challaye.

Emery counted himself among those who condemned the "ancien régime," that is to say the Third Republic. He applauded wholeheartedly Pétain's meeting with Hitler at Montoire and the policy of official collaboration which issued from it. There seemed to be nothing about the Third Republic which Emery would defend; he condemned the venality of the press, what he called the "seductive theory" of the law of the majority, the influence of the communists on French foreign policy, and finally even Parliament itself. Parliament was meant to regulate and control political life, especially in foreign affairs. Instead it was the seat of total confusion about the most important subject, Franco-German relations, and it was "in the worst confusion, in obscurity, in ignorance, that the French people were led to war."[54] His utter condemnation of the Third Republic is seen in the conclusion to a 1942 article:

> If we wish to regain our freedom, remain loyal to the socialist ideal, that is all well and good, but we would be fooling ourselves completely if we linked these goals to a decadent regime which betrayed them while claiming to serve them. Real politics to save and re-establish great social values is not that which borrows from the pseudo-revolutionaries who have suddenly become strangely conservative without even realizing it. In the past we are talking about are many things which need to be rejected without hesitation; the question now is to reorganize a modern State in a Europe which will create new solidarities. Let us hope that the return of at least a relative peace will allow us to give these tasks an ever greater stimulus.[55]

Emery had already gone on record in a speech made in Bordeaux for Déat's Rassemblement national populaire (R.N.P.) as being in favor of the integration of France into Hitler's European dream. "France," he said, "can only be resurrected by a peace that is as quick as possible, a peace which cannot be conceived in any other form than a continental entente in which Germany will of necessity play the principal role. The choice to be made does not depend on our mood, or on our past or present doctrines; it must be made, we must do it despite ourselves through a simple consideration of reality and of the general interests of our country."[56] Vichy was the new beginning after the paralyzing uncertainty of the Phoney War, and Pétain's "words of wisdom, courage and hope" to the defeated nation in June 1940 were heard "with immense relief" by a nation waiting for a "new chance of salvation and renewal." That renewal would be on German terms in a new European order. As Emery told his audience, "we had to decide to attempt as the conquered that which we had not wanted to do before the war when we could have discussed things as equals. The problem remains before us, we all know it is that of a Franco-German collaboration for the realization of peace and the organization of Europe."[57]

A third explanation for the *dérive pacifiste* under Vichy must be the visceral anticommunism of many of the new-style pacifists. Although virtually all of the leaders of the prewar LICP were of the left, not one of them was a member of the Parti communiste français (PCF); in fact, some of them (Georges Pioch, for example) were among those excluded from the party during the Bolshevization drive of the early 1920s. The LICP from its inception had been the object of attacks by the PCF, and the minority members who resigned from the LDH central committee in 1937 were among those who saw clearly what was really going on in the Moscow Purge Trials.[58] The apparent cupidity of Soviet diplomacy in signing the Nazi-Soviet Pact of August 1939 served only to confirm the worst suspicions of most integral pacifists. As Emery said in his speech to the R.N.P. in Bordeaux, even *if* a British victory over Nazi Germany were possible, it would be bought at the price of a very long war of attrition which would bring about the complete exhaustion of Europe; and "in this exhaustion would be born the disorder and the violence which would prepare the invasion of Bolshevism in all its forms. Thus, this supposed victory would in reality be our loss, condemning us to a fate that would make us pine bitterly for that of today."[59]

The anti-Soviet stance was also somewhat paradoxically accompanied by a profound dislike of the Anglo-American alliance. Part of this was probably due to the long-standing distrust of the "City of London," the "powers of money" and the British arms manufacturers which had been grist to the left-wing pacifist mill in the 1930s. The argument took on a sharper focus under Vichy, however. Paul Rives, for example, writing scarcely six weeks before the Normandy invasions, argued that the Second World War was not primarily about territorial gains but about socialism, a project which was completely foreign to the Anglo-American mind-set. "This is why," he wrote, "the Anglo-Americans prefer the more or less sporty terrorism of aerial combat to ground fighting."[60] Emery was even more explicit, regarding the conflict already in the first stages of its death throes in terms as profoundly anti-American as anti-Soviet. Germany was the bulwark against Sovietization, but its collapse would turn the entire European continent into a battleground between the competing forces of Russian and American imperialism.[61]

Fourthly and finally, the continued reliance on prewar pacifist networks and ties of friendship helps to explain some pacifists' collaboration under Vichy. Déat, for example, had been one of the defenders of Gerin when the latter was imprisoned for conscientious objection in 1935. Both were *normaliens.* It was perhaps not unnatural that Gerin should accept a position at *L'Œuvre* writing an occasional literary review column.

The clearest example, however, of the existence of a pacifist network which transcended the politics of Vichy and made very strange bedfellows indeed, must be the story of Michel Alexandre, an assimilated French Jew who was excluded for racial reasons from his position as professor of philosophy at the Lycée Henri-IV in Paris. Alexandre and his wife Jeanne were leading lights in the French peace movement from the Great War onwards. They were active in the SEDCOG, the *Ligue des droits de l'homme*, the *Ligue internationale des femmes pour la paix et la liberté* (LIFPL), the *Comité de vigilance des intellectuels antifascistes* (CVIA) and many other groups during the interwar years. Their commitment to pacifism was unshakable, to the point where in the postwar period Alexandre rose to the defense of pacifist friends who had collaborated with Vichy, notably Emery, Marcelle Capy, and Challaye.

Emery was sentenced to five years in prison, a fine of 12,000 francs, and civic degradation on 28 November 1945. His predicament provoked a very organized campaign on the part of a wide circle of friends, including Michel Alexandre, to secure his acquittal and release.[62] In an examination for discovery before the examining magistrate in late 1944, Emery was accused of having collaborated with a number of newspapers in the northern zone which were directly under the thumb of the Germans, and of having given several public lectures and undertaken certain missions for the R.N.P. He was also accused of antinational sentiments in his private correspondence.[63] Emery defended himself against these charges by arguing that Germany was unbeatable on the continent in 1940, and hence that France had to seek a *modus vivendi*, with a view only later to a mediating role between the Germans and British. He underscored that "this conception of collaboration was obviously exclusive of all acts of warfare whatever they might be, and aspired instead toward the rapid re-establishment of peace." He had done nothing more than be what he called "an obstinate partisan of what is called today the western federation and which is advocated by so many newspapers."[64] In his final statement to the court, Emery declared that "the continuity of my political attitude … cannot therefore have been determined by the defeat and the occupation. I am of those who for twenty years have tried to deflect the catastrophe which we saw returning"; he argued that this in no way meant acceptance of fascism, nazism, or racism.[65]

Alexandre also testified in defense of Challaye in 1945,[66] but privately admitted that Challaye had "nevertheless written some stupid things, which he doesn't even realize."[67] Two years later he wrote again to the courts, this time on behalf of Marcelle Capy, who had suffered at the hands of both the Gestapo and then the courts of the Liberation. Capy was a former president of the LICP. In 1943 she was denounced as a communist in the Lot, arrested, interrogated and had her house searched by the Gestapo. In 1944 she returned to Paris where Claude Jamet, a member of the prewar *comité directeur* of the LICP, asked her to write some "human interest stories" for *Germinal* which she agreed to do in order to earn some money. After the Liberation, charges were filed against her because of these articles, but ultimately they were dismissed as groundless. In 1947 she was surprised not to receive her electoral voting card. When she made inquiries she learned that a second dossier had been opened against her on the basis of the original allegations, and that she had been sentenced to "national indignity" *in absentia*.[68]

Georges Pioch seems to have been one of the few high-profile pacifists of the interwar period to emerge unscathed from Vichy. Despite having written for *L'Œuvre* in the early years of the war, Pioch was forbidden at some point to write in the Parisian press, at least according to a 1943 letter to Alexandre in which he wrote, "I continue to purge, not without a certain intimate pride, the honor which is done me by the passants of the occupation to be booted out of the so-called Parisian press, and, even, forbidden to publish at all."[69]

Conclusion

In December 1939 Jean Nersessian, a former student of Michel Alexandre's and at the time a *khâgneux* in Royan, wrote to his former teacher that "you taught me to think, to be myself, to the extent that that is possible." Alexandre responded with an affectionate note in which he cautioned Nersessian to write "nothing a police colonel could not read without emotion." Times were dangerous, even before the Nazi invasion, and in a prescient foretelling of what was to come, for himself, for other Jews, and for some pacifists, Alexandre wrote "we are headed toward the monasteries."[70]

The rule of silence and the search for refuge were about to become the order of the day—or at least, for some. For others, though—perhaps even for the majority of old-style and new-style pacifists—the rule of silence was broken in strange ways in the collaborationist press or in an acceptance of French defeat. At the same time refuge was provided to old pacifist friends on the run from Vichy or the Germans. Faced with the crisis of war, many French pacifists thus opted for peace as the "ethic of ultimate ends."[71] What is interesting is that they continued to argue their essentially ethical position from a uniquely political perspective which is what distinguishes them from their British counterparts. The prescriptions for the renewal of France—acceptance of the German victory, integration of France within the new European order, a rejection of the militarist tradition in French history, and a visceral anticommunism—were all essentially *political* positions, taken and held by intellectuals and activists for whom, in the words of Henri Jeanson, "la paix prime le droit."[72] Binding them all together, and giving them sense in a nonsensical world, were pacifist networks and ties of friendship stretching back to at least 1914.

Because of the moral and political ambiguities posed by Vichy, Alexandre's withdrawal to the "monasteries" can also be interpreted in a more metaphorical way. It is a prophetic statement of the fate reserved for French pacifism in the postwar world in which the message of peace, hope and national reconciliation has been stripped away from the peace movement.[73] Like the Church before it, French pacifism has been expelled from the body politic in France, silenced and forced back on itself in a retreat to a secular monastery. This is a process which, arguably, began long before the Second World War, but which reached its apotheosis thereafter.[74]

In the final analysis one is left with something of a conundrum in the strange case of the pacifist response to the Second World War. For many pacifists, both old-style and new-style, the coming of war was their worst nightmare come true, the failure of twenty years of political activity aimed at staving off precisely this eventuality. For the new-style pacifists particularly, the advent of war was a bitter confirmation of an historical analysis of French and European diplomatic history which stretched back to the days of the Great War and also drew inspiration from a dissenting view of the French Revolution. For other pacifists, Vichy was something to be accepted and endured, if not perhaps welcomed; feeding this tacit acceptance of Vichy was an anticommunism which also reached back to the early 1920s and had certainly gained strength as the PCF seemed to change its tune on the peace question during the 1930s. For many pacifists, the Second World War was a time of political withdrawal, of *attentisme*, of hoping for better days to come. In many ways, then, French pacifism's response to the Second World War mirrored that of France generally.

Notes

The author would like to thank the Faculty Research and Development Programme at Concordia University for the funding which made the preparation of this chapter possible, as well as Kenneth Mouré, Martin Alexander and Nicolas Offenstadt for their helpful comments on an earlier draft.

1. Norman Ingram, "Ambivalence in the Post-Second World War French Peace Movement, 1946-1952" in *The Pacifist Impulse in Historical Perspective*, ed. Harvey L. Dyck (Toronto, 1996), 397-412.
2. Norman Ingram, *The Politics of Dissent: Pacifism in France, 1919-1939* (Oxford, 1991), 1-16.
3. The seminal work on British pacifism is Martin Ceadel's *Pacifism in Britain, 1914-1945: The Defining of a Faith* (Oxford, 1980).
4. Ingram, *Politics of Dissent*, 6. See also Sandi Cooper, *Patriotic Pacifism: Waging War on War in Europe, 1815-1914* (New York and Oxford, 1990); and Roger Chickering, *Imperial Germany and a World without War: The Peace Movement and German Society, 1892-1914* (Princeton, 1975).
5. Norman Ingram, "Romain Rolland, Interwar Pacifism and the Problem of Peace," in *Peace Movements and Political Cultures*, ed. Charles Chatfield and Peter van den Dungen (Knoxville, 1988), 143-64.
6. There is considerable debate over the definition of "feminist pacifism" in the interwar period. Some writers prefer a broader definition than the one I have used.
7. See the correspondence between Jouve and Romain Rolland in which she details the tribulations of life in occupied Paris in Fonds Romain Rolland, Bibliothèque nationale, Paris.

8. See Henriette Sauret to Jeanne Mélin, Paris, 21 February 1942, in Bibliothèque historique de la ville de Paris (BHVP), Fonds Bouglé, Correspondance Jeanne Mélin, Boite 47(2), in which she recounts the death of her husband, the writer André Arnyvelde, at the hands of the Germans in the Compiègne camp.
9. See below.
10. Théodore Ruyssen, "Et, de nouveau, voici la Guerre … !," *La paix par le droit* (hereafter cited as *PD*), 49, nos. 9-10 (September-October 1939), 251.
11. Ibid., 250.
12. Théodore Ruyssen to Edouard Daladier, Combloux (Haute-Savoie), 4 September 1939, in ibid., 253-4.
13. Théodore Ruyssen, "La Paix qui suivra la Guerre: Appel aux bonnes volontés," in *PD* 50, no. 1 (January 1940), 2. Cf. Ruyssen, "Travaux d'approche pour la Paix future," *PD* 49, nos. 11-12 (November-December 1939), 294-305.
14. Georges Scelle, "La Base de la paix future," *PD* 50, 1 (January 1940), 5.
15. Ibid.
16. Ibid., 6-8.
17. Ruyssen in "Notre Assemblée Générale: Paris, Dimanche 28 janvier 1940 (Suite et Fin)," in *PD* 50, nos. 3-4 (March-April 1940), 72.
18. On *L'Effort* see Yves Bongarçon, "Un Vichysme de gauche? Les débuts de *L'Effort*, quotidien socialiste lyonnais (1940)," in *Cahiers d'histoire* 32, no. 2 (1987), 123-46.
19. Théodore Ruyssen, "La Justice en marche," *L'Effort* I, 37 (9 September 1940), 1. I am indebted to Nicolas Offenstadt for drawing my attention to these articles in *L'Effort*.
20. Ibid.
21. Ibid.
22. Théodore Ruyssen, "Révolution et Tradition," *L'Effort* I, 72 (14 October 1940), 1.
23. Ibid.
24. Ibid.
25. Margueritte, an important although somewhat muddled writer and thinker within the ranks of pacifisme nouveau style, argued early and hard for acceptance of the Vichy regime, as well as for the incorporation of France into a new Nazi-dominated European order. He condemned the Free French and those who attacked Vichy, and strangely seemed to assume that France would take its place in the new Europe almost as if by divine right, thus betraying a misapprehension of what the Germans were actually thinking. See Victor Margueritte, "Deux Routes? Non, une Seule," *L'Effort* I, 24 (27 August 1940).
26. Archives départementales du Gard (hereafter cited as ADG), Série 5 J 8, Théodore Ruyssen to Auguste Laune, the administrator of the Association, Grenoble, 9 June 1946. On 4 June 1946 Laune had already written to Ruyssen that "En ce qui concerne le curriculum vitae en double exemplaire pour les dirigeants, j'ai l'intention de dire que notre président [Ruyssen] remplace à la Fac des lettres de Grenoble l'indésirable Chevalier,—que notre secrétaire g[énér]al [Prudhommeaux] a été nommé conseiller municipal de Versailles à la Libération,—que notre secrétaire de rédaction, rédacteur au Ministère des Aff. Etrang. [J.L. Puech] avait été déstitué par Vichy et que le trésorier [Laune] est un des 4 négociants de vins du Gard qui ont refusé des affaires avec les allemands. Je pourrais leur répondre en outre ce que me disait tout dernièrement Paganelli [Prefect of the Gard and President of the Nîmes group of the APD]: 'Nous sommes des résistants de toujours, d'avant la lettre et leur remettre les No. de la revue' …" See Auguste Laune to Théodore Ruyssen, Nîmes, 4 June 1946, in ADG, Série 5 J 8.
27. Ruyssen to Laune, Grenoble, 9 June 1946, ADG, Série 5 J 8.
28. Jules Prudhommeaux to Auguste Laune, Versailles, 18 June 1946 in ADG, Série 5 J 8.

29. One thinks of André Trocmé, Jacques Martin, Sylvain Broussaudier, among others. Cf Nicolas Offenstadt, "Histoire de la Ligue internationale des combattants de la paix (LICP), 1931-1939," Mémoire de maîtrise d'histoire contemporaine, Université de Paris I—Panthéon-Sorbonne, 1991. Offenstadt argues (p. 265) that "incontestably" more of the leadership of the LICP became collaborators than resisters, and in this he is certainly correct.
30. Sylvain Broussaudier, "Souvenirs d'un Combattant de la Paix," 119. Memoir deposited in the Institut d'Histoire Sociale, hereafter cited as the IHS.
31. See the interesting essay by Peter Farrugia, "The Conviction of Things not Seen: Christian Pacifism in France, 1919-1945," in *Challenge to Mars: Essays on Pacifism from 1918 to 1945*, ed. Peter Brock and Thomas P. Socknat (Toronto, 1999), especially 108-12. Farrugia freely admits that "French religious pacifism of the interwar years was indeed confined to a very small minority," but argues that "The resistance activities of a significant group among French Christians who rejected violence prove that interwar pacifism did not necessarily lead to wartime collaboration."
32. See Ingram, *Politics of Dissent*, 122-5; Emmanuel Naquet, "La Société d'études documentaires et critiques sur la guerre. Ou la naissance d'une minorité pacifiste au sein de la Ligue des droits de l'homme," in *Matériaux pour l'histoire de notre temps* No. 30 (January-March 1993), 6-10. See also Archives de la Préfecture de Police, BA. 1775.
33. See Félicien Challaye, *Georges Demartial. Sa vie, son oeuvre* (Paris, n.d. [1950]), 6-7. There is also an account of the expulsion in "Le Dossier Demartial (défense, témoignage et plaidoirie)," in *Evolution* 30 (June 1928), 34-50.
34. René Gerin and Raymond Poincaré, *Les responsabilités de la guerre: Quatorze questions par René Gerin, ancien élève de l'Ecole normale supérieure, agrégé des lettres: Quatorze réponses par Raymond Poincaré de l'Académie française* (Paris, 1930).
35. See René Gerin, *Honneur et patrie: ou comment j'ai été exclu de la Légion d'Honneur* (Paris, 1934).
36. Norman Ingram, "Defending the Rights of Man: the Ligue des droits de l'homme and the Problem of Peace," in *Challenge to Mars: Essays on Pacifism from 1918 to 1945* ed. Peter Brock and Thomas P. Socknat (Toronto, 1999), 115-33.
37. Georges Demartial, *La légende des démocraties pacifiques* (Paris, 1939).
38. Ibid., 5-8.
39. Ibid., 24.
40. Ibid., 30
41. Cited in ibid.
42. G. Ferrero, *La fin des aventures*, cited in ibid., 31.
43. Demartial, *Légende*, 31 and 32.
44. Ibid., 37.
45. Ibid., 79.
46. Georges Demartial, *1939: La guerre de l'imposture* (Paris, 1941), 15-16.
47. Ibid., 23.
48. Ibid., 36.
49. Ibid., see especially pp. 39-42 on "La Trahison russe".
50. See James Friguglietti, *Albert Mathiez, historien révolutionnaire (1874-1932)*, trans. by Marie-Françoise Pernot (Paris, 1974), 226-7.
51. Georges Michon, "Robespierre et la guerre," *Annales révolutionnaires* (Organe de la Société des études robespierristes), Vol. 12 (1920), 265-311.
52. Georges Michon, *Robespierre et la guerre révolutionnaire, 1791-1792* (Paris, 1937) and Georges Michon, *Le rôle de la presse en 1791-1792: La Déclaration de Pillnitz et la guerre* (Paris, 1941).

53. Georges Albertini, Review of Georges Michon, *Le rôle de la presse en 1791-1792*, in *L'Atelier*, Saturday, 15 November 1941, 6.
54. Léon Emery, "Français, vous avez la mémoire courte," *L'Effort*, 6 August 1942, 2.
55. Ibid.
56. "De Munich à Montoire: Conférence faite à Bordeaux sous les auspices du R.N.P., le 27 juin 1942" by Léon Emery, 7. Typescript in IHS, Archives Léon Emery [hereafter cited as IHS/ALE]: Dossier "Ecrits de la 2e guerre mondiale".
57. Ibid.
58. Ingram, *Politics of Dissent*, 126-7, 205-6, 216, 221-2, and Ingram, "Defending the Rights of Man."
59. Emery, "De Munich à Montoire," 7.
60. Paul Rives, "Avenir Européen du socialisme," *Germinal* no. 1 (28 April 1944), 1.
61. Léon Emery, "Le Socialisme et la paix," *Germinal* no. 2 (5 May 1944), 2. The anti-Soviet/anti-American *Leitmotiv* found an echo in the French peace movement of the Fourth Republic. See Ingram, "Ambivalence in the Post-Second World War French Peace Movement, 1946-1952," in *The Pacifist Impulse in Historical Perspective*, ed. Harvey L. Dyck (Toronto, 1996). Guy Lemonnier says that for him the Americans were a worse threat to France than the Soviets. Interview with Guy Lemonnier, Institut d'Histoire Sociale, 16 July 1998.
62. See IHS/ALE Dossier "Léon Emery. Son Procès."
63. Ibid., "Déclaration du 15 déc. 1944 devant M. le Juge Mallet," 1.
64. Ibid.
65. Léon Emery, "Déclaration finale" in IHS/ALE, Dossier "Léon Emery. Son Procès".
66. See Michel Alexandre to Monsieur le Président (of the Chambre civique perhaps), Limoges, 12 July 1945, in Bibliothèque municipale de Nîmes [hereafter cited as BMN], Ms. 801/VII.1. There is a copy of this letter in the Bibliothèque de documentation internationale contemporaine FΔRés 348. Challaye describes his hearing to Alexandre in a letter dated 24 July 1945 in BMN, Ms. 801/VII.1.
67. Undated handwritten note by Alexandre on the Challaye affair, but certainly written before Challaye's trial. In BMN, Ms. 801/VII.1.
68. See Marcelle Capy to Michel Alexandre, Paris, 13 January 1947 and "Témoignage de Michel Alexandre," dated 22 January 1947 in BMN, Ms. 801/VII.1.
69. Pioch to Alexandre, Paris, 30 December 1943, in BMN, Ms. 801/V.5.
70. Jean Nersessian to Alexandre, Royan, 10 December 1939, and Alexandre to Nersessian, Clermont-Ferrand, early 1940, in BMN, Ms. 801/V.5.
71. This idea, taken from Max Weber, underlies much of Martin Ceadel's analysis of British pacifism. See Ceadel, *Pacifism in Britain.*
72. Henri Jeanson, "La Paix prime le droit," in *La Flèche* (21 March 1936), cited in Charles Rousseau, "La Dénonciation des Traités de Locarno devant le droit international," *PD* 46/4 (April 1936), 198.
73. See Ingram, "Ambivalence," in *Pacifist Impulse.*
74. See the immensely suggestive analysis of Sergio Luzzatto, *L'impôt du sang: La gauche française à l'épreuve de la guerre mondiale, 1900-1945* (Lyons, 1996).

Chapter 8

CRISIS AND CHANGE IN THE JUVENILE JUSTICE SYSTEM, 1934-1945

Sarah Fishman

On 27 August 1934, at the correctional boy's school for juvenile offenders on Belle-Ile, an island off the coast of Brittany, wardens badly beat an inmate for the offense of having begun to eat his dinner before the signal bell. A riot broke out and in the general chaos, all the boys managed to escape. However, they were recaptured after the local police offered townspeople and vacationing tourists a 20 franc reward for the return of any fugitive. Publicity about the incident inspired outrage, prompting Jacques Prévert to write "Children's Hunt," a poem that popular Paris cabaret singer Marianne Oswald set to music.[1]

The public response to the Belle-Ile incident marked a major reversal of attitudes. In the nineteenth century, boys incarcerated for committing crimes met with indifference at best. Yet by the 1930s, public opinion had shifted to one of sympathy. Books and articles consistently referred to public correctional houses for minors as *"bagnes d'enfants"* (children's penal camps), making explicit the comparison with adult penal labor camps (*bagnes*) that were renowned for harsh conditions and cruel wardens.[2]

From 1934 on, scandals continued to rock public institutions for delinquent boys, so called correctional houses (*maisons de correction*). In part, media attention to the issue remained high because a journalist for *Paris Soir*, Alexis Danan, picked up the campaign. After the painful loss of his five-year-old son, Danan found himself drawn to children's issues. The Belle-Ile children's hunt moved

Notes for this chapter begin on page 170.

Danan to dedicate himself to attacking abuse in correctional houses. In 1937, as public interest had begun to flag, Danan exposed the "Eysses Affair," the case of Roger Abel, a 19 year-old inmate at Eysses who died of tuberculosis after being subjected to six months of solitary confinement combined with a severely restricted diet, including an entire week of a diet reduced to dry bread and water on three occasions.

Although juvenile inmates had died in public institutions prior to the 1930s, boys previously written off as incorrigibly bad now gained public sympathy owing to the conjunction of a number of trends.[3] In particular, rising panic about a broadly perceived population crisis had reached a critical point by the 1930s, as demographers finally convinced political leaders of the need to act and elite concern had percolated out into wider public consciousness. Secondly, a circle of experts on juvenile crime from across a spectrum of fields, doctors, psychiatrists, psychologists, legal experts, policymakers, social workers and moral reformers, had pressed for a major overhaul of France's system from the start of the twentieth century. Their efforts attracted little public support until they finally succeeded in linking France's population crisis and its treatment of delinquent youth, which they argued wasted potentially productive future citizens. Fortuitously, the reformers found powerful support in journalists like Danan, who proved exceptionally effective at presenting cases so as to gain maximum public attention and sympathy for incarcerated juvenile delinquents, now referred to as "martyred children."[4] Interestingly, until after World War II, girls in public institutions remained more or less invisible.[5] The much smaller number of girls both in court and in public institutions only partly explains the lack of attention. Their invisibility resulted primarily from two factors, the cultural vision of the delinquent girl as a sexually precocious threat to the social order, and the exclusion of girls from the masculine concept of productive citizens—meaning workers and soldiers—reformers wrote about rescuing.[6]

For delinquent boys, a series of scandals in the 1930s magnified longstanding problems with a system widely criticized in knowledgeable circles. The media focus on correctional house abuses linked the problems to a widely shared sense of cultural pessimism and alarm about youth and family breakdown that intensified in the 1930s. However, while the media scandals sparked Popular Front reform efforts, the Third Republic's political paralysis, combined with strong institutional resistance to change from within the juvenile justice system in the 1930s, prevented deep and lasting changes in the system. Only the crisis of France's defeat in 1940 and the resulting creation of the Vichy government provided the final catalyst. Remarkably, the Vichy government, an ultra-conservative, authoritarian regime fixated on the need for France's moral regeneration, did not react with punitive ardor to the upswing in wartime juvenile crime rates. The evolution of the juvenile justice system illustrates perfectly Pascal Ory's argument that Vichy policy left its deepest marks where, "without knowing or wanting to, it followed in the footsteps of the Popular Front and sometimes, more profoundly, of the entire Third Republic."[7] Vichy proved critical in France's evolution from a primarily punitive system to the current therapeutic and rehabilitative one.

The Evolution of the Juvenile Justice System to 1930

The juvenile justice system, or combination of age-specific laws, separate courts, procedures and institutions for juvenile offenders, only came to be a system in France in the late nineteenth and early twentieth centuries. Article 66 of the Napoleonic Penal Code of 1810 defined 16 as the age of penal majority and created a second distinction based on the notion of "discretion" (*discernement*), which corresponds to our notion of penal responsibility. A minor who knowingly chooses to break the law and understands the potential consequences acts with discretion. Under the age of 16, a minor acquitted under Article 66 as acting without discretion could either be returned to parents or taken to a "correctional house" for a period not to exceed the age of 21. Article 69 stipulated that minors who acted with discretion received a correctional sentence not to exceed one-half the adult sentence. The Penal Code did not require separate courts or procedures for minors.

While it mentioned correctional houses for minors acquitted under Article 66, the Code never mandated separate institutions for minors.[8] By the early nineteenth century, a new view of childhood had emerged that contradicted the Catholic doctrine of children as inherently sinful. Jean-Jacques Rousseau articulated the notion that education profoundly shapes the impressionable but untainted minds of children. Romanticism went a step further, constructing childhood as a special time of innocence. In other words, if a child went astray, adults were probably to blame.[9] Placing wayward children in jails filled with criminal adults only compounded the error. Another broad development relevant to criminal children was the rise of the reforming state. Modern political and economic structures led to the shift from the old regime's sporadic and bloody punishment of offenses to what Michel Foucault described as the carceral universe. The modern prison represented just one of many new institutions, including schools, hospitals, asylum, which attempted to categorize and control individuals.[10]

The new view of childhood combined with the increasingly interventionist state created pressure for a new response to child criminals. Penal administrators slowly worked toward segregating minors and adults, starting in the 1820s with separate quarters for minors. The first prison specifically for minors, La Petite Roquette, opened in Paris in 1836.[11] However what eventually prevailed for child criminals started as a private initiative. Many nineteenth-century observers attributed rising social upheaval and crime to urbanization. They considered overcrowded modern cities an especially unhealthy environment for young people.[12] An agricultural youth colony could correct the pernicious influence of city life, reform young criminals and teach them good work habits by exposing them to the hard but healthy rigors of rural life.[13] The first such institution, Mettray, opened in 1838 and became the model for work farms for criminal children across Europe.

The Second Republic mandated separate institutions for young criminals who acted without discretion. The law of 5 August 1850 on the education and patronage of youthful prisoners created public agricultural penitentiary colonies (*colonies pénitentiaires)* for delinquent minors where they would be raised with "harsh discipline," receive "moral, religious, and professional education," and perform agricultural labor.[14] Although "penitentiary colony" remained the official designation for public institutions for delinquent minor boys until 1927, the term correctional house was more widely used.

By the late nineteenth century, several key developments inspired a rethinking of laws and institutions for minors. First, the Third Republic paid more attention to children than any previous political system. In control of the government by 1880, republicans turned their attention to primary education, creating public schools to mold good republican citizens. Second, the French adopted Stanley Hall's concept of adolescence as a distinct, universal and transitional phase of life, a period of growing mental abilities combined with new and unstable emotions linked to sexuality. According to the theory, adolescence, a phase of "physical and mental anarchy," spawned the rebelliousness that explained behavioral problems like stealing, running away from home or sexual promiscuity. Such a view led many people to advocate new ways of controlling adolescent misbehavior, from trying to extend schooling for the vast majority of young people who finished at age 13, to attempting to stem the erosion of apprenticeships, to using new psychological insights to treat problem adolescents.[15]

Another key late nineteenth-century factor motivated new approaches to the problem of juvenile crime. Secular republicans, enamored of scientific and medical models of society, increasingly viewed France's decline, confirmed by the 1870 defeat, in biological terms. According to historian Robert Nye, secular republicans popularized scientific writings that viewed such factors as reduced geopolitical status, declining birth rates, mental illness and crime, in evolutionary terms as signs of degeneration. But the Lamarckian orientation of French evolutionary theory maintained that degeneracy could be reversed with environmental improvements, ultimately tempering biological determinism. In other words, even those enamored of medical models of crime and deviance believed the damage could be fixed. Those who saw the child criminal as a frightening precursor of evolutionary decline also believed such children represented the best hope for reversing the process.[16]

If a minor's misbehavior resulted from an adolescent crisis, or a medical condition, or from parental abuse, did he or she not deserve treatment rather than punishment? Children's reformers, including Henri Rollet, judge and founder in 1888 of the French Children's Rescue Union, and Paul Flandin, Paris Court of Appeals judge, took up the cause of delinquent children. In 1890, Rollet and Flandin created the first Committee to Defend Children in the Justice System (*Comité de défense des enfants traduits en justice),* inspired largely by developments in America, the birthplace of separate juvenile courts with specialized judges and simplified procedures. Members of the Committee advocated, through books, articles and Rollet's review *L'enfant,* replacing penitentiary colonies for children with specialized, rehabilitative institutions. By the end of the century, the Paris Committee to Defend Children in the Justice System had spawned related committees in Marseilles, Bordeaux, and Lille.

Although by the early twentieth century, most specialists and professionals in the field considered children in the justice system to be victims, the broader public continued to manifest fear of child criminals. In 1900 *Le Petit Parisien* described a band of prowlers in Belleville as "la bande des malfaiteurs, dite bande des Apaches," giving urban youth gangs their designation.[17] By 1908, the popular review *Lecture pour tous* asserted that apaches had produced a veritable "tidal wave of trash and blood …"[18] Alarm about youth gangs hindered the struggle to ease the harsh and punitive nature of public institutions. However, efforts to revise the legal code succeeded on the eve of World War I. The law of 22 July 1912 reflected both the public's punitive desires and the protective concerns of children's activists. To reconcile punishment and protection, the determination of the child's discretion under Article 66 remained in effect.

The law of 22 July 1912 declared that all minors under age 13 acted without discretion and their cases, decriminalized, would be handled by the Civil Court's Advisory Chamber. Minors between 13 and 18 fell under the jurisdiction of a Court for Children and Adolescents (*Tribunal pour enfants et adolescents*) (TEA), a Court of First Instance in each jurisdiction assigned cases involving minors. TEA judges and investigating magistrates were, if possible, to have some expertise in juvenile law. The law required the appointment of a defender to every charged minor. Names, photographs and descriptions of offenses or crimes involving minors could no longer be published, ending the sensationalized accounts of child criminals that until then had regularly appeared in the *Gazette des Tribunaux.*[19]

In line with the new "environmental" view of child crime, the 1912 law required not just an investigation of the crime but also a social investigation of the minor's personality, school performance, work habits, friends, activities, family and neighborhood. Still, for minors 13 to 18, courts first determined discretion. Minors under 16 who acted with discretion received attenuated adult penalties that could be served in juvenile penitentiary colonies. Minors 13 to 18 acquitted as acting without discretion could be sent to private institutions or public juvenile penitentiary colonies to the age of 21, or be returned to their parents with or without probation. Although it rested on the Penal Code's fulcrum of discretion, the 1912 law's social investigation and probation policies reflected significant shifts in ideas about children who commit crime. The application of the 1912 law awaited the end of World War I. By then, however, experts in rapidly developing fields were already disillusioned with the 1912 law's shortcomings.

The Expert View: A System in Crisis

By the eve of World War II, specialists in juvenile crime were profoundly unhappy with France's system. After the fall of France in 1940, as their part in the national search for what went wrong, delinquency experts pointed at France's inability to redeem its wayward children. Nearly everyone who wrote about the problem of juvenile crime in the 1940s agreed first that France had fallen seriously behind countries like Italy, Switzerland, the United States, Belgium, and even Germany.[20] In spite of the 1912 law's improvements, France's juvenile justice system continued to rest on the notion of punishment rather than rehabilitation. Legal specialist André Perreau lamented, "It is unfortunate that the country that gave birth to Descartes has let itself be surpassed in the application of Cartesian principles by countries like England, the United States, Belgium, Italy."[21]

France, the homeland of modern scientific methods, had in the nineteenth century been in the forefront of both child psychology and criminology. In the early twentieth century, French doctor Georges Heuyer pioneered the field of pediatric neuro-psychiatry. In 1914, Heuyer began studying children at a mental institution, in "special education" classes, and at La Petite Roquette, children he eventually designated "abnormal". Heuyer and his students played a critical role in the movement to reform France's juvenile justice system. The neuro-psychiatrists asserted that a criminal act committed by a young person, even in cases involving poverty or abuse, signaled a potential mental or emotional condition. They insisted that the proper response to child crime was not punishment, but observation, testing and rehabilitation, a point affirmed by experts on both sides of the nature/nurture divide. The French considered themselves intellectually advanced, but institutionally backward.[22]

The creation in 1927 of a National Committee to Defend Children in the Justice System signaled the coalescence of criminologists, jurists, social workers, psychologists and psychiatrists interested in juvenile delinquency into an interest group. Coordinating efforts to rehabilitate minors and formulating suggestions for improvements in the system, the National Committee indicated a new desire to bypass turf quarrels between public institutions and private charities, between legal and psychiatric approaches.[23] The juvenile delinquency establishment in the 1930s sponsored a series of meetings and published journals like *Pour l'Enfance Coupable*, *Défense de l'Enfance Malheureuse*, and *Voix de l'Enfant*. Not surprisingly, specialists in juvenile crime hardly spoke with a unanimous voice. Some reformers stressed medical or hereditary causes, some focused on the family, and others on personality. Some reformers advocated rural camps, others favored apprenticeships that would meet practical needs, and one group advocated scouting as a way to reeducate minors. However, nearly all juvenile delinquency specialists believed that minors, with young minds and habits more susceptible to change, could be treated if properly diagnosed.

Alongside changing ideas about childhood, the concept of adolescence and fresh theories about crime, the twentieth century witnessed a major reorientation in prevailing cultural concerns. A new set of social and political fears finally crowded out older anxieties about degeneracy and the born criminal previously triggered by criminal youth.[24] Nationalist concerns had strengthened while the relative size of France's population began to reflect the long decline in France's birth rate. If, as was commonly assumed in France, the size of a nation's population indicated national strength, then the slowed growth of France's population would endanger its world position.[25] The opinion that France needed babies and a healthy population eventually allowed children's reformers to reshape popular attitudes towards children and adolescents who commit crimes. Rather than portraying juvenile delinquents as precociously perverted or degenerate children destined for a life of crime unless firmly repressed, children's activists redefined the problem in demographic terms. France needed the contribution of its entire population and could no longer afford to waste a portion of its youth, whose misdeeds resulted from a widely acknowledged decline in family values.

Writings in the field emphasized that a majority of the children who found themselves in trouble with the law came from broken or otherwise "defective" families. The media echoed experts' ideas. Most minors who broke the law were troubled and in need of protection rather than repression. "The young delinquent, in fact, is more than just a guilty person; most often he is also a victim."[26] Blaming the family for juvenile delinquency anchored the problem to a larger, more popular cause. The breakdown of the French family not only caused the birthrate to drop, it ruined the children who were born. Reformers Fernand and Henri Joubrel stressed the demographic importance of rehabilitating France's youth by citing Goethe. "To save a man is good ... But to save a child is to save a multiplication table."[27]

Events subsequent to France's defeat in 1940, and especially the captivity of 1.6 million French prisoners of war, reinforced the emphasis on broken families. Experts declared that the sudden absence of nearly 600,000 POW fathers caused the threefold increase in the number of minors appearing before the courts. In fact, a careful look at studies done during the 1940s fails to confirm a link between paternal war captivity and delinquency, yet specialists were blinded to the shortcomings of their statistical analyses by their zeal to link delinquency to family crisis. Such a connection popularized the issue, drew government attention, and deflected blame for the juvenile crime wave from the young people involved.

Although experts of the 1940s stressed family breakdown as a primary cause of juvenile crime, they also insisted that nature played a critical role. A child was born with certain innate characteristics, somehow shaped by heredity, further manipulated by early childhood conditions and illnesses, upon which a healthy or unhealthy environment exerted its influence. Most specialists asserted that if a minor committed a crime or a misdemeanor, it most likely manifested some kind of condition or "character trouble" (*trouble de caractère*).[28] Juvenile judge Georges Epron asserted that "80 percent of young delinquents concern the doctor or the psychiatrist" and that a delinquent minor should be considered "a sick person who needs to be made better."[29] My reading of case files casts grave doubt on the validity of assertions that nearly 80 percent of delinquent youth suffered from serious emotional disturbances. Nevertheless, most specialists firmly believed it. Therefore, a system to rehabilitate delinquent minors should respond with diagnosis and treatment, not punishment.

Reformers pressed for changes in the entire juvenile justice system, from the first contact with a minor accused of breaking the law, to judicial procedures, to final placement options. First of all, many people involved with the system criticized the determination of discretion as unimportant and diversionary. The question should not be whether a minor acted with discretion, but what condition caused the minor to misbehave. "The delinquent act matters less than the delinquent. The delinquent act represents the past, the delinquent the future."[30]

Under the 1912 law, minors who had been arrested could be placed in preventive detention during the investigation if they represented a danger to the community. Judges placed most minors in preventive detention in private charities, but some minors landed in separate quarters of adult pretrial detention jails (*maisons d'arret)* for a month or more. Separate quarters notwithstanding, most juvenile delinquency experts viewed preventive detention as unnecessarily punitive and dangerously corrupting. Reformers had a solution for both the lack of information about the minor and the evils of preventive detention: Observation Centers where minors awaiting hearings could be observed and receive medical, intelligence and psychological testing. The Observation Center's report would allow judges, most of whom had no training in child or adolescent psychology, to make better decisions about placement and treatment.[31]

Final placement options also required serious reform. Nearly everyone in the field, including prison administrators, condemned existing public institutions for delinquent youth as ineffective and cruel. Even if correctional houses had not been abusive, most of the juvenile delinquency establishment considered them fundamentally flawed. Juvenile delinquents needed treatment, education, rehabilitation, counseling and job training, not punishment and meaningless labor to break them in. Arguing against Mettray's philosophy of removing children from the cities, experts pointed out the irrelevance of the skills adolescents gained through rural labor and their need for urban occupational skills that would allow them to earn a living after release.[32]

In addition to severing juvenile courts from the rest of the judiciary, some experts began to advocate that the Penal Administration (*Administration pénitentiaire*), the bureaucracy that ran prisons in France, cede control of state juvenile institutions. Severing ties both indicated a new philosophy and allowed a critical change. Institutions for minors would no longer be required to hire personnel from the ranks of prison wardens. So long as those who staffed juvenile institutions had been hired and trained by the Penal Administration and rose through its ranks, juvenile institutions would retain their repressive atmosphere. Even Jean Bancal, Administrative Services Inspector of juvenile institutions run by the Penal Administration, agreed on the need to separate the two administrations.[33]

Despite the level of alarm in the 1930s, reforms had already begun in the late 1920s. For example, while of little immediate import, a decree of 31 December 1927 formally renamed state institutions. Penitentiary colonies instantly became Supervised Educational Houses (*Maisons d'éducation surveillée*). While changing names hardly equaled altering actual practice at these institutions, it articulated the desired outcome. Therapeutic initiatives had also already begun at several public institutions.[34]

Thus the media scandals of the 1930s played nicely into the hands of the reformers, setting Penal Administration officials on the defensive. In 1936, the Popular Front, among its many ambitions, hoped to overhaul the juvenile justice system. Although several efforts to rewrite the 1912 law failed, Popular Front Justice Minister Marc Rucard initiated reforms in two Supervised Educational Houses, Saint-Maurice and Saint-Hilaire.[35] The reformers intended to shift the focus at Supervised Educational Houses away from punishment and towards rehabilitation, education, and job training. Educators, recruited from students attaining their Certificate of Pedagogical Aptitude, replaced prison wardens and provided minors at Saint-Maurice with schooling and job apprenticeships.[36]

Despite the shared desire to undertake serious reforms, turf wars erupted between the ministries of National Education, Justice and Public Health. In addition to ministerial competition, reforming administrators and educators at both Saint-Maurice and Saint-Hilaire met with fierce resistance from within the institutions. Saint-Maurice reformers complained in May 1938 that the director's recalcitrance had prevented them from instituting changes promised during their training sessions, low student-teacher ratios, sports facilities, the end of locked doors, barred windows and corporal punishments. Saint-Hilaire reformers faced similar problems until a new director arrived. François Dhallenne accepted the post in 1938 on the condition that he choose his administrative team. Dhallenne, who described in vivid detail the "lamentable state" of the facilities at his arrival, immediately began the reconstruction of the facility, initiated new pedagogical methods, introduced sports like soccer and basketball, established agricultural training and substituted positive reinforcement for physical punishment and confinement.[37]

The Popular Front took another decisive action. Mettray, once considered the model agricultural colony for boys, finally came to be seen for the stark and brutal labor camp it was.[38] Journalist Alexis Danan had compiled a thick folder on Mettray, replete with cases of children who had died from mistreatment and administrators who pocketed the public funds Mettray received for each ward. Hoping to avoid "incidents concerning children's penal camps that have lately fed the scandal press," the government, after sending inspectors to Mettray, withdrew all public wards, forcing Mettray to close.[39]

The Popular Front, facing severe domestic and international crises, failed to accomplish fundamental legal reforms or to initiate changes at other state institutions. The mid-1930s reformist impulse stalled in 1938, as the rising threat of war increasingly dominated the government's attention. The general mobilization of 3 September 1939 removed most of the younger, reform-minded directors and personnel from Supervised Educational Houses, with occasionally disastrous consequences.[40] However, shortly after France's defeat in June 1940, demobilized reformers returned to both Saint-Maurice and Saint-Hilaire. Developments in the juvenile justice system continued on the previous trajectory from punitive to therapeutic, despite the drastic change of regime in the summer of 1940.

The Vichy Regime and the Juvenile Justice System

A major about-face in that trajectory would not have been surprising, given both the juvenile crime situation after 1940 and the nature of the Vichy regime. After Marshal Philippe Pétain became Prime Minister in the midst of the crisis of June

1940, he destroyed the Third Republic, which he considered a corrupt system responsible for France's defeat. Once the National Assembly voted full powers to Pétain on 10 July, he passed four Constitutional Acts establishing a new government, the French State, with its capital in Vichy. Pétain became the head of state; initially Pierre Laval became the head of the government.

Historians agree that the French State at Vichy had its own domestic program centered on a renunciation of the Third Republic and all its values: democracy, individualism, liberalism and egalitarianism. While Vichy was hardly monolithic and various factions continually clashed, nonetheless more traditional Maurrassian, Catholic conservatives like Georges Lamirand and Paul de la Porte du Theil controlled Vichy's youth and educational policies. They believed that the wrong political system in France had produced a soft population that was accustomed to excessive leisure and debilitated by such dissolute activities as drinking, dancing, jazz, and movie-going. Conservatives considered this factor critical in explaining the debacle of 1940. Because impressionable children and adolescents represented the best hope for reshaping national values, France's youth ranked high in Pétain's list of priorities. His interest in youth dated to the 1930s when Pétain lobbied unsuccessfully to be appointed Minister of National Education in Doumergue's 1934 government.[41] In a December 1940 "Message to Youth" Pétain explained, "The unhealthy atmosphere many of your elders grew up in slackened their energies, weakened their courage … You will learn to prefer the joy of difficulties overcome, rather than easy pleasures."[42]

Vichy quickly directed its attention to the public schools, hoping to emphasize traditional morality, obedience, hierarchy and respect for authority, to restore Catholic Church influence, and especially to inspire reverence for Pétain. However Vichy primarily worked to purge the schoolteaching corps of Jews, free masons and any other teachers disloyal to Pétain. Outside of school, Vichy both created and encouraged certain kinds of youth movements like the Chantiers de la Jeunesse and the Compagnons de la Jeunesse, both of which combined aspects of military boot camp, scouting, and public service.[43]

Vichy officials, conservatives and the fascist press also lashed out at a new youth counterculture that flourished in Paris and several other large cities in the summer of 1940. The *zazous*, France's swing kids, engaged in behavior that rejected Vichy's moral order. The young men grew thin mustaches, wore long jackets and short pants with big baggy knees and narrow ankles over white socks. The young women used heavy makeup and hair dye, wore short, pleated skirts, jackets with large padded shoulders, and heavy, flat shoes, defying the conservative, feminine look promoted by Vichy and women's magazines.[44] The *zazous* constituted an easy target because they so visibly thumbed their noses at Vichy's values. The rebellious youth listened to jazz, an African-American invention, and preferred idling in cafés or dancing in clubs in the Latin Quarter or along the Champs Elysées to working.[45]

The conservatives in charge of youth policy at Vichy wanted clean-living, hard-working youth, with girls focused on marriage and motherhood and boys on contributing both labor and babies to France. Juvenile crime statistics at the very least indicated the bankruptcy of their efforts. The number of minors appearing in court tripled by 1942 from the prewar averages. In the 1930s, the number of minors appearing before juvenile courts hovered between 10,000 and 12,000. By 1940, that number had risen to nearly 16,000 in spite of the disruption of the courts during the Battle of France, and it peaked in 1942 at nearly 35,000 cases.[46]

The combination of a runaway increase in juvenile crime rates and an authoritarian regime insisting on the moral regeneration of France's youth might have triggered a crackdown. Instead, Vichy accelerated efforts to render the system less punitive and more therapeutic. Conservatives projected their anger and frustration at adolescent misbehavior onto the *zazous*. The tendency to blame rising juvenile crime rates on POW absence also mitigated the repressive response, which was ultimately trumped by demographic concerns magnified by the defeat. Juvenile justice reformers argued that France was paying the price for its system's backwardness, successfully linking delinquent minors to cultural alarm about families and France's population. Even though they felt personally maligned by the 1930s correctional house press scandals, two key players at Vichy, Joseph Barthélemy, former chair of Mettray's board of directors who became Minister of Justice in 1941, and Jean Bancal, Administrative Services Inspector, agreed that the system needed change. In another irony, the authoritarian nature of Vichy freed administrators from the need to persuade elected officials or public opinion, enabling them quickly to accomplish certain goals.

First, reforming staff returned to both Saint-Hilaire and Saint-Maurice by the fall of 1940 where they continued their programs. Efforts to ease the penal nature of the institutions received an unexpected boost from Germany. To meet German demands for French labor, in 1943 a law instituted an obligatory labor service, the *Service du Travail Obligatoire* or STO. However, working for the Penal Administration earned an exemption from the STO. As a result, many educated and skilled young men who never would have done so under other circumstances flooded into the ranks of Supervised Education, the bureaucracy that ran correctional houses.

The new monitors drastically changed the atmosphere in Supervised Educational Houses during the last two years of the war. The smaller age gap between the wards and the new monitors, and a sense of shared hardship and insecurity created by the war facilitated closer relations between the two. "In 1943, we had no distractions, we concentrated our lives on the establishment … we shared our pleasures with the kids and they did not try to escape. The German police were everywhere, and events drew us closer together." Historian Jacques Bourquin argues that monitors identified more closely with their wards owing to the era's blurring of the line between acceptable and delinquent behavior. Nearly everyone took part in illegal black market activities. The monitors working for Supervised Education to avoid the STO were skirting, if not breaking, the law. Under those circumstances, monitors, who lived on site with the wards, occupied a similarly gray behavioral zone. One wartime monitor admitted, "Kids arrived at the Supervised Educational Center for misdemeanors that we ourselves sometimes had committed."[47]

The reformers at Saint-Maurice and Saint-Hilaire lightened the penal atmosphere and nurtured greater confidence between monitors and wards. Saint-Hilaire initiated a system based on scouting methods (troops, back to nature projects) while Saint-Maurice pupils created a representative council to make decisions about dividing up extra food and spending money. The improvements brought about by the influx of new monitors avoiding the STO were of necessity short-lived. After France's liberation, most of the new teachers left. Yet Bourquin argues that the experience provided models of what these institutions could become.[48]

A school for boys 13 and under also experienced notable improvement during the war, and, for the first time, the administration showed interest in improving the dismal conditions at public institutions for delinquent girls, called Preservational Schools. Historian Béatrice Koeppel paints a grim picture of the two public girls' institutions, Clermont and Cadhillac, on the eve of the war. By 1943, according to Koeppel, the treatment of delinquent girls underwent "an upsurge of severity that proved to be inhuman, indeed even absurd."[49] However, in 1943 Supervised Education sent Dominique Reihl, psychologist and reformer, to inspect Cadhillac. In October 1944 Reihl took over as director.

Institutional reforms were far from complete by the time of the Liberation in 1944, and were barely underway for girls. But people at all levels of the system accepted the goals of doing away with barred cells, sleeping cages, manacles, corporal punishment, and of providing education, job training, psychological counseling, and even recreation. Movement in that direction continued after the war, eventually resulting in a system that, by the late 1970s, virtually ceased incarcerating juveniles for minor offenses.

Vichy also undertook a major overhaul of juvenile law and procedures. Appointed Minister of Justice in January 1941, Barthélemy quickly appointed two high-level administrators, Jean Bancal from the Administrative Inspection Services, and Fernand Contancin, director of Penal Administration, to draft a new juvenile code. They presented their bill in September 1941 to an appointed

Council, which included nearly all of France's key experts for one day of discussion, revisions and approval.

The resulting ordinance of 27 July 1942, which superseded articles 66-69 of the Penal Code and the 1912 law, ended discretion as the pivot of the system. Rather, the new procedure established a two-tiered system. Minors arrested first appeared before a preliminary court, the Advisory Chamber, that determined either that the case should proceed or that the minor should be released. If the Chamber decided not to release the minor, the case would be forwarded to the Court for Children and Adolescents. In the law's second major innovation, every minor whose case was forwarded to a Court for Children and Adolescents would automatically be sent to an Observation Center, one of which would be available in each region. Thus the Advisory Chamber functioned as a triage, eliminating trivial cases from court dockets. Serious cases could then be given greater attention, allowing for extensive testing and observation of each minor. In other words, an adolescent charged with a crime or misdemeanor received essentially two "trials," in the original meaning of the word, one of the infraction and one of the self, in the Observation Center, both of which determined the minor's final placement. The 1942 law's preamble claimed that the new law definitively replaced the correctional concept underlying the penal code with "reeducation." Article 28 simply stated that Public Supervised Educational Institutions (*Institutions publique d'éducation surveillée*)(IPES) to rehabilitate minors would replace Supervised Educational Homes, giving the same facilities their third designation in fifteen years.

Article 28 did not specify how the newly renamed institutions would operate, but the preamble outlined the goals. Rather than a large, prison-like structure, many small pavilions would house and educate minors in a family-like setting. A minor entering the school would start in a fairly Spartan pavilion that provided few amenities. As the minor improved, he or she graduated to a nicer pavilion with more amenities and privileges. Such a system rewarded good behavior, motivated students to want to improve themselves, and inspired them to emulate the institution's best rather than its worst pupils.[50] While the state could require such a system only in its own institutions, the law also required Justice Ministry accreditation of private institutions. Although three Observation Centers opened in the Paris region and several others in cities across France, Vichy never passed an application decree for the 27 July 1942 law; therefore the courts never adopted the new judicial procedures.

While the 1942 law moved predominantly in a therapeutic direction, it mandated punitive institutions for the most difficult offenders and included three extremely authoritarian provisions. The law limited avenues of appeal, abolished the automatic appointment of a defense counsel to all minors and ended attenuated penal sentences for older minors, making some minors theoretically liable for capital punishment. No doubt the Free French Justice Commissioner in Algiers, Fernand de Menthon, had these provisions in mind when he called certain aspects of the 1942 law "unacceptable."[51]

Post-War Developments

Vichy forced the Provisional Government's hand. Legal scholar Henri Donnedieu de Vabres noted the 1942 law, "had the merit of creating a 'psychological shock,' of provoking salutary emulation …"[52] The 1912 status quo had become unacceptable. If Vichy could overcome resistance to change, interministerial, divisions and professional rivalries to draw up a new code, then the new government in embryo wanted to prove it could do so as well. In April 1944 de Menthon named a committee in Algiers to study the problem of delinquent youth. After the Liberation, de Menthon forwarded the Algiers' report to a Paris committee headed by Hélène Campinchi, notable resister and family law attorney. Within six months the bill had been written, approved and issued as the Law of 2 February 1945, a law that continues to be the foundation of the juvenile justice system in France. The series of reforms that took place in 1945 represented the culmination of many trends dating back to the turn of the century. But the Vichy years represented a critical watershed, reviving the reforming impulses that had nearly disappeared by 1939, paving the way for the 1945 law with changes in the legal code, in placement options, and in institutional operations.

Publicly, however, the postwar Provisional Government renounced everything Vichy had done, concealing the institutional, legal, and personal continuities. For example, in a postwar review of Vichy's 1942 law, the Information Ministry concluded, "in disguising the existing evil, Vichy, rather than abolishing it, aggravated it."[53] Since the experts who had worked on the 1942 law had no interest in calling attention to their wartime roles, they never contradicted the picture presented to the public. Nevertheless, in fundamental ways the 1945 law closely resembles the 1942 law. For example, both laws completely discard the concept of discretion.[54] They both mandate a two-stage procedure to dispose quickly of less serious cases. The 1942 law used the Advisory Chamber, whereas the 1945 law created the Children's Judge (*juge des enfants*), a completely new kind of magistrate, to dispatch simple cases quickly. Like an investigating magistrate, the Children's Judge questions witnesses, collects information about the crime, and orders medical, psychiatric or family reports. After investigating, the Children's Judge can close the case, admonish the child, return him or her to a parent or guardian with or without probation, request further social or medical studies, place the minor in an Observation Center, or order further investigation of the crime. Finally, the Children's Judge forwards serious cases to the Children's Court (*Tribunal pour Enfants*) over which the Children's Judge presides. Over the years, the Children's Judge has become the linchpin of France's system, not just judging, but also counseling, advising, warning, encouraging, and directing to other available resources both delinquent and "at risk" children and adolescents.

Children's Judges send a small number of cases on to the Children's Court, which determines the minor's innocence or guilt. The 1945 law limits the options for minors under 13 who can be returned to their parents, sent to a private institution, or to a public welfare, educational, job-training, or "medico-pedagogical" institution. The Children's Court can place minors aged 13 to 18 in a Public Institution of Professional, Supervised or Correctional Education, the fourth designation since 1927 and one that only loosely corresponded to existing state institutions. If deemed to be in the minor's best interest, Children's Courts can convict minors over 13 and sentence them to criminal penalties, fines, or jail time. All measures can include permanent or provisional probation to age 21.

Most people in France came to believe the version of events proposed by authors of the 1945 law, that the Liberation of France wiped the slate clean, allowing them to create an entirely new system. By the 1970s, the 1945 blank slate interpretation had become gospel to such an extent that nearly everyone in the field greeted Michel Chauvière's book, provocatively entitled *Enfance inadaptée: l'héritage de Vichy*, with shock, anger, and rejection. Chauvière argued that the political and institutional situation at Vichy represented a moment of rupture and innovation. While his book deals primarily with maladjusted children, a sector that tried but initially failed to incorporate delinquent minors, Chauvière also describes the 27 July 1942 law on delinquent children as a key event that capped ten years of effort and gave juvenile penal law its autonomy. "It took circumstances as exceptional as the war, occupation and Vichy to break at the same time, administrative habits and the traditions of private charities, eventually mixing them up under the banner of the interest of society and the superior interests of children."[55]

A recent article on the juvenile justice system referred to the 2 February 1945 law as "the founding act of juvenile justice."[56] But the war and Vichy proved critical to the rapid creation of a total system for many reasons. The shock of the defeat and collapse of the Third Republic, by validating criticism of the previous system, made throwing old systems out conceivable, even necessary. The situation created by the war and occupation, shortages, the black market, a growing wage/price gap, contributed to the huge increase in the number of minors who got in trouble with the law, a situation bound to worry a regime pinning much of its hopes of remoralizing France on the younger generation and obsessed by the size and health of France's population. The Vichy government, despite its regressive and repressive nature, paved the way for deep reforms. Its authoritarian structure removed the roadblocks of parliamentary debate and public criticism. Out of mistrust, Vichy also pushed a powerful player in the field, National Education, to the sidelines. Vichy's clerical impulses forced the integration of Catholic and other religious experts and institutions with the secular authorities and social service agencies. The very fact that Vichy succeeded in writing a new juvenile justice code in 1942 provided major incentive to the resistance authorities to prepare their own reforms even before France was liberated. The Provisional Government felt the need to act quickly to repair the damage done to France's children by the war.[57]

Thus, despite the denial of everything prior to 1945, postwar reforms built on efforts undertaken during the war. Even the highly significant innovation of the Children's Judge actually refined the 1942 law's Advisory Chamber system to clear the docket of less serious cases. An innovative change in 1945, the Children's Judge continues to function as the central figure in the juvenile justice system, determining which minors undergo testing, which cases will be forwarded to the Children's Court, and centralizing information and access to a wide range of social services. Another postwar change, called for since the 1930s and advocated by a key player in 1942, Jean Bancal, was a law in September 1945 that severed Supervised Education from Penal Administration.

Conclusion

The system has evolved considerably, but the 1945 law, still in effect, set the direction, based on the evolution most experts in the 1940s envisioned. Since 1945, the system has continued to become ever less punitive and carceral. In the 1950s, Children's Courts sent some twenty percent of minors aged 16 to 18 to public institutions, although by then most such institutions were halfway houses (*foyers de semi-liberté*), small group homes where minors lived but left to go to jobs or apprenticeships during the day, returning in the evening for schooling or counseling.[58] At that time, the state had 2000 places in its institutions, supplemented by 20,000 places in private institutions.[59]

In the 1970s, public institutions were renamed again, becoming Special Institutions of Supervised Education (*Institutions Spéciales d'Education Surveillée* or ISES). Former Children's Judge Jean Chazal asserted that neither public nor private institutions resembled in any way the former correctional houses. Staffed by specialized educators, under the direction of "psychopedigogical and child neuro-psychiatric technicians," the ISES surrounded delinquent minors with a family atmosphere in a liberal system open to the outside world, based on confidence in the students, the value of the group, and self-government by the students. ISES took occupational training very seriously.[60] The percentage of minors sent to public institutions declined throughout the 1950s, 1960s, and 1970s. By 1973, according to a report by Marc Ancel, courts placed only three percent of delinquents aged 16 to 18 in public institutions.[61] Although it never happened, in 1975 a study commission, chaired by Jean Costa, judge and former director of Supervised Education, proposed "ending all incarceration—preventive detention and prison sentences" for all minors under age 16.[62]

In the 1980s, the Justice Ministry once again initiated a series of reforms. In 1987, a law prohibited the provisional detention of minors 13 to 16.[63] In 1989, the Supervised Education Direction was renamed the Judicial Protection of Youth Direction (*Direction de la Protection Judiciaire de la jeunesse*) highlighting the emphasis on protection rather than supervision or reeducation.[64] Then Justice Minister Pierre Arpaillange instructed a team to study reforming the 1945 law in three ways: improving procedural guarantees for minors; maintaining specialized jurisdictions; and developing "ways for minors to make reparations for damages caused."[65] Until most recently, France's concession to "get tough" policies involved trying to ensure that delinquent minors repay society for the damage they have done, rather than lengthening prison sentences or treating more minors as adults.[66] Arpaillange insisted that he had no intention, despite his call for restitution, of reopening what he called "closed centers" (*centres fermés*), advocating a variety of placement options, institutions and foster families for judicial authorities who needed quickly to remove a child from the home.[67]

For the first time in many years, a series of incidents in 1997 involving minors seriously reopened the question of France's juvenile justice system. In May of 1997, two teenagers stabbed a 15-year-old boy to death in Bondy, Seine-Saint-Denis for refusing to turn over his watch, and later that year a gang of adolescent boys raped a 14-year-old girl in Strasbourg.[68] Intense media coverage of these incidents raised fears in France of a rising number of violent crimes committed by minors. The anxiety centered on France's growing suburban slums facing high unemployment and poverty and populated by poorly integrated adolescents, often children of immigrants.[69] Responding to such concerns, in May 1998 Jean-Pierre Chevènement, Minister of Interior, sent a confidential letter to Prime Minister Lionel Jospin calling for a major overhaul of the 1945 law. Chevènement advocated separating the protective and punitive functions of Children's Judges, repealing the 1987 prohibition of provisional detention, and reopening punitive institutions for certain delinquents. The letter fell into the hands of the left-wing daily *Libération*, which published it, sparking a lively debate between representatives from the Ministries of Justice, Social Affairs and Interior. When appointed Minister of Justice, Elisabeth Guigou had vigorously defended the 1945 law, arguing that its principles "are not outdated."[70] Quickly, powerful forces from within the juvenile justice system, starting with Guigou, mobilized resistance to Chevènement's proposals. Martine Aubry, Minister of Social Affairs, and a large group calling themselves "children's professionals" rallied to Guigou's point of view. Prime Minister Jospin resolved the dispute by ordering a study of the 1945 law with a view to improving but not ending it.

France's juvenile justice system is extremely, perhaps intrusively therapeutic. Doubtless, such intervention exhibits the usual tendencies, empowering white, middle-class judges, social workers and doctors to intrude into, supervise, and attempt to control immigrant and working-class families. Scholars like Jacques Donzelot and Philippe Meyer extend Foucault's analysis into the twentieth century, when the state, via the new "priests" of the scientific era – doctors, psychiatrists, social workers – extends its power into the supposedly private sphere of the family. Meyer considers children's activists instruments of the state. "In the war waged by the State against irregular families … the child is no more than a pretext and a hostage."[71] Their analyses challenge a naively positivist view of reformers as entirely unselfish and humanitarian. Furthermore, the fact that recent events in the United States have led to movement in the exact opposite direction for juvenile offenders, with states tending to favor increasingly punitive options, argues against describing France's evolution as the "modern" or "normal" path of development. But France's experts had, and continue to have, no doubt about which direction they prefer. As early as the 1920s, juvenile delinquency specialists and activists saw clearly what they hoped to accomplish. Capitalizing on the 1930s press scandals and the crisis of defeat, working steadily in the same direction before, during and after the war, they achieved their goals.

Notes

1. "La chasse aux enfants." Henri Gaillac, *Les Maisons de correction 1830-1945* (Paris, 1970), 288-9.
2. Henri Danjou, *Enfants du malheur. Les bagnes d'enfants* (Paris, 1932); Germain Despres, *Bagnes d'enfants* (Paris, s.d.,); Henri Wallon, *Une plaie de la société: Les bagnes d'enfants* (Bourges, 1934).
3. For nineteenth-century views of child criminals, see Patricia O'Brien, *The Promise of Punishment: Prisons in Nineteenth-Century France* (Princeton, 1982); Kathleen Nilan, "Hapless Innocence and Precocious Perversity in the Courtroom Melodrama: Representations of the Child

Criminal in a Paris Legal Journal, 1830-1848," *Journal of Family History* 22 (July 1997): 251-85.

4. "Martyred Children," *Détective,* 23 January 1935. See also Francois Mauriac, "Child Martyrs!" *Le Figaro,* 10 January 1936; *Le Populaire,* 2 December 1935; *Journal de la Femme,* 13 April 1935.
5. Only in the 1950s did a press scandal involve a girl, Marguerite B, who committed suicide at a public institution. Beatrice Koeppel, *Marguerite B: Une jeune fille en maison de correction* (Paris, 1987).
6. Ann-Louise Shapiro, *Breaking the Codes: Female Criminality in Fin-de-Siècle Paris* (Stanford, 1996).
7. Pascal Ory, "La politique culturelle de Vichy: ruptures et continuités," in Jean-Pierre Rioux, ed., *La vie culturelle sous Vichy* (Brussels, 1990), 229.
8. Gaillac, *Les maisons de correction,* 40.
9. Nilan, "Hapless Innocence," Hugh Cunningham, *Children and Childhood in Western Society since 1500* (New York, 1995).
10. Michel Foucault, *Discipline and Punish: The Birth of the Prison,* trans. Alan Sheridan (New York, 1977); Jacques Donzelot, *The Policing of Families* (London, 1980); Philippe Meyer, *The Child and the State: The Intervention of the State in Family Life* (Cambridge, 1983).
11. On this prison, see O'Brien, *Promise of Punishment*; Kathleen Nilan, "Incarcerating Children: Prison Reformers, Children's Prisons, and Child Prisoners in July Monarchy France" (Ph.D: Yale, 1992); Gaillac, *Maisons de correction.*
12. William H. Schneider, *Quality and Quantity: The Quest for Biological Regeneration in Twentieth-Century France* (Cambridge, 1990), 11-19.
13. Nilan describes the anxiety of social observers about the evil effects of urbanization on France's children "Innocence and Perversity," 48.
14. Gaillac, *Maisons de correction,* 100.
15. Kathleen Alaimo, "Shaping Adolescence in the Popular Milieu: Social Policy, Reformers, and French Youth 1870-1920," *Journal of Family History* 17, no. 4 (1992): 419-38.
16. As early as 1885, French doctor of legal medicine Alexandre Lacassagne contested the strict biological determinism of Italian sociologist Cesare Lombroso's theories of the "born criminal." Robert Nye, *Crime, Madness and Politics in Modern France* (Princeton, 1984), 103; Schneider, *Quality and Quantity,* 72-3; Shapiro, *Breaking the Codes,* 17.
17. Michelle Perrot, "Des Apaches aux Zoulous...ou la modernité des Apaches," in *Enfance délinquante, enfance en danger: Une question de justice* (Paris, 1996), 50.
18. *Le Petit Journal,* 17 November 1907; Gaillac, *Maisons de correction,* 252-3.
19. Françoise Lièvois, *La délinquance juvénile* (Paris, 1946), 33-43.
20. See for example Geneviève Mazo, *Le Centre d'observation et la loi du 27 juillet 1942,* (Paris, 1944), 7.
21. André Perreau, *Le mineur pervers de constitution* (Lyons, 1942), 94, 98; See also Georges Heuyer *Délinquance et criminalité de l'enfance* (Paris 1935), 6; Georges-Dominique Pesle, *L'enfance délinquante vue d'un Centre de Triage* (Paris, 1945), 10; Henri Joubrel, *Ker-Goat* (Paris, 1947), 68, 117; Raymond Valet, *Contribution à l'étude du traitement et de l'assistance de l'enfance anormale* (Lyons, 1942), 15.
22. Michel Chauvière, *Enfance inadaptée, l'heritage de Vichy* (Paris, 1980), 12-16.
23. Chauviere, *Enfance inadaptée,* 24; See also Pierre Videau, *Trois maisons de relèvement du ressort de la coup d'appel de Besançon et de quelques suggestions nouvelles en matière de rééducation des mineurs délinquants* (Gap, 1938), 21; André Beley, *De la prophylaxie de l'acte anti-social chez les mineurs instables* (Paris, 1933). Left out of the emerging synthesis until Vichy, the Catholic

Church undertook its own efforts. Exclusion from the National Committee rested on a continuing anticlerical impulse rather than on differing approaches to juvenile crime.

24. Nye, *Crime, Madness and Politics*, 201-2.
25. Schneider examines the peculiar convergence in France of natalism and eugenics which he attributes both to France's demographic situation—depopulation rather than overpopulation—and to the Lamarckian outlook of French eugenics. Schneider, *Quality and Quantity*, 37-46, 116-22.
26. "René Luaire, *Le rôle de l'initiative privée dans la protection de l'enfance délinquante en France et en Belgique* (Paris, 1936), 4.
27. "Sauver un homme, c'est bien… Mais sauver un enfant, c'est sauver une table de multiplication." Henri and Fernand Joubrel, *L'enfance dite "coupable,"*(Paris, 1946), 14.
28. Judge Chadefaux explained, "The criminal act passes to the second level, it remains only the first acute manifestation of serious problems." In Erwin Frey, *L'avenir des mineurs délinquants* (Paris, 1947), 16; See also Georges-Dominique Pesle, *L'enfance délinquante vue d'un Centre de Triage* (Paris, 1945), 19; S. Cotte, "Rapport sur l'enfance délinquant," *Pour l'enfance "coupable"* 60 (July-September 1945): 2.
29. Georges Epron, "Réflexions sur l'ordonnance du 2 Février 1945 sur l'Enfance délinquante," *Pour l'enfance "coupable"* 62 (January-February 1946): 1.
30. Videau, *Trois maisons de relèvement*, 187.
31. Activists also pressed for training juvenile judges. Roger Albernhe, *La nécessité d'un personnel spécialisé pour s'occuper des enfants en justice* (Montpellier, 1938).
32. Luaire, *Le rôle de l'initiative privée*, 419.
33. *Essai sur le redressement de l'enfance coupable* (Paris, 1941), 64.
34. Gaillac, *Maisons de correction*, 351.
35. Secétariat général du gouvernement, Protection de l'Enfance, Archives Nationales (AN), F60: 608 S1 F, 3 February 1937.
36. C. Brunshwig, 16 November 1936, Secétariat général du gouvernement, Education Nationale, AN, F 60: 427 E 11 A.
37. Gaillac, *Maisons de correction*, 313.
38. See the memoir by former ward Raoul Léger, *La colonie agricole et pénitentiaire de Mettray: Souvenirs d'un colon, 1922-1927* (Paris, 1998).
39. *Paris-Soir*, 8 April 1938; Secrétariat général du gouvernement, Protection de l'Enfance, AN, F60: 608 S 1 F; Gaillac, *Maisons de correction*, 290. Mettray's administrative board and its director Barthélemy, future Vichy justice minister, sued Danan and *Paris-Soir* for 350,000 francs damages. Barthélemy won his libel suit but the court, sympathetic to Mettray's critics, only awarded him 1 franc in damages.
40. Inspection générale des services administratifs, AN, F 1a: 3656.
41. Instead he became Minister of War. Thanks to Martin Alexander for pointing this out.
42. Pétain, "Message à la jeunesse de France" 29 décembre 1940, *La France nouvelle* (Montrouge, 1941), 94.
43. On Vichy's youth policy, see W. D. Halls, *The Youth of Vichy France* (Oxford, 1981); Pierre Giolitto, *Histoire de la jeunesse sous Vichy* (Paris, 1991).
44. Emmanuelle Rioux, "Les Zazous, un phénomène socioculturel pendant l'Occupation," (Mémoire de maîtrise, Paris-X Nanterre, 1987), 15-29.
45. Dominique Veillon, *La mode sous Vichy* (Paris, 1990), 236-9; Jean-Pierre Rioux, "Survivre," *L'histoire* 80 (1985): 94; *Gringoire*, 3 July 1942, 3; Rioux, "Les Zazous," 81.
46. Ministère de la Justice, *Compte général de l'administration de la justice civile et commerciale et de la justice criminelle, Années 1944 à 1947*, Melun, 1953), xxii.

47. Bourquin could not determine if Supervised Education jobs protected Jews, although Jewish wards of both institutions avoided deportation. Jacques Bourquin, "Sur la trace des premiers éducateurs de l'Education surveillée: 1936-1947," *Cahiers du CRIV* 2 (October 1986): 34, 39, 36, 38.
48. Bourquin, "Sur la trace," 39, 37-53.
49. Béatrice Koeppel, "Les temps forts de la rééducation des filles (de Cadhillac à Brécourt): 1935-1950," *Cahiers du CRIV* 2 (October 1986): 69.
50. Ordinance of 27 July 1942, *Journal officiel*. Bancal advocated exactly that system, *Essai*, 67-71.
51. Commissariat à la Justice (Algiers), AN, BB30: 1729, correspondance.
52. Henri Donnedieu de Vabres, "Commentaire," *Recueil Dalloz* (Cahiers 35, 36, Législation, 1945), 175.
53. Ministère de l'information, "Le délinquance juvénile en France," *Notes documentaires et études* 173 (29 October 1945), 4.
54. *Journal officiel*, 4 February 1945.
55. Chauvière, *Enfance inadaptée*, 18, 42-3, 141-5.
56. "L'acte fondateur de la justice des mineurs..." and later, "l'ordonnance fondatrice ... qui affirme la primaute de l'education sur la repression." *Le Monde* (29 May 1998): 8; See also the papers from a 1995 Sorbonne colloquium in honor of the 1945 law, *Enfance délinquante, enfance en danger: une question de justice* (Paris, 1996).
57. Mathias Gardet and Yvonne Le Goïc, "Les enfants perdus et le scoutisme de Ker Goat à La Prévalaye, *Le scoutisme et la rééducation dans l'immédiat après-guerre: Lune de miel sans lendemain?*" Document de l'INJEP no. 21, June 1995, 204.
58. Jean Chazal, *L'enfance délinquante* Que sais-je 563 (Paris, 11th edition, 1983), 88.
59. Chazal, *L'enfance délinquante*, 54; Despite ongoing reforms, Jacques Lerouge, arrested for petty theft, described his life in the mid 1950s in a "maison de correction," a term no longer in official use. He attempted suicide but never saw a psychiatrist, hints at sexual abuse and concludes that his two years provided him only with a "passe-partout pour entrer ensuite dans toutes vos prisons!" Jacques Lerouge, *Le condamné à mort* (Paris, 1996), 121.
60. Chazal, *L'enfance délinquante*, 91-2.
61. Cited in Chazal, *L'enfance délinquante*, 120-1.
62. Chazal, *L'enfance délinquante*, 124.
63. *Le Monde*, 29 May 1998, 8.
64. Agathe Logeart, *Le Monde* 168, "Dossiers et documents," special issue, July-August 1989, 8.
65. "Des modes de réparation du dommage causé par un mineur." *Le Monde* 168, "Dossiers et documents," 8.
66. Conversation with Jacques Bourquin, June 1994.
67. *Le Monde* 168, "Dossiers et documents," 8.
68. John-Thor Dahlburg, "Youths Without Hope Shake the French," *Los Angeles Times*, 27 February 1998, *Libération*, 23 May 1997.
69. A study by sociologist Sophie Body-Gendrot and political scientist Nicole Le Guennec confirms that minors increasingly commit certain kinds of crimes, but they blame economic problems, political disempowerment, lack of social integration, the culture of the street. They warn of adopting Britain and America's repressive policies, which they consider shortsighted given the resulting high recidivism rates. "Par ailleurs, la labellisation des jeunes issus des minorités en criminels potentiels est désastreuse pour le civisime d'une nation." *Le Monde*, 27 May 1998, 9.
70. *Le Monde*, 29 May 1998, 8.
71. Meyer, *The Child and the State*, 11.

Chapter 9

The Liberation of France as a Moment in State-Making

Herrick Chapman

The Liberation endures in the popular imagination as a moment of national regeneration when the French people surmounted extraordinary obstacles to embark on a path of postwar renewal. Liberation brought deliverance from Hitler, of course, but also the immense challenge of restoring democracy after the country had succumbed to near civil war in the final year of the Occupation. It also brought a crisis of public order as de Gaulle's Provisional Government sought to reestablish republican justice amid popular zeal to punish collaborators. Even the simplest matters of housing and feeding the population proved formidable. War had made a million people in France homeless.[1] Labor shortages and the destruction of rails, roadways, harbors, and many a farmer's fields had made food scarce. Yet despite hardship and the seething hatreds that continued to inspire vigilantism well into 1945, most people shared a desire to rally behind de Gaulle's call for unity. When the General and fellow Resistance leaders walked triumphantly down the Champs-Elysées on 26 August 1944 to the cheers of a jubilant multitude, hopes soared that Liberation might enable the country to overcome the effects of the Occupation and the shame of defeat in 1940. Inevitably, disappointments followed. Left-wing idealists watched de Gaulle's new Provisional Government reject their more far-reaching ambitions for reform, and de Gaulle himself became disillusioned in 1945 by the Constituent Assembly's refusal to establish a strong presidency for the Fourth Republic. Still, by the time de Gaulle

Notes for this chapter begin on page 194.

resigned as President of the Provisional Government in January 1946, the French had laid much of the institutional foundation for postwar recovery, including social security, works committees in large enterprises, the first of several major nationalizations in banking and industry, and the beginning of Jean Monnet's experiment in economic planning.[2] With considerable justification the Liberation era, stretching from D-Day to de Gaulle's resignation, found its way into the collective memory as a turning point of more enduring consequence than June '36 or the immediate aftermath of the First World War.

Yet on close examination the contribution of the Liberation to a process of national renewal is more ambiguous. We assume too readily that the *trente glorieuse*, the three decades of astonishing postwar economic growth that ended in the mid-1970s, began right after the Liberation. Strictly speaking they did not. Only in 1949 did the French economy break free from the scarcities and monetary instability that shackled it right after the war.[3] The economic miracle of the 1950s and 1960s owed more to developments after 1945 than to Liberation reforms—to such unforeseen initiatives as the Marshall Plan, the Schuman Plan for coal and steel, and eventually the Common Market. Likewise, one can misread the Liberation as a thoroughgoing rupture with the past, forgetting that in constitutional terms the Fourth Republic differed little from the Third, and that many reforms of 1944-45 had roots in the Popular Front and even Vichy. Although the Resistance and Vichy disagreed on fundamental political principles, the two sides shared a fascination with economic planning and business coordination, anticipating much of the business-state cooperation of the Monnet Plan. Many business, professional, and agricultural associations promoted by Vichy went on to form part of the interest-group infrastructure of the Fourth Republic.[4] Seen from this perspective, the Liberation era appears more continuous with what had preceded it, one chapter in a longer story of renewal running from 1936 to the 1950s.[5]

One way to analyze what was unique about the Liberation era in this longer epoque of renewal is to focus on the process of state-making. As later became apparent, the postwar transformation of economic and social life depended on expanding state authority, and yet in the summer of 1944 no one really knew what would happen when the Provisional Government tried to govern in a traumatized country. Nor could anyone predict confidently what kind of political culture would emerge from the work of restoring public order, mobilizing the nation again for the continuing war against Germany, and launching a postwar recovery. Vichy and Nazi authoritarianism had certainly rekindled people's desire for democracy. But memories of the Third Republic made people leery of the old formulas and eager to bring a higher political morality to public life. If after the Normandy invasion it was clear that de Gaulle would reestablish the rudiments of a republic on the heels of the Allied advance, the true character of a restored state—its particular mixture of democratic, paternalistic, technocratic, and even bonapartist qualities—remained to be shaped through the practical business of government.

To explore how public officials and key societal groups grappled with these uncertainties during the Liberation era of 1944-45, this essay examines two key dimensions of state-making—first, de Gaulle's deliberate, systematic effort to restore state authority "from above," and then the more complex, conflictual, often haphazard process of expanding the role of the state "from below" through citizens's initiatives and government action at the local level. I conclude with a brief assessment of how these two aspects of state-making created new opportunities for politicians, state administrators, and technocratic experts to engage in a process of state-making "from within" after 1945.

State-Making from Above

When the Liberation began, no one had a firmer conviction about the need to restore state authority than did Charles de Gaulle. He had concluded that the defeat of 1940 derived above all from "the feebleness of the state." Putting "the state back on its feet" became for him the "*sine qua non* of the country's recovery."[6] Indeed, everything de Gaulle hoped for from the Liberation—civic order, national unity, success in the military campaign against Germany, formal recognition (and respect) from the Allies, and ultimately the reemergence of France as a great power—depended, in his view, on a strong state. This way of thinking drew on a venerable French tradition of seeing the state, especially its administrative hierarchy and its embodiment in law, as the guarantor of social peace and national integrity in a country battered by a history of domestic upheaval and foreign invasion. It was a view that many French military officers, politicians, and government administrators, whether sitting in Vichy, or London, or a prefecture in Bordeaux, had acquired through professional training and public service.

Given this conviction it remained unclear, even to associates in Algiers, how far de Gaulle was willing to go to restore democracy alongside civil administration. In the early days of creating Free France in London he had explicitly refrained from invoking the rhetoric of democracy for fear of evoking associations with the disgraced Third Republic, and his own monarchical style of leadership troubled even his followers.[7] Roosevelt had withheld support for him for what now appears to have been an unseemly amount of time, partly because he appeared to be unreliable as a standard-bearer of a democratic future for France. Yet, by early 1944 he had done a great deal to disprove the doubters: reaching out to the left-wing resisters in France to build a workable, if deeply fractious, alliance between the external and internal Resistance; calling openly for a new republic and putting legal experts to work on constitutional plans; and establishing the Consultative Assembly in Algiers made up of Resistance spokesmen of every persuasion. Still, suspicions lingered. His announcement that post-Liberation elections would only take place after two million prisoners of war, conscripted workers and deportees had returned to France fed fears that he might postpone elections indefinitely.[8] His frequently-uttered insistence that state restoration be the first objective of a Liberation government did little to eradicate the worry that he remained at heart a latter-day Bonaparte.

Although no one in the Resistance took issue with the principle of restoring the state, many resisters emerged from the Occupation divided over the virtues of actually strengthening state authority. The National Council of the Resistance, an alliance of Resistance groups in metropolitan France, advocated a postwar program of social and economic reform, especially nationalizations, that implied the need for new state controls.[9] And leaders of the Socialist party such as André Philip and Léon Blum viewed the Liberation as a chance to revive the agenda of state-led reform from the Popular Front. Yet, many spokesmen for the internal Resistance, especially such leading intellectuals as Albert Camus, Simone de Beauvoir and Emmanuel Mounier, looked to the individual and civil society, not the state, as the key sites for postwar renewal. They hoped their fellow citizens would be inspired to replicate the solidarities they themselves had found in the underground, solidarities that had the potential to overcome divisions of class and politics that had ravaged the country since the 1930s. Resistance intellectuals, moreover, became impassioned champions of human rights and legal protections against the abuses of state power. About the potential virtue of government action they had less to say.[10] Leaders of the new Christian Democratic party (the *Mouvement Républicain et Populaire* or MRP) also preferred to see national renewal come from civil society rather than government.[11] Communists, too, harbored ambivalence. Although they aspired to state power and labored successfully to win posts in de Gaulle's Provisional Government, they feared a concentration of power in a non-Communist executive and sought to limit the state's capacity to repress the party.[12]

Behind the tension between Gaullists in Algiers, who had struggled in exile to lay a foundation for a vigorous state, and resisters within France, who had lived the nightmare of state oppression and remained distrustful of de Gaulle's ambitions, lay a difference in perspective about the basis of legitimacy for a post-Liberation regime. For the internal Resistance the new republic would acquire its authority from the ascendency of a new governing elite, forged in the heroism and moral schooling of the Resistance and given access to power by a thorough purging of collaborators and a proliferation of local liberation committees. For de

Gaulle legitimacy derived, paradoxically, from both rupture and continuity: a break with the political bankruptcy of the Third Republic and with the usurpation of Vichy; and a reaffirmation of administrative continuity and the capacity of new leaders to restore the agencies of the state to their proper functioning. He hoped to foreshorten the life of liberation committees for fear they would enable the Communist party to establish local independent authority, or "dual power," especially in southern France, where the Resistance had enormous influence even before the Allied landings.

De Gaulle had his first chance to reassert state authority on French soil eight days after D-Day when he made an unannounced visit to the Norman town of Bayeux. This first return to mainland France since he flew to London in June 1940 had just the effect on astonished townsfolk that he had hoped for. "At the sight of General de Gaulle," he wrote later in the inimitable third and first person, "the inhabitants stood in a kind of daze then burst into bravos or else into tears. Rushing out of their houses they followed after me, all in the grip of an extraordinary emotion. … We walked on together, all overwhelmed by comradeship, feeling national joy, pride and hope rise again from the depths of the abyss."[13] Although de Gaulle had not yet perfected the charismatic style of the street processional that would become his trademark by September—walking regally, towering over everyone else with his lower arms swinging up rhythmically as if to thank and bless the cheering multitude, "sailing on the swell of the crowd," as his biographer Jean Lacouture put it—he found it easy to elicit an enthusiastic display of public approval.[14] He worked his way to the makeshift public platform, bedecked with a tricolor streamer and Allied flags, where he told the crowd "to continue the fight today as you have never ceased from fighting since the beginning of the war and since June 1940."[15] Such words helped sew the Gaullist myth of an ever-unified, resistant France and gave people license to forgive in themselves and their neighbors the acts of accommodation to the Germans that had been commonplace during the Occupation, especially in conservative Catholic Normandy where the Resistance had been weak.

Beyond this ceremonial effort to confirm his standing as the leader of liberated territory, de Gaulle came to Bayeux with a further ambition. To establish his own administrative beachhead he brought along François Coulet, whom he named on the spot his *commissaire de la république*, or republican commissar, to represent the Provisional Government in Normandy. Coulet promptly replaced Vichy's sub-prefect in Bayeux with the head of the local liberation committee, telling the latter to "establish French sovereignty at once; show the Allies that we can administer ourselves competently."[16] Coulet then bicycled out to nearby towns, as they became liberated, to invest mayors with authority under the auspices of the Provisional Government and establish connections to local liberation committees, well in advance of British or America efforts to preempt him. Coulet proceeded cautiously, seeking more to co-opt local conservative notables than to stigmatize them as collaborators. He kept local policemen and gendarmes in their jobs.[17] Although Coulet failed in his effort to stop British military authorities from putting into circulation a special currency for liberated territory, he succeeded more generally in winning Allied acquiescence to his administrative coup d'état. As some British and American officials quickly acknowledged, Bayeux demonstrated that de Gaulle could establish order far more effectively than could they.[18]

Success in Bayeux validated several imperatives in de Gaulle's strategy for asserting state authority: as territory becomes liberated, install a republican commissar as a super-prefect of a region; exercise moderation in handling local elites and sitting officials; work in alliance with the local Resistance; and stand up to Allied officials when the occasion requires. Of course it was one thing to pursue this approach in Normandy, where the local Resistance was too weak to challenge de Gaulle's monopoly on authority. A number of de Gaulle's eighteen regional republican commissars, especially in the south, had a tougher time establishing their authority and working with local liberation committees.[19] But for de Gaulle himself the most critical challenge awaited him in Paris, where liberation came in the form of a popular insurrection led by the Resistance and not least by its Communist members. If de Gaulle's chief concern in Bayeux had been to stave off Allied administration of liberated territory, in Paris he sought to secure in deed and not just in word the primacy of the state (and hence his own authority) over the internal Resistance.

De Gaulle achieved this aim by using three key instruments for projecting state authority: bureaucracy, the army, and public ceremony. The Provisional Government's command of the state bureaucracy at the moment of liberation came quickly in the course of the Paris insurrection. De Gaulle's pivot man for this operation was Alexandre Parodi, a distinguished young civil servant who served in the Gaullist Parisian underground as the delegate general of the Provisional Government and whom de Gaulle had telegrammed a fortnight before the insurrection: "speak loudly and clearly in the name of the state."[20] Once the insurrection began, Parodi installed new provisional general secretaries, approved in advance by Algiers, to take over each ministry. These men promptly took up the delicate business of reassuring most ministerial personnel who had served under Vichy about their futures while targeting the most egregious collaborators for dismissal or arrest.[21] In late July, de Gaulle had told the Consultative Assembly in Algiers that "[his] government [had] no intention of suddenly making a clean sweep of the great majority of civil servants, most of whom during the terrible years of the Occupation and [Vichy] usurpation had done their best to serve the public interest."[22]

For the most part de Gaulle's policy of a moderate administrative purge prevailed. In the largest sectors of the bureaucracy—the postal service (PTT), education, and the national railroad (SNCF)—where nearly a million civil servants worked, only about 11,000 were eventually sanctioned for their compromising behavior during the Occupation, and fewer than half of them lost their jobs.[23] The purge was likewise restrained in the ministries of Public Works, Transport, Industrial Production, Foreign Affairs and Finance, striking somewhat more deeply in the ranks of the ministries of Justice, Information, and the Interior. The high civil servants of the *grands corps* tried to "wash the dirty linen within the family," as François Bloch-Lainé put it, outside the glare of public trials, and in the end the overwhelming majority of high ranking bureaucrats, apart from people who held the topmost posts in the Vichy government, avoided sanctions.[24] The administrative machinery of the French state remained intact, more so than after the defeat of 1940 and the great insurrectionary upheavals of the nineteenth century.

At the height of the Paris insurrection, however, Gaullist control of the bureaucracy was hardly complete, nor was it sufficient for eliminating the possibility that the internal Resistance would emerge from the street fighting with a plausible claim to national power. De Gaulle used the second arrow in his quiver, military authority, to strengthen his control over the traditional institutions of the state. He convinced General Eisenhower to send General Leclerc and the French Second Armored Division into the city to complete its liberation, an operation designed as much to secure the supremacy of the army over the FFI (*Forces Françaises de l'Intérieur*, the military wing of the internal Resistance) as to restore French honor. Hence it infuriated de Gaulle to discover when he arrived in Paris on 25 August that FFI chief (and Communist) Rol-Tanguy had along with General Leclerc cosigned the formal acceptance of the German surrender of the Paris garrison. After scolding Leclerc for permitting this symbolic equivalence of army and Resistance, de Gaulle then refused to proceed to the Hôtel de Ville where the National Council of the Resistance awaited him. To do so, he felt, would have conferred to the Council an implied power of investiture. Instead he went straight to what he called "the center"—to the War Ministry on the rue Saint-Dominique where he established his presidential headquarters in the same office that Clemenceau had used to preside over the country in the final stages of the First World War. Under pleading by Parodi and his new police prefect Charles Luizet, de Gaulle finally agreed to make the trip at the end of the day to the Hôtel de Ville, but only after paying a ceremonial visit to the prefecture of police, the other symbolic bastion of the forces of order and the site of the police strike the week before that had ushered in the insurrection.[25] De Gaulle made it clear that in restoring the state, the agencies of civil order and national security came first.

The most important assertion of military authority was still to come with the government's efforts to absorb the FFI into the regular army. On 26 August de Gaulle ordered the high command to begin what proved to be an extraordinarily difficult process. Initially, some FFI units literally refused to assimilate into the army, but de Gaulle gave them little choice. More vexing was the challenge of integrating left-wing resistance fighters, steeped in an ethos of illegality, with the ex-Petainist military professionals and colonial infantry that had assembled in North Africa to join the Allied offensive in southern France. Because the FFI had had the feel of a people's army, many left-wing idealists hoped that it would become the core of a new egalitarian army reminiscent of 1792.[26] But integration remained a top-down, conservative affair. In the newly combined army, few Resistance commanders found the rank and responsibility they felt they deserved. Although with political pressure some FFI units were allowed to remain intact as part of larger, regular battalions, many Resistance fighters had to enter the army as isolated individuals. By winter 1945, amalgamation, though cumbersome as a means of enlarging the army, effectively eliminated the FFI as a base of power for the Resistance left.[27]

One step remained for de Gaulle to restore the state's monopoly over the use of legitimate violence. In late October 1944 he ordered the dissolution of the patriotic militias, a large network of Communist-dominated paramilitary units that had proliferated as part of the Resistance during the final year of the Occupation. The party had continued to recruit FFI men into these militias during the early fall of 1944 as a way to root out collaborators, attack the black market, and intensify local pressure on the government. Some militias refused to disband, and indeed some Communists clung to faint hopes of using the militias to keep open a revolutionary path to power. But by January the party hierarchy foreclosed that option unambiguously. Party chief Maurice Thorez, having returned from his wartime exile in Moscow with Stalin's instructions to pursue a politics of moderation, and with de Gaulle's shrewd gift of an amnesty for desertion in 1940, announced it was time to disarm all remaining militias and to accept "one state, one army, one police."[28] With these words the struggle over divided military authority came to a close.

To restore state authority, de Gaulle also made brilliant use of the third political instrument at his disposal: public ceremony. This aspect of state-making proved no less important than administrative control and military consolidation because at the heart of the Provisional Government lay a nagging uncertainty about legitimacy. De Gaulle had reestablished a democratic republic but neither he, nor his cabinet, nor the complex web of Resistance organizations that lent their support to the Provisional Government had acquired a mandate to rule through popular election. Yet, by the eve of the liberation of Paris few could doubt that de Gaulle enjoyed the overwhelming support of the French people to lead the country. To bridge this gap between popular approval and the lack of an official mandate, and to further strengthen his hand with the Resistance left and the Allies, de Gaulle made a ritual of what has since been described as a republican reinvention of the royal entry.[29]

The Bayeux visit had had something of this quality, but it was in Paris that de Gaulle demonstrated his shrewd mastery of the repertoire of public ceremony. When he finally paid his visit to the Hôtel de Ville he refused to proclaim a new republic, as the revolutionary tradition would have had it, and instead paid homage, not to the Resistance, but to a Paris "liberated by its people with the aid of the armies of France."[30] The next day his processional down the Champs Elysées amidst a crowd of two million people, an assemblage never matched before or since, had the feeling of a coronation, complete with a religious service at Notre Dame.[31] Part monarch, part military hero, part guardian of republican institutions going back to 1940, de Gaulle reached out, as it were, over the heads of the parties and the politicians and even the heros of the Resistance to establish a relationship of mutual gratitude with the crowd.

De Gaulle went on to perfect his version of the royal entry in a series of provincial tours during the autumn that took him to the major cities of nearly every region in the country. At all these stops he followed the same ritual. He arrived with little notice so as to keep control over events and lend his visit an added element of mystery. He began with a public greeting of the key state officials in the area, usually the military commander and republican commissar of the region, whose authority he reconfirmed at a time when communications with Paris were handicapped by the physical destruction of the war. He then went to the prefecture to meet with invited guests, again with the aim of asserting his authority in the company of whatever amalgam of old and new local elites had emerged from the liberation. The visit then culminated with a walk through the cheering multitudes and an oration from the balcony of the hôtel de ville, where he stressed the priority of republican order. Each city visit had special objectives. During de Gaulle's crucial first tour in mid-September to the still politically explosive cities of Lyon, Marseille, and Toulouse, he used the ceremonial review of the troops of the FFI to reassert the military hierarchy and put Resistance commanders in their place. A battle-hardened group of Resistance leaders in Toulouse never quite got over how brutally de Gaulle conveyed to them that their work was over.[32] In Nancy he sought to bolster public morale in the face of the fighting taking place nearby, whereas in Normandy he addressed himself to the burdens of reconstruction. But behind all these visits lay a common objective: to recapitulate the legitimation ritual of 26 August. And the public played its role, thronging into the streets for a chance to see, perhaps even to touch, the first resister of

France, and to perform in a patriotic spectacle of national unity at a time when the poison of division still lingered beneath the surface. De Gaulle played these moments artfully. "Are we in agreement, then?" de Gaulle asked a crowd of 50,000 in the Place du Capitole in Toulouse. "Yes!" people shouted in reply.[33]

By the early spring of 1945 de Gaulle had gone a long way to restore the state along the lines he had envisaged during the Occupation. Formal Allied recognition of his government had finally come in October 1944, the Communist party had retreated from its posture of quasi-revolutionary ambivalence with Thorez's speech of January 1945, and the epidemic of extra-legal retribution against collaborators had diminished. The ongoing military campaign against Germany enabled de Gaulle to preside over the country as an active commander-in-chief at the helm of a people drawn together by a common cause as it had not been since 1940. Public opinion polls revealed that his efforts to restore France to the rank of the great powers, though often rebuffed in the winter of 1944-45 by Roosevelt and Churchill, were enormously popular.[34] If his foreign policy often fell short of its international objectives it certainly served the purpose of shoring up his domestic support.

De Gaulle, of course, hardly deserves all the credit for reconstituting state authority during the first six months of the Liberation period. Alongside him a host of officials, especially his republican commissars, prefects, and ministers (including the Communist members of his government, Charles Tillon and François Billoux), made state restoration a palpable reality in their respective geographical and bureaucratic domains. But de Gaulle's method of state-making—its explicitness, its didactical quality of schooling the country in the necessities of republican order, its constant invocations of "state," "nation," and "France" (and not "the people" or the revolutionary tradition) as the organizing categories of the political community, its ruthless subordination of the Resistance to the institutions of law, administration, and the army—lent a conservative tone to the project. At a time when Communists, Socialists, and the more left-leaning stalwarts of the new MRP thoroughly overshadowed the right in national politics, de Gaulle relegitimized a tradition of centralized, hierarchical state authority that might otherwise have suffered disrepute.

State-Making from Below

As de Gaulle's rhetorical exchange with the crowd in Toulouse suggests, restoring the state involved not just efforts to project authority from above, but also the willingness of people to confer authority from below—to consent, convey approval, even invite the regulatory arm of the state into new areas of daily life.

Likewise, people and the many organizations they belonged to—unions, companies, churches, parties, and associations—fought over how the state's authority should be used in localities and where to draw the boundaries of state intervention. This continual skirmishing over the borders of public and private made every community an arena of state-making during the Liberation era. It pulled a wide variety of social groups, often unwittingly, into the process of redefining the strength and reach of the government's authority.

This struggle to define state authority locally first became evident in conflicts between key state officials, especially the prefects and regional republican commissars, on the one hand, and a vast ensemble of local committees, on the other, notably CDLs (*Comités départmentales de la Libération*), CLLs (*Comités locales de la Libération*), and committees overseeing such matters as purges in professions, the confiscation of illicit profits, price controls, internment camps, and the regional press. This flowering of popular participation in the fall of 1944 had a revolutionary aura to it, reminiscent of committee governance in 1830, 1848, and the Paris Commune. It was, of course, an imperfect form of democracy. The CDLs around the country had few rural representatives (about 8 percent) and a scarcity of right-wing members (80 percent of these committees had left-wing majorities), although women made some notable inroads, comprising 7.5 percent of the members, a great deal more than had served on departmental councils before then.[35] Still, this mobilization of Resistance leadership into an improvised network of local quasi-governmental institutions embodied a spirit of democratic renewal that stood in contrast to de Gaulle's centralized, administrative vision of civic order.

The character of conflict between CDLs and de Gaulle's administrators varied by region and over time. Before the Liberation, de Gaulle's strategists had expected to rely heavily on CDLs as partners in the struggle to assert sovereignty vis-à-vis the Allies. When sovereignty returned swiftly, concern shifted to reconciling the aspirations of liberation committees to govern locally with the desire of administrators to restore the supremacy of the prefects. In the north, where CDLs often lacked a large following and where Allied troops rather than the Resistance were decisive in liberating the territory, commissars and prefects quickly established their authority by relegating CDLs to an advisory role. The CDL in the Morbihan in Brittany, for example, was soon doing little more than holding bimonthly meetings.[36] Next door in the Ille-et-Vilaine the CDL petitioned the prefect with hundreds of proposals, but the latter soon realized he could ignore them.[37]

In the south, where the Resistance had played a more important military role, CDLs had sturdier roots in their localities, a preponderance of radical left-wing members, and the backing of a resurgent labor movement. As a result, they kept the pressure up to intensify the purge and police the black market. In some southern towns CDLs supported factory occupations and the requisitioning of businesses, and they even claimed the authority to override the prefect. When the new prefect in Nice, for example, tried to govern by ignoring the CDL and working closely with the American army, the republican commissar had to replace him or face outright rebellion by the local Resistance.[38] In principle, republican commissars had the authority to bring these committees to heel: they had been given full powers to order arrests, grant clemency, and suspend laws. In practice, given the weakness of the state right after the Liberation and the isolation of much of the country from Paris, commissars had to exert authority gradually, often by cultivating cooperative relationships with the local resistance leaders who dominated the committees. This task proved easier for republican commissars like Yves Farge in Lyon and Henri Ingrand in Clermont-Ferrand, who had been resistance heros in the very regions they were now called on to govern, than it was for their counterparts in Limoges, Toulouse, Montpellier, or Marseille. Still, in all the cities of the south, a give-and-take between committees and state officials made state restoration a process of negotiation at the grassroots and not just a process of imposing authority from above.

Consider the local politics of the purge. Republican commissars struggled to put at end to summary executions by creating special courts that would replace the rough justice of FFI courts-martial and popular tribunals. They also interned hundreds of people, in some areas thousands, to protect them from violence. In a climate of pent-up popular outrage against collaborators, even these measures sometimes proved futile. In Alès in the Gard, 5,000 people stormed the local prison in January 1945 and executed four prisoners—an especially dramatic instance of what went on in many towns for nearly a year after the Liberation.[39] What is most striking is that to restore orderly judicial procedures, republican commissars learned to work with, rather than against, the liberation committees. Henri Ingrand was quite open about his dependence on their cooperation. When a renegade resistance group unleashed a wave of assassinations in the department of the Allier in early 1945 Ingrand called for—and secured—the CDL's public condemnation of the group. In Marseille the pressures for swift justice inspired republican commissar Raymond Aubrac to invent streamlined procedures for official courts that helped placate public passions. He also discovered that he could ill afford to continue commuting the death sentences of condemned collaborators, as he had in his first weeks in power, lest protests over his leniency get out of control. A particularly bloody riot after one such commutation helped convince him, as he later wrote, "to refuse clemency whenever granting it would have in my opinion disturbed public order."[40] In Marseille and elsewhere, left-wing Resistance organizations, often with considerable public support, pushed officials to prosecute and punish more vigorously than de Gaulle's policy of moderation inferred. Republican commissars found themselves serving as mediators between a public dissatisfied with what felt like government inaction and a central administration eager to use clemency to bolster right-wing support for the regime.

As intensive as local pressures were to hasten trials and carry out death sentences, they had little long-term effect on the judicial system itself. Nor did the purge lead to a permanent expansion of the judiciary or alter it as a site of interaction between citizens and the state. In three other areas, however, popular politics had an impact on the shape of the state apparatus and the reach of its authority. The first concerned the police. In fall 1944 republican commissars faced the task of reorganizing local police units disgraced for having served Vichy. French police had long enjoyed a tradition of surviving regime changes relatively unscathed. But this time a police culture of obedience to the state failed to insulate its members from the purge.[41] True, the insurrectionary strike of Parisian police during the city's Liberation did much to redeem the reputation of the force, as did the support many policeman had given to the Resistance. Even so, police responsibility for carrying out Vichy's most heinous policies made it imperative to bring new leadership into local units, recruit more manpower, and let the purge root out the worst collaborators. New blood would also help counteract the timidity in police units that republican commissar Henri Ingrand detected in Clermont-Ferrand, where policemen seemed fearful of taking risks lest some purge in an unknown future call them to task.[42] Meanwhile, the proliferation of patriotic militias, recruited largely from the Communist resistance, offered republican commissars both a danger and an opportunity: a danger, because these units of militant former resisters might serve as the basis of a "people's police" outside the control of the Interior Ministry; an opportunity, because if brought under state supervision they could supplement ordinary police units overwhelmed by burdens of arresting alleged collaborators, requisitioning illicit property, tackling the black market, and providing what amounted to social work in communities disrupted by war.

Several commissars experimented with ways to use militia men to bolster the police—a tactic designed to boost manpower and coopt the local Resistance. In Lyon, Yves Farges brought 800 FFI men and 400 patriotic militiamen into a special police unit under his command.[43] Even in the more politically tranquil Norman department of the Eure, the prefect made similar use of a "*groupe républicaine de sécurité*."[44] In Burgundy, republican commissar Jean Mairey found himself having to tolerate a "*garde civique républicaine*" in Besançon that residents had organized out of frustration with the inadequacies of the local police.[45] The most elaborate use of the militia movement, however, emerged in Marseille, where commissar Aubrac and local Resistance leaders created the *Forces Républicaines de*

Sécurité (FRS), police units supervised by prefects for each department in the region. By the end of September, 3000 men, mostly former members of the Communist resistance, joined mobile FRS brigades. The idea proved so successful that Aubrac thought it would become a model for the rest of France.[46]

To an extent he was right. Manpower needs and a desire to coopt the militias led the Interior Ministry in December 1944 to create a new branch of the national police, the CRS (*Compagnies Républicaines de Sûreté*). Organized into regional battalions under the command of the republican commissars, CRS policemen served in mobile emergency units to handle all kinds of public disturbances, including strikes and demonstrations. Unlike the FRS in Marseille, the new CRS was designed to amalgamate left-wing militiamen and regular policemen who had served under Vichy. Aubrac resented the new structure because amalgamation compromised the political integrity of what he had built in the FRS. But in fact the new CRS, especially in southern France, drew many of its members from the left-wing Resistance, and despite its later association with riot control it initially acquired the image of a "police in the service of the people."[47] Maurice Thorez endorsed it in January 1945 as part of the Communist leadership's decision to accept the unitary authority of the Provisional Government.[48] Indeed, because the CRS helped to integrate party followers into the government branch most commonly associated with republican order, it served to legitimize the party as a responsible partner in government and bolster the image of the national police in the eyes of the party's constituents. Although all this would change during the insurrectionary strikes of 1947 when the Interior Ministry purged the CRS of Communists, the desire of local Resistance fighters to become part of the national police system and the pressure state officials felt to accommodate them gave state restoration a left-wing populist dimension, especially in the volatile south.

So, too, did a wave of working-class agitation in the wake of the Liberation that led to the government seizure of factories and the proliferation of union-dominated management committees—actions that drew state officials into the business of workplace administration well in advance of the major nationalizations of 1945-46. This second arena of grassroots participation in state-making emerged all over France, but it happened most prominently in two places: in the coal fields of the Nord and the Pas-de-Calais, where miners made it clear right after their territory was liberated that they would not go back into the mines unless the government nationalized the region's coal industry; and in several southern towns where the CGT's newfound power and the purging of employers triggered a crisis of authority in dozens of enterprises. Workers took over the Fouga plant in Bézier, as did their counterparts at several firms in Montluçon. Miners in Alès pressured the republican commissar to nationalize seven local mine companies, whereas in Lyon, Yves Farges requisitioned a number of companies, most notably Berliet, and put them under the control of union-led factory liberation committees. In Marseille strike threats and CGT lobbying with purge committees inspired Raymond Aubrac to requisition fifteen companies, a concession to labor militants that eventually led Paris to remove him from his job. In Toulouse labor pressures prompted the socialist mayor to declare all local utilities municipal services, while at the same time a powerful campaign for employee-run management committees in the local aircraft industry led commissar Pierre Bertaux to negotiate the Accord de Toulouse—an agreement to establish management committees throughout the region in airplane factories and other key plants. The management committee movement in Toulouse was in fact only the most spectacular instance of a larger pattern, and by early 1945 labor militants succeeded in bringing a hundred companies under the broad oversight of these new union-led committees.[49]

Despite its revolutionary flavor, this wave of factory takeovers did little to challenge the process of state restoration that de Gaulle promoted in the feverish fall of 1944. On the contrary, the same (usually Communist) labor militants who pushed for requisitions and management committees regarded the state as a necessary partner in their undertaking, and they were eager to return to orderly production in their factories, especially for the war effort. Labor militants viewed requisitions as a way to remove hated, collaborating employers and to bring their company under the stewardship of the state. They were usually content to see management committees serve in powerful advisory bodies rather than to run the factory directly. And they counted on republican commissars to respect these new committees and protect their authority. The Accord de Toulouse explicitly called for "a qualified representative of the government" to arbitrate conflicts between the management committee and a factory director.[50] In the fall of 1944, as in the great strike movement of June 1936, the drive to give workers a more formalized advisory role in running their enterprises went hand in hand with labor's desire to expand the supervisory role of the state. This experience in what we could call grassroots nationalization enhanced labor's expectations that workers would win greater influence in the workplace when parliament passed the big nationalization programs in 1945-46 for coal, gas, electricity, banking and insurance.

In addition to policing and factory seizures, a third arena emerged where popular pressures reinforced an expansion of state authority—in the pricing and distribution of supplies. As the Allies drove the Wehrmacht to the eastern border of France, people expected relief from the hunger, food lines, and black market price gouging that had made daily life miserable during the Occupation. Instead, problems worsened. War damage continued to disrupt transport and destroy crop land, the army drew laborers from the fields, and a brutal winter in 1944-45 took its toll. Shortages also raised the specter of galloping inflation, despite price controls put into place in the mid-1930s and expanded under Vichy. What to do about scarcities became the most divisive issue of the Liberation era. Urban consumers, eager for effective controls, found themselves at odds with farmers and retailers, anxious to see price ceilings lifted. De Gaulle's prefects offered conflicting advice: some of them, especially in better off agricultural areas, urged price liberalization, whereas others argued for tighter controls.[51]

In this climate of divided opinion, working-class consumers took to the streets to push for stronger state action against coal and food shortages. Between October 1944 and May 1945, 221 demonstrations took place around the country, and disturbances over supplies continued, if with lesser frequency, into 1948. Most protests took the form of marches to prefectures and town halls, such as one in the western town of Niort in November 1944, where a thousand people assembled amid placards calling for "heat for the old folks," "sugar for our children," "against the black market."[52] Demonstrations in Saint-Etienne, Clermont-Ferrand, and Nancy in early 1945 each drew as many as fifteen thousand people. Some protests crossed into the realm of the coal or food riot, as happened in Denain, near Lille, where a crowd of 1200 broke into a mine and stole 150 tons of coal and then a smaller group of 350 housewives went on to a refinery where they tried to seize sugar.[53] In Toulouse women looted supermarkets after storming the stalls of an open-air market.[54] Nantes witnessed some of the biggest protests in 1946—a huge demonstration in January and a rampaging crowd of several thousand in August that damaged hotels, restaurants, and cabarets suspected of supported the black market.[55]

Such protests revealed how strongly many urban residents felt about the need for tough government action to redress inequities in pricing and distributing of supplies. To be sure, left-wing organizations often were instigators. Local CGT militants organized about fifteen per cent of the protests that took place between October 1944 and May 1945, and in doing so they pursued the trade union's strategy of channeling working-class discontent into issues of consumption rather than production during the continuing war effort. Two women's organizations, the Communist-oriented UFF (*Union des Femmes Françaises*) and the Catholic *Mouvement Populaire des Familles*, played an even more prominent role. They regarded the supply issue as a way to mobilize working-class housewives politically for the upcoming municipal elections of May 1945.[56] Still, much of the impetus for protest came from local residents themselves, especially women struggling to feed families and incensed by a food distribution system that seemed to privilege some districts over others, even, as rumors had it, to favor German POWs over local residents.[57] They often marched with precise, practical goals in mind, like the protesters in Le Puy who sought to push the prefect to boost the supply of green vegetables and coal, or the demonstrators in Meurthe-et-Moselle who targeted the department's dearth of wine.[58] So powerful were popular passions that activists often found themselves racing to keep up with local initiatives that had escaped their control. The Communist Party in fact seems to have tried to keep protests localized, since the party feared alienating peasant supporters they had done so much to cultivate during the Occupation.[59] The protests, then, though hardly constituting a serious threat to political stability, still revealed a solid reservoir of urban, mostly working-class sentiment supporting tougher state action to keep prices under control.

Despite this pressure, and in the hope of avoiding a rebellion in rural and bourgeois France, the government continued to follow a cautious middle-of-the-road policy in 1945 that made neither side happy. The government kept up the struggle to enforce controls but failed to mount a serious attack against the biggest black marketeers. To head off the threat of postwar inflation de Gaulle opted for the easy, and insufficient, route of issuing bonds to absorb the currency, rejecting as politically too risky the tough road of tight money that Minister of National Economy Pierre Mendès France had recommended (with the support of most republican commissars).[60] But political expediency came at a cost. By the fall of 1945 the threat of inflation was becoming a reality: three attempts to liberalize controls in the food sector, including an ending to bread rationing, brought soaring prices and a return to restrictions.[61] As a result, even de Gaulle's extraordinary popularity began to erode, and his republican commissars offered conflicting advice about whether to toughen or loosen controls.[62] The first formally-elected governments of the Fourth Republic continued to struggle improvisationally down the long path toward price liberalization and the end of rationing amid periodic waves of popular protest, even violence. Not until 1948 did anything like normalcy return to the food markets of France.

If popular pressures had the effect of enhancing police capacity and state's involvement in industrial management, its effects in the realm of market regulation were more complex. Urban agitation for price controls and tough action against the black market encouraged the government to make state regulation effective. It also legitimized a form of state intervention that, until the Liberation, bore the stain of Vichy. Although many of these controls disappeared by the late 1940s, some continued for decades, and this extension of the state's regulatory authority owed something to its public approval in urban France during the Liberation. Still, protest proved insufficient to alter the balance in the internal debate over whether to pursue Pierre Mendès France's ambitious plan for more rigorous restrictions. François Bloch-Lainé, who witnessed the debate from his post in the Treasury, wrote years later that de Gaulle might have convinced the public to accept such a course, much as the Belgian government succeeded in doing in the fall of 1944.[63]

Indeed, the republican commissar in Nancy reported that many people in his region admired the Belgians' use of tough restrictions.[64] Had urban protest been greater, perhaps de Gaulle would have seen a policy of austerity and tighter controls as an antidote to disorder, rather than the potential threat to order that he feared it to be. As it was, public agitation remained contained, partly because the Communist party hoped to avoid widening the political gulf between urban and rural France. Significantly, the party also opposed the policy proposed by Mendès France. In the end, public protests over pricing did as much to expose the weakness of the state in this domain as to prod the government to enforce controls.

Conclusion

The two aspects of state-making we have examined here—de Gaulle's rush to restore state authority systemically from above and the more fragmentary, less self-conscious efforts of local groups to encourage state involvement in matters of justice, policing, and the economy—complemented and conflicted with each other. The complementarity is easy to see. De Gaulle's speed in establishing the sovereignty of the Provisional Government owed a great deal to the willingness of local Resistance groups to work through, rather than against, local commissars and prefects. As a national leader De Gaulle remained popular, even in the unruly south, until the persistence of economic problems began to tarnish his image in the summer of 1945. His notion of strengthening the executive, moreover, found more support at the grassroots than among national party leaders who came to regard the General as too autocratic after a year in power.

But plenty of conflict surfaced as well between these two aspects of state-making. Although state-centric in his vision of France and fiercely determined to restore state authority, de Gaulle proceeded cautiously in expanding the practical role of government. In the fall of 1944 he lacked a clear agenda for reform, despite all the planning his colleagues in Free France had done in Algiers.[65] As we have seen, the first nationalizations occurred improvisationally under political pressure, and in early 1945 de Gaulle surprised his Socialist and Communist partners in government by deciding to postpone the big nationalizations of energy and finance until after the first national elections.[66] Much of the legislative work on the nationalization of coal, gas, and electricity happened after he left the presidency. True, de Gaulle set Pierre Laroque to work revamping the social insurance system, and, shortly before resigning in early 1946, he gave Jean Monnet approval to start working out what would later become the Monnet Plan.[67] His new atomic energy commission began the country's long march to the nuclear bomb. But from de Gaulle's point of view these were carefully circumscribed initiatives that applied traditional modes of centralized administrative leadership to pressing problems.

The logic of state-making from below in 1944-45 pointed in a different direction, or rather in two directions at once: toward strengthening the state as an instrument of reform and toward promoting democratic representation. Resistance fighters who entered the CRS in Marseille, factory militants who won appointments to management committees in Toulouse, housewives who stormed the prefecture in Tours, and many people like them who clamored in dozens of towns for vegetables, tougher purges, the requisition of the factories of business "fifth columnists"—all these citizens did not make up a coherent popular movement for reform, much less the constituency of a single party. Nor did they speak for shopkeepers, industrialists, or farmers who sought less rather than more state regulation. But they did share a common desire to make government more responsive to them as workers and consumers. The innovations they supported—management committees, nationalizations, price controls, purges—called for strengthening the connection between local citizens and assertive government. The feverish atmosphere of the first few months of the Liberation era certainly fed these aspirations, and much of this public enthusiasm for active, democratic government continued to find expression in the strong left-wing showings at the polls in the municipal elections of April-May 1945 and the elections to the Constituent Assembly the following fall.

Both approaches to state-making fell short of transforming the relationship between state and society in France in 1944-45. When de Gaulle resigned from the presidency he had lost his crusade for a strong executive, and his plans for a modernized, well-funded army to restore the stature of France had collapsed amid political pressures to husband resources for domestic recovery. As for state-making from below, it never evolved into a coherent strategy with major spokesmen and an organized constituency. Although the Communist and Socialist parties sought ways to combine greater democratic representation and stronger government intervention, they equivocated for fear of alienating small producers eager to constrain the state.

These two aspects of state-making did, however, help facilitate the subsequent emergence of what could be called state-making from within—the efforts of high civil servants, politicians, and interest-group leaders to thrash out policies between 1945 and the early 1950s that further reshaped the role of the state in postwar society. This third aspect of state-making derived much of its momentum from the modernizing ambitions of economists, engineers, lawyers, and demographers working in ministries and such places as INSEE (*Institut national des statistiques and des études économiques*) and INED (*Institut national des études démographiques*). Along with key Socialist and Communist politicians such as

André Philip and Marcel Paul, these ascendant technocrats would enhance state authority through innovations in social security, family policy, nationalization and economic planning, and the recruitment and regulation of immigrant labor. Inspired by what they had seen of the wartime economies of the United States and Britain, and motivated too by their understandings of the failures of France, they approached postwar reconstruction more willing to try new ideas than were their predecessors in the interwar years, when many technical experts showed the same reluctance to question orthodoxies as had political leaders in the Third Republic.[68] The shame of defeat in 1940 and subsequent yearning for national renewal, the rising stature of experts in the elite circles of both Vichy and the Resistance during the Occupation, and the sheer technical complexity of the economic and social issues facing France after the Liberation—all these factors put technocrats in a strong position to assert themselves in policy-making in the Fourth Republic. But it was the peculiar dynamics of state-making in 1944-45 that expanded the political space in which they would operate. De Gaulle's methods of state-making from above relegitimized the state administration, sheltered the *grands corps* from a potentially crippling purge, and reinvigorated the myth of the state as guardian of the national destiny. By the same token, his refusal to establish a Gaullist party helped perpetuate a weak party system where parliamentary leaders would depend on state administrators, outside experts, and interest-group spokesmen to be key figures of continuity in the policy-making process. De Gaulle, in short, both enhanced the potential for state-centered policy innovation and left a leadership vacuum in his wake—to be filled by an emerging elite of policy specialists, men like Jean Monnet (economic planning), Pierre Laroque (social security), and Raoul Dautry (urban reconstruction and nuclear power) who worked with party leaders and interest-group leaders across much of the political spectrum to shape the modernization drive of the postwar years.

Just as de Gaulle paved the way for the likes of Laroque, so too did state-making from below make it easier for administrators, politicians, and interest-group spokesmen to envision a more active regulatory role for government. Popular pressures in cities and towns served as a counterweight to the more conservative, anti-statist sectors that had held such sway in the Third Republic and that had lobbied successfully for reducing state regulation of the economy after the First World War. True, the broad consensus in 1945 for enlarging the role of the state owed a lot to the shock of defeat in 1940. But it also reflected the powerful groundswell of popular support for Communists, Socialists, and the left-wing Christian Democrats who promised to resume the work of economic and social renovation that the Popular Front had only feebly begun. This political earthquake, made manifest in the elections of spring and fall 1945, did not in itself give state administrators a mandate to rule. But it did create a fluid political climate where the principle question became not whether government should steer the postwar renewal, but how.

If state-making from below and the resurgence of the left strengthened the hand of those who hoped to use the state to renovate the economy, these popular pressures also raised people's expectations, especially in the labor movement, that democracy itself could be enhanced. It is beyond the scope of this essay to examine how postwar reconstruction transformed state-society relations after 1945.[69] Suffice it to say that when de Gaulle left office in early 1946 it remained unclear whether expanding the role of the state would merely concentrate authority in the hands of expert administrators or create new ways to democratize France. Would nationalizations both facilitate modernization and give employees a voice? Would social security simply enlarge the bureaucratic reach of the state or provide citizens with a new arena for democratic participation and social solidarity? By the end of 1945 public support for an expansion of the state's role in many areas of economic and social life had never been greater. And yet beyond this consensus lay sharp disagreements over how to handle the tension between an administrative and a democratic approach to governance. To some extent, of course, this conflict had a long pedigree, reaching back to the French Revolution. But the politics of state-making in 1944-45 brought it out with special intensity. The tensions between top-down and bottom-up efforts to restore authority left people deeply at odds over how to combine a state-led modernization drive with an effort to cultivate economic and social democracy.

Notes

1. Dominique Veillon, *Vivre et survivre en France 1939-1947* (Paris, 1995), 289. I am grateful to Liz Cohen, Ken Mouré, and Martin Alexander for their helpful comments, and to Julie Fette, Josh Humphreys, and Mary Lewis for research assistance. For financial support I wish to thank the National Endowment of the Humanities, the German Marshall Fund of the United States, and New York University.
2. On Liberation-era reforms see especially Andrew Shennan, *Rethinking France: Plans for Renewal 1940-1946* (Oxford, 1989); Jean Bouvier and François Bloch-Lainé, *La France restaurée, 1944-1954: Dialogue sur les choix d'une modernisation* (Paris, 1986); and Richard F. Kuisel, *Capitalism and the State in Modern France: Renovation and Economic Management in the Twentieth Century* (New York, 1981).
3. Michel Margairaz, "Finances, financement et financiers de la reconstruction en 1945: L'ancien et le neuf," in Christiane Franck, ed., *La France de 1945: Résistances, retours, renaissances* Actes du colloque de Caen (17-19 mai 1995) (Caen, 1996), 315.

4. The classic account stressing parallel aspirations in Vichy and the Resistance is Stanley Hoffmann, "The Effects of World War II on French Society and Politics," *French Historical Studies* 2 (Spring 1961): 28-63.
5. On continuities in reform from the 1930s to the late 1940s see, for example, Hoffmann, "The Effects of World War II"; Kuisel, *Capitalism and the State*; Robert O. Paxton, *Vichy France: Old Guard and New Order, 1940-1944* (New York, 1972); Philippe Mioche, *Le Plan Monnet: Genèse et élaboration, 1941-1947* (Paris, 1987); and Herrick Chapman, *State Capitalism and Working-Class Radicalism in the French Aircraft Industry* (Berkeley, 1991).
6. Charles de Gaulle, *The Complete War Memoirs* trans. Jonathan Griffin and Richard Howard (New York, 1959), 6-7, 646, 689.
7. Jean-Louis Cremieux-Brilhac, *La France libre: De l'appel du 18 juin à la Libération* (Paris, 1996), 195-7.
8. Gordon Wright, *France in Modern Times* Fifth Edition (New York, 1995), 393.
9. On the CNR program see Claire Andrieu, *Le programme commun de la Résistance: Des idées dans la Guerre* (Paris, 1984); Henri Michel and Boris Mirkine-Guetzévitch, *Les idées politiques et sociales de la Résistance* (Paris, 1954), 215-18.
10. James D. Wilkinson, *The Intellectual Resistance in Europe* (Cambridge, Mass., 1981) 45-6, 52-5; André Bendjebbar, *Libérations rêvées, libérations vécues 1940-1945* (Paris, 1994), 44-5.
11. Andrew Shennan, "The Origins of Postwar France," *The Historical Journal* (December 1984), 1043.
12. On French Communist attitudes toward the state see Chapman, *State Capitalism*, 10, 59-63, 302-6; Tony Judt, "Une historiographie pas comme les autres: The French Communists and their History," *European Studies Review* 12, 4 (October 1982), 464-5; Philippe Buton, *Les lendemains qui déchantent: Le Parti communiste français à la Libération* (Paris, 1993), 237-42. On Communist ambitions to diminish the repressive capacity of the state see Jean-Marc Berlière, "L'épuration dans la police," in *Le rétablissement de la légalité républicaine (1944)* Actes du colloque organisé par la Fondation Charles de Gaulle, la Fondation nationale des sciences politiques, l'Association française des constitutionalistes (et la participation de l'université de Caen) 6, 7, 8 octobre 1994 (Paris, 1996), 499.
13. De Gaulle, *The Complete War Memoirs*, 564.
14. Jean Lacouture, *De Gaulle: The Rebel, 1890-1944* trans. Patrick O'Brian (New York, 1990), 530; Cremieux-Brilhac, *La France Libre*, 846. On arm gesturing, see de Gaulle, *The Complete War Memoirs*, 654.
15. Quoted in Robert Aron, *France Reborn: The History of the Liberation, June 1944 – May 1945* trans. Humphrey Hare (New York, 1964), 50. On de Gaulle's visit to Bayeux, see also René Hostache, "Bayeux, 14 juin 1944: Etape décisive sur la voie d'Alger à Paris," in *Le rétablissement*, 231-42; and Charles-Louis Foulon, *Le pouvoir en province à la Libération* (Paris, 1975), 101-6.
16. Aron, *France Reborn*, 53. The new sub-prefect, Raymond Triboulet, recounts his experiences in *Le rétablissement*, 249-50.
17. Herbert R. Lottmann, *The Purge* (New York, 1986), 66.
18. On the impact of the Bayeux visit on the Roosevelt administration see Kim Munholland, "The United States and the Free French," in Robert O. Paxton and Nicholas Wahl, eds., *De Gaulle and the United States: A Centennial Reappraisal* (Oxford, 1994), 91.
19. On the republican commissars, see Foulon, *Le pouvoir en province*, and Steven Philip Kramer, "The Provisional Republic, the Collapse of the French Resistance Front and the Origins of Post-War Politics: 1944-1946" (Ph.D. dissertation, Princeton University, 1971).
20. Charles de Gaulle to "Quartus" [Alexandre Parodi], 31 July 1944. Fondation nationale des Sciences politiques (FNSP), Archives Alexandre Parodi, PA 11.

21. See Diane de Bellescize, "L'intérim gouvernemental des secrétaires généraux," in *Le rétablissement,* 129-63.
22. De Gaulle, "Discours prononcé devant l'Assemblée Consultative Provisoire, 25 juillet 1944," in *Oeuvres complètes: Discours et messages* Vol. 3 (Paris, 1970), 84.
23. François Rouquet, *L'épuration dans l'administration française: Agents de l'Etat et collaboration ordinaire* (Paris, 1993), 116-17; Henri Rousso, "L'épuration en France: Une histoire inachevée," *Vingtième siècle* 33 (January-March 1992): 78-105.
24. Bloch-Lainé and Bouvier, *La France restaurée,* 74. On purges in the administration, see also Peter Novick, *The Resistance Versus Vichy: The Purge of Collaborators in Liberated France* (London, 1968), 89-90; Paxton, *Vichy France,* 333-43; and Marc Olivier Baruch, *Servir l'Etat français: L'administration de France de 1940 à 1944* (Paris, 1997), 570-5. On purges in the Finance Ministry, see also Jean-Paul Scot, "La 'Restauration de l'Etat' (juin 1944-novembre 1945): Quelques recherches, quelques enseignements," *Cahiers d'histoire de l'Institut Maurice Thorez* (1982), 181-2.
25. Accounts of August 25 can be found in Serge Berstein, "L'arrivée de de Gaulle à Paris," in *Le rétablissement,* 365-8; de Gaulle, *The Complete War Memoirs,* 643-51; Lacouture, *De Gaulle* Vol. 1: *The Rebel,* 571-6; Aron, *France Reborn,* 287-98.
26. On hopes for a new army and a *levée en masse,* see H. R. Kedward, *In Search of the Maquis: Rural Resistance in Southern France, 1942-44* (Oxford, 1993), 225-6; Grégoire Madjarian, *Conflits, pouvoirs et société à la Libération* (Paris, 1980), 113-14.
27. On the difficulties of army integration, see Jean Delmas, "La réunification de l'armée," in *Le rétablissement,* 543-52; Col. Pierre Le Goyet, "Quelques aspects du problème militaire français pendant la liberation du territoire," and Lt.-Col. Roger Michalon, "L'amalgame F.F.I. – 1re armée et 2e D.B.," in *La Libération de la France* Actes du colloque international tenu à Paris du 28 au 31 octobre 1974 (Paris, 1976), 559-84 and 593-665; and Madjarian, *Conflits,* 103-14; Alexander Werth, *France 1940-1955,* (London, 1957), 233-5.
28. As quoted in Philippe Buton, "Le PCF à la fin de l'année 1944," in *Le rétablissement,* 745. On dissolving the patriotic militias, see Jean-Pierre Rioux, *The Fourth Republic, 1944-1958,* (New York, 1987), 47-8; Madjarian, *Conflits,* 145-64; Kramer, "The Provisional Republic," 103-4; and Foulon, *Le pouvoir en province,* 228-9.
29. On de Gaulle's reinvention of the royal entry, see Laurent Douzou and Dominique Veillon, "Les déplacements du Général de Gaulle à travers la France," in *Le rétablissement,* 652-9.
30. De Gaulle, "Discours prononcé à l'Hôtel de Ville de Paris, 25 Août 1944," in *Oeuvres complètes* vol. 3: *Discours et messages,* 91-2.
31. On the parade as coronation see Fred Kupferman, *Les premiers beaux jours, 1944-1946* (Paris, 1985), 78-9; and François Bédarida, "De Gaulle and the Resistance, 1940-1944," in Hugh Gough and John Horne, eds., *De Gaulle and Twentieth-Century France* (London, 1994), 32-3.
32. Pierre Laborie, "La Libération de Toulouse vue par le pouvoir central," in Rolande Trempé, ed., *La Libération dans le midi de la France* Actes du colloque organisé par les Universités Toulouse-Le Mirail et Paul Valéry de Montpellier les 7 et 8 juin 1985 (Toulouse, 1986), 166-7; Aron, *France Reborn,* 397.
33. As quoted from the newspaper, *La République du Sud-Ouest,* 17 September 1944, in Douzou and Veillon, "Les déplacements," 650.
34. George H. Gallup, ed., *The Gallup International Public Opinion Polls: France 1939, 1944-1975* Vol. I: *1930, 1944-1967* (New York, 1976), 13-14, and 18-19; Hadley Cantril, ed., *Public Opinion, 1935-1939* (Princeton, 1951), 260. See also the bimonthly reports from republican commissars in Chalon-sur-Marne of 1 February 1945 and 15 April 1945 (Archives du Ministère de l'Intérieur, Administration Générale, Service central des commissariats de la

République, F1a 4020), in Dijon of 16 January 1945 (F1a 4021), and in Nancy of 15-31 March 1945 (F1a 4024).

35. Charles-Louis Foulon, "La Résistance et le pouvoir et l'Etat dans la France libérée," in *Le rétablissement*, 192.
36. Charles-Louis Foulon, "Prise et exercice du pouvoir en province à la libération," in *La Libération de la France* Actes du colloque international tenu à Paris du 28 au 31 octobre 1974 (Paris, 1976), 509. On regional variations in the strength of CDLs, see also Jacqueline Sainclivier, "Le pouvoir résistant (été 1944)," in Buton and Guillon, eds., *Les pouvoirs en France*, 31-4.
37. Rioux, *The Fourth Republic*, 46.
38. Maurice Agulhon and Fernand Barrat, *C.R.S. à Marseille: "La police au service du peuple" 1944-1947* (Paris, 1971), 45.
39. Foulon, *Le pouvoir en province*, 153.
40. Raymond Aubrac, *Où la mémoire s'attarde* (Paris, 1996), 134. On Ingrand's experience, see the report of the republican commissar in Clermont-Ferrand, 23 January 1945, F1a 4021; and Foulon, *Le pouvoir en province*, 153. On the purge in Marseille, see the reports of the republican commissar, 15 November, 2 and 15 December 1944, F1a 4023; and Lottman, *The Purge*, 125-8. On the pressures for purges locally, see also Megan Koreman, "The Collaborator's Penance: The Local Purge, 1944-45," *Journal of Contemporary History* 6, 2 (July 1997): 177-92.
41. Berlière, "L'Epuration dans la police," 502-3.
42. Report of the republican commissar, Clermont-Ferrand, 28 April 1945, F1a 4021.
43. Report of the republican commissar, Lyon, 13 September 1944, F1a 4022.
44. Georges Carrot, *Le maintien de l'ordre en France au XXe siècle* (Paris, 1990), 217.
45. Report of the republican commissar, Dijon, 16 January 1945, F1a 4021.
46. Reports of the republican commissar, Marseille, 15 October, 15 December 1944, F1a 4023; Agulhon and Barrat, *C.R.S. à Marseille*, 46-97; Carrot, *Le maintien de l'ordre*, 216-18; Aubrac, *Où la mémoire s'attarde*, 131-2.
47. Carrot, *Le maintien de l'ordre*, 219-21, 256-8. See also Claude Angeli and Paul Gillet, *La police dans la politique – 1944/1954* (Paris, 1967); Dimitri-Georges Lavroff, "Les Compagnies républicaines de sécurité," *Recueil Sirey* (November 1959), in the archives of the Ministère de l'Intérieur, MI 25590; Philip John Stead, *The Police of France* (New York, 1983), 90-1.
48. Buton, *Les lendemains qui déchantent*, 181-4.
49. On the labor movement for management committees and requisitions, see Antoine Prost, "Un mouvement venu d'en bas," and "Le retour aux temps ordinaires," in Claire Andrieu, Lucette Le Van, and Antoine Prost, eds., *Les nationalisations de la Libération: De l'utopie au compromis* (Paris, 1987); and Madjarian, *Conflits*, 165-82; and Buton, *Les lendemains qui déchantent*, 148-54; Robert Mencherini, *La Libération et les entreprises sous la gestion ouvrière* (Paris, 1994).
50. Chapman, *State Capitalism*, 257-61; see also Rolande Trempé, "Aux origines des comités mixtes à la production: Les comités de libération d'entreprise dans la région toulousaine," *Revue d'histoire de la deuxième guerre mondiale* 131(1983): 41-63.
51. Note on "Marché libre et suppression de certaines taxations," 5 June 1945, in the dossier on CDLs in (F1a 4020). See also, Kramer, "The Provisional Republic," 133-151; and the report of 15 June 1945 from the republican commissar in Chalon-sur-Marne (F1a 4020).
52. Report of the republican commissar in Poitiers, 17 November 1944, F1a 4026. On popular attitudes toward the black market during the Occupation, see Lynn Taylor, "The Black Market in Occupied Northern France, 1940-44," *Contemporary European History* 6, 2 (July 1997): 153-76.
53. Werth, *France, 1940-1955*, 237.
54. Danielle Tartakowsky, "Manifester pour le pain, novembre 1940-octobre 1947," *Les Cahiers de l'IHTP* 32-33 (May 1996), 475.

55. Foulon, *Le pouvoir en province*, 241; Tartakowsky, "Manifester," 475.
56. For a general picture of the 221 demonstrations, as well as a description of the role of the UFF and the Mouvement Populaire des Familles, see Tartakowsky, "Manifester," 472-3.
57. Report of the republican commissar in Nancy, 15-31 May 1945, F1a 4024.
58. Report from the Commissaire de Police, Chef du Service des Renseignements Généraux de la Haute-Loire to the Préfet de la Haute-Loire au Puy, 31 January 1945, F1a 4021; report of the republican commmissar in Nancy, 15-31 May 1945, F1a 4024.
59. Madjarian, *Conflits*, 281; Tartakowsky, "Manifester," 471.
60. On the rejection of Mendès France's economic policy and his subsequent resignation from the Provisional Government see Michel-Pierre Chélini, *L'inflation, État et opinion en France de 1944 à 1952* (Paris, 1998), 266-281; Kuisel, *Capitalism and the State*, 191-9; and Bouvier and Bloch-Lainé, *La France restaurée*, 66-84. On support from republican commissars see Foulon, *Le pouvoir en province*, 185.
61. Michel Margairaz, "L'Etat et les restrictions en France dans les années 1940," *Les Cahiers de l'IHTP* 32-33 (May 1996), 38-40.
62. Kramer, "The Provisional Republic," 140; the report of the republican commissar in Lyon, 15 October – 15 December 1945, F1a 4022; Rioux, *The Fourth Republic*, 26; Veillon, *Vivre et survivre*, 297.
63. Bouvier and Bloch-Lainé, *La France restaurée*, 84. Jean Monnet doubted the feasibility of austerity in such a depleted economy. See Margairaz, "Finances, financements, et financiers," 319.
64. Report of the republican commissar in Nancy, 15 October – 15 December 1944, F1a 4024.
65. Shennan, *Rethinking France*, 68.
66. Kramer, "The Provisional Republic," 270-2.
67. William I. Hitchcock, *France Restored: Cold War Diplomacy and the Quest for Leadership in Europe* (Chapel Hill, 1998), 33-4.
68. See, for example, Nathalie Carré de Malberg's analysis of the financial conservatism of state administrators in "Les Inspecteurs des finances et la défense du franc (1934-1935)," Comité pour l'histoire économique et financier de la France, *Du franc Poincare à l'écu* Colloque tenu à Bercy les 3 et 4 décembre 1992 (Paris, 1993), 125-69.
69. In the book I am writing on the economic and social reconstruction of France after the war I explore the tension between technocratic and democratic approaches to governance in several policy arenas.

Chapter 10

MODERNIZING POLITICS IN THE FOURTH REPUBLIC

Women in the Mouvement républicain populaire, 1944-1958

Patricia E. Prestwich

In 1946, Marie-Madeleine Dienesch, a deputy in the Christian Democratic *Mouvement républicain populaire* (MRP), declared that "the MRP is a family party, the great party of the French family, and it is a feminist party." Her statement was in response to complaints by women party activists (*militantes*) that they never heard a woman's voice in National Assembly and that, less than two years after gaining the right to vote, they were "awfully disillusioned."[1] Since these women had already reproached their party for not seeking women candidates or discussing women's issues, Dienesch's assurances were probably met with less-than-polite skepticism. The women's grievances were well-founded: in 1946, Dienesch was one of only nine MRP women deputies in the National Assembly, although the party, with 158 seats, was the second largest party in France.[2] By 1951, only three MRP women deputies remained. One of these deputies, Francine Lefebvre, tried to console *militantes* by pointing to the slow political progress of American women, who had achieved the vote in 1920.[3] By 1958 and the establishment of the Fifth Republic, the MRP had collapsed, and it was formally dissolved four years later. About the only bright spot in the MRP's bleak record of electoral nonrepresentation of women was its appointment, in 1947, of Germaine Poinso-Chapuis, an interwar Catholic suffragist, as Minister of Health.

Notes for this chapter begin on page 217.

She became the first woman minister in the history of France, and thereafter campaigned under the slogan of "First Feminist of France."[4]

Given the MRP's record, it would be tempting to dismiss Dienesch's statement as political cant. Indeed, the MRP seems an unpromising site for even the most generously defined feminism, particularly in comparison with the Communist party, which was larger and had more women deputies.[5] As a Christian Democratic party that had emerged from the Resistance in 1944 and disappeared with de Gaulle's return to power in 1958, the MRP has been inextricably linked with the political failures of the unlamented Fourth Republic. Although the MRP was instrumental in constructing the postwar welfare state and European integration, it became increasingly conservative after 1947, much to the disappointment of many of its members.[6] In fact, historians have suggested that the party attracted large numbers of right-wing voters who had previously supported the Vichy regime.[7] The MRP has not fared much better with historians of feminism, despite the fact that the party attracted proportionally more women voters than any other party.[8] The MRP's strongly Catholic political base and its espousal of traditional family values have led these historians to categorize it as simply another conservative party dedicated to championing *la femme au foyer* (the unpaid homemaker and mother).[9] Its large female electorate has, in consequence, been taken as evidence of women's political conservatism and hostility to feminism in the Fourth Republic.

Yet, if one looks beyond the party's record at the national level to the efforts of its women activists and their organizations, the picture is less discouraging. In fact, the MRP's party structures provided more opportunities for women than did those of other parties in the Fourth Republic, including the Communist party.[10] Between 1946 and 1951, these structures enabled women activists to develop their own political culture and a platform that defended women's interests both as mothers and as workers. In terms that would become more familiar during the second wave of French feminism in the 1970s, MRP *militantes* argued that women had the right to work, whatever their economic circumstances, and that the duty of the party was to promote women's freedom of choice. Moreover, these party activists established their program in a period of national concern about population growth when, as General de Gaulle proclaimed, France needed twelve million babies in ten years. The MRP as a party may not have been feminist, but its women's section was.

The establishment of a small feminist group within an increasingly conservative party that would not survive the political crisis of 1958 must rank, at best, as an ambiguous achievement. The history of these women party members is a striking example of what has been called the "difficulties of the encounter of Frenchwomen with citizenship."[11] But these difficulties have not arisen because of women, but because of definitions of French citizenship that originated with the French Revolution. Therefore, the experience of MRP women in the Fourth Republic illustrates a continuing crisis in French democracy that has extended from the false promises of renewal in 1944 to current anxieties about French political "backwardness."

Women's Citizenship and Modernization: From Renewal to Backwardness

On April 21, 1944, shortly before the Normandy invasions, General de Gaulle issued an ordinance declaring that women had the same civic rights as men, thereby ending more than 150 years of women's exclusion from official politics. Frenchwomen voted for the first time in the local and regional elections of April 1945, and the Constitution of 1946 reaffirmed their political rights. This dramatic change in French democracy, which more than doubled the electorate, occasioned widespread public approval, but little comment. The reform was long overdue, and perhaps the lack of comment reflected relief that France had now caught up with other western democracies. It is also possible that the event was overshadowed by the immediate challenges of political and economic reconstruction. Or perhaps there was no need for comment because women's suffrage was such a ready-made symbol of renewal after the crisis of defeat and occupation. The proclamation of women's suffrage immediately distanced the 'new' France from the masculinist Vichy regime that had sought to restrict women's activities to the domestic sphere, and from the equally discredited stalemate society of the Third Republic, whose Senate had systematically blocked the enfranchisement of women in the interwar years. It also sent a reassuring message that, after four years of authoritarian rule, the republican model of democracy developed during the French Revolution was satisfactory: it merely had to be reestablished and extended to this hitherto-excluded group in society. Significantly, women's enfranchisement was rationalized on the basis of their wartime service, particularly their contribution to the Resistance, with no reference to the long and frustrating campaigns for women's suffrage during the Third Republic.

For more than forty years after the Liberation, the enfranchisement of women continued to evoke little interest. In history texts, in fact, it was frequently stated that universal suffrage had been established in France in 1848 when all men over the age of 21 were given the right to vote. When texts did refer to the establishment of universal adult suffrage in 1944, the event was often treated parenthetically, either as further evidence of modernization in postwar France or as a topic of interest only to women.[12] Nor has women's official entry into politics gained a place in public memory, at least to judge by the commemorative history in which the French excel. In 1994, for example, during widespread public ceremonies to mark the fiftieth anniversary of the liberation of France (including a reenactment of the liberation of Paris), the enfranchisement of women was barely noted.

This comforting representation of women's official entry into politics as a worthy, albeit unmemorable, event has not remained unchallenged. In 1992, a group of Frenchwomen, including politicians, charged that the abysmal record of women's participation in politics since 1944 was proof of French political backwardness and an embarrassing example of "difference". They pointed to the fact that in the fifty years since Frenchwomen received the right to vote, they had comprised no more than six percent of the National Assembly, a record of participation that placed France last within the European Community.[13] (In fact, women's highest representation was achieved in 1946; by 1958, in the new Fifth Republic, their representation had fallen to 1.3 percent and it would not rise beyond two percent until the 1970s.[14]) Their arguments were reinforced in 1995 by a report of the United Nations that ranked France thirty-first in the world in terms of the participation of women in political life, behind Cuba, China, and the Philippines.[15]

In the face of such dismal statistics, drastic action appeared necessary. Therefore, these women launched a campaign for parity, that is, the allocation of fifty percent of seats in the National Assembly to women. The parity movement's leaders emphasized that this was not a demand for quotas; it was an attack on a fundamental concept of French republican democracy, that of the universal, single, disembodied individual. Rather than a universal symbol, they argued, the hypothetical republican individual has been a synonym for masculinity and a means of excluding women from politics. Consequently, the universal individual must become two-sexed and the National Assembly must be divided equally between women and men. As one spokesperson explained, "Women are neither a group nor a lobby. They constitute half of the sovereign people, half of the human species."[16] Most politicians have rejected this demand for a radical rethinking of French democracy, but they have admitted the need for more women in politics. The Socialist party has tried to increase the number of its women candidates through the use of quotas, and, in 1997, women formed nearly one-third of Lionel Jospin's new Socialist government. In 1998, after electoral gains by the right-wing National Front, President Jacques Chirac declared that it was time to modernize French politics, and he called for the increased participation of women in public life.[17]

The enfranchisement of women in 1944 is equally problematic when viewed in the context of women's history. A generation of scholarly research has provided ample evidence that, in western societies, wars and revolutions do not result in significant gains for women.[18] Such crises may temporarily weaken gender barriers and allow women to assume new roles, but the return of stability has been accompanied by reinforced limits on women's opportunities and rights. In France, women did not receive the right to vote after the First World War, despite arguments by suffrage advocates that it was an appropriate reward for women's wartime efforts.[19] Instead, women faced a new abortion law that restricted their rights over their bodies and accusations that they had not done enough to prevent the carnage.[20] The emergence in the 1920s of a new image of the modern woman—the *garçonne* or flapper—provoked much debate and anxiety, but did not reflect any real change in the position of Frenchwomen.[21] The women who served in the French Resistance during the Second World War demonstrated their patriotism and their commitment to basic human values, but they did not achieve roles of leadership, and they were unable to breach well-established gender barriers.[22] Nor is there evidence that the Resistance paid much attention to women's rights in their plans for a postwar society. For the estimated 790,000 wives of prisoners of war, the period from 1940 to 1944 was not one of liberation but of adversity. With the return of their husbands, these women welcomed the resumption of their traditional roles as wives and mothers.[23]

Furthermore, research on women and the public sphere has undermined the interpretation that women's enfranchisement was a simple expansion of politics to include those previously excluded, and that, by implication, women's lack of political experience would delay their advancement in this new world of elections and party politics. The work of Jürgen Habermas has led a number of historians and political scientists to redefine traditional politics as the monopoly of white, bourgeois men,[24] and to argue the unions, peace movements, and associations for social reform have constituted alternative publics for those excluded from official politics.[25] The extensive networks of women's organizations in the nineteenth and twentieth centuries have therefore been interpreted as political and public spaces that allowed women to define their identity, hone their political skills, and, in the words of one historian, find "circuitous routes to public life."[26] A recent study of women's political activities in interwar France by Siân Reynolds has extended this analysis to argue that women were not outside politics, even as formally defined, and to demonstrate that participation in youth organizations, social work, and peace movements expanded the sphere of women's political action. The enfranchisement of women in 1944, she argues, can be seen as a logical consequence of women's "political energy" and success before 1940.[27]

Women's prewar accomplishments did not, however, translate into postwar success in electoral politics. Historians, writing either from the perspective of the Third Republic or from that of second-wave feminism after 1970, have variously portrayed the period of the Liberation and the Fourth Republic as a simple continuation of Third Republic feminism; as a black hole of feminist inaction; as a period of missed opportunities; or, somewhat more charitably, as a necessary apprenticeship before the renewal of feminism and the expansion of women's rights in the 1970s. Yet, given the entrenched resistance to women's suffrage during the Third Republic and the importance that prewar women activists attached to the vote, it would be difficult to claim that de Gaulle's ordinance of 1944 was not a turning point for women. This was certainly the view of women who joined the MRP at the Liberation. Their experiences in the period from 1944 to 1958 suggest that neither backwardness nor renewal are adequate concepts for understanding the challenges of women's newly acquired political citizenship.

The Experience of Politics: From Optimism to Disillusionment

As Frenchwomen entered the world of official politics in 1944, they had good reason to be optimistic. They brought with them an ideology that, from the early days of the suffrage movement, had emphasized that women, because of their different nature, could make a unique contribution to politics. Women, it was argued, were by nature self-sacrificing, tenacious, and eminently practical. In the words of Germaine Poinso-Chapuis, women would bring "the resources of their heart to the solution of social problems; their good sense and domestic practicality to the problems of the national economy."[28] This doctrine was reiterated at the founding congress of the MRP in 1944 by the national representative of women's groups in the party, Simone Rollin. In public life, Rollin stated, women were equal as human beings but, as women, they were complementary to men because of "fundamental physiological and psychological differences."[29] At the time of the Liberation, this doctrine had a certain appeal to those searching for a new way of doing politics. In 1945, one family movement argued that women had to be elected to public office in large numbers because: "an exclusively masculine society reflects the characteristics of the male mind. *It tends to become a sort of mathematical equation where everything is regulated by intelligence.* A mechanical order dominates which excludes all emotion. *Peace without love is not Peace.*"[30] (emphasis in text) The knowledge that women constituted over 53 percent of the electorate also bolstered women's confidence.[31] As one MRP *militante* argued, "women, by their numbers, can clean up politics." But she also warned that in this "political world that is new to them and that is often synonymous with scheming and lies", women had to preserve "all their natural qualities."[32] For women, therefore, the task was not to integrate into the male world of politics, but to transform it.

This reputedly female approach to politics complemented the MRP's vision of its role, and it is not surprising that the party attracted a large number of women voters, particularly younger women. A new party, with many supporters drawn from prewar Catholic Action groups that had long distrusted parliamentary politics, the MRP saw itself as a party committed to redefining the meaning of politics. As the National Secretary, André Colin warned party leaders in March 1946, "for us, political action must consist of doing something practical every day." An unnamed supporter agreed, bluntly warning that "the masses don't care about ideals."[33] The MRP's structures were designed to keep its leaders in contact with ordinary citizens and their needs through a series of *équipes* or teams that represented rural voters, workers, youth, small business, and, of course, women. The party's strong commitment to the defense of the family was also a potential attraction for women, and not just conservative women. Dienesch's claim that a family party could be a feminist party was not necessarily a facile slogan. As a number of scholars have demonstrated, the relations between motherhood and feminism are particularly complex, and, in France, the feminist movements of the Third Republic had strongly emphasized women's sexual difference and the importance of their maternal roles.[34]

From its founding, the MRP welcomed women and promised them "complete equality" within the party,[35] but equality was to be channeled through separate women's sections, or *Equipes féminines.* It was naturally assumed, by both men and women, that women were best qualified to speak to women and that women would vote for women. Therefore, every branch of the MRP was to have its women's team that would recruit women into the party, appeal to women voters, and bring issues of particular interest to women to the party's regional and national congresses. These *Equipes féminines* were also to maintain contact with nonpolitical women's organizations, including feminist groups. The activities of the *Equipes féminines* were coordinated at the national level by a woman's representative and a national committee composed of female deputies and departmental representatives. Simone Rollin was the first national women's representative; in 1947, she was replaced by a young war widow, Germaine Touquet, who coordinated women's efforts until 1959.

Separate women's organizations, either independent or within a party, have historically offered both advantages and disadvantages to women. They have long acted as "training grounds"[36] for women, allowing them to define their interests, develop their strategies, and, most importantly, to speak. Since the voices of women party members were noticeably absent from the records of MRP congresses, this last advantage should not be underestimated. But separate organizations within a party increase the risk of marginalization: women can easily be portrayed as a special interest group or find themselves restricted to so-called "women's issues." The danger of marginalization was embedded in the structures of the MRP, for the *Equipes féminines* did not have a representative on the party's Central Bureau, which made the key political decisions. Finally, in organizing within a party, women committed themselves to partisan politics and restricted their ability to cooperate with women in other parties. Such solidarity across party lines could, as historian William Guéraiche sardonically notes, "splinter the framework of the political game."[37]

From its inception, the MRP attracted talented women who did not readily fit the traditional image of the *femme au foyer*. At both the national and local levels, many party members had distinguished themselves in the Resistance or had been politically active before the war in social Catholic organizations, such as the *Jeunesse ouvrière chrétienne* (JOC), or in the MRP's political predecessor, the *Parti démocrate populaire* (PDP). Of the nine women deputies elected to the National Assembly in 1946 only two were married with children, and both had long been active outside the home. Six were single women with careers in teaching or the civil service. Francine Lefebvre, who had the longest parliamentary career of any MRP woman deputy, had founded a branch of a Catholic trade union in her factory at the Liberation, and she entered politics as a consequence of her union activities. The most experienced of the new women deputies was undoubtedly Germaine Poinso-Chapuis.[38] One of the first women lawyers in Marseilles, she was a founding member of the French Soroptimist Club, an organization for professional women. She had campaigned for women's suffrage in the 1930s, and, as one of the directors of the PDP, she had fought to establish a women's section within the party.[39] During the Occupation, she carried on the legal practice of a Jewish colleague, and defended Communists and Trotskyites before the Vichy courts. Poinso-Chapuis was also a gifted public speaker: typically, after one of her speeches to party members, the recording secretary simply wrote that it was impossible to capture the brilliance of her words.[40] A determined and politically skilled woman, Poinso-Chapuis was reputedly described by her opponents as "the only man in the MRP"—that dubious compliment designating a talented woman as an honorary man.

Although the paucity of party archives on the women's sections makes it difficult to assess the qualifications of ordinary members, a number of experienced women leaders emerged at the local level. Marthe Gouffé, a party leader in the Paris region, had been active in the prewar PDP. In the Nord, a stronghold of the MRP, Marie Van Der Elst led the workers' section and was a prominent spokesperson for the party on many issues.[41] In the Bouches-du-Rhône (where the party's membership cards have been preserved), the women who joined the MRP came from diverse backgrounds. Some were wives of party members, but many were unmarried, and a number had careers in education or the social services. Since the MRP deliberately sought to recruit women through contacts with women's organizations, it is likely that the party attracted a number of women with experience in alternative politics who saw the vote as a means of enacting much needed social reforms for women and the family.

But if the women who entered the MRP at the Liberation were optimistic about their new political roles, they quickly became angered, frustrated, and disillusioned. Like their female colleagues in more established parties, they soon discovered that official politics remained a male preserve. As the Parisian activist Ita Marbeau complained in 1950, "the reins of government, whether those of the nation or of the family, remain in the hands of men because they are more powerful."[42] Despite the rhetoric of the Liberation, the wartime experience had not eliminated a stubborn opposition among the political classes to women's suffrage. This opposition was apparent even in 1943, when the issue of women's civic equality provoked lengthy debate in the Consultative Assembly in Algiers.[43] Enfranchisement came through decree, not as the result of parliamentary action, and it was not accompanied by changes in the Civil Code, which continued to restrict women's rights.

Even in the newly-established MRP, male leaders were concerned that women might form an autonomous group within the party. These fears persisted and women had to refute charges that the *Equipes féminines* created divisions within the party, or that they were not doing valuable political work. In the Federation of the Seine, for example, Marthe Gouffé reported that when the *Equipe féminine* was established in her section of the party, it seemed as if there were "two clans, one male, the other female." Women, she complained, were only given responsibility for organizing fund-raising activities or social events. Gouffé told her male colleagues to stop considering women as inferior: "In the Middle Ages or at the time of Louis XIV, this was fashionable. In 1949, after the war and the occupation, it is no longer acceptable, and they know it."[44] Gouffé, however, also decided that it was better for women not to meet as a separate group. Other women, such as Francine Lefebvre and Marie Van Der Elst, avoided the problem by making worker groups the focus of their activities.

Militantes also had to fight the persistent fear, among both men and women, that their entry into politics transgressed well-established gender roles—that is, in becoming equal to men, women would become men. This anxiety can be seen even in a fashion advertisement that appeared in the party newspaper in 1945: a sketch of a pantsuit for women was accompanied by the advice that "this outfit has been very popular among female voters, female municipal councillors, and female deputies."[45] Women replied, as they had done before the war, that equality did not mean identity; they would keep their feminine nature and would not, in the words of one *militante*, become "raging suffragettes."[46] When possible, women candidates were photographed with their children or grandchildren. This insistence on a traditional femininity may represent a continuation of prewar feminism, which emphasized women's importance as mothers. But it should also be seen within the context of a persistent hostility to women's presence in politics. Today, women politicians in France complain that they are seen first as sexual beings and are judged on their elegance or "femininity".[47] This pressure to maintain traditional gender roles suggests the enduring conservatism of the political world and, as Joan Scott has argued, the importance of sexual difference to the preservation of traditional republican politics.[48]

Judging by their complaints, women were more disturbed by the hostility they faced within the party, particularly at the local level, than by any hostility from the electorate. Not surprisingly, this hostility was most evident when the party came to prepare its lists of candidates for elections. The MRP's electoral lists usually contained a token woman, but often in fifth or sixth place, where the possibility of success was nonexistent.[49] The early electoral victories of women in 1945 and 1946 were, in part, the result of the MRP's difficulty, as a new party, in finding candidates. But in 1946, when the MRP became the second largest party in the Assembly (after the Communist party), competition for nominations was fierce and women fared badly. Simone Rollin complained bitterly of the absence of women candidates, and told the party's executive in 1946 that women were needed to enact the practical reforms that the MRP espoused. She warned that the party had to rid itself of "outdated ideas that women are incapable of taking responsibility, that women are timid, that they cannot speak or effectively represent the movement." It was not enough, she argued, to place only one woman candidate on an electoral list. Women could also represent workers, youth, or rural society on electoral lists, and they could head a list as the party's representative.[50] Even prominent women faced a battle to retain their favored position on party lists. In 1945 Simone Rollin had been elected to the Constituent Assembly because she had been placed second on a list. In the 1946 elections for the National Assembly, she was put in third place only after she and other women protested the lack of women candidates on the list. Rollin was not elected, and by 1948 she had left the MRP. Francine Lefebvre, a deputy from Paris, expressed a widespread disillusionment when she compared women's entry into political life "to that period of engagement before marriage, when everything looks rosy."[51] Others were less gracious, and accused the MRP of being a typical party of the Third Republic.

The fate of Germaine Poinso-Chapuis could only reinforce women's disappointment with the MRP and with parliamentary politics. In November 1947, only three years after women had obtained the right to vote, Poinso-Chapuis was appointed Minister of Public Health and Population in the government of

Robert Schuman. She was the first woman minister in the history of France, and her appointment was greeted with widespread approval in the press. (Poinso-Chapuis immediately appointed women to half the positions in her ministerial cabinet.) Yet, within ten months, her ministerial career had ended as a result of the MRP's attempt to support Catholic schools by providing funding to the parents of students. Although Poinso-Chapuis had not initiated the decree for this funding and was not convinced of its wisdom, the decree was issued in her name by Prime Minister Robert Schuman. (The next day, he sent her the decree to sign.[52]) Not surprisingly, given the long history of republican anticlericalism, the result was a political crisis that threatened the MRP's position in the government coalition. Poinso-Chapuis was forced to resign as Minister of Health, and the crisis ended her ministerial career, much to the dismay of her colleagues, both women and men. This sacrifice of the MRP's most prominent woman could not help but send a message to women. As Germaine Touquet, the MRP national representative for women, later remarked of this incident, "it is always easier to sacrifice a woman minister."[53] Had the Communist party remained in the coalition government after 1947, the Fourth Republic might have had another woman minister. It was not until 1974, sixteen years after the founding of the Fifth Republic, that Simone Veil became France's second woman minister, again as Minister of Health.

The barriers that women faced in the MRP were common to all political parties, although it might have been more disillusioning for women to encounter them in a new party. But MRP *militantes* faced a particular problem because this party, which continually proclaimed itself to be the "great party of the French family," appeared to define the family as traditional and patriarchal. In 1945, as women voted for the first time, the MRP was seriously debating the merits of a family vote, a proposal that would accord the (usually male) head of the family an extra vote in elections. An early propaganda leaflet on family issues that was directed to workers made it clear that the rights and needs of women were subordinate to those of the family, and in particular to the interests of husbands. Work outside the home, the brochure argued, destroyed women's charm and modesty: it gave them a comportment and liberties that "deflowered" them. What workers needed, the pamphlet continued, was "tender wives, belonging to them alone, … those guardians and queens of the hearth that any worker, like any man, hopes for."[54]

Even in 1945, this vision of women's citizenship was too restrictive for most *militantes*, including some of the more conservative ones. Simone Rollin, a mother of five and an activist in Catholic parents' associations, probably came closest to the image of the *femme au foyer*, and it is not surprising that she was appointed by MRP leaders as the first national representative of women. In her keynote speech at the party's founding congress, she argued that "women's essential mission is beside their children," and she urged women to see dishwashing and mending as "beautiful tasks" because they represented an ideal of the family. Nevertheless, Rollin also insisted that women were not to be slaves within the family, but equals, and she demanded modern appliances and pensions for homemakers.[55] Rollin was appalled by the drudgery of housework and the burdens it placed on women's health. After she left the party in 1947, she had a successful career promoting the use of laborsaving household appliances. In 1990, at the end of her life, she still maintained that equality for women in society could only come after equality within the family, and she was encouraged by the fact that more young couples shared housework and family responsibilities.[56]

Rollin's statements have been cited as representative of the party's conservative view of women's roles,[57] but they were not, in fact, well received by a number of *militantes.* These women responded that most women had no other means of survival except their work, and they demanded the right to work in dignity and security. In September 1946, shortly before the second referendum on the constitution and legislative elections, the *Equipes féminines* began to debate the thorny question of whether equality meant identity with men or whether, in the interests of equality, there should be different functions for women and men.[58] The absence of a consensus within the party on women's roles is illustrated by an early memorandum to local organizers of campaign meetings for women. The room, the note instructed, should be decorated with photographs portraying women as both mothers and workers, and with the words of female deputies.[59]

The Political Achievement: Building a Modern Feminism

By 1951, the women's sections of the MRP had built a coherent platform that attempted to avoid the pitfalls of an equality based either on identity or on difference. Rather than portraying women uniquely as workers or as homemakers, the *Equipes féminines* argued, as would feminists of the 1970s, that women had two roles in society: as mothers and wage earners. Moreover, work was not simply an economic necessity; all women, whether single or married, had "the absolute right to work, as does any human being."[60] The national representative of women in the party, Germaine Touquet, stated bluntly that in a democracy women had to be free to define their own lives, and that the duty of the MRP was to protect women's freedom of choice.[61] This larger conception of women's roles and rights was accompanied by the development of a purportedly female political culture that served to distance women from traditional and, by implication, male political practices. The catalyst for these changes was not the crisis of defeat and occupation but rather the political crises that confronted the MRP and its women activists from 1946 to 1951, as the party began to decline in power.

By 1947, the MRP faced strong competition for votes on the Left from the Communist party and on the Right from the Gaullist *Rassemblement pour la France.* Ideologically and politically, it was the left-wing challenge that preoccupied party strategists. As André Colin warned the party, "if we don't appear as a party of progress and youth, it will be the Communists."[62] Similarly, the party's women strategists saw themselves as trapped between two unacceptable definitions of women's roles: the Communist party offered women an equality based on identity with men, while the Right preached a doctrine of difference that restricted women to the home. Despite the appeal of Gaullist doctrines to a number of Catholic women, it was the Communist threat that MRP women activists took most seriously. At a time when France faced massive economic reconstruction, the Communist party offered women economic progress and full citizenship through paid work. The party also portrayed itself as a defender of the French family, but with a difference: it argued that all mothers—whether legitimately married or not—deserved assistance. Given the high rate of consensual unions within the French working classes, this was a realistic policy; it was also a policy that the MRP, which believed in the sanctity of marriage, found difficult to counter. The Communist party was also successful in recruiting women, particularly through its women's organization, the *Union française féminine,* and it had the largest number of women deputies in the National Assembly. In 1949, Poinso-Chapuis—who frequently criticized her own party for spending more time on principles than on action—pointed to the Communist party's "excellent work" in promoting women as she tried to convince MRP leaders to pay more attention to women.[63] MRP *militantes* had already emphasized the importance of paid work to women, but the Communists' electoral success made the defense of women workers a political necessity.

The Communist and Gaullist challenges to the survival of the MRP coincided with a realization that the majority of the MRP's electorate (nearly 60 percent) was female, but that women voters had a high rate of abstention. As early as 1946, women activists had warned the leadership that the women's vote was crucial to the MRP's electoral success, and that more women candidates were necessary. Only in 1950, after several academic studies of voting patterns confirmed the MRP's popularity with women voters, did party leaders begin to pay attention to these warnings. But the issue was complicated by the higher rate of abstention among women voters. This phenomenon, which continued until the 1970s, has been noted by scholars, but it has often been interpreted as evidence of women's inexperience in politics or their conservatism. Only in the 1970s, it has been argued, as women entered higher education and the work force in larger numbers, did they become more politically aware. This was not, however, the perception of the MRP's women activists. As early as 1946, they had warned party leaders that women, and particularly younger women, were not disinterested in politics but rather disgusted by it. Just before the crucial referendum of October 1946 on the new constitution, the women's sections spoke of a "civic defeatism" among women electors, characterized by the feeling that voting would change nothing.[64]

The *Equipes féminines* spent considerable time trying to comprehend women's aversion to electoral politics and devising new means of attracting women voters. They concluded that women had a different definition of politics: women were only interested if they saw that political action would resolve the concrete problems of daily life, and they made little distinction between governmental and administrative action. Therefore, party propaganda directed to women would have to emphasize such practical issues as food shortages or the lack of adequate housing. As well, to attract women, the party would have to abandon large public meetings or election rallies and approach women directly, through women's organizations or through committees that dealt with local problems. The most thoughtful analysis of women's evident disinterest in official politics came in 1956, when the national women's representative, Germaine Touquet, reviewed the results of ten years of women's suffrage. Touquet focused on a voting pattern of women that political scientists would later call the "swing vote."[65] She argued that, because women were attracted less by principles than by concrete actions, they were an unstable voting group. But she went on to emphasize that women's lack of involvement in parliamentary politics was the result of fundamental inequalities in society. Women became voters in 1944 not because the majority of women had demanded it, but because it had been accorded as part of the Liberation. These new rights had imposed additional responsibilities, and were therefore not an emancipation but an obligation.[66]

Redefining politics to appeal to women voters hastened the development of a distinctive political culture within the women's sections of the MRP. Prewar suffrage groups had always asserted that women would bring something different to politics, and, in 1947, one MRP activist challenged women to acquire "a true political personality."[67] The necessity of creating a separate female identity within the party was accentuated by the widespread concern among ordinary supporters, both women and men, that the MRP was losing its moral bearings in its struggles to stay in power. The new "political personality" that emerged in the women's sections of the party was epitomized by the figure of the *technicienne*, the practical, efficient, and politically neutral reformer. The *technicienne* was someone who understood the technical complexities of an issue, whether it was marriage law or the Marshall Plan, but who could also explain the problem clearly, dispassionately, and in a way that suggested possible solutions. It was this pragmatic approach that *militantes* most admired in their women deputies and sought to emulate. After Germaine Poinso-Chapuis gave one of her typically spellbinding speeches to a meeting of party women, Germaine Touquet praised the speech for bringing, "in its form and expression, a new clarity to the problem."[68]

This concept of the *technicienne* had many advantages. It incorporated the belief of the prewar suffrage movement that women were determined, hard-working problem-solvers who would bring a different approach to politics. Yet it avoided the earlier movement's emphasis on women as mothers and its housewifely images of women "cleaning up" politics. In postwar France, where the emphasis was on economic reconstruction through state planning, the *technicienne* was a more modern and more scientific embodiment of women's functions. Women would become the technocrats of politics. As such, their expertise would not be limited to so-called women's issues or to women's meetings. At the local party level and beyond, women were encouraged to become experts on a variety of issues, including international relations and economic policy, and to speak on these issues both in women's groups and in general party meetings. As their models, they could look to their women deputies, who were knowledgeable on a range of issues: Francine Lefebvre was an expert on labor legislation, Marie-Madeleine Dienesch championed educational reform, and Germaine Poinso-Chapuis had mastered an impressive number of problems, from alcoholism to economic planning.

The *technicienne* was also a useful device to convey women's dislike of partisan politics and the practices of traditional male politicians. Women's experience with party politics in the Fourth Republic could only confirm a distaste for the political "game" that had been evident in the prewar suffrage movement. As Germaine Poinso-Chapuis had argued in the 1930s, "[i]f politics means insulting one's neighbors, scuffling in stormy meetings, and being engulfed in quarrels and insults, women don't want it."[69] Women activists within the party rejected what they saw as the demagogy of parliamentary politics, with its emphasis on the appearance of candidates, on emotional appeals to the electorate, and on beguilingly simple solutions. In their view, electors, whether male or female, needed to be informed of the complexity of political problems in order to make rational decisions. When José Dupuis, a former deputy, gave a speech to party women explaining the difficult initial steps toward European integration, one *militante* responded that Dupuis, a model *technicienne*, had demonstrated that such problems could be solved if men would only treat them in a "simple and objective manner."[70] This sharp criticism of their male colleagues was not simply the result of the discrimination that women faced within the party. It also reflected a widespread crisis among party supporters, both women and men, who were angered that party leaders ignored grassroots opinion and who feared that they were abandoning the MRP's democratic ideals. In 1948, for example, the feisty Marie Van Der Elst castigated MRP leaders Robert Schuman and Georges Bidault for speaking "in the language of politics," and for not listening to the rank and file of the party, who "bring the practical perspective." Party members, she concluded, were as disgusted as the general populace was by politics.[71]

Women party members consciously adopted a different political language, one that avoided sentimentality and maternal images. In their speeches and reports, they frequently described themselves as "realistic" or "intransigent." This somewhat cold tone was counterbalanced by references to women's special talent for empathy: women were better, it was claimed, at listening and at understanding. Sometimes this quality was described as innate; at other times it was attributed to women's extensive involvement in the problems of daily living. In contrast to the game of politics, with its "quarrels and insults", MRP women stressed the importance of friendship in politics and the welcoming atmosphere of their meetings. This insistence on friendship may have allayed their discouragement, but it also served as a criticism of contemporary political practices. As one report explained: "[t]his friendship applies to everyone. We do not have several leaders welcoming ordinary party members with a friendly 'paternalism'. No, we are simply a group of committed women, all inspired by the same ideal and by the same desire to 'serve'." The report went on to say that this manner of working together—which clearly refuted stereotypes about "feminine rivalry"—was the realization of "a true team" where individual actions matter less than what could be achieved by working together.[72] For women activists, the *Equipes féminines* embodied the original democratic ideals of the MRP.

This avowedly female approach to politics was most effectively developed in the annual general meeting of women in the party, the *Journées nationales féminines,* held every February. As the MRP declined in power and membership, the *Journées nationales féminines* became the most important means of recruiting new members and of generating the practical reforms needed to attract women voters. Party organizers made an effort to attract women from all over the country, often urging local leaders to provide childcare or prepare family meals so that women would be free to travel to Paris. These annual national meetings were specifically designed to draft legislation that would improve women's lives. Each year, a limited number of issues was selected for study by the national organizing committee, which sent detailed questionnaires to all local and regional *Equipes féminines.* Nonpolitical organizations and unions were invited to take part in the discussions at all levels. To encourage such participation, invitations emphasized that these were not political meetings but rather gatherings of women to discuss improvements in women's lives. The national committee compiled detailed reports from the questionnaires, and these reports were debated at the *Journées nationales.* After much discussion, the meetings passed a series of motions that were subsequently introduced as bills in the National Assembly by the party's women deputies. The national women's meeting of 1950, for example, was the source of Germaine Poinso-Chapuis's bill to remove inequalities in marriage legislation. In other years, the *Journées nationales féminines* studied part-time employment, vocational training for young women, and the problems of rural women. During elections, party propaganda emphasized how much women deputies had worked for women by listing the bills that they had introduced in the National Assembly. Given the MRP's declining membership and resources, these national meetings were an effective way of maintaining activity in the women's sections. Whether women voters were impressed by these necessary, but often very technical, legislative reforms is impossible to say.

The *Journées nationales* served to emphasize political action at the national level, but a number of women in the party argued that municipal politics was more rewarding or, in some cases, more suited to "feminine" talents. When Marie-Louise Weber lost her seat in the National Assembly in the elections of 1951, she returned to Mulhouse, where she served as the only woman municipal councillor. She later remarked that, "in a certain sense, action at the municipal level is more satisfying than parliamentary battles—which are so unpleasant and risky—for the results are almost always tangible and effective."[73] Increasingly after 1951, the women's sections of the MRP publicized the achievements of women in local politics. In part, this reflected an obvious disenchantment with parliamentary politics. It was also a necessity: after 1951, only three MRP women deputies remained, and the possibility of effective action at the national level was limited. Such publicity may also be an indication of expanded opportunities for women at the local or regional level. Historians are only beginning to acknowledge the importance of municipal action in matters of health and welfare, such as the antituberculosis campaigns before the First World War.[74] After 1945, as rationing continued, as the state began to construct low-cost public housing, and as the system of social security was put in place, events at the local level became increasingly important to the lives of voters, whether women or men.[75]

The concept of women as the resolutely practical and tenacious technicians of politics gave MRP activists of the 1940s and 1950s the distinct political identity that they sought. Like their defense of women's dual roles as mothers and workers, this identity could be qualified as feminist in that it continues to appeal to women in politics throughout the western world. In the 1980s, the French political scientist Mariette Sineau analyzed the attitudes of women politicians in several western countries, and found that they consistently described themselves, in her words, as the "specialists in daily life."[76] In 1997, when 120 women were elected to the British Parliament (double the previous number) these new members spoke of their ambition to improve relations between the people and parliament, and to enact reforms that would establish a balance in women's lives between their work and their family responsibilities. One new M.P. said: "Women are more cooperative in the way they work. They're not so into scoring points, and more interested in hearing different points of view to get the best policy." She finished with a phrase that would have been applauded by Germaine Poinso-Chapuis and other MRP *militantes*: "it's time to modernise Westminster."[77]

Despite its modern tone and continuing appeal, this concept of women as the technicians of politics recalls earlier suffrage arguments that women would bring something new to politics because they were mothers. Both arguments are based on a theory of difference, and both risk being labeled as essentialist, that is, attributing certain qualities to women simply because they are women. It is difficult, and perhaps impossible, to determine whether MRP women and their suffrage predecessors truly believed that women had innately different capabilities or whether they were making a valid claim to a special competence based on their daily experience as workers and as mothers. Furthermore, the question of essentialism obscures a more important issue, namely how such concepts functioned and what they tell us about the situations women faced. Historians have underlined the difficulties that women faced in trying to find "the right formula" to win political rights.[78] Joan Scott has succinctly identified their dilemma: "when women (among others) were denied citizenship on the grounds of their difference, how could they demand change as human individuals without invoking the difference that excluded them?"[79] The continuing appeal of the argument that women will bring a seasoned practicality to public life underscores women's continued exclusion from politics, and the persistent inability of the political system to modernize. As Jacques Chirac admitted in 1998, "political life must be closer to that of ordinary citizens."[80]

Conclusion

The women who joined the MRP never doubted that the right to vote was a turning point. They preferred to be a small feminist group within a party that did not appreciate their skills or reflect their values than to be excluded from official politics. At one dinner, after a large and particularly successful meeting, they gleefully pictured the horrified reaction of senators in the Third Republic to this gathering of over a hundred *militantes*.[81] Moreover, it was the necessity to act politically—to attract party members and voters—that had given them the opportunity to establish within the MRP a more inclusive and more modern approach to women's issues. In interviews, surviving MRP activists, now in their 80s, remember their political lives with pride and a certain nostalgia. They also see themselves as pioneers of women's rights and, except on the issue of abortion, tend to identify with the younger generation of feminists.[82] Their experiences suggest that support for women's equality in the France of the 1940s and 1950s was more widespread than previously thought.

Yet it is impossible to ignore the historical evidence of their disillusionment with politics and their bitterness at being excluded from power in a party that depended on the votes of women for its success. Their early disenchantment with politics and their argument that, by 1946, their female electorate (primarily younger women) shared this view challenge the argument that women in the Fourth Republic were either conservative or apolitical. Their experiences raise the interesting question of how women reacted to rejection. A number of women stayed in the party, undoubtedly reasoning that if it took 150 years to achieve the vote, it might take more than ten years to reform politics. Others may have simply dropped out of politics, swelling the ranks of the politically alienated. But it is also plausible that women's postwar efforts at reform were again channeled into the world of alternative politics that had flourished in the Third Republic. Before drawing conclusions about postwar politics or feminism, it would, therefore, be worthwhile to study women's organizations, student movements, peace organizations, consumer advocacy groups, the civil service, and any other source of possible political activity by women. It might also be advisable to study groups that have traditionally been seen as conservative, such as Catholic family associations. As the history of women in the MRP demonstrates, you never know where you will find a feminist.

Notes

The research for this article was made possible by research grants and leaves provided by the University of Alberta. I am also grateful to Madame Germaine Touquet for sharing her experiences with me and to Professor Jean Chélini for granting me access to the Federation of the Bouches-du-Rhône (MRP) archives in Marseilles.

1. In French, "joliment désabusées." Archives nationales, Archives privées, Fonds du Mouvement républicain populaire, 350AP/57, 10 March 1946.
2. The Communist party, with 165 seats, was the largest party in 1946. It had 23 women deputies. Maurice Larkin, *France Since the Popular Front. Government and People, 1936-1996*, 2nd ed., (Oxford, 1997), 152; Jean Pascal, *Les femmes députés de 1945 à 1988* (Paris, 1990), 59.
3. *MRP Vous Parle*, March 1951, 7.

4. Poinso-Chapuis was the first woman to have full ministerial responsibilities. In 1936 Léon Blum appointed three women as Undersecretaries of State, and in 1946 Andrée Vienot was named Undersecretary of State for Youth and Sports.
5. Definitions of feminism abound and are a constant source of debate. The current emphasis is on reconciling women's need for equality and their equally strong need for a recognition of their difference. As Joan Scott has noted, since the French Revolution, feminists have argued for their right, as human beings, to equality, while also proclaiming a superiority based on difference. Joan W. Scott, "'La Querelle des Femmes' in the Late Twentieth Century," *The New Left Review*, no. 226 (1997), 14. Good introductions to the complexities of defining feminism are: Karen Offen, "Defining Feminism. A Comparative Historical Approach," in *Signs*, vol. 14, no. 1 (1988): 119-57, and Gisela Bock, "Challenging Dichotomies: Perspectives on Women's History," in *Beyond Equality and Difference: Citizenship, Feminist Politics and Female Subjectivity*, Gisela Bock and Susan James, eds. (London, 1992), 1-23.
6. For the MRP see R.E.M. Irving, *Christian Democracy in France* (London, 1973); for a view of the MRP as conservative from the beginning, see Richard Vinen, *Bourgeois Politics in France, 1945-51* (Cambridge, 1995), 137-72.
7. Larken, *France Since the Popular Front*, 135. Richard Vinen sees the MRP as a conservative party but does not think it attracted former Pétainists. Vinen, *Bourgeois Politics*, 155-7.
8. Women composed 58 percent of the MRP's electorate in 1946 and 61 percent in 1951. In comparison, in 1951, women made up 52 percent of the Gaullist RPF's electorate. Claire Duchen, *Women's Rights and Women's Lives in France 1944-1968* (London, 1955), 39. Richard Vinen argues that more elderly women were attracted to the RPF, while the MRP attracted younger women. Vinen, *Bourgeois Politics*, 54.
9. Duchen, *Women's Rights*, 33-63.
10. William Guéraiche, "La Question 'femmes' dans les partis (1946-1962)," *Historiens & géographes* 88, no. 358 (1997): 245-6. For the ways in which the Communist party used its women's organization to control women members, see Renée Rousseau, *Les femmes rouges: chronique les années Vermeersch* (Paris, 1983).
11. Francoise Thébaud, "Les Françaises, quelle citoyenneté," in *Provence historique*, vol. 46 (1997), 576.
12. Siân Reynolds, *France Between the Wars. Gender and Politics* (London, 1996), 212-13.
13. Joan W. Scott, "'Querelle des Femmes'," 7. The elections of 1997, which saw an increase in the number of women deputies, raised France to the next to last place, ahead of Greece and slightly behind Italy. *L'Européen*, no. 11, 3-9 June, 1998, 22.
14. Duchen, *Women's Rights*, 54.
15. *Le Figaro*, 18 August 1995, 6.
16. Scott, "'Querelle des Femmes'," 10-12, quote from 11.
17. *Le Monde*, 25 March 1998, 6.
18. See, for example, Margaret Randolph Higonnet, Sonya Micheland Jane Jenson, and Margaret Collins Weitz, eds., *Behind the Lines. Gender and the Two World Wars* (New Haven, 1987).
19. For women's suffrage and feminism in France, see Christine Bard, *Les filles de Marianne: Histoire des féminismes 1914-1940* (Paris, 1993); Steven Hause and Anne Kenney, *Women's Suffrage and Social Politics in the French Third Republic* (Princeton, 1984); Laurence Klejman and Florence Rochefort, *L'égalité en marche: Le féminisme sous la Troisième République* (Paris, 1989); and Paul Smith, *Feminism and the Third Republic. Women's Political and Civil Rights in France 1918-1945* (Oxford, 1996). A useful survey of the issues is Karen Offen, "Women, Citizenship, and Suffrage in France Since 1789," in *The Transformation of Modern France*, ed. William B. Cohen, (Boston, 1997), 125-41.
20. Norman Ingram, *The Politics of Dissent, Pacifism in France 1919-1939* (Oxford, 1991).

21. Mary Louise Roberts, *Civilization Without Sexes. Reconstructing Gender in Postwar France, 1917-1927* (Chicago, 1994), 215.
22. Paula Schwartz, "Redefining Resistance: Women's Activism in Wartime France," in *Behind the Lines*, in Higgonet et al., eds., (New Haven, 1987), 147.
23. Sarah Fishman, *We Will Wait: Wives of French Prisoners of War, 1940-1945* (New Haven, 1991), xviii-xix.
24. See, for example, Nancy Fraser, "Rethinking the Public Sphere: A Contribution to the Critique of Actually Existing Democracy," in *Habermas and the Public Sphere*, Craig Calhoun, ed. (Cambridge Mass., 1992), 109-42.
25. Fraser, "Rethinking," 123.
26. Mary P. Ryan, "Gender and Public Access: Women's Politics in Nineteenth-Century America," in *Habermas and the Public Sphere*, 284.
27. Reynolds, *France Between the Wars*, 198.
28. Mlle Germaine Chapuis, "Pourquoi nous sommes Partisans du Suffrage féminin" (Paris, n.d.), 14.
29. MRP Brochure, "Un Grand Congrès, une Grande Espérance," Archives of the Federation of the Seine (MRP), Box "Groupe parlementaire."
30. Archives départementales des Bouches-du-Rhône, M6 11577, brochure of the *Mouvement populaire des familles*.
31. Duchen, *Women's Rights*, 35.
32. Archives de la Fédération des Bouches-du-Rhône, Carton 21, "Organization départementale," n.d.
33. AN, 350AP/57, 9 March 1946, 3, 20.
34. See, for example, Anne Cova, "Féminismes et maternité entre les deux guerres en France," *Les Temps modernes*, no. 593 (1997): 47-75 and Karen Offen, "Depopulation, Nationalism and Feminism in Fin-de-siècle France," *American Historical Review*, vol. 89 (1984): 648-76.
35. AN, 350AP/55, 8 April 1945.
36. Fraser, "Rethinking," 124.
37. William Guéraiche, "Des femmes en politique à la Libération: vers de nouvelles représentations féminines?" *Les Temps modernes*, no. 593 (1997), 99.
38. For her life, see Association Les Femmes et La Ville (sous la direction d'Yvonne Knibiehler), *Germaine Poinso-Chapuis. Femme d'Etat (1901-1981)* (Aix-en-Provence, 1998) and Stéphanie Arnaud, "Germaine Poinso-Chapuis, une marseillaise en politique, 1901-1981," Maîtrise d'histoire, Université de Provence, 1994-1995.
39. Jean-Claude Delbreil, *Centrisme et democratie-chrétienne en France: Le Parti démocrate populaire des origines au M.R.P. 1919-1944* (Paris, 1990), 57.
40. Archives de la Fédération des Bouches-du-Rhône (MRP), Carton O, "Vie des Sections."
41. Bruno Béthouart, *Le M.R.P. dans le Nord-Pas-de-Calais, 1944-1967* (Westhoek, 1984), 136.
42. *MRP Vous Parle*, February 1950, 7.
43. William Guéraiche, "Les femmes politiques de 1944 à 1947: quelle libération?" in *CLIO: Histoire, femmes et sociétés*, no. 1 (1995): 165-86.
44. *MRP Vous Parle*, September-October 1949, 6.
45. *L'Aube*, 16-17 December 1945.
46. *MRP Vous Parle*, April 1950, 7.
47. Mariette Sineau, "Des Femmes en Politique, Rapport pour le CNRS, Avril 1986," 14-15; Elisabeth Guigou, *Etre femme en politique* (Paris, 1997), 102ff.
48. Scott, "'Querelle des Femmes'," 5.
49. The electoral system established in the Fourth Republic was based on a list of candidates from each party for each department, rather than an individual party candidate for a single constituency. Larkin, *France Since the Popular Front*, 138-9.

50. AN, 350AP/57, 10 March 1946.
51. *MRP Vous Parle*, April 1948, 3.
52. Stéphanie Arnaud, "L'Eloignement de la politique," in "Germaine Poinso-Chapuis, Femme d'Etat (1901-1981), Colloque organisé par L'Assocation "Les Femmes et la Ville," 138-9.
53. Interview with the author, 17 November 1997.
54. AN, 350AP/124, "Les problêmes de la famille ouvrière."
55. AN, 350AP/55, "Discours de Simone Rollin."
56. Interview with the author, 31 May 1990.
57. Duchen, *Women's Rights*, 102.
58. AN, 350AP/119, "MRP à l'Action," 15 September 1946.
59. AN, 350AP/119, "MRP à l'Action," 15 August 1946.
60. *MRP Vous Parle*, April 1950, 7.
61. *Pour l'information féminine*, March 1954, 6.
62. AN, 350AP/59, 9 January 1949.
63. AN, 350AP/59, 8 January 1949.
64. AN, 350AP/119, "MRP à l'Action," 10 October 1946.
65. Offen, "Women, Citizenship, and Suffrage," 137. In the 1970s, all political parties became preoccupied with this pattern of voting.
66. *Pour l'information féminine*, April 1956, 5.
67. AN, 350AP/119, "MRP à l'action," 15 January 1947.
68. *Forces nouvelles*, 27 February 1954, 9.
69. Chapuis, "Pourquoi nous sommes Partisans," 21.
70. *Forces nouvelles*, 27 February 1954, 9
71. AN, 350AP/58, 25 September 1948.
72. *Pour l'information féminine*, April 1956, 2.
73. *Forces nouvelles*, 11 April 1953, 8.
74. See, for example, Lion Murard and Patrick Zylberman, *L'hygiène dans la République. La santé publique en France, ou l'utopie contrariée 1870-1918* (Paris,1996).
75. Women were not alone in believing that reform could be more effective at the local level. In 1936, Henri Sellier, the dynamic mayor of the Parisian suburb of Suresnes became Minister of Health, but the experience reputedly left him with many doubts about the possibility of enacting social change at the national level. Reynolds, *France Between the Wars*, 154.
76. Sineau, "Des Femmes en Politique," 192.
77. *The Guardian*, 11 May 1997.
78. Offen, "Women, Citizenship, and Suffrage," 132.
79. Scott, "'Querelle des Femmes'," 17.
80. *Le Monde*, 25 March 1998, 6.
81. AN, 350AP/119, "MRP à l'Action," February (II) 1950.
82. Not surprisingly, these Catholic women did not address the issue of women's freedom to control their own bodies. It was only in 1962 that a younger generation of party women began to discuss the issue of birth control, much to the dismay of some older women, who complained that, in a party that was barely surviving, there were more urgent political issues.

Chapter 11

Crisis and Modernization in the Fourth Republic

From Suez to Rome

William I. Hitchcock

I

The link between crisis and modernization is perhaps nowhere as strong as in the history of the French Fourth Republic. This much-disparaged regime, established in October 1946 after two years of partisan wrangling over its constitutional attributes, won few adherents during its short existence. It was beset by an almost uninterrupted series of crises, both internal and external, and was finally laid low by the worst of them, the Algerian War. Few mourned its passing. Charles de Gaulle, who worked assiduously to weaken the Republic during the 1940s and 1950s, routinely engaged in polemics against it throughout his tenure as president of its successor, his own Fifth Republic. In 1954, U.S. President Dwight Eisenhower referred to postwar France as a "helpless, hopeless mass of protoplasm." The British viewed France as the "sick man" of Europe, reduced to the level of the nineteenth-century Ottoman Empire. Commentators routinely bemoaned France's institutional instability, and subsequent historians—aware of the ultimate demise of the Republic—generally consider this period in French history as, in the title of one survey, "the locust years." Crisis became the leitmotif of the regime.[1]

Notes for this chapter begin on page 237.

Recent works, however, have returned to this woeful period to show that the foundations of France's *trente glorieuses*—the almost thirty years of economic growth France enjoyed from the end of the war through the early 1970s—were laid during the 1940s.[2] Hence the paradox of French recovery: a weak, divided regime managed to chart a successful national strategy of recovery and pursue it with effectiveness, so much so that when the European economies really began to take off in the late 1950s, France's was one of the most dynamic. During the decade of the 1960s, French average annual growth of GDP, at 5.8 percent, exceeded German (4.9 percent), American (3.9 percent), and British (2.9 percent). Between 1950 and 1985, France's GDP increased 306 percent, a figure that compares favorably to Germany's growth (374 percent) and more than doubled Britain's (129 percent).[3]

Explanations for this stunning French postwar recovery vary. The memoirs of leading economic officials from the period, such as Jean Monnet, Pierre Massé, Robert Marjolin, François Bloch-Lainé, and Jean Fourastié, underscore the impact of a young, innovative technocratic elite that led the French government to accept indicative planning, state investment, and an ambitious program of industrial modernization. New men and new measures overcame traditional French *malthusianisme*.[4] J.-J. Carré, P. Dubois, and E. Malinvaud, in their comprehensive analysis of French economic growth, suggest that France profited from a happy convergence of economic, social, and international developments, such as an increase in French productivity, the upsurge of long-suppressed demand for goods by postwar consumers, and a favorable international environment that saw the United States assist France with some $5 billion in loans and grants and, just as significant, new techniques of production and management. The heavy investment by the state in the modernization of the nation's productive plant was a major factor, as was the presence of a dynamic economic team at the helm of the French administration.[5] More recent scholarship, acknowledging these points, has broadened the picture by giving particular emphasis to the shift in economic thinking within French government and industry that took place from the mid-1930s right through to the end of the 1950s; a shift in *mentalités* was the prerequisite to changes in economic behavior. This approach has placed the evolution of French economic thinking into the context of the long-running social, political, and economic trauma that France experienced in this period and that began to heal only with the stabilization of international politics in the early 1950s. These accounts also stress the influence of the United States in pressing new models of economic management upon France during the period of postwar reconstruction.[6] Finally, France's adhesion to the 1957 Treaty of Rome, the founding document of the European Economic Community (EEC), has been seen as a critical element in France's postwar economic success. The EEC led directly to the expansion of France's foreign trade, increased industrial competition, encouraged specialization, and improved productivity. As William James Adams has pointed out, French growth was already on the rise by 1950, but the increase between the advent of the EEC in 1958 and 1985 is especially impressive. In this period, the percentage increase in volume of GDP in France surpassed every other industrialized country except Japan.[7] Clearly, a combination of new ideas and personnel, external aid, domestic restructuring and modernization, and trade policy all aided French growth.[8]

To make this tale still more remarkable, it must be remembered that this economic recovery was engineered in the face of numerous political and international crises that left French governments with little room for maneuver. In fact, the desperate need to address the ongoing political and economic crises of the period forced the pace of policy-making, and served to galvanize political opinion around innovative and even radical solutions to the problem of recovery. The Monnet Plan offers the best example. In 1945-46, France, politically immobilized by partisanship within the National Assembly, faced a severe balance of payments crisis, a coal shortage, and the security threat posed by a worsening of US-Soviet relations. The Monnet Plan, which received Cabinet approval in January 1947, was by no means an answer to all of these challenges, but it provided the government with a new institutional mechanism for national reconstruction. It removed economic decision-making from the often-competing ministries, and outlined a strategy of recovery that encompassed economic planning, investment, and international loan agreements all in one. It also framed France's diplomatic strategy toward Germany, because the Monnet Plan set industrial targets that were dependent upon imports of German coal—compelling the government to pursue a hard line on German economic recovery with its fellow Allied occupation powers. Crisis had served to spur on innovation in policy-making.[9]

So too with the Schuman Plan of 1950. When Robert Schuman came to the Foreign Ministry in mid-1948, he initiated a period of rapid improvement in Franco-German relations based on the principle that France had to grant Germany economic and political independence so that Germany, in repaying France's trust, would engage itself to Western Europe. In early 1950, however, as the United States and Great Britain began to press for German rearmament, Schuman's policy of rapprochement appeared severely threatened. If a near-sovereign Germany, then showing signs of an impressive economic recovery, were granted the privilege of restoring its armed forces, the European balance of power would swing radically in Germany's favor, rendering meaningless the sacrifices Schuman had made to improve relations. Schuman's response was to seek immediate German entry into a binding economic community, centered on the production of coal and steel, that would ensure a continuing balance of economic power between the two adversaries. France, with the Schuman Plan secured, could weather the future debate on rearmament knowing that Germany's coal and steel producing capacities were linked to France's own.[10] In the case of the Monnet and Schuman Plans, crisis offered political actors an important lever with which to persuade reluctant parliamentary, industrial, and agricultural circles to press ahead with radical solutions. The two plans became the twin pillars of France's new economic policy, joining indicative planning at home with a broader, Europe-wide strategy of integration and sector-specific economic cooperation.

Like its better known predecessors, the Treaty of Rome of 1957 was also born in an atmosphere of political and international crisis—a crisis which in fact catalyzed French acceptance of the Treaty itself. Though the process of arriving at France's commitment to the common market was a long and difficult one, the timing and the swiftness with which Guy Mollet's government moved to embrace the customs union was determined by an economic and especially an international crisis that left France, in late 1956, feeling vulnerable, insecure, and at a crossroads with respect to its national identity and its future prospects as a European power. The most visible manifestation of this crisis was the failed attempt in November 1956 to invade Egypt and reassert western control over the Suez Canal, which had been nationalized by the Egyptian leader Gamal Abdel Nasser in July.

Scholars remain divided over how much emphasis to place on the impact of the Suez crisis in triggering French acceptance of the Treaty of Rome. Hanns Jürgen Küsters has suggested that the negotiations on the Treaty were stalled, and that "the successful outcome of the EEC negotiations was an historical accident, initiated by Nasser's Suez crisis in November 1956."[11] Britain, by sacrificing its French ally in a moment of high international drama, pushed France into Germany's waiting arms. Recent studies by Frances Lynch and Andrew Moravcsik, however, reject the influence of Suez, suggesting that French officials had already arrived at the decision to press ahead with a gradual reduction of tariffs before the November 1956 crisis, after a long internal debate about the respective merits of protectionism versus external competition.[12] This chapter tries to chart a middle course, showing that Suez was the acute phase of a longer crisis that had been running throughout 1956, during which French planners had begun to accept the need for a tighter economic relationship among the states of Western Europe. The shift was driven by strategic, colonial, and economic considerations. The Suez crisis served this process by placing French weaknesses in stark relief and offered a powerful tool to Mollet and his advisers for bringing the long, difficult, and then stalemated negotiations over the common market to a swift and profitable conclusion.

II

When in the spring of 1955, Belgian Foreign Minister Paul-Henri Spaak raised the proposal for the establishment of a common market between the Schuman Plan Six, the idea was met with widespread hostility in France. The political appeal of linking West Germany, since 1955 a near-sovereign state, more closely to the western powers was undeniable, but the price to be paid seemed prohibitive. France, with its long tradition of protectionism, was leery of opening up its markets to international competition through the means of a customs union. By contrast, the Benelux countries and Germany, whose gross national product was to a far greater extent linked to foreign trade, were more favorable toward a common market, and it is no accident that the idea was first mooted in 1953 by the Dutch Foreign Minister, Johan Willem Beyen. The French were not only concerned about the impact such a plan might have economically; many in French political circles sought to avoid another lengthy debate on Europe so soon after the rejection of the European Defense Community. The battle over the EDC had left French prestige battered and the parliament divided. Indeed, it remains hard to explain why the French government, which evinced considerable hostility to the common market proposals of 1955, came in the end to sign the Treaty of Rome in March 1957, an accord that was promptly ratified by the French parliament.

Compared to the Monnet and Schuman Plans, the European Economic Community has received less attention from historians.[13] The memoirs of key players tend to stress the role of individual "Europeanists" such as Monnet and Spaak in "re-launching" the movement toward European integration in the wake of the EDC debacle. These men kept the idea of "Europe" before public opinion, especially through Monnet's lobbying group called the Action Committee for the United States of Europe, which during 1956 and 1957 kept up a steady drumbeat in favor of integration.[14] Further research on the origins of the common market has shed light on the role of Guy Mollet, a longtime advocate of European integration who became premier in January 1956. Mollet pursued a deft strategy, urging on his reluctant technical advisers to engage in negotiations, and using the prospect of Euratom, which many in France liked because of its restrictive features on Germany's atomic potential, as a lure to catch the bigger fish, the common market. Mollet's foreign minister, Christian Pineau, preferred another analogy: Euratom was a smokescreen behind which progress on the common market could be made.[15] In explaining Mollet's adhesion to the common market idea, scholars have pointed to his socialist credentials, his belief in the need to promote Europe as a Third Force in the East-West conflict, and his own national political strategy, which played off of resentment toward the United States for its meddling role in France's colonial affairs. Mollet was also eager to extend the common market to France's African colonies so as to promote African development and thereby entice these colonies to remain loyal to the metropole.[16] In these explanations, economic factors were less prominent in Mollet's thinking than power-political ones.

Economic factors, though, were not by any means absent from French bureaucratic thinking on the common market. New research by Frances Lynch outlines the debate within the French administration on the common market. On the one side stood the protectionists, who sought to quash any lowering of external tariffs for fear of bringing on an unwanted rush of foreign competition into the French economy. They feared economic dislocation and social unrest, which a weak Fourth Republic, already institutionally enfeebled by war and political partisanship, would be ill-equipped to handle. On the other side of the debate stood the modernizers, who argued that in order for France to keep up with Germany economically, and to profit from the already-visible postwar European boom, the country had to make itself more competitive, and this could only be done by submitting itself to the cold shower of international competition. The era of protectionism was an anachronism and would not serve to promote French power in the long run. According to Lynch, this debate was ultimately resolved in favor of the modernizers, who then led the charge in bringing France around to support the formation of the EEC. Crucial to the successful conclusion of the EEC treaty, then, was a conversion of economic thinking within the French government in the mid-1950s.[17]

These three explanations for France's eventual adhesion to the common market—the role of individual "Europeanists," the power-political and colonial strategy of Mollet, and the conversion of economic thinking within the administration—help explain the gradual shift in elite opinion toward a policy of European integration and liberalization. But the transition was not a smooth one. Like the Monnet and Schuman Plans, the common market needed a crisis before these trends converged upon a point of action. That crisis was the one at Suez in late 1956. Without Suez, the EEC may well have been born, but not as soon as it was, nor as easily. Suez helped Mollet persuade the parliament that France, whose British ally had proven weak and irresolute and whose American patron had stabbed France in the back, now needed new friends. United with its European neighbors, France could lay the foundation for a reneweal of French and European independence. The prerequisite to such independence lay in economic strength, and that, Mollet and his team argued, could only come from increased competition with, and broader access to, European markets. Crisis once again served to concentrate the French mind.

III

When Paul-Henri Spaak began his effort to "relaunch" the European integration effort that had been so badly hurt by the EDC fiasco, he knew that it would be unwise to push for anything too ambitious, given the state of public opinion in France. He thought that progress could be made in integrating certain sectors of the Western European economies, notably in the areas of transportation, electricity, and atomic energy. He also pointed out to the French that given the current international climate—the Austrian state treaty on unification and neutralization of that once-occupied country had just been completed and the Soviets were making noise about a four-power meeting to do the same for Germany—the time was propitious to link Germany more securely to the West.[18] The French government was receptive to these overtures, but knew that hostility to supranationality would severely curtail any major new effort on European integration. Initiatives would have to be limited to specific sectors of the economy.[19] But Spaak pressed forward, and on 18 May 1955, in conjunction with his Dutch and Luxemburger counterparts, proposed that the six Schuman Plan countries meet to discuss both further sector-specific cooperation in energy and transportation, and the institution of a customs union between the six ECSC countries.[20]

The French government quickly warmed to the idea of a European agency for atomic energy. This scheme seemed to have many of the same advantages that the Schuman Plan had offered in 1950. A European atomic program would restrict the development of an independent German one; it would put an end to the bilateral scramble to establish a special "atomic" relationship with the United States that, for example, the Belgians had already undertaken; and it promised to spread the costs of research and development among a broad base of states. Provided that the European effort would not prohibit the development of a French atomic weapon, planning for which was already underway, Euratom offered France significant advantages.[21] It was no surprise, then, that the Germans should be considerably hostile to the scheme. Enjoying their newfound freedom in the international system, the Germans were reluctant to place this emerging new technology, which appeared to hold vast implications for German economic expansion, under a restrictive, French-controlled regime.[22]

The attitudes of the two countries were, however, precisely the reverse when considering the second topic raised by Benelux: a common market between the six ECSC countries. Aside from the political problem—there remained a high degree of residual hostility to integration within the French parliament—the French bureaucracy raised numerous objections on economic grounds. The common market required a common external tariff, but would this be set at the low level favored by Benelux or the high rate imposed by France? Also, the costs of production were higher in France due to its generous social benefits for the labor force (paid holidays, shorter working week, better pay for women); this social legislation would have to be adopted by France's neighbors in order to level the playing field. The problem of opening the heavily-protected agricultural sector to competition raised serious objections, as did the possibility that a common market in Europe could weaken France's ties to its overseas territories. Finally, the French saw in the common market scheme a creeping supranationalism: once instituted, it would require a common political authority and perhaps a central bank, a prospect that would be thoroughly reviled by the National Assembly.[23] By contrast, the Germans were cautiously in favor, as Chancellor Konrad Adenauer and his State Secretary for Foreign Affairs Walter Hallstein believed that more sector-specific cooperation along the lines of the Schuman Plan would complete the linkage of Germany into Western Europe. Still, the Germans wanted to be sure that in agreeing to enter into the joint atomic research and development plan of Euratom, they also gained concessions from France that would open up European trade—a boon for Germany's export-oriented economy.[24] Despite the public stance of Euro-philia evident at the six-nation Messina conference, convened in early June 1955 to examine the Benelux proposals, serious battles about the two proposals lay ahead.

While dubious about the prospects for a customs union, the French government did not want to reject it out of hand. During the long-running talks on Euratom and the common market [they met in Brussels intermittently from July 1955 until the spring of 1957] the French searched for ways to accept the Benelux proposals but within a treaty that offered certain safeguards and protections to French interests.[25] Why this effort to be conciliatory? Perhaps this stance reflects the French view that they could secure significant concessions from the five partners, just as France had been able to do throughout the EDC debate. The common market idea had no substantial form, and the French technocrats sought to craft a treaty that provided significant protections for French interests to cushion the blow of a common market.[26] Further, the French grew increasingly attached to the Euratom project. They saw in this scheme a way of reinvigorating European integration, reclaiming some prestige for France following the EDC crisis, and above all, they saw it as a useful and constructive way to contain German independence—and possibly the evolution of a special German-American relationship—in a field that was considered to have huge future importance in the European balance of economic power.[27] But in order to get Euratom, the French were going to have give the Germans and Benelux the common market. The linkage between the two treaties had become explicit by the winter of 1955-56, and the French were well aware of this.[28]

International factors also help explain French willingness to pursue the common market talks. The French were very concerned about the failure of the four-power talks held in Geneva during the second half of 1955 on German unification. High hopes had been raised in July when Khrushchev appeared conciliatory toward the issue of unification; by November, however, he had soured on the idea. French policy-makers feared that the disappointment among the West German public would create pressure upon the government to search for an all-German settlement, at the expense of the Western Alliance. Without speedy and concrete results to give the Germans a sense that they belonged in the Western community and that they stood to gain from deeper association with it, the Germans might drift toward neutralism and appeasement of the East.[29] As one French official noted, "In Germany, time is working on the side of nationalism."[30]

The government may also have been motivated to press ahead with the negotiations by Britain's attitude. The British reaction both to Euratom and the common market project was totally hostile, as Prime Minister Eden made clear in his talks with President Eisenhower in January 1956. The British and French had long tussled over the best means to secure European cooperation: the British favored the intergovernmental approach of the OEEC, while the French preferred integrative mechanisms that clearly bound Germany, such as the Schuman Plan. The British expressed little interest in Euratom, quietly pooh-poohing the meager accomplishments of their continental neighbors in the area of atomic energy; but the prospect of a common external tariff clearly scared them, especially because they believed that France would use its influence to ensure that this tariff was set at a high level.[31] The persistent British effort to deny the validity of integration as a means to underpin a Franco-German settlement caused irritation in Paris. The French always wished to have Britain join the new institutions of "Europe," the better to balance out Germany's preponderant role. But by keeping Europe at an arms length, the British only made the French conclude that binding, supranational mechanisms to control Germany were all the more imperative.[32]

These external factors offered a political case for the common market that was badly needed, because the technical services of the French administration continued to produce cautious, if not downright hostile, memoranda concerning the economic dimensions of the plan. When in April 1956 the Brussels conference finally produced a detailed proposal on how the common market was to be put into practice—a document called the Spaak Report—French experts condemned it quite harshly. The same objections were raised then as had been raised a year earlier: the French economy would be swamped by foreign competition that French business was ill-equipped to handle. This in turn would compel "profound transformations, which may be beneficial, but which will create social and economic dislocations [*bouleversements*] which must not be underestimated." Once again, a desire to see Euratom succeed, and a distinct fear of being seen as anti-Europe, meant that France could not reject the EEC completely; but serious safeguards would have to be built in to any future treaty.[33]

Progress was still further delayed during the summer of 1956, as two issues in particular almost scotched the talks. First, the French began a sustained effort to bring their overseas territories—to which some 50% of their exports still went—into the common market. The reason for this was that the French had concluded that the common market could be used as a tool to effect the modernization of the export industries in the French empire. France now wanted a modernization fund, to be funded by the Six, in return for opening up its colonial markets. The Germans were hostile to the idea of being associated with colonialism in any form, while the other countries all felt that they had better things to do with their national budgets than contribute to the modernization of the French empire.[34]

The second tough issue that slowed progress on the treaties related to Euratom. The French parliament, in July 1956, passed a resolution supporting the principles of Euratom, but insisting that the agency in no way restrict the development of an atom bomb by France, should France wish to proceed with one.[35] The Germans were galled by this blatant double standard. The French would be able to profit from a European funded project to pursue their own national military ends. This explains why the French wanted a strong Euratom, having a monopoly over the importing [from the United States] of fissionable material and its eventual production in Europe. The Germans, by contrast, sought a much looser Euratom, one that simply coordinated national projects.[36] In retaliation for these French efforts to manipulate the treaty to their own advantage, the Germans adopted an inflexible stance in the common market negotiations. The Germans now opposed the harmonization of labor legislation as demanded by the French, for this, as German Economics Minister Ludwig Erhard argued, would foist the inefficiencies of the French social welfare system onto the rest of Europe. By September 1956, progress on the common market and Euratom had broken down, and the subsequent meeting of the six foreign ministers on 20-21 October 1956 did nothing to break the logjam.[37]

IV

Within a few weeks, however, this unpromising state of affairs was completely reversed when, at a meeting in Paris on 6 November, Chancellor Adenauer and Premier Mollet managed to broker a compromise that saved the EEC/Euratom treaty. In order to explain why this stalemate was broken so quickly in late 1956, it is important to recall the general state of political and economic affairs in which the Mollet government was operating. In retrospect, we can see that 1956 was a year of intensifying crisis, the year when the death knell of the Fourth Republic started to toll. The crises were interlocking: first came the political crisis triggered by the advent of Mollet to power in January 1956, which in turn worsened the situation in Algeria. As Mollet committed ever more resources to fight in North Africa, the economy began to buckle under the strain. Economic troubles only highlighted the growing asymmetry between French and German power, for across the Rhine the economic recovery was in full force. The Suez crisis, then, came only at the end of a year filled with assaults on French power and influence, and the country's political and economic stability. These elements of the 1956 crisis require some comment if Mollet's decision in late 1956 to forge ahead with the common market and break the deadlock is to be understood.

The first dimension of the 1956 crisis was political. Guy Mollet became premier on 5 February 1956, with a commanding vote of 420 deputies backing his leftist "*Front républicain*" government. This vote disguised the tumult that had led to his premiership, however, and the political damage that Mollet's ascendancy had caused. The country had wanted the Radical Pierre Mendès France, the man who had ended the Indochina war, to be premier, as voter polls showed. The Republican Front was conceived by supporters of Mendès France, especially Jean-Jacques Servan-Schreiber's review *L'Express*, working in conjunction with the Socialists, François Mitterrand's UDSR, and dissident Gaullists under Jacques Chaban-Delmas. It was a loose coalition of interests given coherence by Mendès France's assertion that he sought to bring peace in Algeria, continue modernization, defend the interests of the middle class, and restore French influence. Above all, his public declaration that he would throw himself into a search for conciliation in Algeria found strong support among the public. Yet the elections, as was always the case in the Fourth Republic, produced no clear-cut verdict. The Communists remained France's largest party, with over 25% of the vote, and the Socialists and Radicals won about 15% each. But the left faced the hostility of the MRP, the right-wing independents, and the new political force of Pierre Poujade whose grass-roots right-wing movement now held 51 seats in the Assembly. Nonetheless, the public saw these results, in which the Radicals had gained over a million votes since 1951, as a statement in favor of a *Mendésiste* government. It was not to be. For Mendès to gain a majority, he would have to accept Communist votes, which he had famously rejected when he became premier in June 1954. Without the PCF, he would need the MRP, the Christian Democratic party that still hated Mendès for having killed "their" EDC project. The parliamentary arithmetic was such that only the Socialist leader, Mollet, would have a chance at winning a majority. He did, but the public was thereby denied the one genuinely popular leader that the Fourth Republic had put forward; the parliament once again had thwarted the will of the people.[38]

The second link in the ongoing 1956 crisis was forged in Algeria. In the fall of 1954, the Algerian independence movement had begun a military uprising against the French colonial establishment in Algeria. After a particularly vicious assault on European civilians in Philippeville in August 1955, the French army took revenge on the Muslim population, leaving thousands dead and radicalizing the situation. On 6 February 1956, the day after receiving his investiture from the parliament, Mollet flew to Algiers to show his commitment to crafting a settlement there. During the election, he had made unguarded comments about "this stupid war" and had even raised the possibility of independence for Algeria. Indeed, these comments had brought the PCF to support his bid for the premiership. They also created massive unease in Algiers, and when Mollet arrived there he was mobbed by the middle and lower class European settlers who bombarded the prime minister's car with tomatoes, rotten fruit, and stones. The civilian government was only rescued from the crowd by the intervention of the army—a telling moment when the army's strength and the government's weakness were starkly evident. Shaken by the violence against him, and now aware of the hostility of the Europeans to any political settlement, Mollet appointed as resident general in Algiers Robert Lacoste, a fellow Socialist who announced a tough policy of fighting the rebel movement while offering palliatives to the Muslim population. If Mendès France had offered the brief hope of a lasting solution in Algeria, Mollet now delegated the problem to Lacoste, who was granted the power to govern by decree. By July 1956, over 400,000 French military personnel were serving in Algeria. Mollet had gone to war, and the promise of the Republican Front was a distant memory.[39]

Mollet's policy in Algeria led to the third dimension of the 1956 crisis. Since the end of World War II, France had been fighting a tough battle with its external finances, and by the mid-fifties, appeared to be winning. In 1954-55, France established a balance of payments equilibrium, even briefly enjoying a modest surplus in 1955. But the war in Algeria, requiring in 1956 300 billion francs of expenditure, undid this achievement by boosting inflation. This in turn exacerbated the trade deficit which ballooned to $890 million by the end of the year. This had to be covered by drawing upon currency reserves, which dwindled dangerously. At the same moment, the seizure of the Suez Canal in July 1956 by Nasser placed a choke-hold on French imports of oil, 90% of which passed through the Canal, and boosted prices of petroleum products on which France was highly dependent. Added to these external troubles, Mollet now faced the challenge of fulfilling his ambitious social policies like improved health benefits to the poor and elderly, a third week of paid vacations for employees, and increased construction of public housing. By the end of the year, the French budget deficit approached one trillion francs.[40]

These, then, were the circumstances facing the Mollet government as it entered the acute phase of the 1956 crisis. In this environment, the common market question gained immense significance, coming to represent a crossroads for French national strategy. In fighting for Algeria, France was still fighting a rearguard action for Empire, for protectionism, for the traditional trappings of great power status. Euratom and the common market, by contrast, offered not only innovative ways to remedy the energy problem, to enhance competition and promote trade; it would also signal a new effort by France to augment its national power through economic growth and modernization rather than through war and imperial preference. Mollet had come to discover the meaning of Mendès France's slogan: *gouverner, c'est choisir.*

It was time, then, to break the stalemated negotiations and make progress toward the common market. Mollet, like all his Fourth Republic predecessors, was fortunate to have Konrad Adenauer as a counterpart. Mollet and Adenauer, both strongly pro-Europe since the EDC experience, had also found common ground in their suspicion of the Soviet Union and their distaste for heavy-handed American diplomacy.[41] When in late September, Mollet and Adenauer also concluded an agreement on the return to Germany of the French-annexed Saar territory—a region that had long poisoned Franco-German relations—the way seemed open to compromise on European integration as well.[42] Mollet, in a letter to Adenauer of 31 October, told the chancellor that now was the time to "show our people and world opinion our common determination to promote together the construction of Europe." The issues were not technical but political, Mollet believed, and required intervention by the politicial leaders to be solved.[43]

Thus, the Suez crisis, as it began to unfold in the fall of 1956, found the French and German leaders—against the judgment of their advisors—primed to forge a compromise on the remaining issues on the common market and Euratom. Suez proved to be the catalyst for a swift resolution of the outstanding issues. Even before the actual Franco-British-Israeli invasion of the Canal zone took place in November 1956, Adenauer had begun to fulminate against American policy. He was already irritated by what he saw as U.S. neglect of a European role in world affairs. He thought the Americans were too willing to accept, in tacit agreement with Moscow, a divided and nuclearized world. While the Europeans earned the wrath of the Third World for fighting communism there, the Americans stood aloof, expressing disinterest in the fate of Europe. The Suez crisis in Adenauer's mind only underscored the need for Europe to join together in a tight political union, so as to chart more effectively a European foreign policy that was not subject to judgment from Washington.[44]

The meeting between Mollet and Adenauer in Paris on 6 November came at a moment of immense tension for France. On 29 October, the Israeli airforce launched an assault on Egyptian military targets in the Sinai peninsula; by 5 November, the Israelis had reached the Suez Canal, as well as the Straits of Tiran on the southern tip of Sinai. On 5 November, French and British aircraft came into the battle, ostensibly as "peacemakers," but in fact in direct collusion with the Israelis in a plan to topple Nasser and seize control of the Canal. On 6 November, French and British troops landed on Egyptian beaches at Port Said and Port Fuad. At this very same moment, starting on 4 November, the Soviet Union began its massive and bloody repression of "national communism" in Hungary.

It was natural, then, that Adenauer and Mollet, who had come together to examine European issues, should have been sidetracked in their talks by the international crisis. And once again, the French-German meeting provided an opportunity for Adenauer to vent his anger at the United States. Suez, he claimed, was the fault of the Americans to start with, because of their mishandling of the Aswan Dam affair; but now the Europeans were the ones losing face. It was time, he said, to unite "against America." The Americans, he continued, had lost hope in a united Europe and were seeking a "pax atomica" with the Russians. The unwillingness of the United States to oppose Soviet repression in Hungary was evidence of that. In the midst of Adenauer's rantings, Mollet was called out of the room to take a telephone call from British Prime Minister Anthony Eden. As recounted by Foreign Minister Christian Pineau, this call totally deflated Mollet, for Eden was calling to tell him that Britain—at the insistence of the United States—had unilaterally decided to call off the invasion. It was, Pineau wrote, "un coup dur" for Mollet, and for any hope of independent European action in world affairs. Returning to the room, Mollet told Adenauer what had happened, and after an awkward silence, Adenauer gently encouraged his French counterpart with the telling phrase: "Now, it is time to create Europe!"[45]

Pineau saw this meeting as a turning point: "Starting from this moment, when Western Europe felt, rightly or wrongly, that it could no longer count on the United States when its security was threatened, the only solution was the union of the Six, and the creation of institutions capable, if not of assuring their own defense, at least of bringing these countries closer and more tightly together on the economic plane." The actions of Nasser, Khrushchev, Eisenhower, and Eden—coming at the end of a year filled with political and economic crisis for France—pushed the French and Germans together. That very day, upon orders from Mollet and Adenauer, the common market negotiators resolved many of their differences—largely in favor of the French position. Within two days of the Mollet-Adenauer meeting in Paris, Pineau could report that the Germans had softened their attitude on Euratom, on harmonization of social policy, and on the safeguard clauses associated with the lowering of tariffs. When Hallstein continued to object to bringing the French overseas territories into the common market because of the likely increase in costs of German imports of tropical products, Adenauer quickly stifled him. "Hallstein," he is reported to have said during the final negotiations on the common market, "stop boring us with your bananas, your coffee, your cocoa. The work we are engaged in is too important to be compromised by such minor economic considerations." Never had the political nature of the compromise wrought at the end of 1956 been more apparent.[46]

Of course, there still remained a number of hurdles for the EEC and Euratom treaties. Despite Adenauer and Mollet's intervention, the technical services remained reluctant to give in so swiftly, and negotiations continued on through February 1957.[47] The Suez crisis, however, seemed to add more weight to the French argument that Europe needed Euratom and the common market as a means of offsetting American power. The French continued to argue for a powerful Euratom that would control all fissionable material and would not be constrained by the United States in any way. This, Mollet told Adenauer, would insure that "the relations between Europe and America develop on an equal basis."[48] And on the common market, as Alan Milward has noted, the French got almost everything they wanted, including control over the pace at which tariffs were lowered, commitments to equalize the social costs of production (i.e., welfare and labor benefits) across the Six, preferential treatment for the French empire, and an investment fund for modernizing these overseas territories. This latter concession was especially impressive. From December 1956 to February 1957, the French and Belgians pressed hard for the investment fund against heavy Dutch resistance; the Germans, reluctant to be associated with colonialism, were now too committed to the treaty to let this issue block an accord.[49] It was a sign of how good the deal was for France that the National Assembly, notoriously divided on every major issue of the day, nonetheless handily passed a resolution in favor of the government's European policy, with only the Communists and Poujadists in opposition. Christian Pineau, in speaking to the parliament, framed the issue in terms of French power and influence. "You must choose between Europe and the uncertain future of an isolated France," he told the Assembly. "The recent events [of Suez] have shown that only through unity can the European countries meet threats" such as the one thrown down by Nasser. Mollet too, in taking the podium, stated that the only alternative to Europe was "autarky, a slowdown, asphyxiation, and disaffection of the overseas population." In light of the Assembly's positive reaction to these arguments, the other five partners—so used to having European integration held hostage by the French—moved quickly to meet France's final desiderata: a five-year investment fund for overseas development, into which the six would pay $581 million, and from which France would take $512 million for her own territories.[50]

On 25 March 1957, the six nations signed the Treaty of Rome. Clearly, the EEC was not a response to the Suez crisis. The idea of a customs union and an atomic pool had been in the air for three years, and intense negotiations had been under way since the spring of 1955. But these talks had stalled at the end of 1956, and the Suez affair, coming at the end of a year filled with political challenges and economic troubles, created the conditions in which agreement could be reached. It brought Adenauer and Mollet together at a time of high drama, compelling Adenauer to make major concessions to France just at a time when the French badly needed a "European" success to offset the humiliation at Suez. And it allowed Mollet and Pineau to argue for the treaty from the perspective of French power and international stature, rather than engage in a piece-by-piece adumbration of a highly technical treaty with which most deputies were, as Jacques Fauvet noted in *Le Monde*, quite unfamiliar.[51] Mollet and Pineau recognized the value of the Suez crisis in bringing public opinion around to support the treaty. Suez did not blaze the path to Rome. The Six had already begun to proceed down that road. Yet the failure at Suez paradoxically smoothed the way and hastened the pace of the travelers.[52]

It was typical of the regime that international crisis had been needed to create political momentum in favor of new and untested policies. The Fourth Republic could at least take credit for having made a virtue of necessity. As a source of legitimacy, however, this strategy was deeply flawed. The regime's successes in facing down crises and promoting economic growth could never be translated into popular political support or an enduring commitment to the 1946 Constitution which routinely deprived the people of its favored leaders (Pinay and Mendès France especially) and offered instead a carousel of twenty-six different governments between de Gaulle's departure in 1946 and his return in 1958. The events in 1958 in Algeria revealed the dangers of using crisis as a tool of governance: sometimes it could backfire. Surely a large part of the reason that de Gaulle's bid for power in 1958 came off so smoothly was precisely because the French people had grown weary of a regime that was too preoccupied with crisis to enjoy the fruits of the postwar expansion that was already taking hold by the end of the 1950s. Modernization and crisis need not be paired forever. As Jean-Pierre Rioux has said, France, in supporting de Gaulle and his Fifth Republic constitution, expressed "a deep-seated desire to be governed strongly and well."[53] Governance was the heart of the issue. For despite the many international problems that France faced in the ten years after the war, the chief source of crisis came from within, from a divided public and a divided political establishment that simply could not overcome ideological, class, and regional divides to offer some degree of national unity and consensus. The Fourth Republic's achievements, tragically, did not redound the credit of the regime because they had in most cases been accomplished in spite of it. De Gaulle stood for, and indeed provided, the much-longed for *rassemblement* that had been missing in France for at least a generation and, perhaps, since 1914. In searching for a new postwar national identity, France sought to embrace modernization, expansion and growth, and leave the crisis years behind.

Notes

The author wishes to thank William G. Gray for his assistance.

1. Frank Giles, *The Locust Years: The Story of the Fourth French Republic, 1946-1958* (New York, 1991). For works that examine the institutional weaknesses of the regime, see Philip Williams, *Crisis and Compromise: Politics in the Fourth Republic* (Hamden, CT, 1964); Georgette Elgey, *La République des illusions, 1945-1951* (Paris, 1965) and her *La République des contradictions, 1951-1954* (Paris, 1968); and Jacques Fauvet, *La IVème Republique* (Paris, 1959); Alexander Werth, *France, 1940-1955* (London, 1956); and Paul-Marie de la Gorce, *L'après-guerre, 1944-1952* (Paris, 1979) and his *Apogée et mort de la IVème République* (Grasset, 1979). For Ike's comment, see Rolf Steininger, "John Foster Dulles, the European Defense Community, and the German Question," in Richard H. Immerman, ed., *John Foster Dulles and the Diplomacy of the Cold War* (Princeton, 1990), 88. On de Gaulle's hostility to the regime, see Jean Charlot, *Le Gaullisme de l'opposition, 1946-1958* (Paris, 1983), and Claude Mauriac, *The Other de Gaulle: Diaries, 1944-1954* (New York, 1973).
2. Pierre Gerbet, *Le relèvement, 1944-1949* (Paris, 1991); Gérard Bossuat, *La France, l'aide américaine et la construction européenne, 1944-1954* (Paris, 1992); Irwin Wall, *The United States and the Making of Postwar France, 1945-1954* (Cambridge, 1991); Richard Kuisel, *Capitalism and the State in Modern France: Renovation and Management in the Twentieth Century* (Cambridge, 1981); Michel Margairaz, *L'Etat, les finances, et l'économie: Histoire d'une conversion* (Paris, 1991); and William I. Hitchcock, *France Restored: Cold War Diplomacy and the Quest for Leadership in Europe, 1944-1954* (Chapel Hill, N.C., 1998).
3. Fernand Braudel and Ernest Labrousse, eds., *Histoire économique et sociale de la France*, vol. 4, part 3, (Paris, 1982), 1012; William James Adams, *Restructuring the French Economy: Government and the Rise of Market Competition since World War II* (Washington, D.C., 1989), 4.
4. Jean Monnet, *Memoirs* (Garden City, 1978); Pierre Massé, *Le Plan, ou l'anti-hasard* (Paris, 1965); Robert Marjolin, *Memoirs, 1911-1986: Architect of European Unity* (London, 1989); François Bloch-Lainé, *Profession: Fonctionnaire* (Paris, 1976); Jean Fourastié and J-P Courtheoux, *La planification économique en France* (Paris, 1968).
5. J.-J. Carré, P. Dubois, and E. Malinvaud, *French Economic Growth* (Stanford, 1975), 495-506.
6. There is a large literature on this topic, but the best recent work is Margairaz, *L'Etat, les finances, et l'économie*; Philippe Mioche, *Le Plan Monnet: Genèse et élaboration, 1941-1947* (Paris, 1987); Bossuat, *La France, l'aide américaine, et la construction européenne*; and Richard Kuisel, *Capitalism and the State in Modern France.*
7. Adams, *Restructuring*, 4, 6, 269; and see Carré, Dubois, and Malinvaud, *French Economic Growth*, 393-416.
8. Charles de Gaulle, not wishing to acknowledge the achievements of his predecessors, stressed the role of the financial and monetary reforms he initiated in December 1958 upon taking

office as chief of state of the Fifth Republic. Charles de Gaulle, *Mémoires d'espoir*, vol. 1 (Paris, 1970), 146-58.

9. On these themes, see two especially useful articles: Frances Lynch, "Resolving the Paradox of the Monnet Plan: National and International Planning in French Reconstruction," *Economic History Review* 37, no. 2 (May 1984), 229-43; and Philippe Mioche, "Aux origines du Plan Monnet: Les discours et les contenus dans les premières plans français," *Revue historique* 538 (April-June 1981), 405-38. Also Alan S. Milward, *The Reconstruction of Western Europe, 1945-1951* (Berkeley, 1984), 126-41; and Hitchcock, *France Restored*, 29-40, 54-62.
10. William I. Hitchcock, "France, the Western Alliance, and the Origins of the Schuman Plan, 1948-1950," *Diplomatic History* 21, no. 4 (Fall 1997), 603-30.
11. Hanns Jürgen Küsters, "West Germany's Foreign Policy in Western Europe, 1949-1957: The Art of the Possible," in Clemens Wurm, ed., *Western Europe and Germany: The Beginnings of European Integration, 1945-1960* (Oxford, 1995), 69.
12. Andrew Moravcsik, *The Choice for Europe: Social Purpose and State Power from Messina to Maastricht* (Ithaca, 1998), 86-7, 103-22; Frances Lynch, *France and the International Economy: From Vichy to the Treaty of Rome* (London, 1997), 169-83, 214-15.
13. Though this is changing. For a recent assessment of the literature, see the useful survey by Pierre Gerbet, *La France et l'intégration européenne: Essai d'historiographie* (Berne, 1995).
14. Monnet, *Memoirs*, 405-17. The Action Committee held its first meeting in January 1956—six months after the Messina conference had broached the topic of a common market and atomic pool. François Duchêne, one of Monnet's former collaborators and his most recent biographer, shows Monnet thought that the common market would never get anywhere in France and so concentrated his efforts on establishing Euratom. Through Euratom, Duchêne argues, Monnet kept alive the European idea and therefore created the environment in which later initiatives on tariffs could succeed. *Jean Monnet: The First Statesman of Interdependence* (New York, 1994), 284-306. Pierre Uri in his memoirs makes a claim to have been the chief author of the common market. Pierre Uri, *Penser par l'action: Un fondateur de l'Europe* (Paris, 1991), 113-37.
15. He made this comment in 1987, at a symposium marking the 30th anniversary of the Treaty of Rome. "I can say today what I never would have said at the time: Euratom was for us a smokescreen that hid the common market." This suggests a high degree of tactical organization on Mollet's part. Pineau's intervention came during the debate in the symposium: Enrico Serra, ed., *Il Rilanco dell'Europa e i Trattati di Roma* (Milan, 1989), 282-3.
16. Among the best work on Mollet's strategy in 1956 is René Girault, "Decision Makers, Decisions and French Power," in Ennion Di Nolfo, ed., *Power In Europe? vol. II: Great Britain, France, Germany and Italy and the Origins of the EEC, 1952-1957* (Berlin, 1992), 66-83; and Pierre Guillen, "Europe as a Cure for French Impotence? The Guy Mollet Government and the Negotiation of the Treaties of Rome," in *ibid.*, 505-16. Also Gérard Bossuat, "La vraie nature de la politique européenne de la France (1950-1957)," in Gilbert Trausch, ed., *Die Europäische Integration vom Schuman-Plan bis zu den Verträgen von Rom* (Baden-Baden, 1993), 191-230; and Gérard Bossuat, "Guy Mollet: la puissance française autrement," *Relations internationales* 57 (printemps 1989), 25-48. On Mollet's thinking about European connections to Africa, see René Girault, "La France entre l'Europe et l'Afrique," in Serra, *Il Rilancio*, 351-78.
17. Lynch, *France and the International Economy*, 169-83; and her essay, "Restoring France: the road to integration," in Alan Milward, Frances M.B. Lynch, Federico Romero, Ruggero Ranieri, and Vibeke Sørensen, *The Frontier of National Sovereignty: History and Theory, 1945-1992* (London, 1993), 59-87. This emphasis on the internal economic debate appears also in Alan S. Milward, *The European Rescue of the Nation-State* (Berkeley, 1992), 196-223.

18. *Documents diplomatiques français* [hereafter *DDF*], *1955*, vol. I (January-June), Rivière to Pinay, 1 April 1955, doc. 163: 377-8; Spaak to Pinay, 4 April 1955, doc. 171: 399-400; Garnier to Pinay, 26 April 1955, doc. 228: 517-18. For Spaak's account, see Paul-Henri Spaak, *The Continuing Battle: Memoirs of a European, 1936-1966* (London, 1971), 227-31, 238-52.
19. *DDF 1955*, vol. I, Note du Département, 7 April 1955, doc. 181: 418-21; and note 2, 418. Foreign Minister Antoine Pinay, meeting with his British counterpart Harold Macmillan, made precisely the same point: in light of the Austrian treaty, it was important to give the Germans the idea that European integration was not dead; the West had to have something to offer. On the other hand, Pinay said that new initiatives must not be "utopian," but concrete, and limited to areas such as energy and transport. *DDF 1955, Annexes*, vol. I (January-June), Pinay-Macmillan talks, 21 April 1955: 28-9.
20. *DDF 1955*, vol. I, Note de la Direction des Affaires Economiques et Financières, 18 May 1955, doc. 288: 665-70.
21. *DDF 1955*, vol. I, Note du Département, n.d. [beginning of May 1955], doc. 239: 546-51. For a full discussion of French policy toward Euratom, see Pierre Guillen, "La France et la négociation du traité d'Euratom," *Relations internationales* 44 (hiver 1985), 391-412.
22. *DDF 1955*, vol. I, François-Poncet to Pinay, 25 May 1955, doc. 297: 683-6.
23. *DDF 1955*, vol. I, Note de la Direction des Affaires Economiques et Financières, 18 May 1955, doc. 288: 665-70; and Note du Department, 26 May 1955, doc. 301: 692-3.
24. *DDF 1955*, vol. I, Pinay to major embassies, 10 June 1955, doc. 332: 756-8. The German Economics Minister, Ludwig Erhard—a vigorous advocate of free trade—fought a stiff rearguard action against the common market, arguing that it would merely extend protectionism to the member states. For a full discussion of German views and policy toward both Euratom and the common market, see the work of Hanns Jürgen Küsters, *Die Gründung der europäische Wirtschaftsgemeinschaft* (Baden-Baden: Nomos, 1982).
25. See for example the instructions delivered to the French delegation to the Brussels talks. These were strongly in favor of Euratom, and cautious—but not opposed—to the common market idea. *DDF 1955*, vol. II (July-December), Note du Service de Coopération Economique, 5 July 1955, doc. 13: 19-23.
26. See, e.g., *DDF 1955*, vol. II, Rivière to Pinay, 20 July 1955, doc. 48: 112-15; and Note de la Direction des Affaires Economiques et Financières, 13 Oct. 1955: 658-63. Indeed, the French made considerable gains for their views in the talks, securing assurances that the lowering of tariffs would at first only be partial, and spaced out over a four or five year period. *DDF 1956*, vol. I (January-June), Note de la Direction Générale des Affaires Economiques et Financières, 2 Feb. 1956, doc. 67: 135-40.
27. *DDF 1956*, vol. I, Note de la Direction Générale des Affaires Economiques et Financières, 6 April 1956, doc. 222: 526-8. A European atomic agency was "eminently desirable," this memo concluded.
28. *DDF 1955*, vol. II, Note de la Direction des Affaires Economiques et Financières, 7 Sept. 1955, doc. 179: 437-9; and *DDF 1956*, vol. I, Rivière to Pineau, 6 February 1956, doc. 87: 178.
29. *DDF 1955*, vol II, Note de la sous-direction d'Europe centrale, 21 November 1955, doc. 379: 836-9.
30. *DDF 1956*, vol. I, Christian de Margerie to Pineau, 23 March 1956, doc. 199: 478-80. "Every day," de Margerie wrote, "ever more aware of the strength of their country, a good number of [German] politicians ... are turning away from the European idea. They think it more profitable for their country not to submit to new supranational authorities and to try its luck on the plane of free, open competition."

31. *FRUS 1955-1957*, vol. XXVII, Memorandum of Conversation, Dulles, Eden, et al., 30 January 1956: 619-20. Foreign Minister Selwyn Lloyd described the British view as "hostile" to the common market.
32. *DDF 1955*, vol. II, Note du Service de Coopération Economique, 5 July 1955, doc. 13: 19-23. On British policy and the origins of the EEC, see John Young, "Towards a New View of British Policy and European Unity, 1945-1957," in R. Ahmann et al., *The Quest for Stability: Problems of West European Security, 1918-1957* (Oxford, 1993), 435-62; and Milward, *Rescue*, 424-33.
33. *DDF 1956*, vol. I, 17 April 1956, doc. 251: 610-13; 21 April 1956, doc. 265: 636-40; 25 April 1956, doc. 269: 645-54; and 7 May 1956, doc. 302: 725-31. These four memoranda emanated from the Direction Générale des Affaires Economiques et Financières in the Quai d'Orsay—an office which since the late 1940s had held a strongly liberal view of political economy and viewed *dirigisme* with some scepticism.
34. See the excellent discussion of French imperial economic policy and the EEC in Lynch, *France and the International Economy*, 202-6.
35. *DDF 1956*, vol. II, Pineau to major embassies, 13 July 1956, doc. 38: 88-9. The vote was 332 to 186.
36. *DDF 1956*, vol. II, Note du Département, 15 October 1956, doc. 277: 596-7.
37. Maurice Faure, the Secretary of State for Foreign Affaires (Pineau's deputy) traveled to Bonn in mid-September to meet with German officials. On 16 September, Erhard told him he would oppose an exact harmonization of social legislation; the next day, Foreign Minister von Brentano and his deputy Hallstein announced their opposition to an explicity discriminatory Euratom treaty. See *DDF 1956*, vol. II, 16 September 1956, doc. 184: 384-7; and 17 September 1956, doc. 188: 392-6. Franz-Josef Strauss also made clear his opposition to French demands, 18 September 1956, doc. 192: 404-7. Adenauer, interestingly, gave Faure much more encouraging signs, suggesting a "good cop/bad cop" tactic on the part of the Germans. Faure to Pineau, 17 September 1956, doc. 185: 387-8. In any case, the Germans were right: the French economic policy-makers told their military colleagues that Euratom would be a boon to France's own atomic program. Rather than hamstring the French atomic program, it would help it and was therefore "the condition for greater national independence." *DDF 1956*, vol. I, Note du Cabinet du Secrétaire d'Etat aux Affaires Etrangères, 25 June 1956 (conversation between Faure, Marjoilin, and French military advisers), doc. 430: 1051-3.
38. For a discussion of the politics of 1956, see Jean Pierre Rioux, *The Fourth Republic, 1944-1958* (Cambridge, 1987), 254-63; and Jean Lacouture, *Pierre Mendès France* (New York, 1984), 352-61.
39. Rioux, *Fourth Republic*, 263-72; John Ruedy, *Modern Algeria: The Origins and Development of a Nation* (Bloomington, 1992), 156-67; Bernard Droz and Evelyne Lever, *Histoire de la guerre d'Algérie, 1954-1962* (Paris, rev.1984), 59-133.
40. Robert Frank, "The French Alternative: Economic Power through the Empire or through Europe?" in Di Nolfo, *Power in Europe?*, 160-73.
41. On Mollet's European ideas, see Denis Lefebvre, *Guy Mollet: Le mal aimé* (Paris, 1992), 269-75; and Sylvie Guillaume, "Guy Mollet et l'Allemagne," in Bernard Ménager et al., *Guy Mollet: Un camarade en république* (Lille, 1987), 481-97. Mollet visited Adenauer in June to share with him his impressions of his recent trip to Moscow. Mollet reported that Khrushchev was now totally hostile to German unification, brazenly stating that he would rather have the 18 million East Germans on his side than 70 million united Germans arrayed against him, or even neutral. Mollet also came away from Moscow believing that while the Soviet Union was now much less likely to present a military threat to western Europe, the Russians were preparing for an economic offensive, designed to bolster production of industrial and agricultural goods,

placing themselves in a better position to challenge the West in the global competition for markets. These considerations only enhanced Mollet's belief that the West needed a united and productive Europe now more than ever. On Mollet's visit to Moscow, *DDF 1956*, vol. I, May 16-19, 1956, doc. 329: 791-822. On meeting with Adenauer, 4 June 1956, doc. 364: 881-7.

42. There is a great deal of documentation on the Saar in the *DDF* volumes, but on the improvement in relations see Couve de Murville to Pineau, 2 October 1956, *DDF 1956*, vol. II, doc. 233: 488-9.
43. *DDF 1956*, vol. III, Mollet to Adenauer, 31 October 1956, doc. 75: 121-2.
44. *DDF 1956*, vol. II, Pineau to major embassies summarizing Mollet-Adenauer talks, 2 October 1956, doc. 235: 493-6; and Couve to Pineau, 10 October 1956, doc. 261: 553-4. It is also true that Adenauer was facing an election scheduled for mid-1957 and wanted to see a treaty presented to the Bundestag before that time. For more on Adenauer's views at this period, see Hanns Jürgen Küsters, "Adenauers Europapolitik in der Gründungsphase der EWG," *Vierteljahrshefte für Zeitgeschichte* (1983, vol. 4), 646-73; and Sabine Lee, "German Decision-Making Elites and European Integration: German 'Europolitik' during the Years of the EEC and Free Trade Area Negotiations," in Anne Deighton, ed., *Building Postwar Europe: National Decision-Makers and European Institutions, 1948-1963* (London, 1995), 38-54.
45. The French *procès-verbal* only includes the first part of the Adenauer-Mollet conversation; the exchanges after Eden's call are not included. *DDF 1956*, vol. III, 6 November 1956, doc. 138: 231-8. But Christian Pineau gives a lively rendering of the meeting: Christian Pineau and Christiane Rimbaud, *Le grand pari: L'aventure du Traité de Rome* (Paris, 1991), 221-3.
46. Pineau and Rimbaud, *Le grand pari*, 223-6. On the French assessment of the German concessions, *DDF 1956*, vol. III, Pineau to major posts, 8 Nov. 1956, doc. 146: 249-51. Another factor in making the French still more favorable to Euratom than ever before was that the Suez crisis had dramatically underscored French dependence upon imported Middle Eastern oil. Suddenly, atomic energy appeared to be a prerequisite to national independence. Mollet to Adenauer, 13 Nov. 1956, doc. 165: 288-9.
47. On the persistent objections of many in the French government and parliament to the principles behind the common market, see Marjolin, *Memoirs*, 276-307. Marjolin's story would appear to undercut Lynch's argument that there had been a conversion within the French government in favor of the common market. Rather, the treaty could only be sold to the public chiefly on its foreign policy merits.
48. *DDF 1956*, vol. III, Mollet to Adenauer, 13 November 1956, doc. 165: 288-9. It was clear that despite the Suez crisis and Adenauer's tough talk with Mollet, the Germans feared worsening the US-European rift by focusing too heavily on Euratom's independence from US oversight. German public opinion had been strongly against the Anglo-French invasion of Suez. See Couve de Murville to Pineau, 24 November 1956, doc. 231: 405-6.
49. See *DDF 1956*, vol. III, Pineau to major posts, 24 November 1956 and 1 December 1956, docs. 228 and 253: 401-2 and 451-52.
50. On the Assembly debate, and the mechanics of the overseas investment fund, see *Le Monde*, 20 and 24 January, and 21 February 1957. France and Germany both agreed to put $200 million each into the fund, with the Netherlands and Belgium giving $70 million each, Italy $40 million, and Luxembourg $1.2 million; of the total $581.2, France would receive $512 million [a net gain of $312 million].
51. *Le Monde*, 19 January 1957.
52. See the comments of Pineau and Pierre Guillen, in Serra, *Il Rilancio*, 528-9; and for a similar assessment, Marjolin, *Memoirs*, 297.
53. Rioux, *The Fourth Republic*, 313.

Chapter 12

SEEKING FRANCE'S 'LOST SOLDIERS'

Reflections on the French Military Crisis in Algeria

Martin S. Alexander

'Lost soldiers' was first offered as a conceptual framework, to help us study the mid-20th Century French military, by an American political scientist, George Armstrong Kelly of Princeton, in 1965. Kelly employed the epithet 'lost' to depict an army without firm direction and without an internally or externally accepted mission. In this frame of reference Kelly examined 'the French army and empire in crisis,' from the 1940s to Algerian independence in July 1962. He saw the process of army politicization as a function of outrage at successive imperial defeats and retreats, turning into a cancerous malady afflicting the custodians of French national security.[1] However, as Olivier Forcade noted, over 30 years after Kelly: 'Engagement in political action is not a majority phenomenon in the officer corps from the Third to the Fifth French Republic … [but] The armed forces were never so plunged into politics as during the 1950s and 1960s.'[2]

To revisit the notion of France's postwar army as 'lost soldiers' is to reaffirm the relevance of Kelly's identification of an era of unclear loyalties and ethical/disciplinary crisis. Yet it is also to move, as quizzical historians should, beyond his excessively monolithic or unitary typecasting of the French army in the Algerian War era. Raoul Girardet, while the crisis was still in progress, called into doubt the notion of an undifferentiated bloc, 'the army,' or even 'the officers.'[3] Jean Planchais, *Le Monde's* well-informed reporter on the military dimensions of the Algerian War, warned in a symposium in 1998 to mark the fortieth anniversary of the

Notes for this chapter begin on page 259.

advent of the Fifth Republic: 'I am always a bit worried when I hear talk of "the army" or "the military." The army is in reality a very composite body, this being true more than ever in 1958.'[4]

With access available to the Algerian War documents of the *Service Historique de l'Armée de Terre* at Vincennes, it becomes plain that France's 'lost soldiers' of the Algerian years belonged to several 'tribes' or 'castes' within what was, formally, 'the Army' (restrictively defined, here, as the land forces or *armée de terre*).[5] The decomposition that occurred in the 1950s meant the different elements accommodated each other uneasily. Historians must, therefore, seek to identify and understand a diversity of backgrounds, terms of engagement, mentalities, and experiences in North Africa. In the crisis provoked by Algeria, the French army showed that generational factors, geographical origins, social roots, rank attained, branch of service, and attendant sub-culture, 'profoundly nuance the idea of a monolithic officer corps.'[6]

Scholars have yet to establish a convincing typology of France's soldiers in the anguished era of its wars of decolonization.[7] The temptation is to suggest that there were as many French military experiences in Algeria from 1954 to 1962 as there were individuals who wore a French uniform. What size, then, was the French army in this era, and how much of it undertook duties in Algeria? In November 1954 some 54,000 French troops garrisoned Algeria. After the outbreak of the 'rebellion,' this total was rapidly expanded. By March 1957 the land forces there stood at 12 divisions in three corps commands (Oran, Algiers, Constantine), along with a large theater reserve. The average size of the career army officer corps was some 30,000, but many of them never set foot in North Africa.[8] On 1 March 1959 there were 429,000 French servicemen in Algeria. In all, about 2.5 million men served there at some point in the war; of these, about 25,000 were reservist officers, several hundred thousand were reservist other ranks, and some 1.2 million were conscripts.[9] A full-scale sociological study of these soldiers would require a large research team and a very large research grant.[10] Thankfully, serious exploration of experiences and attitudes of conscripts in Algeria now has a reliable point of departure in the project *Soldats en Algerie*, conducted by Jean-Charles Jauffret and his research students at the Université de Montpellier III (Paul-Valéry) and the *Institut d'Etudes Politiques* at Aix-en-Provence.[11]

Nevertheless, as John Cairns once acknowledged about research on the crisis of 1940, historians must set themselves manageable tasks.[12] This essay therefore acknowledges the much more detailed work of Jauffret and cautiously proposes a possible three-fold typology of the 'armies within the army.' It suggests some connections between the divisions discernible in the army and the outcome of the Algerian War, and the longer-term issue of loyalty to the Fifth Republic and its institutions. First there was the traditional or classical officer corps. Second, there was a tough young warrior caste mostly found in elite formations with an assumed collective identity and ethos all their own.[13] Third were the reservists and conscripts, sent south across the Mediterranean in May 1956 by the Government of Republican Defense under a Socialist, Guy Mollet. Thousands came home profoundly alienated, some rendered dysfunctional, by brutalities they had perpetrated in the name of 'French civilization' while in Algeria—and they returned home to a France that wished to forget them and 'their' war.[14]

The Classical Officer Elite

To consider the first military group, the traditional officer corps, we must limit ourselves to officers of senior rank in the mid-1950s. Most were metropolitans, whose service since 1945 had been in France itself or in the French zone in Germany. Some had made careers mainly overseas. Among them a distinction must be drawn between, on the one hand, the officers and cadres of what was loosely termed the *Armée d'Afrique* (who spent one tour or more, sometimes most of a career, in the units of French North Africa) and, on the other, the officers and cadres of *La Coloniale*. The latter joined specifically *coloniale* infantry and artillery regiments (largely volunteer, long-service regulars) and made their whole careers in *La Coloniale*, either with *coloniale blanche* regiments, or with black African or Indochinese *tirailleurs* regiments. They were different types of soldier. Socially, *La Coloniale* officers typically hailed from lower socioeconomic groups, and often from southern France.[15] *Armée d'Afrique* cadres, however, included officers from fashionable branches, such as the cavalry, and from families of the haute bourgeoisie. To generalize about their politics, few officers of the *Armée d'Afrique* zealously adhered to the collaborationist regime of Marshal Henri-Philippe Pétain. Many, however, were conservative/authoritarian, their loyalty gravitating towards General Maxime Weygand, Vichy's proconsul in North Africa in 1940-41, and General Alphonse Juin, its Resident-General in Morocco. Officers of *La Coloniale*, in contrast, were often Gaullist, producing such notable figures as General Legentilhomme and General de Boislambert, Colonel Edgard de Larminat and the young Captain (later General) Jacques Massu.[16]

Many of the army generals of the Algerian War era had been stationed in overseas territories before 1940. Some had remained in the French overseas territories during the Second World War—among them, some in the Vichy forces that defended Madagascar in 1942, others in Indochina under Vichy's proconsul, Admiral Jean Decoux.[17] Some of these officers had served in Indochina between September 1945 and the final withdrawal in May-June 1954 after the humiliating surrender at Điện-Biên-Phu.[18]

For others, however, their formative experiences occurred under more uplifting conditions, in de Gaulle's Free French Forces from 1940 to 1945. These men included colonial veterans such as Philippe Leclerc de Hautecloque's original *coloniale* force that crossed the Sahara from Chad and rallied to de Gaulle in 1940. This nucleus grew into the renowned 2e DB, the French 2nd Armored Division, whose Sherman tanks were first to enter Paris at the Porte d'Orléans in August 1944.[19] One wartime 2e DB company commander, Massu, subsequently became the general commanding 10th Parachute Division that jumped into the Suez Canal zone in November 1956. After another pride-wounding withdrawal from Egypt, and aware that Nasser provided training camps for the Algerian FLN-ALN (*Front de Libération Nationale-Armée de Libération Nationale*), Massu directed the infamous 'cleansing' of insurgents from the Algiers Casbah in 1957.[20] Other officers had fought in General Pierre Koenig's Free French brigade with the British 8th Army in the Desert in 1942. They also counted personnel from the French Expeditionary Corps led by Juin in Italy in 1943-44.[21] Others still had spent World War Two in Vichy's 'Armistice Army,' the 100,000 man force permitted to Pétain's regime by Germany in June 1940; or as prisoners of war after the collapse of France in 1940, 1.6 million French soldiers of that campaign spending the next five years as captives of the Third Reich.

Emblematic of senior 'colonial' officers was Raoul Salan. He had come to prominence by heading France's imperial military counterintelligence bureau from 1937 to 1941. Salan's story was one 'of conflicting loyalties, like that of a number of French soldiers. The conflicts began in 1940 and were revived in a sombre form during the Algerian civil war.' In French West Africa in 1939, Salan served Vichy before switching to the Free French in 1943. A Freemason, fluent in Oriental languages, he attracted the soubriquet of 'The Mandarin' or 'The Chinaman' and was 'a politically-minded general known for his cunning and inscrutability.'[22] He was widely distrusted by fellow officers. Intransigently anticommunist and a champion of the French 'civilizing mission' overseas, Salan followed Marshal Jean de Lattre de Tassigny as high commissioner and commander-in-chief in Indochina in 1952-53.[23]

While in Saigon, Salan became physically and morally rotted by a drug addiction. The Fourth Republic nonetheless assigned him to Algeria as military commander-in-chief, widening his powers in 1957 by appointing him to succeed the erstwhile trade union official, Robert Lacoste, as government resident-general.[24] Suspect in de Gaulle's eyes after his intrigues during the 13 May 1958 crisis, Salan could not give unfettered loyalty to a head of government (soon to be head of state) unwilling to pay any price to preserve French Algeria. In December 1958 de Gaulle transferred Salan back to France as Inspector-General of National Defense.[25] Seeking to strengthen himself by practicing 'divide and rule,' de Gaulle then split the military and civil functions in Algeria. Paul Delouvrier became delegate-general of the government. Maurice Challe, an air force general, was appointed military commander-in-chief.

This separation of powers was significant. It revealed de Gaulle's mistrust of senior army officers steeped in years of overseas service, remote from the modernizing dynamics of metropolitan France and its increasingly European orientation. De Gaulle feared their appetite for politics, whetted in bringing about his own return in the May 1958 'Operation Resurrection.'[26] He also understood that 'France won't put up with having half a million of her children in Algeria for the next fifty years,' in contrast, he suspected, to key army officers. Salan was not the most uncompromising exponent of this 'war-with-no-holds-barred' mentality. But when interviewed by Jean-Jacques Servan-Schreiber in 1957, Salan instructed him to carry a 'clear and simple message' to Paris:

> Let them know that the army of France […] knows that it is going to win this war. It is enough to hold on, as the Resident-General Robert Lacoste has so pertinently noted, through "the last quarter of an hour". It would be unforgivable to let go—and *the army will not allow it !* The fate of France will henceforth be determined in Algiers, not Paris. If there's a battle of wills, it's Paris that'll have to bend, and no longer Algiers […] Tell them this plainly—The army will let nobody steal their victory from them.

Servan-Schreiber asked to quote Salan verbatim. The general hesitated, perhaps realizing how his words might be construed in the quite different ambiance of Paris, as a 'declaration of war against the authority of the Republic.' Salan nevertheless acceded: he knew he had burnt his boats. Leaving their meeting, Servan-Schreiber pondered 'who would bring Salan before a military tribunal, for this was inevitably the destiny of the man. [He was] In the phrase that would become famous, "a lost soldier" [*un soldat perdu*].'[27]

Combat and Revolutionary War Officers—a 'Warrior Caste'

Of the factions into which the Algerian War split the army, top-ranking 'colonialist' generals typified by Salan were not the most menacing for the survival of the Fourth Republic or the authority of the Fifth. As Planchais of *Le Monde* warned, in early 1958:

> Among those [in the Army] who might be driven by ambition or exasperation to quarrel with the present regime, the most sensible would prefer not to become personally involved. They would gladly welcome a change, would give the utmost assistance to the new regime, but would prefer not to be regarded as its backers. The High

> Command, with its low prestige, would soon be overthrown. It is rarely the generals nowadays who start military revolts, even if they provide the figure-heads. Revolutions are now made by Captains and Colonels.[28]

A second sub-caste within the French army, the 'warrior professionals', cohered as the longer the struggle wore on against the *Front de Libération Nationale* (FLN) and its military wing, the *Armée de Libération Nationale* (ALN). For this group, Algeria was a mission about honor—a mission to expunge the memory of defeat, withdrawal and humiliation in Indochina.[29] They also sought to protect Moslems who had fought for France: well after the last French units returned to metropolitan soil in 1962 'even the officers the most remote from political involvement were disturbed by the memory of the Moslem soldiers they had commanded.'[30]

Among field-grade operational officers the battle-toughened, uncompromising captains, majors and colonels of the Foreign Legion parachutists and the marine infantry were to the fore. Examples included Pierre Château-Jobert, Roger Trinquier (the principal architect, along with Charles Lacheroy, of the counter-insurgency doctrine of 'revolutionary war'), Jean Gardes, Antoine Argoud, Pierre Jeanpierre, Marcel 'Bruno' Bigeard, and their subordinate company commanders such as Major Hélie de Saint-Marc and Captain Pierre Sergent.[31] Shared characteristics or group-think within this 'revolutionary war school' turned on two factors. The first was anti-communism. 'Bored by what they saw as the mediocrity of post-war France [...] they were obsessed by the war against communism and the idea that the future of the Western world was being played out within the French Empire.'[32] The second was their bonding around a shared experience of war in Indochina. Especially influential and energetic, even idealistic by their own lights, were younger professional officers hardened by experiencing Indochina during the denouement of the war there, in 1952-54. They arrived when the French military command and wider community in Indochina were basking in the success won by the French Expeditionary Corps against the Vietminh in 1951, the 'Year of de Lattre.' Young lieutenants and captains had their first encounter with the Orient at Haiphong or Saigon in 1952-53 and found it scented with the perfume of a possible victory.

Thus Diên-Biên-Phu and subsequent imprisonment by the Vietminh under appalling conditions was doubly traumatic.[33] It injured the captured officers physically; but it also affected them psychologically. The operational lessons drawn by theorists of *guerre révolutionnaire* became overlaid with a sense of distrust toward contemporary France.[34] In particular, for those such as Château-Jobert, Bigeard, Argoud, de Saint-Marc and Sergent, a bitterness took hold that French conscript troops had not been committed to Indochina. Many felt defeat could have been avoided by greater resolve—had Indochina been made a cause of the whole French people. Behind the failure to respect the Clausewitzian precept of a unity of army-people-nation, embittered field commanders and psychological warfare experts smelled the pusillanimous politics of the Fourth Republic.[35] Cadres repatriated from Indochina nursed a sense of unnecessary defeat, a sense that comrades had died in vain.[36] It was just a short step to believing in a stab-in-the-back 'made in France.'[37] As Colonel Pierre Langlais, a Diên-Biên-Phu veteran, wrote: 'the defeat was not down to this or that general, this or that government,' but down 'to the entire country for abandoning its professional army and getting its elite cadres massacred.'[38]

Hélie de Saint-Marc was another of the captains and majors of 1954 that France sent to Algeria—'not new men, their objectivity intact, but bitter, hardened men who had been at war for 15 years, each weighed down by personal dramas.'[39] This was a super-fit and plainspoken 'warrior caste'. They were not, in the main, drawn from ancient military families, with generations of service to the French flag behind them. Their socioeconomic backgrounds and family status were modest, even humble. Château-Jobert, a Breton, was an artillery private (second class) aged 24, in 1936. When France was attacked in 1940 he was still just a lieutenant, 28 years old, attending the Air Observers' School at Dinard.[40] For him and his peers, the dislocation of the traditional, socially-exclusive officer corps by the events of summer 1940 and the liberating 'adventure' of Free France, offered rapid promotion and upward social and class mobility. In their origins and attitudes towards fighting and politics, the warrior cadres had little need of patrons among a generation of top generals largely discredited, retired or imprisoned in 1940-45. They had little innate sense of military subordination to the state.

These officers and non-commissioned officers (NCO's) had been what sociologists term a 'functional elite.'[41] Combat professionals, they had no time for the snobbery and spit-and-polish of traditional colonial soldiers. But they were just as ill-at-ease with the cadres of the *Direction Générale de l'Armement* and the increasingly favored *ingénieurs-généraux*. The latter were not warriors but a technocratic manager-elite. Theirs was the culture gaining ground in the Defense Ministry in Paris in the late-1950s. They left combat officers feeling out-of-sorts in armed forces that were being shaped by specialists in weapons engineering, military technology, and nuclear science, by képi-wearing functionaries.[42] Gladwyn Jebb, British ambassador at Paris, remarked just before de Gaulle's return to power in 1958:

> ambitious young French officers are probably influenced by two considerations. First, military planning in the North Atlantic Alliance centres largely around nuclear warfare, while the French are almost completely engaged in an elementary guerilla conflict. Secondly, this guerilla conflict is, at least in their opinion, the only NATO battle at present being fought—and France is apparently fighting it alone. Thus,

> however illogically, the French officer feels that he is bearing the brunt of Western defence, while at the same time being totally outstripped in the techniques of modern warfare by his other Atlantic colleagues whose countries are not at war.[43]

Jebb had identified part of the malaise among the warrior cadres at the sharp end in Algeria. But he failed to grasp that the combat professionals believed their conception of soldiering was the 'true path'. They felt their NATO allies were being distracted, their doctrine and training inordinately focused on literally fantastical, unimaginable scenarios of nuclear war. Meanwhile they, under-resourced and inadequately supported by NATO or French politicians, were mired in the inevitably dirty reality of 'modern warfare' (in Trinquier's telling title to his treatise on counterinsurgency). In the view of these French soldiers, ballistic missiles and nuclear weapons provided at best a superpower standoff. At worst they had established an umbrella to deter not just nuclear exchanges but also major conventional wars, an umbrella beneath which low-intensity conflicts and insurgencies—armed and financed by Moscow and Beijing and ruthlessly waged with unlimited ideological and military techniques—might cost the West the Cold War. They conceived the battle against the FLN/ALN as, in Martine Lemalet's formulation, a 'struggle against terrorist troubles, behind which they saw the hand of Moscow.'[44]

These officers assumed practical direction over the war's conduct in 1959-60, just as a chasm was opening between those in the *métropole* who would end the war and the diehards. In France people increasingly favored independence for Algeria. In the army were, on one side, 'certain career soldiers who supported the OAS [the *Organisation armée secrète*, formed in February 1961 as a diehard riposte to de Gaulle's triumphant referendum of 8 January] and who reasoned in terms of defeat, abandonment and treason.'[45] On the other stood more recent St. Cyr officer classes without direct experience of Indochina. For them, Diên-Biên-Phu was already history, not a personal affront to honor. Whereas for Indochina veterans Algeria was a 'war that could not be lost,' for some younger officers Algeria seemed broken-backed by 1961.[46] Its origins and early controversies (the Philippeville massacre of 1955; the deployment of the conscripts in 1956; the Battle of Algiers in 1957) antedated their commissioning. By 1961-62, as P.-M. de La Gorce perceptively noted:

> most officers of lower rank [had] had no part in the Indochinese War. Thus they do not share the feeling of being abandoned that so affected their elders. They are not attracted by ideological warfare or by the prospect of actual conflict with communism [...] These younger men even feel less bound to Algeria than the older men did to Indochina [...] Perhaps, too, the officers who knew only the Algerian War do not feel the same need for revenge as do those who made their way out of Diên-Biên-Phu.[47]

The April 1961 putsch-attempt marked the final call by *guerre révolutionnaire* 'ultras' to rally a majority of officers, and stop the ending the Algerian War at the price of another French retreat. In this crisis most French officers neither actively supported nor actively opposed the 'dissidence' in Algiers.[48] They awaited the outcome, many privately wishing success to the anti-Gaullists. Insubordination—many preferred the ambiguous but more resonant word 'resistance'—had been legitimated by de Gaulle's own defiance of the legal authorities in France in June 1940.[49] And the wait-and-see posture widespread among officers during the dramas in Algeria was rooted in an *'attentisme'* that had become commonplace under Vichy (1940-44).[50]

As the Algerian drama came to a climax, many officers experienced a crisis of conscience about France's Moslem *Harki* auxiliaries.[51] But few admired the settler society or lamented the fate of the Europeans who took ship for Marseille in 1962-3 because they risked massacre in independent Algeria.[52] Paul-Marie de La Gorce noted how 'the same affection [...] aroused in them by remote Indochina was rarely felt by officers for the soil of Algeria [...] They seldom cared for the European groups.'[53] Idealists who had embraced the doctrine of Franco-Algerian 'integration,' articulated by the Gaullist politician Jacques Soustelle (Algerian governor-general in 1955-56), were disillusioned by the non-implementation of the full franchise and equal rights for Moslems of the 1947 Algerian Statute.[54]

Distaste for the *pieds-noirs* (European colonists in Algeria) was a rare point of agreement between the ideologically-motivated apostles of revolutionary war and the conscript rankers. It found its counterpoint in the dawning awareness among some thoughtful settlers of their isolation from mainstream military and metropolitan politics. Some *pieds-noirs* saw that the Moslem-European rift was widening because of the tactics of the soldiers—supposedly their guardians. The Algerian-born writer Jules Roy visited Kabylia in 1960 to see his brother, a farmer. He observed a total alienation between the two communities, caused by the ruthless methods of the army in seeking 'victory.'[55] The youngish operational officers and psy-war experts 'felt they were the defenders of the West'; Algeria was where destiny called them to halt Communism's advance once and for all.[56] But the calm in the towns was artificial: it depended on military patrols of the streets and souks. Neither this nor uprooting the Moslems by their hundreds of thousands to protected encampments or 'regroupment centers' could achieve peace and reconciliation. 'In the countryside,' noted Roy, 'my brother had to stick sheet-iron behind his windows every night.' The brutality of the paratroopers, felt Roy, meant that 'the Arabs, who people said had no nation, had suddenly got a country.' France's visage had become cruel and exacting; Moslem families were astonished to see a French person 'who was neither soldier nor tax inspector.'[57]

The diversity of wartime experiences, the fracturing of memory and the polarizations must again be underlined. It is no surprise that the French army in general, and its career officers and NCO's in particular, displayed the antisocial traits of abandoned children between the early 1950s and the early 1960s. For these were men who, in their formative years, had undergone the military equivalent of spells in remand centers and foster homes.[58] The wars, defeats and retreats of the late-1940s and 1950s were not likely to build a united officer corps and cadres that were disciplined, well-adjusted 'soldier-citizens.' Their memoirs, diaries and letters show how embittered and adrift many became, while remaining convinced to the end of the rectitude and honor of their conduct.[59]

There was, at best, a guarded, opportunistic allegiance in early 1961 to France's political leaders: de Gaulle and his prime minister, Michel Debré. Then, as in the last years of the Fourth Republic, British ambassador Jebb was right to remark that 'French Army officers have little use for politics and none for French politicians.'[60] There were few signs of positive enthusiasm in 1961 and in some barracks there were indications of festering, potentially violent anti-Gaullism.[61] During the interlude between signature of the Evian Accord (18 March 1962) and Algeria's independence (1 July 1962), de Gaulle asked the plainspoken Aimé Paquet, deputy for the Isère: 'What does the Army think?' 'President, the Army hates you,' Paquet replied.

De Gaulle's pragmatic decision to cut and run from Algeria permanently damned him in the eyes of many officer veterans of the war. Roger Goepfert, president of the 1st, 5th, 9th and 17th Algerian Tirailleurs' Veterans Association, noted after the death in February 2000 of Maurice Bénos, commander of the 17th Algerian Tirailleurs in 1961-62: 'the ceasefire of 19 March 1962 was not the sort we were hoping for. Instead of the promised peace, it only prompted massacres, executions and humiliations.' Bénos, 'viscerally opposed to de Gaulle's policy of abandonment,' made the only gesture left to him, resigning his commission on 2 July 1962—the day after Algerian independence.[62] Soldiers like Bénos understood that de Gaulle had won. De Gaulle knew this too. His new breed of technocrat commanders, personified by General Charles Ailleret, were now in key posts. 'One does not make policy', he had contemptuously told Aimé Paquet, 'with majors, captains, lieutenants and NCO's.'[63] He had faced down the worst that his opponents could throw at him. Ultimately, as John Cairns noted perspicaciously in 1965: 'de Gaulle would never win the Army to him, for he had ended its illusions. His object was rather to win it back to France [...] it was military statesmanship of a high order.'[64]

'Reluctant Warriors': the Reservists and Conscripts

Behind malcontent officers were the increasingly reluctant conscripts. Drawn largely from metropolitan France, most wished only to return home quickly, lives and limbs intact. Alongside French troops' womenfolk (wives, mothers, fiancées of reservists and draftees), ALN combatants and the *Harkis*, conscripts remain the most neglected participants of the Algerian War.[65] These veterans did not disembark at Marseille to parades, marching bands and a grateful national embrace. They were cold-shouldered. France was embarrassed by them, ashamed about the war, eager to fix its gaze on Europe and move on. As already noted, even scholars paid scant attention to the reservists and conscripts till the 1990s. Among groups involved in France's twentieth-century wars, those from Algeria have had their experiences smothered by a historical chloroform administered by the French state itself. Happily, Benjamin Stora's work has pioneered a recovery of much that was 'forgotten' or 'unremembered' about Algeria among French military veterans and other participants.[66]

The voices heard from the 1990s recount how the Algerian War was hated on all sides. Most ordinary Moslems were not militants in the ALN 'politico-administrative organization' (OPA). Most shared the revulsion of reservists and draftees for the French command's use of torture, 'free-fire zones' (*zones interdites*) and forcible population displacement—but also condemned ALN bombings, throat-cutting and disembowellings. The gathering of veteran testimonies is enabling scholars to track the networks, informal communities and self-help associations that sprang from the ever-widening conscript hostility, sometimes erupting into overt protest, against Algerian war service.[67]

Scaling the wall of 'silence and shame,' in Bernard Sigg's phrase, is possible now. Intimate accounts by rank-and-file troops offer insights into what they underwent in Algeria.[68] Vivid primary sources include the interviews transcribed by Jean-Pierre Vittori, and the work of Maurice Matéos-Ruiz.[69] Even more direct are testimonies in the letters published by Martine Lemalet in 1992—raw realities from Algeria shared whilst the war was on with family and loved ones in France. As soldiers-in-spite-of-themselves, reservists and conscripts had emphatically *not* chosen to be in Algeria. Writing of his return to France in 1957, from General Jacques Paris de Bollardière's division, Servan-Schreiber described Algeria as 'a jail, alas, to hundreds of thousands of young conscript soldiers who will remain scarred for life by the decadent experience they've undergone, defenseless and entirely despite themselves.'[70] The 'Djebel generation' had suffered the terrible luck of reaching military age between 1955 and 1962.[71]

One infantryman's diary noted on 23 January 1961, two weeks after de Gaulle's referendum on Algeria's future, that his company commander had been transferred for campaigning in his post's hinterland for a 'No' vote (for which he had raised a score of 80 percent). The diarist evidently detested his captain for the political role he had assumed, and detested the cause of French Algeria. Subsequent entries record this soldier's skeptical response to the April 1961 events: 'The coup has failed. For better or worse! The putschistes had promised to free the conscript contingent after 18 months service if they succeeded. For me, that was freedom; but would they have kept their word ?'[72] Just as loyalty and trust in the high command and French political leadership had evaporated among middle-rank warrior-caste officers, so too, a wider distrust of the activists had spread and completed the disenchantment of the rank-and-file. As one commentator remarked soon after the war: 'Almost everywhere [...] were the outward and visible sign that the draftees were hostile to the putsch [...] Had these soldiers felt very differently on May 13 [1958] or January 24 [1960—'Barricades Week'] ? Probably not. But peace appeared to be so close, in April 1961, that this military coup d'état took on the aspect of an outrageous attempt to prolong the war.'[73]

The conscript's diary noted above further illustrates the problems for historians seeking to reconstruct the collective state of mind of just part of the army. 'Since the coup d'Etat, the mail no longer gets through to us [...] I've become blind, deaf, mute, no longer know how to read or write; a portcullis of indifference has dropped between the world and me!'[74] If, in the latter stages of the war, conscripts found themselves deprived of word from home, so too—but for much longer—until the 1990s, the French people received little word from the 'Djebel generation.'

This was because as Stora, Claude Liauzu and Martin Evans suggest, France's official silence and nonrecognition of the war muted the voice of conscript veterans after 1962.[75] Through an edict from de Gaulle in 1963 to deny the war *as a war,* reservists and draftees lacked basic rights to which they would have been entitled by war veteran status. Treating Algerian events from 1954-62 merely as 'operations to restore public order,' France excluded veterans from ex-servicemen's status and thus from practical benefits, pensions and disability allowances, as well as from symbolic recognition through medals and monuments. Because of the state monopoly over French broadcasting down to the 1980s, veterans found the means to have their own say denied or 'confiscated.'[76]

In November 1984, the thirtieth anniversary of the Algerian War's outbreak, there was political and press furor in France at the decision to send Claude Cheysson, then foreign minister, to attend a commemoration in Algiers.[77] But no comparable furor surrounded the French state's continuing refusal to add the Algerian War to the 11 November Armistice ceremony or to VE Day (8 May). Autonomous bodies such as the FNACA (*Fédération Nationale des Anciens Combattants d'Algérie,* set up in 1958), had to continue their work as unofficial lobbyists and self-help organizations for Algerian War ex-servicemen. By exercising the political muscle their numbers gave them in certain towns, the FNACA and similar groups got streets and squares named for the 19th March 1962, the date of the ceasefire in Algeria. They articulated the physical, psychological and monetary claims of some six to seven million French people (including widows and dependents as well as ex-soldiers). Successes included the concession of ex-servicemen's identity cards to Algerian War combatants in 1974.[78]

Several factors account for the failure of the Algiers putsch and the start of the process of ending the war. One was a rising tide of anti-war demonstrations during 1960-61 in metropolitan France, led by intellectuals, trade unionists and youth movements.[79] The French were tired of the Algerian War.[80] Unsurprisingly the conscripts—civilians-in-uniform, after all—shared this fatigue. A second was an awareness of the shifting mood and its political significance throughout the barracks across Algeria. In deciding events on the ground at the key moment of April 1961, conscript resistance played a crucial part in preventing any broad mobilization in favor of the coup.[81]

Crucial, too, was de Gaulle's resolute stance and his skill in employing the new mass media (leading Servan-Schreiber's *L'Express* to dub this 'the transistor radio war'). There is compelling evidence that de Gaulle and Debré prevailed because they won 'the battle of the air waves.' The former dramatized the crisis, theatrically appearing on television in his general's uniform to denounce the illegality in Algiers as the doings of a quartet of military has-beens, '*un quarteron de généraux en retraite.*'[82] He demanded obedience and order and, like Debré, spoke over the radio into the conscripts' barracks.[83]

In 1961 the army's apolitical tradition of silence remained influential. What caused concern in Paris was that de Gaulle himself had shown in 1940 that behavior close to constitutional vigilantism could be legitimate. His example inclined soldiers to act according to personal instincts or political nostrums (whether in favor of 'The Republic' or for a 'French Algeria'). The divergent traditions emanating from the army's fragmentation between 1940 and 1944 meant that obedience had lost some of its force; it had become conditional, contingent, a saleable commodity.[84] This spread uncertainty and indecision.

The only officers who were able to act according to clear nostrums when loyalties became unclear were those in 'elite' units such as Foreign Legion and Chasseur-Parachutists. These troops lived an almost sealed, semi-monastic, highly-motivated existence within their own esprit de corps and traditions. They stood proudly and self-consciously apart from the bulk of the army.[85] The officers of such units and numerous soldiers who followed their lead held a singular view of the army's 'duty' *in extremis* to 'save the nation' from the state. This usually very self-serving interpretation of 'duty' saw the rootless or 'lost' field officers and diehard colonialist generals release themselves from the normal imperative to obey the constituted political authority and carry out its policy.[86] Their fixation with the Cold War resonated less loudly, however, with civilians in the metropole. Politicians and commentators noted a thaw, a détente, under Khrushchev. De Gaulle's efforts, from 1959, to steer an independent foreign policy line, found favor. The metropolitan public balked at 'halting Communism' in Algeria, even finding the idea faintly ridiculous.[87] De Gaulle found it cutting across his plans to act as a bridge between the Super Powers.

So the problem for 'warrior' and *guerre révolutionnnaire* officers in Algeria was that, by 1960-61, not only metropolitan civilians but also their own troops wished to end the war—even at the price of another defeat. 'Conscripts, totally uncommitted to any concept of *Algérie Française*, sabotaged certain equipments [in April 1961], disobeyed, and arrested officers known to sympathize with the coup leaders.'[88] About 20 per cent intended to exercise their rights as first-time voters to support the French Communist Party at the ballot box as soon as they were demobilized, and they did not have long to wait, for de Gaulle called referenda and parliamentary elections in 1962.

Nor did draftees care about the fate of the settlers, so deeply was the war in Algeria detested. North Africa was no longer an exotic 'other' of romance and grandeur; it was an alien land where young Bretons, Parisians, Lyonnais or Corrèziens risked pointless injury or death. The *pieds-noirs* were viewed askance by warrior officers as early as 1955-57 for refusing to embrace fundamental reforms. They were loathed by the conscripts by 1960-61 for blocking peace with the FLN.[89] Service in Algeria was a bleak and dangerous way to waste 28 months of one's youth. Naturally, efforts were made to persuade enlisted men of the war's importance (using the propaganda specialists of the 5e Bureau and the army newspaper in Algeria, *Le Bled*).[90] In 1958 one psy-war expert, Captain Souyris, invented the formula: 'Every French soldier is a propagandist.'[91] But reservist and conscript hearts and minds were not converted, let alone enough native Algerians. 'The Navy and Air Force remained largely unaffected, and among Army officers, very many of all ranks agreed only with the tactical concepts of the doctrine, and either ignored or rejected their wider, nonmilitary implications [...] NCO's and privates were even less convinced.'[92]

The deep disgust at being in Algeria resonates loudly in the accounts of reservists such as Georges Mattéi and Daniel Zimmermann.[93] Gérard Périot, a drafted private in the 14th *Tirailleurs* served in Algeria from July 1958 to early 1961. He expressed his loathing for the place and a universal urge to get home, which meant that the 'morale of the ordinary troops was never up to much.' Only one home leave of 23 days was permitted in the whole tour—whose length bred fear about the odds of surviving.[94] Other conscript memoirs, such as that by Pierre Paulian, confirm the horror of night patrols, the hostile terrain and harsh weather.[95]

Evidence of the drafted men's outlook was not hard to find in the barracks. It should not have surprised the para and Legion malcontents at the head of the 1961 putsch that their call to resist de Gaulle—just when conscripts could see he would achieve both Algeria's independence and their own release from the army—fell like a stone. Slogans daubed on the walls of barracks in Algiers, Bône, Constantine and other garrison cities during the crisis days of April 1961 were eloquent: *'le contingent ne marche pas,' 'le contingent bouge pas,' 'le contingent s'en fout.'* A conscript's diary from spring 1961 recounted rumors that French/FLN talks would resume on 20 May—they had been tried unsuccessfully at Melun in 1960—at Evian:

> I think frequently of the duplicity of my role here: psychological war in the village: the good conscience of France. Who's taken in? Not the fellaghas. War in the field: operation or ambush: the virile face of France. I realize the ambiguity of my situation; what does it matter? My action in the village is not calculated. I act only for myself—yes, and for the women and children of Imardabar. So much the better: I give an honorable impression of my country. My action makes sense only if it remains mine as an individual and not mine as the representative of an army. Here the face of the army is repugnant. I don't know what goes on beyond the ridge-line of the Djebel [...] The resignation, the acceptance, the externalized and internalized obedience of most of my fellow detainees breaks my heart and strikes terror into me [...] The respect for authority transforms many of my fellows in misfortune into unfeeling robots. Whether hunting men or hunting rabbits, they show no qualms of conscience. When I really hit rock-bottom, I find myself envying them.[96]

Legacies: Army, Veterans and Fifth Republic Politicians

De Gaulle knew, when he returned to power in 1958, that he had a restless, unreliable army on his hands.[97] As he emerged from the Algerian crisis he knew he had an army broken into pieces. It would need to be rebuilt, not simply glued together from the bits into which it had fragmented. Disbanding the 1st Legion Parachute Regiment after the 1961 putsch and early-retiring over 200 older and senior officers was not a sufficient remedy.[98] Age was not the chief determinant of political behavior among the French officers. The Algerian War did not fracture the French army along tidy generational lines. Instead it spread fissures throughout the ranks and across the arms of service. These rendered the whole brittle, disaggregated. There was the split between those officers who had served mostly in Europe or metropolitan France in the years since 1945 (in the French zone of occupation in Germany, for example, or in NATO postings), those who had been dispatched to

Algeria only late in the drama, and those with long, often bitter, experience of overseas service, of defeats and retreats, from Indochina and perhaps Madagascar, through Morocco to Algeria.[99] There was the split caused by ideology, the ideologues forming a small but influential army sub-caste.[100] 'Active malcontents' numbered recently-retired generals such as Zeller and Salan in their sixties, but also field officers such as Saint-Marc, Sergent and Durand-Ruel in their twenties and thirties. In James H. Meisel's words, 'ultimately the French army did not follow the insurgents. It [...] remained loyal, in an apathetic way. Among the officers the Few did not prevail over the Many, even though—or [...] because—the Many were so hopelessly divided.'[101]

De Gaulle decided in 1960-1 that the Algerian War was unwinnable (and also, given the frailty of France's public finances, unaffordable).[102] He decided to end it swiftly, and turn France's energies back to Europe. By the summer of 1961 he was convinced that French destiny lay in Europe—but also in a redefinition of a global role, one of equilibrium between East and West, with France providing influence, even leadership, over the Non-Aligned Movement that took shape after 1955. De Gaulle was growing ever less trustful of the USA. This led him, despite his fears of Communism, to withdraw the French Mediterranean fleet from NATO in 1959—a step on the path to comprehensive French disengagement from NATO's integrated military structures in 1966.[103] De Gaulle's military thinking was consistent with his statecraft. He always prioritized Europe above the French Empire and Overseas Departments, in his scheme of national priorities. In 1919-25 when many officers of his generation served in Morocco, Syria and Lebanon, de Gaulle was in Poland and Paris.[104] In fact, he had never served in Africa: highly unusual for a French general of his era. And the Algerian settler community, with few exceptions, had supported Vichy, especially in 1940-41.[105]

Events during 1961 proved doubly fortuitous to de Gaulle's desire for a decisive shift in French grand strategy. Only four months after the Algiers putsch's failure, the USSR challenged Western security by erecting a wall between East and West Berlin. This crisis gave de Gaulle a heaven-sent pretext for troop redeployments. On 23 August he told Ambassador Hervé Alphand that he was meeting the Berlin crisis by reinforcing military dispositions in Europe, bringing 45,000 troops home from Algeria. Of these, 15,000 were to raise France's two divisions in Germany to full strength, and the other 30,000 to strengthen the rapid-reaction units in metropolitan France.[106] The new dispositions symbolized a wider policy shift, away from North Africa.

De Gaulle's appointment of Pierre Messmer, a dependable Gaullist political 'baron,' as defense minister in February 1960 (a post he held until May 1969), and of General Ailleret to command all forces in Algeria in the key transitional year to independence (April 1961 to April 1962), announced a new order in

French civil-military relations and the ascendency of a new military caste.[107] Ailleret was associated, above all, with the French nuclear force: he personally directed the detonation of France's first two bombs at Reggane, in the Algerian Sahara, in February and April 1960. He typified a fresh breed of officers for the post-Algerian era. The years after 1962-3 saw both doctrinal and professional renewal, directed by men in Ailleret's mould. The new leaders were strategic thinkers, deterrence theorists and educators, nuclear technicians and aeronautical engineers, such as Generals André Beaufre, Pierre Gallois, and Michel Fourquet in the 1960s (the last succeeding Ailleret as chief of the armed forces staff in 1968), Jean Callet, Jeannou Lacaze and Maurice Schmitt in the 1970s and 1980s.[108] With new men came new priorities. The first was to restore French leadership to the core of what came to be termed the 'European pillar' of NATO. The second was to operationalize the *force de frappe* into an air-ground-submarine nuclear triad, making France a 'superpower in miniature.'[109]

Algeria fulfilled its purpose in de Gaulle's plans for French renewal, vital strategic facilities being retained in North Africa till the late-1960s.[110] Algeria's other great strategic asset—oil—could be obtained elsewhere and all the more easily, de Gaulle reasoned, if France drew closer to Middle East nations by taking the Algerian poison out of Franco-Arab relations. Alphand asked him in August 1961 about the fate of Algeria's oil. 'We'll try to get it,' replied de Gaulle. 'If we don't succeed, too bad! There's oil in other parts of the world.' And, inquired Alphand, 'if you follow such a policy, what future has France got? Primarily a European one?' 'Without a doubt,' rejoined de Gaulle, 'but also a global one.'[111]

By December 1961 the senior ministers steering Algerian policy were confident of the prospects of an acceptably peaceful transfer of sovereignty to the new Algeria. Crucial to the new-found equanimity in Paris was the relief of Fifth Republic leaders that the army had been tamed—'under government control,' in the phrase of Louis Joxe, minister of state for Algerian affairs.[112] As Alphand mused in his diary in July 1962 (prophetically, in light of the bloodshed in Algeria during the 1990s): 'the Algerian problem, or the "Algerian question", has simply changed its appearance. It has not been resolved. It [...] will continue to exist long after us. But [...] mostly life is actually all about trying to live with problems, with as little difficulty as possible.'[113]

The events of 1954-62 left the ALN-FLN commanders—the officers of the new Algerian army—with a determining role in their nation's politics.[114] But 'defeat and retreat' in 1961-2 ended such a role for the French army. Unpaid debts were eventually settled by de Gaulle—especially those to the loyalist Massu who successfully insisted, after the 'events' of May 1968, upon the release from prison at Tulle and La Santé of Argoud, Salan, Challe, Georges Robin the 'rebel major,' and other military and OAS dissidents.[115] For these 'lost soldiers,' however, walking free from jail was no prelude to walking back into the army. Algerian independence signified the loss of their careers, the loss of their cause and the loss of the military's capacity to play political king-maker in France. A few were irredeemably alienated. They plunged into a murky, sometimes racist *pied-noir* subculture in Provence. The most notorious example was Pierre Sergent—a vice-president of the *Front National* of Jean-Marie Le Pen (himself an Indochina War paratroop veteran)—elected deputy for Orange when France experimented with proportional representation for the National Assembly from 1986 to 1988.[116]

Since the 1980s a few veterans, together with some *pieds-noirs* and their descendants, have been significant in fashioning a politics of alienation on the French right. This politics reflects a postmodern malaise at the Republic's 'establishment' parties: first at the way they have bred, or tolerated, corruption by ministers from Henri Emmanuelli, and Christian Nucci to Roland Dumas; second, at their failure to allay FN voters' fears of long-term high unemployment and immigration.[117] But whether prompted by malaise or by a real crisis-in-the-making, political change at the close of the twentieth century would not be led by the military.[118] This was thanks to the post-Algerian War eradication of what Planchais memorably termed 'the malaise of the army.'[119] Expunging the 'political fantasies' of French soldiers was a significant and lasting achievement, after the military crises and renewals since 1919. As the Fifth Republic reached middle age, it was 'lost politicians' who urgently needed to reconnect and relegitimate themselves with the people of France.

Notes

* For helpful comment on a draft of this chapter, I am indebted to Dr Martin Thomas, University of the West of England, Bristol, Dr Anthony Clayton, De Montfort University, Professor J. F. V. Keiger, University of Salford, and Ken Mouré.

1. G. A. Kelly, *Lost Soldiers. The French Army and Empire in Crisis, 1947-1962* (Cambridge, MA, 1965), 13-30, 359-72.
2. 'Introduction,' in O. Forcade, E. Duhamel, P. Vial, eds., *Les militaires en république, 1870-1962. Les officiers, le pouvoir et la vie publique en France* (Paris, 1999), 28-9.
3. R. Girardet, *La société militaire française contemporaine de 1815 à nos jours* (Paris, 1953); idem, *La crise militaire française, 1945-1962* (Paris, 1964).
4. In *L'avenement de la Ve République. Entre nouveauté et tradition* (Paris, 1999), 119.
5. See Service Historique de l'Armée de Terre, *Introduction à l'étude des Archives de l'Algérie* (Vincennes, 1992); J.-C. Jauffret, H. Baudoin, J. Roucaud, M. Hardy, eds., *La guerre d'Algérie par*

les documents. Tome 1: L'avertissement, 1943-1946 (Vincennes, 1990); J. Nicot, P. Schillinger, C. Obert, *Inventaire des Archives de l'Algérie. Sous-série 1H. Tome II (1945-1967)* (Vincennes, 1994); J.-C. Jauffret, H. Baudoin, J. Roucaud, A. Porchet, eds., *La guerre d'Algérie par les documents. Tome 2: Les portes de la guerre, 1946-1954* (Vincennes, 1998); P. Boureaux, A. Chablat-Beylot, 'Etat des sources relatives à l'Indochine conservées par le Service Historique de l'Armée de l'Air (SHAA),' in SHAA, *Regards sur l'Aviation militaire française en Indochine, 1940-1954. Recueil d'articles et état des sources* (Vincennes, 1999), 363-441.

6. Forcade, in *Les militaires en république*, 29.
7. See A. Clayton, *The Wars of French Decolonization* (Harlow, 1994); A. Horne, *A Savage War of Peace. Algeria, 1954-1962* (London, 1977); J. Talbott, *The War Without a Name. France in Algeria, 1954-1962* (New York, 1980).
8. J. Frémeaux, *Le monde arabe et la sécurité de la France depuis 1958* (Paris, 1995), 41; A. Clayton, *France, Soldiers and Africa* (Oxford, 1988), 189-90.
9. Frémeaux, *Le monde arabe*, 30-1, 247-8; Talbott, *War Without a Name*, 38-55, 245-7. A draftee's tour lasted 24 months, later extended to 28 (but only 27 for *pieds-noirs*, a source of resentment among their metropolitan comrades-in-arms).
10. A study of the men of France's far smaller Indochina Expeditionary Corps needed 3 major volumes when published: M. Bodin, *La France et ses soldats d'Indochine, 1945-1954* (Paris, 1996); *Soldats d'Indochine, 1945-1954* (Paris, 1997); *Les combattants français face à la guerre d'Indochine, 1945-1954* (Paris, 1998).
11. J.-C. Jauffret, *Soldats en Algérie, 1954-1962. Expériences contrastées des hommes du contingent* (Paris, 2000), based on a CNRS-funded analysis of 430 ex-conscripts' responses to a 152-point questionnaire, follow-up interviews and some 40 sets of unpublished notebooks and letters.
12. J. C. Cairns, 'Some recent historians and the "Strange Defeat" of 1940,' *Journal of Modern History* 46, no. 1 (March 1974), 60-85.
13. J.-C. Jauffret, 'The War Culture of French Combatants in Algeria, 1954-62,' in M. S. Alexander, J.F.V. Keiger, and Martin Evans, eds., *The Algerian War and the French Army, 1954-62: Experiences, Images, Testimonies* (Basingstoke, forthcoming in 2001). I also acknowledge the work of Dr Eckard Michels of Birkbeck College, University of London, as a source for this notion of a 'warrior elite' or 'warrior caste.'
14. S. Groussard, *La guerre oubliée* (Paris, 1974), is a bitter first-hand lament. Not until 16 Oct. 1977 were the remains of a symbolic 'Unknown Soldier' from France's N. African war dead interred at Nôtre-Dame-de-Lorette (Pas-de-Calais). See M. Evans, 'Rehabilitating the Traumatized War Veteran: The Case of French Conscripts from the Algerian War, 1954-1962', in M. Evans and K. Lunn, eds., *War and Memory in the Twentieth Century* (Oxford, New York, 1997), 73-85; D. Joly, *The French Communist Party and the Algerian War* (Basingstoke, 1991), 100-6, 115-29.
15. E. Bergot, *La coloniale du Rif au Tchad, 1925-1980* (Paris, 1982).
16. Clayton, *France, Soldiers and Africa*, 133-5; D. Porch, *The French Foreign Legion* (New York, 1991), 466-85, 494-504.
17. See M. Thomas, *The French Empire at War, 1940-45* (Manchester, 1998), esp. 45-116, 139-54, 191-217; J. Valette, *La guerre d'Indochine, 1945-1954* (Paris, 1994); Y. Gras, *Histoire de la guerre d'Indochine* (Paris, 1979); A. Ruscio, *La guerre française d'Indochine* (Brussels, 1992).
18. The essentials of Bodin's socioprofessional analysis of the Indochina expeditionary corps may be found in his article, 'Le combattant français du corps expéditionnaire en Extrême-Orient (1945-1954),' *Guerres mondiales et conflits contemporains*, 168 (Oct. 1992), 175-93.
19. See A. Clayton, *Three Marshals of France. Leadership after Trauma* (London, 1992), 39-63, 123-38; E. Bergot, *La 2e DB* (Paris, 1977); P. C. F. Bankwitz, 'French Defeat in 1940 and its Rever-

sal in 1944-1945: The Deuxième Division Blindée,' in J. Blatt, ed., *The French Defeat of 1940. Reassessments* (Providence and Oxford, 1998), 327-53.

20. Talbott, *War Without a Name*, 79-89; J. Massu, *Huit ans avec Leclerc* (Paris, 1974); *idem, La vraie bataille d'Alger* (Paris, 1971); *idem*, with H. Le Mire, *Vérité sur Suez, 1956* (Paris, 1978); P. Pelissier, *La bataille d'Alger* (Paris, 1996).
21. Clayton, *Three Marshals*, 65-91, 139-95; P. Messmer, *Après tant de batailles ... mémoires* (Paris, 1992), 75-136; P. Vial, 'Un ministre paradoxale: le général Koenig (19 juin/14 août 1954—23 février/6 octobre 1955),' in *Les militaires en république*, 255-89.
22. *The Times* (4 July 1984), 16.
23. A. Gandy, *Salan* (Paris, 1990), 133-226; R. Salan, *Mémoires: Fin d'un empire. 1: Le sens d'un engagement* (Paris, 1970); *2: Le Viet-minh, mon adversaire* (Paris, 1971); *Indochine rouge. Le message d'Ho Chi Minh* (Paris, 1975).
24. J.-J. Servan-Schreiber, *Passions*, vol. 1 (Paris, 1991), 364. Servan-Schreiber was a journalist and founder-editor of the weekly news magazine, *L'Express*. His contemporary memoir of reservist service in Algeria from July 1956 to Jan. 1957, *Lieutenant in Algeria* (London, 1958), eloquently presents a disaffected junior officer's perspective.
25. Gandy, *Salan*, 317-29. On 27 May 1958, Gen. André Dulac, Salan's emissary, met de Gaulle, supposedly winning the latter's approval to extend the army's 'Operation Resurrection' to the *métropole* if necessary. His account of the de Gaulle-Salan rupture predictably sides with Salan (described as 'finding himself in a false position as delegate-general of a government that totally disagreed with him on the matter upon which the entire struggle was coalescing'). A. Dulac, *Nos guerres perdues. Levant 1941, Indochine 1951-53, Algérie 1958-60* (Paris, 1969), 127-30; also R. Salan, *Mémoires. 4: L'Algérie, de Gaulle et moi* (Paris, 1974), 173-98.
26. Dulac, *Nos guerres perdues*, 69-151; R. Rémond, *1958, le retour de De Gaulle* (Brussels, 1998); O. Rudelle, *Mai 1958, de Gaulle et la République* (Paris, 1988); C. S. Maier and D. S. White, eds., *The Thirteenth of May: The Advent of de Gaulle's Republic* (New York, 1968).
27. Servan-Schreiber, *Passions*, 1, 364-6.
28. J. Planchais, *Le malaise de l'Armée* (Paris, 1958), quoted in Gladwyn Jebb, British Ambassador, Paris, to Selwyn Lloyd, Foreign Secretary (11 Mar. 1958), Public Record Office Kew, London [hereafter, PRO], Foreign Office General Correspondence, FO 371/137300 (1201/9/58) WF1202/3, para. 14.
29. Kelly, *Lost Soldiers*, 143-65
30. P.-M. de La Gorce, *The French Army: A Military-Political History*, trans. by K. Douglas (New York, 1963), 548.
31. See M. Bigeard, *Pour une parcelle de gloire* (Paris, 1976); *idem, De la brousse à la jungle* (Paris, 1994); P. Château-Jobert, *Feux et lumières sur ma trace. Faits de guerre et de paix* (Paris, 1978); R. Trinquier, *La Guerre moderne* (Paris, 1961); *idem, Le temps perdu* (Paris, 1978); A. Argoud, *La décadence, l'imposture et la tragédie* (Paris, 1974); H. de Saint-Marc, *Mémoires. Les champs de braises* (Paris, 1995), 177-8, 235; *idem, Les sentinelles du soir* (Paris, 1999) 152-3; L. Beccaria, *Hélie de Saint-Marc* (Paris, 1988), 152-5, 162-5.
32. M. Evans, 'The French Army and the Algerian War: crisis of identity,' in M. Scriven, P. Wagstaff, eds., *War and Society in 20th Century France* (Oxford, 1991), 153. Cf. P. Paret, *French Revolutionary Warfare from Indochina to Algeria* (Princeton, NJ, 1964), 3-8, 11-19, 33-51.
33. Beccaria, *Hélie de Saint-Marc*, 148-50; J. Pouget, *Le manifeste du Camp No. 1* (Paris, 1969); J. Ferrandi, *Les officiers français face au Viet-minh* (Paris, 1966).
34. Paret, *French Revolutionary Warfare*, 7-8; Kelly, *Lost Soldiers*, 54-75, 107-42.
35. Maier and White, *The Thirteenth of May*, 111-122; for a senior Diên-Biên-Phu veteran who hated the Fourth Republic but doubted that the army's wholesale conversion to *guerre révolu-*

tionnaire, or 'Maoism turned on its head,' was the correct response, see P. Langlais, *Diên-Biên-Phu* (Paris, 1963), 252-7.

36. Of 37,000 from the expeditionary corps who became Viet POWs, only 11,000 survived. 309 Legion officers, 1,082 NCO's and 9,021 soldiers died in Indochina. The Legion comprised 35 per cent of the European troop strength of the expeditionary corps, over 30,000 legionnaires serving at some point from 1946-54 in Indochina. The burden of these losses on Legion officers' subsequent outlook may be inferred, for total Legion dead in Algeria (a war of near-identical duration) were 'only' 65 officers, 278 NCO's and 1,633 soldiers. Beccaria, *Hélie de Saint-Marc*, 148-9.
37. J.-M. Marill, 'L'Héritage indochinois: adaptation de l'armée française en Algérie (1954-1956),' *Revue historique des armées* no. 187 (June 1992), 26-32. I am grateful to Lt. Col. Frédéric Guelton, SHAT, Vincennes, for this article. Cf. A. Zervoudakis, 'From Indochina to Algeria: Counter-insurgency lessons,' in Alexander, Evans, Keiger, eds., *The Algerian War and the French Army*, chap. 2.
38. Langlais, *Diên-Biên-Phu*, 252
39. Beccaria, *Hélie de Saint-Marc*, 149.
40. P. Château-Jobert, *Manifeste politique et social* (Paris, 1964).
41. See R. Hudemann, G.-H. Soutou, eds., *Eliten in Deutschland und Frankreich im 19 und 20 Jahrhundert: Strukturen und Beziehungen* (Munich, 1994), à propos which D. L. Augustine noted: 'The most important distinction made is that between power elites, which exercise real power, and *functional elites, which carry out elite functions but do not necessarily possess power*' (Review for H-German@H-Net.msu.edu, 1998), emphasis added.
42. See Michel Martin, *Warriors into Managers: The French Military Establishment since 1945* (Chapel Hill, NC, 1981); M. S. Alexander and P. C. F. Bankwitz, 'From *politiques en képi* to military technocrats: de Gaulle and the transformation of the French Army after Indochina and Algeria,' in G. J. Andreopoulos, H. E. Selesky, eds., *The Aftermath of Defeat: Armed Forces and the Challenge of Recovery* (New Haven and London, 1994), 79-101.
43. PRO, FO 371/137300, Jebb to Selwyn Lloyd (11 Mar. 1958), 1201/9/58, WF1202/3, para. 12. Cf. Paret's comment (*French Revolutionary Warfare*, 5) that 'Despite its shortcomings, it does offer one of the most coherent and detailed analyses [...] of what may be called unconventional, sublimited warfare—subversion, insurrection, and revolution—whose tools lie at the opposite end of the spectrum from rockets and the hydrogen bomb.'
44. M. Lemalet, *Lettres d'Algérie, 1954-1962. La guerre des appelés, la mémoire d'une génération* (Paris, 1992), 267; Beccaria, *Hélie de Saint-Marc*, 149. Trinquier's book was *La guerre moderne* (Paris, 1961) translated as *Modern Warfare*, trans. Daniel Lee (New York, 1964).
45. Lemalet, *Lettres d'Algérie*, 281.
46. Kelly, *Lost Soldiers*, 143-235; P. Pelissier, *St. Cyr, génération Indochine-Algérie* (Paris, 1992).
47. De La Gorce, *The French Army*, 550.
48. M. Vaïsse, *1961. Alger, le Putsch* (Brussels, 1983); J.-H. Levame, *Putsch. Algérie, 22 avril 1961* (Paris, 1997).
49. Cf. *Resistance: The political autobiography of Georges Bidault* (London, 1967) (French original entitled, *D'une résistance à l'autre*). This, though from a civilian, is an instance of the self-conscious appropriation of 'resister' discourse for legitimation, in this case of a man with an impeccable record as the authorized head of the *Conseil National de la Résistance*, the CNR, in 1943-45—before he revived the title for the clandestine organisation he led against de Gaulle's Algerian policy in 1961-63.
50. A point made by John Cairns himself in his *France* (Englewood Cliffs, NJ, 1965), 154-5. However, de Lattre and some French military intelligence veterans rallied by Col. Louis Rivet, the former *2e Bureau* chief, courageously rejected *attentisme* (Clayton, *Three Marshals*, 95-101).

51. Notably Maurice Challe, an air force general and commander-in-chief in 1959-60, who directed massive and *militarily* successful operations, 'The Challe Plan,' that ended the ability of ALN armed commandos to function within Algeria. See his memoir, *Notre révolte* (Paris, 1974); also de Saint-Marc, *Les champs de braises*, 289-92; Beccaria, *Hélie de Saint-Marc*, 202-4; Clayton, *Wars of French Decolonization*, 157-61; Frémeaux, *Le monde arabe*, 244-6; M. Khellil, 'Le parcours d'un combattant,' *Histoire et défense. Les cahiers de Montpellier* 25/1 (1992), 109-16. Some 300,000-400,000 *Harkis* and dependents fled permanently to France, fearing for their lives in 1962-63.
52. Some 900,000 European Algerians relocated to a *métropole* where most had never set foot. See A. Figueras, *Les pieds-noirs dans le plat* (Paris, 1962); Frémeaux, *Le monde arabe*, 243-4. On the settlement of French Algeria generally and attitudes to it in French political circles, see B. Stora, *Histoire de l'Algérie coloniale, 1830-1954* (Paris, 1991) and *Histoire de l'Algérie depuis l'indépendance* (Paris, 1994); J. K. Gosnell, *The Politics of Frenchness in Colonial Algeria, 1930-1954* (Ann Arbor, MI, 1998); J. Ruedy, *Modern Algeria. The Origins and Development of a Nation* (Bloomington and Indianapolis, IN, 1992), 45-195.
53. De La Gorce, *The French Army*, 550.
54. S. Tyre, 'The Gaullists, the army and Algeria before 1958: common cause or marriage of convenience?' in *Journal of Strategic Studies* 25, no. 1 (Mar. 2002).
55. J. Roy, *Mémoires barbares* (Paris, 1989), 559-63 (*Livre de poche* edn.). A study using newly-opened French archives at Vincennes, of the disputes among the French authorities in 1957-60 over the notorious policy of 'resettling' Algeria's rural population to army-protected enclaves, is K. Sutton, 'Army Administration Tensions over Algeria's *Centres de Regroupement*, 1954-1962,' *British Journal of Middle Eastern Studies* 26, no. 2 (1999), 243-70.
56. Beccaria, *Hélie de Saint-Marc*, 149.
57. Roy, *Mémoires barbares*, 563-5, 566-7.
58. If these officers felt disowned, outcast, bastardized, compare de Saint-Marc's taxonomy of the operations that have faced his successors—French field officers of the 1990s in the Gulf, Bosnia, Rwanda—as 'orphan-wars, for which no one is willing to assume paternity, their stakes obscured beneath polemics and media manipulation'. (*Les Sentinelles*, 109-15). Cf. Beccaria, *Hélie de Saint-Marc*, 287-94.
59. Cf. autobiographies by career captains and majors who sided with the 1961 putsch: H.-J. Loustau, *Guerre en Kabylie. 1956-1961* (Paris, 1985); P.-A. Léger, *Aux carrefours de la Guerre* (Paris, 1983); M. Delacour, *Cavalier en Algérie* (Paris, 1992).
60. PRO, FO 371/137300, Jebb to Selwyn Lloyd (11 Mar. 1958), 1201/9/58, WF1202/3, para. 10.
61. A. Gribius, *Une vie d'officier* (Paris, 1971), 278-81; Vaïsse, *1961. Alger*, 33-5.
62. Col. R. Goepfert, 'Hommage au Lieutenant-Colonel Maurice Bénos, ancien commandant du 1er BTA, avril-mai 1958, et du 17e BTA, 1961-62,' in *Bulletin de Liaison de l'Amicale des 1er, 5e, 9e et 17e Régiments de Tirailleurs Algériens*, no. 198 (28 April 2000), 21-2.
63. J.-R. Tournoux, *Le tourment et la fatalité, 1958-1974* (Paris, 1974), 111-12; for anti-Gaullism more generally, J. Jackson, 'General de Gaulle and his Enemies: Anti-Gaullism in France since 1940,' *Transactions of the Royal Historical Society*, 6th ser., 9 (Cambridge, 1999), 43-65.
64. Cairns, *France*, 155-6.
65. There is nothing comparable to S. Fishman, *We Will Wait. Wives of French prisoners-of-war, 1940-45* (New Haven, 1991). The French army had 17,456 officers, NCO's and men killed and 64,985 wounded in Algeria. To this must be added the dead among indigenous North Africans who fought as French auxiliaries: Algerian and Moroccan *tirailleur* and *spahi* units, and the *Harkis*. The Algerians reckon their losses, mostly civilians and some ALN fighters, at nearly 1 million, from a population of almost 10 million. These statistics remain disputed. See G. Pervillé, 'Combien de morts pendant la guerre d'Algérie?' *L'Histoire*, 54 (1983), 89-92; Beccaria,

Hélie de Saint-Marc, 292; B. Stora, *La gangrène et l'oubli. La mémoire de la guerre d'Algérie* (Paris, 1991), 275-6; Clayton, *France, Soldiers and Africa*, 188-9. On the *Harkis*, see M. Faivre, *Un village de Harkis, des Babors au pays drouais* (Paris, 1994); *idem, Les combattants musulmans de la guerre d'Algérie* (Paris, 1995); G. Fleury, *Le combat des Harkis* (Paris, 1989).

66. H. Bellet, 'La mémoire, mot-clé de la culture', *Le Monde* (1 June 1999), 18; B. Stora, *Histoire de la guerre d'Algérie (1954-1962)*, (Paris, 1993), 97-100; M. Bodin, 'D'une guerre à l'autre: L'évolution de l'état d'esprit des soldats algériens (1947-1956),' *Guerres mondiales et conflits contemporains* 177 (Jan. 1995), 167-83.
67. P. Rotman, B. Tavernier, *La guerre sans nom. Les appelés d'Algérie, 1954-1962* (Paris, 1992); also E. Bergot, *La guerre des appelés en Algérie, 1956-1962* (Paris, 1980).
68. B. W. Sigg, *Le silence et la honte. Névroses de la guerre d'Algérie* (Paris, 1989).
69. J.-P. Vittori, *Nous les appelés d'Algérie* (Paris, 1983); M. Mateos-Ruiz, *L'Algérie des appelés* (Biarritz, 1998).
70. Servan-Schreiber, *Passions*, 1, 366; also Col. R. Barberot, *Malaventure en Algérie avec le Général Paris de Bollardière* (Paris, 1957).
71. X. Grall, *La génération du Djebel* (Paris, 1962); for a critical look at the validity of the concept of 'the Algerian generation' see P. Thibaud, 'Génération algérienne?' in J.-P. Rioux, ed., *La guerre d'Algérie et les français* (Paris, 1990), 608-16.
72. Lemalet, *Lettres d'Algérie*, 278, 280 (23 Jan., 24 April 1961: Journal de Claude P.).
73. De La Gorce, *The French Army*, 544.
74. Lemalet, *Lettres d'Algérie*, 280 (Journal de Claude P., 28 April 1961).
75. C. Liauzu, 'Le contingent entre silence et discours ancien combattant', in Rioux, ed., *La guerre d'Algerie*, 509-16.
76. C. Mauss-Copeaux, *Appelés en Algérie. La parole confisquée* (Paris, 1999).
77. D. Geddes, 'French anger at Cheysson visit to Algeria,' *The Times* (30 Oct. 1984), 6; editorial: 'Exploiting painful memories,' *ibid* (1 Nov. 1984), 17
78. With 310,000 members (40 per cent of all organised Algerian veterans), the FNACA was the largest Algerian War ex-servicemen's body by 1989. It was strong in Paris, the Isère, the Loire and Brittany. F. Rouyard, 'La bataille du 19 mars,' in Rioux, ed., *La guerre d'Algérie*, 545-52. Note the contrast between draftee readiness to celebrate and commemorate the ceasefire (as a date that lifted their fear of death and endless service in Algeria), and the warrior officers' contempt for it (as a date signifying defeat, dereliction and dishonor).
79. D. Tartakowsky, 'Les manifestations de rue,' in Rioux, ed., *La guerre d'Algérie*, 131-43.
80. J. Talbott, 'French public opinion and the Algerian War: a research note,' *French Historical Studies* 9, no. 2 (Fall 1975), 354-61.
81. A. Frémont, 'Le contingent: témoignage et réflexion,' Equipe IRESCO-Guerre d'Algérie; 'De jeunes militants dans le contingent: l'enquête des organisations de jeunesse de 1959-60,' in Rioux, ed., *La guerre d'Algérie*, 79-85, 86-98.
82. Vaïsse, *1961, Alger*, 35-9; J. Grandmougin, 'Il y a 20 ans: Paris mate Alger,' *Historia* no. 413 (Apr. 1981), 37-50; J. Fauvet and J. Planchais, *La fronde des généraux* (Paris, 1961).
83. Clayton, *France, Soldiers and Africa*, 185; R. J. Bookmiller, 'The Algerian War of Words: Broadcasting and Revolution, 1954-62,' *The Maghreb Review*, 14, nos. 3-4 (1989), 196-213.
84. R. Girardet, 'La désobéissance légitime (1940-1962);' C. Levisse-Touzé, 'Les chefs militaires face à la défaite (16 juin-10 juillet 1940);' J. Delmas, 'Les officiers en Résistance et en politique,' in *Les militaires en république*, 547-52, 645-52, 661-6.
85. Beccaria, *Hélie de Saint-Marc*, 164.
86. E. Michels, 'From one crisis to another: the morale of the Foreign Legion during the Algerian War,' in Alexander, Keiger and Evans, eds., *The Algerian War and the French Army*, chap. 5; *idem*, 'Die Bundesrepublik und die Franzosiche Fremdenlegion, 1949-1962,' in E.-W. Hansen,

G. Schreiber, B. Wegner, eds., *Politischer Wandel, Organierte Gewalt und Nationale Sicherheit. Beiträge zur Neueren Geschichte Deutschlands und Frankreiches. Festschrift fur Klaus-Jurgen Müller* (Munich, 1995), 447-61; *idem, Deutsche in der Fremden Legion 1870-1965: Mythen und Realitäten* (Paderborn, 1999).

87. See Paret, *French Revolutionary Warfare*, 4-5; Beccaria, *Hélie de Saint-Marc*, 149-50.
88. Clayton, *France, Soldiers and Africa*, 185.
89. G. Périot, *Deuxième classe en Algérie* (Paris, 1962), 182-3. Cf. de Saint-Marc, *Les champs de braises*, 189-90, 193-7, 245-8; and his bitter reflection that 'after the 1961 revolt I never bumped into any of the ambitious and glib-tongued die-hards from Algiers pacing the gangways of my prisons' (*Les sentinelles du soir*, 71-7, 163).
90. H. Descombin, *Guerre d'Algérie 1959-60. Le Cinquième Bureau ou 'le Théorème du Poisson'* (Paris, 1994); F. Géré, *La guerre psychologique* (Paris, 1997), 265-300.
91. Géré, *Guerre psychologique*, 272.
92. Paret, *French Revolutionary Warfare*, 8.
93. G. M. Mattéi, *La guerre des gusses* (La Tour d'Aigues, 1995); D. Zimmermann, *80 exercices en zone interdite* (Paris, 1961), reworked and reissued as *Nouvelles de la Zone Interdite* (Paris, 1988; reprinted Arles, 1996).
94. Périot, *Deuxième classse*, 220-2; J.-C. Jauffret, ed., *Journal de marche du Sergent Paul Fauchon. Kabylie, juillet 1956 – mars 1957* (Montpellier, 1997).
95. P. Paulian, *800 jours dans l'Ouarsenis. Un appelé dans les djebels* (Paris, 1995), 31-44, 46-65, 69-80.
96. Lemalet, *Lettres d'Algérie*, 281-2 (Journal de Claude P., 8 May 1961).
97. General A. Bach, 'Une armée en fronde,' in *L'avènement de la Ve République*, 105-118.
98. Kelly, *Lost Soldiers*, 309-29, 359-72.
99. See P. Boyer de Latour, *De l'Indochine à l'Algérie. Le martyre de l'Armée française* (Paris, 1962); and analysis in Clayton, *France, Soldiers and Africa*, 185-6.
100. For an evocation of Legion Para officers and NCO spirit, see de Saint-Marc, *Les champs de braises*, 208; Beccaria, *Hélie de Saint-Marc*, 161, 164-5; also P. Sergent, *Je ne regrette rien. La poignante histoire des Légionnaires parachutistes du 1er REP* (Paris, 1972); *idem, Ma peau au bout de mes idées*, 2 vols. (Paris, 1967-68); *idem, Lettre aux officers* (Paris, 1975).
101. J. H. Meisel, *The Fall of the Republic. Military Revolt in France* (Ann Arbor, MI, 1962), 195-6.
102. I am indebted to Dr. Martin Thomas for drawing me to this economic dimension or, in Paul M. Kennedy's phrase, 'reality behind diplomacy.'
103. Frémeaux, *Le monde arabe*, 38-9; M. Vaïsse, *La grandeur. Politique étrangère du général de Gaulle 1958-1969* (Paris, 1998), 66-7, 381-95; C. G. Cogan, *Forced to Choose. France, the Atlantic Alliance and NATO—Then and Now* (Westport, CT and London, 1997), 123-6.
104. Clayton, *France, Soldiers and Africa*, 106-111, 114-19.
105. Thomas, *The French Empire*, 237-43.
106. H. Alphand, *L'étonnement d'être. Journal, 1939-1973* (Paris, 1977), 362-6; Vaïsse, *La grandeur*, 26-63, 162-224.
107. Messmer, *Après tant de batailles*, 251-348.
108. Kelly, *Lost Soldiers*, 373-81; D. Mongin, 'Le rôle des militaires dans le choix de l'arme atomique avant 1958,' in *Les militaires en république*, 89-97; C. Ailleret, *L'aventure atomique française. Souvenirs et réflexions* (Paris, 1968); *idem, Général du contingent. En Algérie, 1960-1962* (Paris, 1998); A. Beaufre, *Mémoires. 1920—1940—1960* (Paris, 1969); P. M. Gallois, *La stratégie de l'âge nucléaire* (Paris, 1960); *idem, Le sablier du Siècle. Mémoires* (Paris, 1999), esp. 307-413; J. Callet, *L'honneur de commander* (Paris, 1990), esp. 69-126; J. Lacaze, *Le Président et le champignon* (Paris, 1991); M. Schmitt, *De Diên-Biên-Phu à Koweit City* (Paris, 1994).

109. D. Mongin, *La bombe atomique française, 1945-1958* (Brussels, 1997); *L'aventure de la Bombe. De Gaulle et la dissuasion nucléaire, 1958-1969. Colloque organisé à Arc-et-Senans par l'Université de Franche-Comté et l'Institut Charles-de-Gaulle, les 27, 28 et 29 septembre 1984* (Paris, 1985); B. Goldschmidt, *L'aventure atomique. Ses aspects politiques et techniques* (Paris, 1962).
110. Evian left France the Saharan nuclear facilities, the Hammaguir aerospace center and Mers-el-Kebir naval base, used until Feb. 1966, July 1967 and Feb. 1968 respectively (Frémeaux, *Le monde arabe*, 24-8, 33-7, 42-5). Cf. J. Lacouture, *1962, Algérie: la guerre est finie* (Brussels, 1985), 101-7.
111. Alphand, *L'étonnement*, 365.
112. *Ibid.*, 370-1. Cf. O. Dard, 'L'armée française face à l'Organisation Armée Secrète (O.A.S.),' in *Les militaires en république*, 687-99; J. Ferrandi, *600 jours avec Salan et L'OAS* (Paris, 1969), 128-283.
113. Alphand, *L'étonnement*, 378-9.
114. France trained over 1,000 Algerian army officers at the *Ecole militaire interarmes* at Coëtquidan between 1965 and 1978, at the express request of the second President of Algeria, Col. Houari Boumediene (Frémeaux, *Le monde arabe*, 48).
115. See J. Massu, *Baden, mai 1968: Souvenirs d'une fidelité gaulliste* (Paris, 1983); G. Menant, 'Il y a dix ans: le jour où de Gaulle a disparu, 29 mai 1968,' *Paris-Match* no. 1510 (5 May 1978), 90-3, 110; G. Robin, *'Commandant Rebelle'. Algérie, 1958. De l'obéissance à la révolte* (Paris, 1998).
116. The FN held 35 National Assembly seats from 1986-88. See G. Bresson and C. Lionet, *Le Pen: Biographie* (Paris, 1994), 151-245, 421-43; A. Douglas, 'Le Pen, Jean-Marie (1928-),' in W. Northcutt, ed., *Historical Dictionary of the French Fourth and Fifth Republics, 1946-1991* (Westport, CT, 1992), 262-4; A. Chebel d'Appollonia, *L'Extrême-Droite en France de Maurras à Le Pen* (Brussels, 1988), 293-308, 328-39; J. Marcus, *The National Front and French Politics: The Resistible Rise of Jean-Marie Le Pen* (Basingstoke, 1995).
117. R. Gildea, *France since 1945* (Oxford, 1996), 190-1. By 1998-99, however, the FN itself was consumed by fratricidal conflict between Le Pen and his self-styled political heir, Bruno Mégret. See V. Rillardon, 'Front contre Front,' *Modern & Contemporary France* 8, no. 1 (Feb. 2000), 99-102.
118. J. Guisnel, *Les généraux. Enquête sur le pouvoir militaire en France* (Paris, 1990); S. Cohen, *La défaite des généraux. Le pouvoir politique et l'armée sous la Ve République* (Paris, 1994).
119. Planchais analyzes his own role as war correspondent in Algeria in 'Du technique au politique: à la rubrique 'Défense' du journal *Le Monde* (1945-1965),' in *Les militaires en république*, 529-45. On the Fifth Republic's travails in the 1990s, see B. Jenkins and P. Morris, 'Political scandal in France,' *Modern & Contemporary France* NS 1, no. 2 (1993), 127-37; M. Maclean, 'Dirty dealing: business and scandal in contemporary France,' *ibid.*, 161-70; L. Jaume, 'Le gaullisme et la crise de l'Etat', *ibid.*, NS 8, no.1 (2000), 7-18.

Chapter 13

'UNE JOURNÉE PORTÉE DISPARUE'

The Paris Massacre of 1961 and Memory

Jim House and Neil MacMaster

On the evening of 17 October 1961 a peaceful demonstration by 30,000 Algerian immigrants, organized by the *Front de Libération Nationale* (FLN), converged on central Paris. Met by an extremely violent police repression, at least 50 Algerians were to die or 'disappear' that night, while a further 11,538 men were savagely beaten and herded into sports stadia.[1] This was probably the largest 'peacetime' massacre in Western Europe in the twentieth century.

Since public knowledge of these 'lost' events slowly resurfaced in the 1980s two central questions have been asked: firstly, how was it possible that state murder on this scale could take place under the aegis of a Western democratic power and in the very heart of a capital that stood as the symbol of culture and civilized values? Secondly, how could a large scale and public massacre be so thoroughly covered up and expunged from official and public memory that almost every trace was effectively lost for twenty years? Our aim is to provide some answers to these questions and to show how the systematic organization of amnesia eventually gave way to a process of recovery and commemoration of 'lost memory.'

One of the limitations of most earlier accounts of the events of 17 October is that they have been interpreted within a short time-scale and a central preoccupation has been—in the face of official denial—to assemble data to prove the scale of the killings and to establish the responsibility of the authorities. This forensic preoccupation with the immediacy of the killings tends to overlook or

Notes for this chapter begin on page 285.

obscure an analysis of the broader political context which can make sense of this otherwise 'incomprehensible' event.

The following analysis locates the October massacre in relation to four chronological phases. Firstly, the event can be interpreted as the terminal crisis in a long process of racialization of Algerian immigrants, linked to the deepening crisis of colonialism from c.1920 onwards and to the violent tensions generated during the Algerian War (1954-62). The crucial agents of state violence were senior police officers and government officials who introduced into Paris forms of violence, torture, and repression that had been routinized in colonial North Africa. In a second phase it is argued that the killings were not restricted to the night of 17 October, as often assumed, but that the massacre was a peak in a longer period of systematic police murders that lasted from late August until late November 1961.[2] This phase of unlawful terror, tacitly encouraged by government, can be linked to an internal crisis within the Paris police force and to an ultimate and murderous trial of strength between the FLN and the French state in the final stages of the Algerian War. A third phase examines the processes by which the massacre was repressed and expunged from official and mainstream memory, including the major parties of the left and the Algerian state, in the six-month period after October 17. In a fourth, long phase, from March 1962 down to the 1990s, in spite of official French occultation and Algerian state ambivalence, an underground counter-memory of October was kept alive by immigrant communities and by small numbers of French activists who had been involved in anti-colonial, pro-Algerian solidarity networks (Trotskyists, worker-priests and *porteurs de valises*). This counter-memory was largely private, rather than public, until it was resurrected and redeployed as a strategic resource by antiracist and immigrant rights groups from 1979 onwards. Commemoration of the massacre, as well as a campaign for access to official archives, has provided a rallying point for various racialized groups who now see in 17 October a symbol of contemporary French racism and of official reluctance to accept responsibility for the repressive functions of colonial/post-colonial governance.

Phase 1. Colonialism and Police Repression (1945-60)

By 1958 there were some 120,000 Algerians in Paris and its suburbs, including 13,000 women and children, a community which was radically segregated from the surrounding French society. The immigrants sought a solution to the severe housing crisis which they faced through the construction of large squatter settlements or *bidonvilles* located in the industrial wastelands of the Paris suburbs.[3] Algerian spatial segregation within the urban fabric was further compounded during the Algerian War as the FLN sought to assert its absolute control over the immigrant *quartiers*, particularly with the aim of raising funds for the Liberation Army in North Africa. A highly sophisticated pyramidal structure extended down to local cell leaders and the *Comités de justice* that controlled daily life in the enclave with an iron fist.[4] The FLN sought to weld the immigrant enclaves into a self-contained 'counter-society' that would prove impenetrable to police and intelligence operations and provide a secure zone for FLN organizers.

The residential segregation of Algerians meant that most French inhabitants of Paris had little direct experience of the 'ghetto' zones. Apart from some contact in the workplace, French and Algerians inhabited radically separate urban and social spheres and each group remained ignorant of the life of the other. As a consequence French workers and employers had little direct experience of the ferocious repression and '*ratonnades*' that Algerians were subjected to on an almost daily basis by police patrols within their delimited *quartiers*.[5]

However, the low level of French public response to police violence during October arose less from its 'invisibility' than from growing indifference towards the colonial war and the plight of the immigrants. A highly racialized stereotype of Algerians had become deeply entrenched within French metropolitan society during the first half century before the outbreak of the Algerian War.[6] This racism deepened after 1954 as daily news reports emphasized the savagery of FLN 'terrorism' first in Algeria and then in the metropolis as the opening of a 'second front' in August 1958 led to the assassination of police officers.[7]

It was against this background of radical segregation that the FLN leadership decided, in a dramatic gesture, to break out from the ghetto zones and to march into central Paris during a critical and final phase of the War. One central intent of the FLN strategy was to break the lines of invisibility by 'invading' and contesting the symbolic spaces of the central city. The media and the French public, it was thought, would be unable to ignore the thousands of immigrant men, women, and children who, by marching peacefully through the *Grands Boulevards*, would demonstrate the total solidarity of the Algerian community with the FLN and strengthen its negotiating hand with the French government.

With a few individual exceptions, the general response of the Parisian public to the Algerian demonstrators was one of racist venom and encouragement of police violence mixed with resentment that such inferior types were daring to 'invade' the prestigious spaces of the central city, reserved to the French, and presenting a challenge to the 'geography of exclusion.' While public hostility or indifference was a factor in the process by which the massacre was later covered up and expunged from official memory, the most crucial response to the strategy of invasion came from the government and the security forces, who clearly recognized the political significance of the challenge. The ruthlessness of the police response was not, as Maurice Papon claimed, a reflection of the public order threat that 'terrorists' offered to the sites of central state power, but arose from the determination to replay the notorious *Bataille d'Alger* as the *Bataille de Paris* and to crush the morale and public assertiveness of the FLN. This police response needs to be understood within the long term context of colonial repression, state apparatuses and institutionalized police racism.

Police racism towards Algerians was not solely a product of the special conditions of the 'war without a name' but had a history that went back into the 1920s. A specialized *Brigade nord-africaine*, composed primarily of police officers from North Africa, was established in 1925 and introduced colonial 'hard' policing tactics to counter nationalist and left-wing influences among the immigrant workers.[8] Although the *Brigade* was disbanded in December 1945 because of its collaborationist role, the right-wing Prefect of Paris, Jean Baylot, was eventually able to reconstitute it in 1953 in the form of the *Brigade des agressions et violences* (BAV).[9] Throughout his period as Prefect of Police (1951-4) Baylot's chief aid (*secrétaire général*) was Maurice Papon, who transferred from Algeria where he had served as Prefect of Constantine during 1949-51. The long career of Maurice Papon, always within the ambit of the Ministry of the Interior between 1935 and 1967, is 'exemplary' of the technocratic high functionary who not only survived every change of régime, but amalgamated the efficient techniques of collaborationist policing under Vichy (identification and deportation) with those of colonial repression, mass resettlement and 'anti-terrorist' strategies honed in the colonial theater.[10]

Under the direction of Baylot and Papon the Paris police forces became widely tainted by a right-wing, racist and anti-Maghrebian ethos. From 1947 onwards the police engaged in huge stop and search operations to counter Maghrebian 'criminality', and these *rafles* passed seamlessly into actions to combat the 'political criminality' of nationalist demonstrations.[11] Under Baylot the techniques and scale of repression deepened, and in 1953 police fired on the Algerian section of a Bastille Day march killing seven men. Although Algerians had French citizenship under the law of 7 May 1946, in practice, police actions seriously eroded their rights and liberties and created a widespread tolerance or normalization of street-level violence, the *chasse au faciès* by which immigrants were stopped on the basis of their 'Arab looks', searched, insulted, beaten up or arrested.

The Algerian War was to see a deepening of the cycle of repression. By early 1958 tension was growing among the Paris police at their vulnerability to FLN attacks and, following an unruly march by 2,000 officers to the National Assembly, the government immediately replaced Lahillonne as Prefect of Police by Papon, who was flown in from Algeria. By 1958 Papon had gained a fearsome reputation for his harsh counter-terrorist tactics in Morocco (1954-6) and as super-prefect (IGAME) of Constantine (1956-8).[12] In Algeria Papon played a key role in the dangerous process by which the police mission, the protection of persons, was confused and subordinated to that of the army mission, the 'destruction of the enemy.'[13]

From March 1958 onwards, and in particular with the FLN 'second front' campaign in mainland France after 25 August, Papon brought to the capital his considerable expertise in the management of colonial repressive techniques and a willingness to deploy extra-legal methods. He secretly flew in from Algeria counterinsurgency specialists who rapidly established an intelligence network the SAT (*Service d'assistance technique*) to cut the FLN off from its base in the immigrant community.[14] In January 1959 Papon created the *Centre d'identification de Vincennes* (CIV) where rounded up Algerians were incarcerated without any judicial process, interrogated, and beaten. This was soon followed by the creation of the infamous *Force de police auxiliaire* (FPA) or *harki* units that began to engage in systematic torture in the 13th and 18th arrondissements from the spring of 1960.[15] Until August 1961 the systematic use of violence and torture was largely restricted to certain specialized police units, notably the FPA and the intelligence service, the *Direction de la surveillance du territoire* (DST),[16] but a conjunctural crisis created a highly dangerous and volatile situation in which the systematic use of violence and murder began to spread into the 'ordinary' forces, the municipal police in particular.

Phase 2. The Crisis of August-October 1961

The 'crisis within a crisis' of the late summer of 1961 needs to be understood within the context of the deep tensions, largely invisible to the French public, generated by the final phase of the Algerian War in which both sides were moving towards negotiation but at the same time playing a game of brinkmanship in order to maximize their own gains from any final settlement.

Peace negotiations between the Algerian Provisional Government (GPRA) and the French had broken down on 26 July 1961, partly over claims to the oil-rich Sahara. The three month period from late July through to the resumption of talks between the two sides from 28 October 1961 witnessed a phase of unprecedented tension and violence inside France. Both Algerians and French seemed determined to reinforce their future negotiating position by a show of strength.

At Tripoli in August 1961 the President of the *Conseil national de la révolution algérienne*, Ferhat Abbas, was replaced by the 'hard-line' Ben Khedda who maintained that only a reinforcement of armed struggle would bring about meaningful negotiations. This immediately translated into a resumption of the assassination of police officers in Paris and between late August and early October eleven officers were killed and seventeen wounded. Against a background of growing violence throughout September, Maurice Papon issued on 5 October a directive 'to neutralize terrorism' by imposing a curfew on Algerians between 8:30 p.m. and 5:30 a.m.[17] The central committee of the FLN *Fédération de France* decided that the ban provided an ideal opportunity to achieve a range of objectives. Firstly, the curfew had to be broken at all costs if the FLN networks were to continue to operate effectively.[18] Secondly, the aim was to demonstrate the strength of the FLN support base in Paris to a wider French public and, with a view to a future bid for post-independence power sharing, to the GPRA in North Africa. This would reinforce the position of the FLN as the legitimate voice of the Algerian people, its sole representative, in the negotiations with the French government. Thirdly, a decision of 7 October to halt the assassination of police officers was indicative of a deeper shift in FLN strategy towards 'olive-branch' negotiation. The huge mobilization of 17 October was planned meticulously; in particular demonstrators were to carry no weapons of any description, men wore their 'Sunday' best, and the presence of women and children was a guarantee of pacific intent.[19]

Finally, the attitude of the GPRA towards de Gaulle was one of profound ambiguity. By October it was evident to the FLN that he held the key to a negotiated settlement but that the General's own position was still potentially fragile and exposed to forces from the far right (an attempt on 8 September 1961 to assinate de Gaulle by the *Organisation armée secrète* (OAS) came close to success) and from senior Gaullists like Debré who were sympathetic to *l'Algérie française*. De Gaulle's crucial recognition on 5 September of the Algerian claim to the Sahara was a clear signal of an inexorable move towards peace. It was no longer in the FLN interest to destabilize de Gaulle's position within the government or the French community. The FLN strategy of entente was also a reassurance of Algerian good intent towards the *pieds-noirs* in the post-independence settlement.

However, what the external FLN leadership had got horribly wrong was the capacity of the police to overstep the limits of 'normal' violence. This capacity for extreme, 'extra-legal' violence was not, as often argued, largely a matter of police units running out of control like free-booting hit squads, but was indirectly but knowingly facilitated by government at the highest level.

In a penetrating analysis of the Gaullist strategy during the autumn of 1961 Brigitte Gaïti has argued that, during a phase of suspended talks and uncertainty, the General deliberately played a cunning poker game in which he sent contradictory messages in order to outmaneuver both the French 'ultras' and the FLN.[20] Although settlement was increasingly certain, de Gaulle could not afford to appear weak if he was to reinforce his negotiating position. The signal that he wished to send was one of uncompromising harshness: as Raymond Aron stated with acidity, 'General de Gaulle makes war in order to save the style in which he surrenders.'[21] This 'hard-line' position also served de Gaulle's interest well in so far as it lulled the camp of *l'Algérie française* and masked the underlying shift towards independence.

De Gaulle's strategy of ambivalence, of both concession and severe repression, was crucial to the events of 17 October. Firstly, a cabinet reshuffle on 24 August in which the 'liberal' Minister of Justice, Edmond Michelet, was removed meant a victory for the 'ultras' led by Michel Debré and signaled that de Gaulle accepted a hardening of repression. Michelet's removal further weakened the legal system and enabled the Prefecture to cover up torture and killings with impunity.[22] There can be no doubt that de Gaulle and his ministers were fully aware of the extensive use of state violence, of torture and abuse of human rights in Algeria and France throughout the period 1958-61. As the war deepened opposition intellectuals analyzed the creeping 'gangrene', the institutional acquiescence in systematic violence.[23] The Prime Minister, Michel Debré, a hard-line defender of *l'Algérie française* in 1957, felt that a veritable 'revolutionary war' was underway against terrorism in Paris, a battle that he likened to the Crusades against Islam, and he hinted that this desperate struggle justified all means, including torture.[24] He was fully behind the repressive operations mounted by Papon and gave him considerable autonomy to smash the FLN in Paris—as had the army in Algiers.

However, while the government created the conditions under which a massacre could take place, the evidence would suggest that neither it nor Papon planned or intended the 'embarrassing' killings of 17 October. The answer to this large-scale '*bavure*' must be found in the deteriorating conditions within the Paris police force. By early September an unusually tense and angry climate was growing even among the moderate officers of the major union, the *Syndicat général de police* (SGP), and there was talk of forming 'commandos' that would take affairs into their own hands. A new sinister, and murderous, phase in the repression of the FLN appeared and almost daily from 6 September onwards North Africans arrested by the police were later found dead in the Seine or in the canals of Paris.

At this juncture Papon, instead of trying to calm the nervous tension that was growing, deliberately encouraged a spirit of revenge among the rank and file. A note by the Prefect, disclosed by the Mandelkern Commission, shows that he began to coordinate special repressive measures as early as 5 September.[25] On 2 October, in a speech to officers in the Prefecture and during a round of inspection of local police stations, Papon made it quite clear that he would use his authority to ensure that the police would be '*couverts*' or protected for any actions they might take against Algerians, a term that was widely understood by the rank and file to give the green light to the most violent forms of action.

Police eyewitness accounts, as well as trade union minutes of the SGP, make it clear that Papon's guarantee did indeed translate into violence. The perpetual danger of assassination from late August onwards created a high level of nervous tension among officers, and the realization that Algerians were moving en masse into the central city on 17 October was seen as both a 'provocation' as well as an opportunity for revenge.[26] Normally routine police violence against North Africans was tempered by the fact that Algerians could not always be easily identified by appearance, and other nationalities could be assaulted by 'mistake.' Hence the particular *acharnement* of the police when confronted with Algerian nationalist demonstrations. As the officer Raoul Letard remarks, the police dreamed of the day when the Algerians would 'be stupid enough to come into the open all together.'[27] Knowing that they were 'covered' by Papon, the city police ran amok, but in most instances the descent into murder appears to have been triggered by the units of practiced killers, *harkis* and extreme 'ultras', who opened fire with calculation.[28]

It seems unlikely that Papon planned or coordinated the killings of 17 October: he did not need to do so.[29] After the demonstration what concerned him was less the scale of murder, but rather the fact that it had not been properly concealed and thus opened the way to a potential political scandal.[30] Just as de Gaulle and his ministers, through granting autonomy of action to Papon, could disclaim all knowledge of state violence and maintain a rather uneasy 'clear conscience,' so Papon in turn guaranteed a certain autonomy to officers further down the chain of command. However, what officers were permitted to do with that freedom of action was spelled out in no uncertain terms.[31]

The brutality and killings of the 17 October did not appear out of the blue, but were the culmination of a lengthy period of torture and murder during which police officers had become habituated to both violence and to a feeling of routine impunity. October 1961 represents the moment that levels of systematic violence that were quite widely accepted within the colonial theater erupted into the 'civilized' center of empire. Traditionally the French government, like other colonial powers, had practiced a 'two-track' deployment of State power—the overtness of violence in one sphere (the massacre of Sétif in 1945, of Madagascar in 1947, for example) contrasting with the supposed 'absence' of violence in the metropolis. It was this reassuring myth that led to one widespread reaction to the October massacre: it was simply 'unbelievable' or 'impossible'.

Phase 3. The Suppression of Memory (October 1961-February 1962)

Within six months of the October massacre a combination of factors contributed to the remarkably successful erasure of the event from public memory. One cru cial factor at work was the ability of government, during a period of 'national emergency', to suppress the truth and to successfully block any attempt at official investigation. De Gaulle said hardly a word, but tacitly upheld the police, and through the following years continued to show the highest regard for Papon.[32] The government provided strong and consistent support for Papon's actions, using a strategy of prudent silence or maintaining the Papon smokescreen: the FLN had fired first, only two Algerians died, and bodies in the Seine were victims of Algerian fratricidal killings. The government was therefore able to impose its own definition of the political situation, namely, that 'the demonstrations ... were threats to public order and the police and government had acted as they should have done.'[33] Those civil servants who dissented, such as Michel Massenet—head of social policy towards Algerians—were brushed aside by the Minister of Justice and the police hierarchy, and chose not to publicize their disagreements.[34]

Papon and Roger Frey were able to block judicial procedure, aided by the complicity of the judicial apparatus.[35] Papon nullified the Senate's decision of 31 October to establish a commission of inquiry by suddenly opening twenty-seven judicial inquiries. No commission could investigate evidence that was already under judicial inquiry: all investigations led eventually to the dead end of an official dismissal,[36] reinforced by subsequent amnesty legislation. Despite some initial, but concealed, division the security forces quickly closed ranks behind their colleagues.[37] Those covering up the massacre also had the initial advantage that the nature of repression on and after 17 October, spread out across Paris and the suburbs, in both public and restricted areas, meant that it took some time before oppositional testimonies could be coordinated. It was only ten days after the massacre, when sufficient publicity in the national press had been given on the nature of police violence, that there was a more general awareness of the fact that an unusually murderous repression had taken place. Papon then made full use of his unusual powers to seize journals and books that contained detailed and harrowing accounts of police violence (for example *Vérité-Liberté, Les Temps modernes, Partisans, Témoignages et Documents* and Marcel Péju's book *Les Ratonnades à Paris*).

While government moves to throw a blanket of silence over the October events may not appear unexpected, what does seem more inexplicable is why the FLN hierarchy should have abstained from making a public outcry and, far from seeking to make long-term political capital out of the massacre, almost colluded in the official conspiracy of silence. A number of factors were at work. Firstly, the organization of the demonstration may well have been a serious tactical error: it did not reinforce the negotiating position vis-à-vis the French government. Indeed, internal FLN documents from the period confirm that repression had led to very serious dislocation of its structures.[38] Secondly, although the FLN was certainly aware of the scale of the killing, the FLN leadership appears to have acknowledged that public opinion was so alienated or habituated to the killing and torture of Algerians that further revelations would make little impact.[39] There were some public protests, notably on 20 October, when several thousand Algerian women and children attempted to gather in central Paris to protest at the violence of the 17th and the continuing detention of family members,[40] and some small-scale protests in eight provincial *départements* on 18 and 20 October.[41] Nevertheless, the deaths in Paris have to be placed in the wider context of the Algerian War and the many hundreds of thousands of Algerians who lost their lives.[42] This policy of relative quiescence in the face of violence was clearly dictated to the Paris FLN by the French Federation leadership in Germany.[43]

Lastly, and most crucial of all to the official FLN 'silence', was the resumption of negotiations. Whether the October events had any impact whatsoever in bringing either side back to the negotiating table is hard to say, but in less than two weeks after the October massacre the GPRA resumed talks in Basle, discussions that were to lead to the definitive peace accords of Evian. The FLN leadership, against this background, had every interest in marginalizing the October massacre both at the time and while in power in post-independence Algeria (see below).

A third major element in the process of forgetting was the disunity within and across the mainstream and alternative left. The mainstream French left did not ignore the massacre entirely, but suffered from an endemic disunity which stemmed from the Cold War, the attitude to adopt towards de Gaulle, and the (linked) question of how to support French 'disengagement' from Algeria.[44] As will be shown, it was only around the question of antifascism, as a defensive strategy, that such disparate constituencies could and would unify.

Communist and most union responses were largely formal: *L'Humanité* published both a PCF declaration on 19 October calling for solidarity protests with Algerian workers, and a CGT (*Confédération générale du travail*) text calling for similar action.[45] There were some spontaneous protests in factories in the Paris suburbs, but it is unclear to what extent union (i.e. CGT) coordination was involved.[46] The CGT was preoccupied by wage disputes, to which its leaders decided to give priority.[47] On 30 October, when many trade unions and the national leadership of the UNEF (*Union nationale des étudiants de France*) did publish a united appeal to the government, the text simply warned that any future police repression would bring widescale union response.[48] The CFTC (*Confédération française des travailleurs chrétiens*) published the highly critical *Face à la répression*, which summarized the anonymous testimonies of demonstrators and witnesses.[49] Elsewhere, minutes of the Parliamentary Socialist Group meetings in the weeks after 17 October show that while most members were aware that the official death figures were false, they agreed that proving widespread killings was very difficult, and considered criticizing the security forces politically ill-timed.[50]

The only left party to react with any spontaneity was the PSU (*Parti socialiste unifié*), which occupied a liminal position in relation to the mainstream/alternative left. While the PSU leadership sought to encourage solidarity with Algerians, the divisions on the left preventing such solidarity were noted at its national executive meeting of 25 October, which regretted the 'near impossibility of holding any truly unified rally.'[51] The problem of rallies being banned was secondary to the disunity of the left, although censorship undoubtedly limited the efficacy of intellectual intervention based around petition signing, brochure publishing and the holding of public meetings.[52] This disunity was well illustrated by the short (banned) protest the PSU organized at Place Clichy on 1 November involving a few thousand activists, followed by a rapid wreath-laying ceremony outside the Rex cinema where several Algerians had been shot dead on 17 October;[53] later the same day, a different protest took place, organized by the *Comité Audin* and *Témoignages et Documents* in the Latin Quarter.[54]

The 'traditional' divisions of communist/noncommunist left were further complicated by the existence of various smaller, far-left or unaligned anti-war constituencies which already had close links with Algerians—students, intellectuals, *porteurs de valises*, antiracists, Trotskyists, left-wing Catholics and pacifists.[55] These groups reacted with more vigor than the main left parties and unions, but were devoid of any mass following and their counter-narratives were thus unable to exert significant pressure on the government or Papon. The antiracist association MRAP (*Mouvement contre le racisme, l'antisémitisme et pour la Paix*) attempted to coordinate a disunited mainstream and alternative left by organizing a commemorative ceremony on 11 November, and holding a protest meeting at the Salle Lancry on 8 December which brought together representatives from thirty left organizations.[56] But even the MRAP's relative previous success in stressing the parallel between the state racism of Vichy and that towards Algerians, failed to unite all oppositional vectors after 17 October.[57] Marginalized and largely uncoordinated, and in the face of the well-oiled tactics of the state cover-up, the various constituencies of the alternative, antiracist left experienced a crisis of mobilization.

The fourth key element in the 'memory repression' of October was the extent to which the death of demonstrators at Charonne on 8 February 1962 overlay and obfuscated the earlier event. The growing historiography on the period of the late Algerian War (1961-62) contrasts the limited reactions to 17 October with the mass-scale reactions on the left to the killing by the police of nine protesters (seven of whom were PCF members) at the Charonne métro station and Place Voltaire.[58] But while the left was (and is) far from free of anti-Algerian racism, the left's amnesia over 17 October does not stem uniquely from its own anti-Algerian hostility; between October 1961 and February 1962, there was an important change in the political context which saw the mainstream left unite temporarily around the linked themes of antifascism and an end to the Algerian War.

The activism which demanded peace in Algeria, protested against police brutality in repressing the UNEF-inspired demonstrations of 18 November and 6 December, and which condemned OAS atrocities, saw the PCF, *Section française de l'Internationale ouvrièie* (SFIO), CGT and CFTC rally together in a defensive movement to underline the dangers to democracy that the war's continuation posed.[59] A large unitary (banned) anti-OAS demonstration involving 60-70,000 demonstrators on 19 December was repressed with great violence.[60] The problems of how to achieve unity on the left could be removed when it was a question of demonstrating against police or OAS violence.[61] This defensive action did not mean the left necessarily identified with the Algerian cause.[62]

November/December 1961 was therefore a key transitional period which was perhaps only possible due to the continuation of well-established state violence now targeting the French left as well as Algerians. The general strike of 13 February 1962 to bury the victims of Charonne, saw the largest political demonstration since February 1934, and served in fact to relaunch and reunify an antifascist movement which had peaked in December 1961.[63] After Charonne, the left could refer to the opposition to the extreme right in 1934, the *Front Populaire* rallies, and the revised antifascism of recent campaigns against Pierre Poujade.[64] In contrast, there was no well-established tradition of republican antiracist campaigning against colonial racism, with easily identifiable dates, themes or well-known key figures which could have provided an ideological anchorage for moral protest after 17 October. Tellingly, the PCF henceforth sought to keep alive the memory of Charonne, celebrating this unitary action of which the PCF considered itself the instigator, while highlighting the 13 February demonstration as much as the massacre itself. In February 1963, a PCF-organized commemorative demonstration representing 'antifascist unity' attracted 100,000 people.[65] Thereafter, PCF publications commemorate Charonne with the same attention.[66] There was no first anniversary of 17 October in *L'Humanité* in October 1962. In 1982 and 1983, *L'Humanité* could still evoke Charonne and 'forget' 17 October.[67]

It is also important to consider certain structural factors which further ensured that Charonne would be engraved more strongly on French minds. The number of demonstrations on 17 October 1961, in sites dispersed in the suburbs (Nanterre, Colombes, Courbevoie), as well as in Paris *intra muros*, have made it difficult to choose a particular location on which annual commemoration can be focused, while Charonne was already familiar as a métro station and a central location in the social imaginary of the mainstream left, equidistant from République and Nation.

Phase 4. Counter-Memory: From the Underground to Public Remembrance, 1962 to the Present Day

By the spring of 1962 a congruence of factors, both on the side of government as well as of the FLN and the French political left, appears to have led to a remarkable erasure of the October massacre from public memory. The fourth and final phase analyzed here studies briefly how official discourse subsequently negated the massacre, and how successive post-independence Algerian regimes evoked 17 October partially and inconsistently. This section will also show how and why the private memory of the October massacre survived over the ensuing two decades to provide the basis for the eventual public 'recovery' and re-commemoration of the October events from the early 1980s onwards, through antiracist and immigration rights associations. The memory of the massacre has therefore evolved as a counter-memory, first private and underground, then public, and illustrates Pierre Nora's conclusion to *Les lieux de mémoire*, namely, that the memorial and historical initiative has increasingly moved from the state to civil society over the past thirty years.[68]

The instrumental elision of 17 October from official memory can be understood as part of a wider process of organized forgetting by the French state, one covering the Algerian War in its entirety. This process has no doubt been aided by the lack of many of the memory frameworks (*cadres sociaux de la mémoire*) central to the conceptualization of memory offered by Maurice Halbwachs—the essential structural elements of space, time, and language which provide predispositions to remember or forget.[69] For the Algerian War, it is difficult to find a single memorial site either in France or Algeria, any clearly definable dates with which actors could identify, just as the French state is only beginning to accept that the conflict was a 'war' (see Conclusion). The War was so divisive that there are multiple collective memories which will not and cannot crystallize into a national memory.[70] Furthermore, a combination of misinformation (see above) and amnesty legislation has shaped the perception of the War's events and made highly unlikely the prosecution of those suspected of atrocities.[71]

Post-independence Algerian regimes, on the other hand, certainly attempted to legitimate themselves through recourse to an official, mythologized historiography of the War, and the 17 October was declared *Journée nationale à l'émigration* in 1962.[72] However, the place of 17 October within this instrumentalized national history has been marginal:[73] successive Algerian regimes have maintained an ambivalent relationship with Algerians and their families resident in France,[74] an ambivalence partially explainable by the late conversion of many Algerians in France to the FLN from the previously dominant rival movement the Messalist-inspired MNA (*Mouvement National Algérien*).[75] Generally speaking, a more pluralist, inclusive history of the Algerian War has been tolerated since the 1980s.[76]

The powerful FLN satellite organization, the *Amicale des Algériens en France*, has used the 17 October as a symbol to unify the 'Algerian community'[77] and the *Amicale*'s publication has called for the memories of both 17 October and Charonne to be closely associated.[78]

For Algerians in France in the period to the late 1970s, the major vector of memory transmission was the family.[79] That this private, familial memory should have survived is all the more remarkable, given the many factors proper to the situation of emigration which have affected memory transmission across the generations: intense socio-economic disadvantage, geographical mobility and uprootedness, rehousing, the return of migrants to Algeria due to deportation, labor rotation or retirement, and lack of access to cultural resources in the French context. More generally, as Abdelmalek Sayad has shown, the status of the immigrant is pregnant with a certain number of silences over the hardships endured.[80] These familial memories are not homogeneous. In general, 17 October is remembered by most participants as a crisis, due to the severe physical, emotional, economic and political consequences the repression caused. However, for some, 17 October may be remembered more positively, as an example of self-affirmation in the public sphere,[81] or, for some Algerian women, of a spatial and political visibility from which they were often excluded.[82] If some Algerian parents may have deliberately tried to 'protect' their children from knowing the full extent of the massacre,[83] silence is of course not forgetting.[84]

The proof that the memory was handed down to their children lies in the public evocation of the massacre as an important theme within antiracist and immigrant politics since the late 1970s. Neither formalized, closed nor institutionalized, the memory of 17 October was available to be used by Algerians and other racialized groups as a strategic resource in their contestation of racism in France. These 'memory activists', born during the 1950s and early/mid 1960s, have used their cultural capital via the alternative media to highlight the continuity of anti-Algerian and anti-immigrant racism, but in changed historical circumstances, thus creating intergenerational and transversal solidarity, and autonomy from the mainstream left.[85] A 'community of suffering'[86] would be forged between primary emigrant Algerians, their children and grandchildren, and other racialized groups, themselves the target of discrimination, surveillance, and often physical violence at the hands of the security forces or the general public.[87] Such 'memory activism' has served to highlight how institutional racism, public hostility (or general indifference) have been renewed, and racist memory transmitted, from the colonial to the post-colonial era.[88] Furthermore, rather as the cause of *l'Algérie française* had done during the Algerian War, the emergence of the *Front national* has crystallized the diverse racist constituencies within French society and added greater urgency to antiracist activism.

The countercultural media project *Sans frontière* (1979-1985) (SF), through its publication of the same name, was the first main vector of this memory activism.[89] SF activists possessed the cultural capital to express demands in the French public sphere, and some activists had previously belonged to the radical left *Mouvement des travailleurs arabes* (1972-1977) which had fought the developing anti-North African racism of the early 1970s and kept alive the memory of 17 October.[90] Writing in 1984, Farid Aïchoune, one of the project's founders and who, as a child, had been taken on a demonstration of solidarity with Algerians in the days following 17 October, stated: 'from the killings of 14 July 1953 to the massacre of 17 October and the assassinations of Maghrebians over the past few years, the same hatred appears to span the generations, within certain sectors of the population. Our roots are dripping with blood.'[91] Aïchoune's comments illustrate Fentress and Wickham's observation that 'the way memories of the past are generated and understood by given social groups is a direct guide to how they understand their position in the present.'[92] Interestingly, *Sans frontière* always maintained that 17 October and Charonne should be commemorated by all groups, since 'one group's blood cannot wash away another's.'[93]

SF aimed to remind the young people active within the autonomous anti-racist social movements of 1980-1985, that their action should be situated within a tradition of political activism and defense of rights by (in particular) Algerians in France.[94] Receptivity to SF's longer-term approach to the history and memory of migration was no doubt increased by the consequences of the official ending of primary immigration in the post-1974 period, and the fading of the 'myth of return' harbored by many immigrant parents. These developments brought most of the descendants of Algerian immigrants to conceive of their futures in France rather than elsewhere and therefore to seek to better understand their parents' trajectories.

SF was not the sole vector of this memory activism. The first significant commemoration of the massacre was held on 17 October 1984 next to the Canal Saint-Martin and was organized by the *Collectif jeunes*, supported by *Radio-beur*, *Sans-frontière* and the *Association de la nouvelle génération immigrée*. The MRAP leant support to these initiatives stemming from the flourishing associational activity of the early 1980s as a result of the law of 9 October 1981, which extended the rights of non-nationals to form associations. *SOS-Racisme*'s awareness of 17 October, and the association's subsequent commemorations of the massacre, certainly drew on this memory transmission within the Algerian immigrant comunities, but also showed that the massacre had remained as an important symbolic event within student politics (UNEF) in which *SOS-Racisme* founders Harlem Désir and Julien Dray had previously campaigned, and within Maoist, Trotskyist and other far-left organizations.[95]

Other factors intervened in the 1980s to ensure that the memory of 17 October resurfaced within the socialist left. Many former far-left activists reintegrated the *Parti socialiste* (PS) and reinfused the PS with the memory of 17 October, as Mitterrand's presidential candidature and subsequent victory in 1981, and the ensuing return of the left government in the same year, ended three decades of Gaullist-inspired rule.[96] The growth in France of unofficial public memories of the Algerian War throughout the 1980s further created a climate conducive to the commemoration of 17 October.[97]

A combination of all these memory vectors and evolving political circumstances explains the visibility of the thirtieth anniversary of the massacre in 1991. A large gathering in Paris followed the symbolic route from the Canal Saint-Martin to the Rex cinema. This march, a colloquium at the Sorbonne, the publication of the most detailed book to date—Einaudi's *La Bataille de Paris*—and widespread media publicity, all ensured that the massacre resurfaced as an important theme in the 1992 commemorations of the thirtieth anniversary of the end of the Algerian War.[98] This renewal of interest has helped reveal the historical complexity of the massacre, its aftermath, and the Algerian War more generally.[99] Fictional representations of the massacre have also increased its visibility.[100] In 1991 the PCF recognized the symbolic importance of the memory of 17 October within the fight against racism.[101]

Memory activism has not, however, been limited to commemorations. Specific demands have been addressed to successive left and right-wing governments. The demonstrators on 17 October 1991 claimed 'the right to memory'[102] and a deputation to the Assemblée Nationale was organized, demanding access to official archives, a key claim of both the MRAP and the association *Au nom de la mémoire* throughout the 1990s. Such access has yet to be widely granted (see Conclusion). The MRAP's call for Papon to be tried for his involvement in the massacre is highly unlikely to succeed, due to the aforementioned amnesty legislation. As our Introduction stated, one main aim of memory activism and its associated publications has been to prove that the official number of deaths is a gross underestimation, and to provide evidence of official complicity—notably of Papon—and through the figure of Papon therefore evoke the parallels and differences between Vichy state racism and that of the post-1945 period. As during the Algerian War, not all agree that such parallels can or should be made: Richard J. Golsan has criticized what he sees as the conflation of Vichy and 17 October through such an argumentative repertoire.[103]

The need for state recognition of the extent of the massacre and subsequent cover-up has been another central theme of antiracist campaigning. The MRAP's president, Mouloud Aounit, used the anniversary on 17 October 1997 to call for the setting-up of a 'Truth committee' on 17 October. He declared: 'symbolic reparation is needed for what happened. Everyone needs to share the memory of 17 October. Victims of the massacre need official recognition, and this recognition needs accepting by all groups within society.'[104] The very opposite of nostalgia and its glorification of the past, such memory activism stresses that any future project for French society can only be realized once the plurality of visions of France's colonial legacy have been officially recognized.[105] Such recognition would of course also significantly undermine the consensual and superficially reassuring assertion that racism can exist only on the far right, rather than at the heart of republican institutions. The example of October 1961—as event and memory—shows how conjunctural crises exacerbate racist ideologies and practices already deep-seated within colonial and then post-colonial state and society.

Conclusion

As the scale of the October killings began to be established through the 1980's, an incredulous public began to ask how it was possible that such a barbaric event could be so radically expunged from memory. Investigators like Levine and Einaudi began to discover how the Gaullist régime continued into the post-colonial era apparently unaffected and undisturbed by an event that might have been expected to have triggered both a national and international outcry. It could be argued that the October events, a 'small detail'—to borrow Jean-Marie Le Pen's notorious phrase—within the broader crisis of the Algerian War and the transition to the Fifth Republic, was *not* experienced by the contemporary political system as a crisis at all.

However, a growing function of the historian in the second half of the 20th century has been the disclosure, through archival research, of the secret workings of the state and the extent to which governments have all too frequently been able to use their considerable powers for 'crisis management' by preventing scandals, misgovernance, and inter-ministerial divisions from spilling over into the public domain. On one level, that of policing and counter-FLN operations in the capital, the French government was faced with a crisis. This crisis stemmed, not as Papon and the government officially claimed in 1961, from a danger of FLN insurrection to the security of Paris and the very seat of government, but from a phase of extreme tension and demoralization within the police force itself. Papon moved to both resolve and harness the growing anxiety of officers subjected to FLN hit-squads by seeming to channel their fear and frustration into acts of extreme brutality. But this apparent 'blind-eye to murder' created a further level of division in the Paris police as a significant body of officers, shocked and sickened by the systematic brutality, threatened to expose the situation.[106] It was with some difficulty that Papon was able to impose a cover-up by appealing in person to the traditions of silence and *esprit de corps* of 'la maison.'

In spite of this, it seems quite probable that the October events did leave an indelible mark on the collective memory and modus operandi of the Paris police. Although Papon continued as Prefect of Police until 1967 his successor, Maurice Grimaud, was strongly opposed to Papon's 'hard' policing methods and the culture of violence that had become systematized in the ranks.[107] Commentators have frequently remarked on the surprising fact that the extraordinary scale of street-level violence in May 1968 led to only one death in Paris. The absence of a blood-bath, and of a further deepening of the May crisis, was linked to a key shift in command attitudes to repression.[108] Individual acts of police brutality and even murder of Algerians have continued down to the present, but the systematized state violence that accompanied the crisis of decolonization ended in 1961.

The most significant legacy of the October events has, however, been as a 'crise larvée,' a slowly ticking time-bomb that finally erupted in the 1980s. Against the odds of official silence, censorship and legal blockage, an apparently weak or disempowered minority of Algerians and oppositional groups served as the vectors of memory and finally made their voice heard. The lid has now been definitively taken off the October massacre and the event is annually commemorated. However, we ought to reflect on the disparity between the partial acceptance of the French state's complicity in the deportation of Jews and the continuing reluctance to face up to France's colonial past.[109] This was well-illustrated during the course of the Papon trial in Bordeaux (8 October 1997 to 2 April 1998). The prosecution decided to reinforce its case, that Papon was fully capable of inhuman acts against Jews in 1944, by bringing in expert witness on the October events. However, in spite of a flurry of press reporting on the massacre during the two days it was debated in court (16 and 21 October), it quickly disappeared from media attention and was submerged by the Vichy syndrome and the 'guerre franco-française.'[110] The promise by Socialist ministers to make a full disclosure of archive sources on October culminated, after the trial, in the damp squib of the Mandelkern report. The commission, far from facilitating public access to official sources, mainly catalogued the range of files, while providing a highly dubious gloss on a few selected items.

What this indicates is both the on-going lack of a full recognition of state involvement in the massacre, as well as a general unwillingness in French society to engage in a wider reassessment of colonial history and the Algerian war.[111] The failure to address the issue, to seek reconciliation through coming to terms with past acts of barbarism, is integrally linked to the continuing depth of anti-Algerian racism and islamophobia in French society. In this sense, the final act of the October drama is still to be played out.[112] But, as General Pinochet was to discover in December 1998, the past has the unpleasant habit of springing back in the most unexpected ways. In the words of Richard Terdiman, 'although memory sustains hegemony, it also subverts it through its capacity to recollect and restore the alternative discourses the dominant world would simply bleach out and forget.'[113]

Notes

1. The number of deaths is still a matter of controversy. The official "Mandelkern Report," *Rapport sur les archives de la Préfecture de Police relative à la manifestation par le FLN le 17 Octobre 1961* (6 June 1998),17, arrived at a figure of thirty-two possible victims, but the report has been much criticized and underestimates the true number: see *Libération*, 22 October 1997 and 5 May 1998; *Le Monde*, 5 May 1998.
2. That 17 October was a peak within a wider "crisis of killing" that accelerated from 6 September onwards is confirmed by the Mandelkern *Rapport*: 17 and Annex IV.
3. On the shanty towns see M. Hervo and M.-A Charras, *Bidonvilles* (Paris, 1971); A. Sayad, *Un Nanterre algérien, terre de bidonvilles* (Paris, 1995); A. El Gharbaoui, "Les travailleurs maghrébins immigrés dans la banlieue nord-est de Paris," *Revue de Géographie du Maroc*, no. 19 (1971): 3-56.
4. On the complex FLN structure in France see Benjamin Stora, *Ils venaient d'Algérie. L'immigration algérienne en France, 1912-1992* (Paris, 1992): 335-55; A. Haroun, *La 7e Wilaya. La guerre du FLN en France, 1954-1962* (Paris, 1986), 47-65.
5. Poor French living alongside Algerians in certain "ghettos" like the 18th arrondissement were aware of police violence but they were "voiceless" or lacking in the means to influence public opinion: see P. Péju, *Les Harkis à Paris* (Paris, 1961), 114-15.
6. N. MacMaster, *Colonial Migrants and Racism: Algerians in France, 1900-62* (London, 1997), chaps. 7, 8.
7. On French public opinion and the Algerians in France see C.-R. Ageron, "L'Opinion française à travers les sondages" and "Les français devant la guerre civile algérienne" in J.-P. Rioux, ed., *La guerre d'Algérie et les français* (Paris, 1990), 25-44, 53-62.
8. On the *Brigade* see MacMaster, *Colonial Migrants*, chap. 10.
9. On Baylot see J.-L. Einaudi, *La bataille de Paris: 17 octobre 1961* (Paris, 1991), 45-6; B. Violet, *Le dossier Papon* (Paris, 1997), 65.
10. A career spanning Vichyite collaboration and colonial policing in North Africa was not uncommon, as in the cases of Papon's associates, Maurice Sabatier, Pierre Somveille, René Gazagne and Jean Chapel: see Violet, *Dossier Papon*, 24-5, 96; G. Boulanger, *Papon. Un intrus dans la République* (Paris, 1997), 261-3. On the ability of Vichyite functionaries to survive the *épuration* and to be quietly integrated into the Gaullist régime: see N. Weill, "L'épuration à deux vitesses de la police parisienne," *Le Monde*, 18 October 1997; M.O. Baruch and N. Weill in "Supplément: Le Procès Papon," *Le Monde*, 1 October 1997, 3, 7.
11. See H. Moscat and M. Péju, "Du Colonialisme au Racisme: Les Nord-Africains dans la Métropole," *Les Temps modernes* 8, no. 83 (September, 1952): 468-507; J.R. House, "Antiracism and Antiracist Discourse in France from 1900 to the Present Day" (Ph.D. dissertation, University of Leeds, 1997), chap. 5.

12. On Papon's role in Morocco and as *Inspecteur général de l'administration en mission extraordinaire* (IGAME) in Algeria see Violet, *Dossier Papon*, chaps. 5 and 6.
13. See Jacques Delarue, "La police en paravent et au rempart," in Rioux, ed., *La guerre d'Algérie*, 260. In May 1956, on his arrival as IGAME in Constantine, Papon announced a total war: "The time is now ended when one had to distinguish civilians from military [opponents]..," Boulanger, *Papon*, 237.
14. MacMaster, *Colonial Migrants*, 196-7.
15. On the operations of the FPA see Péju, *Les Harkis*; and Stora, *Ils venaient*, 303-6.
16. On the use of torture by the DST see H. Hamon and P. Rotman, *Les porteurs de valise. La résistance française à la guerre d'Algérie* (Paris, 1979), chap. 8.
17. For the full text of the curfew order see Einaudi, *Bataille de Paris*, 85. Papon had already experimented with such a curfew in Algeria in September 1957, see Violet, *Dossier Papon*, 89.
18. The FLN defiance was probably influenced by its earlier success in breaking a curfew imposed by Papon on 1 September 1958; see House, "Antiracism," 241.
19. "Circulaire du comité fédéral de la Fédération de France du FLN," 10 October 1961: full text in Einaudi, *Bataille de Paris*, Appendix 3, 301-3.
20. B. Gaïti, "Les ratés de l'histoire. Une manifestation sans suites: le 17 octobre 1961 à Paris," *Sociétés contemporaines* nos 18/19 (1994):11-37.
21. R. Aron "Adieu au gaullisme," *Preuves*, October 1961, quoted in *Le Monde*, 25 October 1961.
22. On the departure of Michelet see J. Rovan, "Témoignage sur Edmond Michelet, Garde des Sceaux," Rioux, *Guerre d'Algérie*, 276-8; Einaudi, *Bataille de Paris*, 28-30, 62-3. During September and October Papon told the Paris police that the departure of Michelet meant that he now had the full support of government and that they were 'covered': Boulanger, *Papon*, 356.
23. See B. Stora, *La gangrène et l'oubli. La mémoire de la guerre d'Algérie* (Paris, 1991), 32-4.
24. Einaudi, *Bataille de Paris*, 25.
25. Mandelkern, *Rapport*, 14.
26. Evidence of a police officer in *Le Monde*, 19 October 1997.
27. "La confession d'un policier," *L'Express*, 16 October 1997, 18-19. See also the Commander of the Third Police District of 5 November 1961 in Mandelkern, *Rapport*, 12.
28. The Paris police was infiltrated by pro-OAS elements. To counter the *gangrène* in the police in Algeria untrustworthy elements were removed to France and replaced by metropolitan officers who respected judicial procedure: see Delarue, "Police en paravent" in Rioux, *La guerre d'Algérie*, 262, 264. The CFTC noted how this weakened the police cadres in Paris who respected the rule of law and Republican legitimacy, while those transferred from Algeria brought a "racist and fascist mentality, trained to employ the methods favored in colonial wars," *Le Monde*, 2 November 1961.
29. Extreme-right wing "ultras," who operated within the radio car units, broadcast disinformation that police officers had been shot and killed by Algerians, information that triggered a "counter-violence" in separate locations. Papon, who was present in the central operations room of the Prefecture, probably heard these transmissions but took no steps to counter their lethal impact. The tape recordings of the control center were not made available to the Mandelkern Commission.
30. After 17 October, a real threat to Papon's position came from a serious division within the police force, especially from officers who were shocked by the scale of calculated violence: see the penetrating article by Michel Legris, "Un profond malaise règne dans la police parisienne," *Le Monde*, 14 November 1961.
31. See the minutes of the *Conseil syndical* of the SGP, 7 November 1961, which contain detailed information on the degree of 'cover' offered by the Prefecture: quoted by Einaudi, *Bataille de Paris*, 250; also the evidence of an officer in *L'Express*, 16 October 1997, 19.

32. See Einaudi, *Bataille de Paris*, 253-4. Papon prepared a report on the massacre for the Minister of the Interior and for the Prime Minister. The Mandelkern Commission found that this report had "disappeared." See *Libération*, 5 May 1998. On de Gaulle's high regard for Papon, see Boulanger, *Papon*, 256.
33. Gaïti, *"Les ratés,"* 27.
34. Archives Nationales, Centre d'archives contemporaines (CAC), Fontainebleau, 770391, article 8, dossier "divers-événements — SAT." See also V. Viet, *La France immigrée. Construction d'une politique 1914-1997* (Paris, 1998), 215-17 passim.
35. M. Heurgon, *Histoire du PSU, 1. La fondation et la guerre d'Algérie* (Paris, 1994), 338.
36. Einaudi, *Bataille de Paris*, 253-65 passim.
37. Ibid., 243-53 passim.
38. See Haroun, *La 7e Wilaya*, 370 on the report from FLN zone 212 that between 60% and 100% of FLN activists had been arrested, including "all our cadres, from sector to cell level."
39. See the significant admission of Haroun, *La 7e Wilaya*, 416 footnote 1. The FLN was opposed to the publication of Péju's *Les ratonnades à Paris*; see Einaudi, *Bataille de Paris*, 293.
40. Einaudi, *Bataille de Paris*, 209-10.
41. Stora, *Ils venaient*, 310-11.
42. Probably about half a million Algerians died during the war: see Stora, *La gangrène*, 184.
43. Einaudi, *Bataille de Paris*, 166-7.
44. See Hamon and Rotman, *Porteurs de valises*, 373-7 passim, and D. Joly, *The French Communist Party and the Algerian War* (Basingstoke, 1991). Einaudi nevertheless devotes a whole section to French protests in *Bataille de Paris*, 232-43 passim.
45. Einaudi, *Bataille de Paris*, 197.
46. Paris public transport workers protested at the use made of vehicles, and transport authority cleaning staff refused to work in blood-soaked buses; see ibid. 198-9.
47. Ibid., 236.
48. Ibid., 236 and 194-9 passim.
49. Brochure reproduced in *Les Temps modernes*, no. 187, (December 1961): 784-802.
50. Archives du Groupe Parlementaire socialiste, minutes of 18, 30 October and 7 November 1961 meetings (Fondation nationale des sciences politiques [FNSP], Archives d'histoire contemporaine, Paris).
51. Archives Daniel/Cletta Mayer, 2M 1.1, minutes of PSU national executive committee, 18 and 25 October 1961 (FNSP, Archives d'histoire contemporaine, Paris).
52. See Einaudi, *Bataille de Paris*, 224-5 and Alain Monchablon, "Syndicalisme étudiant et génération algérienne," in Rioux, *Guerre d'Algérie*, 175-90 passim. On intellectual intervention, see J.-F. Sirinelli, *Intellectuels et passions françaises. Manifestes et pétitions françaises au XXè siècle* (Paris, 1990).
53. Heurgon, *Histoire du PSU*, 341-3 passim.
54. Einaudi, *Bataille de Paris*, 238.
55. See Hamon and Rotman, *Porteurs de valises*, also M. Evans, *The Memory of Resistance. French Opposition to the Algerian War (1954-1962)* (Oxford, 1997).
56. See A. Lévy, "Pas de ça chez nous," *Droit et Liberté* no. 203, (1961, 15 November-15 December): 1, 5; House: chaps. 5 and 6 passim. In 1987, the MRAP's title changed to *Mouvement contre le Racisme et Pour l'Amitié entre les Peuples.*
57. Compare the appeal dated 18 October 1961, *Les Temps modernes*, no. 186 (November 1961), 624-8 passim and "Contre la barbarie," *Esprit* 29e année no. 11 (November 1961), 667-70 passim.

58. See Heurgon, *Histoire du PSU,* 340; F. Guidice, *Arabicides. Une chronique française 1970-1991* (Paris, 1992), 339; Hamon and Rotman, *Porteurs de valises,* 379; P. Mann, "Les manifestations dans la dynamique des conflits," in P. Favre, ed., *La manifestation,* (Paris, 1990), 302.
59. See Heurgon, *Histoire du PSU,* 334-54 passim.
60. Ibid., 353-4.
61. D. Tartakowsky, "Les manifestations de rue," in Rioux, *Guerre d'Algérie,* 140.
62. J. Rancière, "The Cause of the Other," *parallax* 4, no. 2 (1998): 25-33.
63. Heurgon, *Histoire du PSU,* 370. Tartakowsky has recorded 196 protest demonstrations throughout France concerning Charonne in the period 9-13 February 1962; "Les manifestations", 142.
64. On antifascist repertoires see D. Tartakowsky, *Le pouvoir est dans la rue. Crises politiques et manifestations en France* (Paris, 1998).
65. See *Le Monde,* 15 February 1963.
66. See *L'Humanité,* 14 February 1963, 14 February 1964, and 8 February 1972. *L'Humanité*'s attack on Roger Frey, Interior Minister for both 17 October and Charonne, does give equal weight to both massacres, see *L'Humanité,* 15 September 1964.
67. I. Lambert, "Vingt ans après," in Rioux, *Guerre d'Algérie,* 554-5.
68. P. Nora, "L'ère de la commémoration" in P. Nora, ed., *Les lieux de mémoire* 111 (3): *Les France* (Paris, 1992), 986-7.
69. M. Halbwachs, *Les cadres sociaux de la mémoire* (Paris, 1925/1994); G. Namer, ibid, "Postface", 297-367.
70. J.-P. Rioux, "La flamme et les bûchers" in Rioux, *La Guerre d'Algérie,* 501-3. See also Stora, *La gangrène.*
71. G. Manceron and H. Remaoun, *D'une rive à l'autre. La guerre d'Algérie de la mémoire à l'histoire* (Paris, 1993), 35-36.
72. Giudice, *Arabicides,* 340.
73. F. Soufi, "La fabrication d'une mémoire: les médias algériens (1963-1995) et la guerre d'Algérie," in C.-R. Ageron, ed., *La guerre d'Algérie at les Algériens* (Paris, 1997), 289-303.
74. M. Stone, *The Agony of Algeria* (London, 1997).
75. See Stora, *La gangrène,* 228.
76. Ibid., 230. See also H. Remaoun, "Pratiques historiographiques et mythes de fondation: le cas de la Guerre de libération à travers les institutions algériennes d'éducation et de recherche," in Ageron, ed., *La guerre d'Algérie et les Algériens,* 305-22.
77. *Actualité de l'Emigration* no. 13 (16 October 1985), 1.
78. "La force de la solidarité et de l'unité," *Actualité de l'Emigration* no. 13 (16 October 1985), 18-19.
79. S. Bouamama, *Dix ans de marche des Beurs. Chronique d'un mouvement avorté* (Paris, 1994), 26.
80. A. Sayad, *L'immigration ou les paradoxes de l'altérité* (Brussels, 1991), 141.
81. I. Avran, "La Guerre d'Algérie il y a 30 ans," *Différences* no. 121 (October 1991), 1-2.
82. A. Tristan, "La répression de la manifestation algérienne à Paris," *Le Monde,* 20-21 October 1991, 2.
83. See Einaudi, *Bataille de Paris,* 290-291; Aïchoune interviewed in M. Levine, *Les ratonnades d'octobre. Un meurtre collectif à Paris* (Paris, 1985), 220; M.-L. Colson in *Libération,* 17 October 1991, 36.
84. Bouamama, *Dix ans de marche des Beurs,* 71.
85. On transversalism see N. Yuval-Davis, "Ethnicity, Gender and Multiculturalism," in P. Werbner and T. Modood, eds., *Debating Cultural Hybridity. Multicultural Identities and the Politics of Anti-Racism* (London, 1997), 203-6; C. Lloyd, *Discourses of Antiracism in France* (Aldershot, 1998), 244.

86. P. Werbner, "Essentialising essentialism, essentialising silence: ambivalence and multiplicity in the constructions of racism and ethnicity," in Werbner and Modood, eds., *Debating Cultural hybridity*, 243.
87. See Giudice, *Arabicides*; M. Silverman, *Deconstructing the Nation: Immigration, Racism and Citizenship in Modern France* (London, 1992); P.-A. Taguieff, *La force du préjugé. Essai sur le racisme et ses doubles* (Paris, 1990); M. Wieviorka, *La France raciste* (Paris, 1992).
88. See Einaudi, *Bataille de Paris*, 346-49.
89. The most detailed analysis of *Sans frontière* is C. Polac, "Quand les 'immigrés' prennent la parole," in Pascal Perrineau, ed., *L'engagement politique. Déclin ou mutation ?* (Paris, 1994), 359-86 passim.
90. On the MTA, and the *Comités-Palestine* which proceeded it, see Giudice, *Arabicides*, 55-124 passim; C. Mauriac, *Le Temps immobile* 3. *Et comme l'espérance est violente* (Paris, 1986): Part 2, 259-592; Polac, "Quand 'les immigrés' prennent parole."
91. "La mémoire et l'oubli," *Sans frontière* no. 88-89 (1984), 27.
92. J. Fentress and C. Wickham, *Social memory* (Oxford, 1992), 126.
93. F. Aïchoune, "Le temps des charognes," *Sans frontière* no. 49 (12-18 February 1982), 5.
94. On the 1980s antiracist movements, see Bouamama, *Dix ans de marche des Beurs*; A. Jazouli, *L'Action collective des jeunes maghrébins de France* (Paris, 1986).
95. Interview with Harlem Désir, Paris, 24 August 1995.
96. Einaudi, *Bataille de Paris*, 277-9 passim.
97. See Stora, *La gangrène*; P. Dine, *Images of the Algerian War. French fiction and film, 1954-1992* (Oxford, 1994).
98. See *Libération*, 12-13 October 1991, 21-28 passim.
99. See in particular the film *Drowning by Bullets* (1993) by Philip Brooks and Alan Hayling shown on national television in France and Britain.
100. See, amongst others, D. Daeninckx, *Meurtres pour mémoire* (Paris, 1984); M. Lallaoui, *Les beurs de Seine* (Paris, 1985); N. Kettane, *Le sourire de Brahim* (Paris, 1985).
101. See *L'Humanité*, 17 October 1991, 5.
102. See *Le Monde*, 19 October 1991.
103. R. J. Golsan, "Memory's *bombes à retardement*: Maurice Papon, Crimes against Humanity and 17 October 1961," *Journal of European Studies* 28, nos. 109-10 (March-June 1998), 168-71 passim.
104. "Sortir de l'oubli," *Différences* no. 190 (November 1997), 1.
105. M. Lallaoui, *Libération*, 8 May 1995.
106. Einaudi, *Bataille de Paris*, 178, 245, 309-313.
107. Violet, *Dossier Papon*, 183; Boulanger, *Papon*, 256.
108. In an interview for *L'Express*, 19 March 1998, Grimaud emphasized his role in May '68 in preventing police gun-fire in response to any "provocation." He also revealed that a second, right-wing student had died from a grenade, but his father requested police silence so that the left could not exploit the death of his son.
109. E. Conan and H. Rousso, *Vichy, un passé qui ne passe pas* (Paris, 1994); H. Rousso, *La hantise du passé* (Paris, 1998).
110. A special *Le Monde* dossier on the Papon trial published in March 1998, compiled from six months of reporting, centered exclusively on Vichy and removed the key articles on the October massacre.
111. An official recognition that the Algerian War was indeed a "guerre" was only acknowledged for the first time in a commemorative plaque located at the Arc de Triomphe in early 1999; see *Le Monde* 20 October 1998.

112. On 4 February 1999 Papon began civil court proceedings against Einaudi, who had been a witness against him at Bordeaux, for his claim in a *Le Monde* article that Algerians had been killed by the police, "under the orders of M. Papon." During the hearing journalists from *L'Humanité* discovered skeletons on wasteland, thought to be a mass grave of Algerian victims buried on the night of 18 October 1961. The libel action had all the marks of an attempt to muddy the waters during a period when Papon's appeal against his ten year prison sentence is under review. Ironically, through his action, Papon may well have succeeded in bringing an unprecedented media attention to bear on the massacre, and in a focused way that is free from the traditional preoccupation with the "Vichy Syndrome." For the first time the state accepted, through the public prosecutor, that there had indeed been a "massacre." See *L'Humanité*, 4, 6, 11, 12 February 1999; *The Guardian*, 15 February 1999.
113. *Past Present. Modernity and the Memory Crisis* (Ithaca, NY and London, 1993), 19-20.

CONTRIBUTORS

Martin S. Alexander is Professor of International Relations in the Department of International Politics, University of Wales, Aberystwyth (UK). He has written *The Republic in Danger: General Maurice Gamelin and the Politics of French Defence, 1933-1940* (1993), edited *French History Since Napoleon* (1999), and is co-editor of *The Algerian War and the French Army, 1954-1962: Experiences, Images, Testimonies* (2001).

Philip M.H. Bell is Senior Research Fellow in History at the University of Liverpool (UK). He is the author of *A Certain Eventuality: Britain and the Fall of France* (1974); *The Origins of the Second World War in Europe* (2nd ed. 1997); *France and Britain, 1900-1940: Entente and Estrangement* (1996); and *France and Britain, 1940-1994: The Long Separation* (1997).

Joel Blatt is Associate Professor of History at the University of Connecticut, Stamford Campus. He edited and introduced *The French Defeat of 1940: Reassessments* (1998), and has published widely on Franco-Italian relations and on Carlo Rosselli. He is currently working on two books: *French Foreign Policy in the Interwar Period, 1918-1940* and *The Assassination of Carlo and Nello Rosselli.*

Herrick Chapman is Associate Professor of History and French Studies at New York University. He is the author of *State Capitalism and Working-Class Radicalism in the French Aircraft Industry* (1991), co-author with Peter Stearns of *European Society in Upheaval: Social History Since 1975* (1992), and has co-edited (with George Reid Andrews) *The Social Construction of Democracy, 1870-1990* (1995), and (with Mark Kesselman and Martin Schain) *A Century of Organized Labor in France: A Union Movement for the Twenty-First Century?* (1998). He is currently writing a book on the social and economic reconstruction of France after the Second World War.

Sarah Fishman is Associate Professor of History at the University of Houston. Her research focuses on the social impact of World War II in France. She is the author of *We Will Wait: Wives of French Prisoners of War 1940-1945* (1992), and has co-edited a volume centered on the debates surrounding the Vichy era, *France at War: Vichy and the Historians* (2000). She has recently completed a manuscript, *The Battle for Children: World War II, Youth Crime and Juvenile Justice in Twentieth-Century France.*

William I. Hitchcock received his Ph.D. from Yale University and teaches in the History Department at Wellesley College. He is the author of *France Restored: Cold War Diplomacy and the Quest for Leadership in Europe* (1998), and co-editor of *From War to Peace: Altered Strategic Landscapes in the Twentieth Century* (2000). He is completing a historical survey of Europe since 1945, to be published by Doubleday.

Jim House lectures in French Studies at the University of Leeds (UK). He completed his Ph.D. in 1997 on the history of antiracism in France and has published on racism, antiracism and the history of immigration. His current research is on memory of migration, on social policy towards Algerian immigrants in France 1947-1969, and is completing research for a book (with Neil MacMaster) on the Paris massacre of 17 October 1961.

Talbot Imlay is a National Security Fellow at Harvard University's John M. Olin Institute for Strategic Studies. He is completing a manuscript for publication entitled *The Test of War: Strategy, Domestic Politics, and the Political Economy in France and Britain Before and During World War II.*

Norman Ingram is Associate Professor and Graduate Programme Director in the Department of History at Concordia University in Montreal. He is the author of *The Politics of Dissent: Pacifism in France, 1919-1939* (1991) and numerous articles on French pacifism. He is presently working on a book examining the transmission of pacifist ideas into mainstream French society during the interwar period.

William D. Irvine is Professor of History at York University in Toronto. He has published *French Conservatism in Crisis: The Republican Federation of France in the 1930s* (1979), *The Boulanger Affair Reconsidered* (1989), and many articles on right-wing politics during the Third Republic. He is currently completing a book on the *Ligue des Droits de l'Homme.*

Neil MacMaster lectures in Contemporary European Studies at the University of East Anglia (UK). His most recent book is *Colonial Migrants and Racism: Algeri-*

ans in France, 1900-62 (1997), and he is currently writing a history of *Racism in Twentieth Century Europe.* He is carrying out research with Jim House for a book on the Paris massacre of 17 October 1961, and in the field of contemporary French Islam, Islamophobia and the Algerian crisis.

Sally Marks's studies of interwar European diplomacy include *The Illusion of Peace: International Relations in Europe, 1918-1933* and *Innocent Abroad: Belgium at the Paris Peace Conference of 1919.* She is currently completing a global survey of the ebbing of European pre-eminence, 1914-1945.

Kenneth Mouré is Associate Professor of History at UC Santa Barbara. He is the author of *Managing the Franc Poincaré: Economic Understanding and Political Constraint in French Monetary Policy, 1928-1936* (1991), published in a revised and expanded edition as *La politique du franc Poincaré (1926-1936)* (1998). He is completing a book on France, the Bank of France and the international gold standard, 1914-1939.

Patricia Prestwich is Professor of History at the University of Alberta. She has published extensively on alcoholism and on psychiatry in France, including *Drink and the Politics of Social Reform: Antialcoholism in France Since 1870* (1988). She is currently completing a book on a Parisian psychiatric hospital (1867-1914) and continuing research on Catholic women in politics after 1945.

Special Note: The editors wish particularly to thank **Josh Ashenmiller,** graduate student in History at UC Santa Barbara, for his speed and precision in compiling the index, and to thank the UCSB Academic Senate Committee on Research for providing funding.

Index

G

M

N

O

P

V

W

Y

Z